HOUSE

European Union Committee

12th Report of Session 2003-04

EU Development Aid in Transition

Report with Evidence

Ordered to be printed 20 April and published 29 April 2004

Published by Authority of the House of Lords
London : The Stationery Office Limited
£22.00

HL Paper 75

The European Union Committee

The European Union Committee is appointed by the House of Lords "to consider European Union documents and other matters relating to the European Union". The Committee has seven Sub-Committees which are:

Economic and Financial Affairs, and International Trade (Sub-Committee A)
Internal Market (Sub-Committee B)
Foreign Affairs, Defence and Development Policy (Sub-Committee C)
Agriculture and Environment (Sub-Committee D)
Law and Institutions (Sub-Committee E)
Home Affairs (Sub-Committee F)
Social and Consumer Affairs (Sub-Committee G) (established in December 2003)

Our Membership

The members of the European Union Committee are:

Baroness Billingham   Lord Marlesford
Lord Bowness   Lord Neill of Bladen
Lord Brennan   Baroness Park of Monmouth
Lord Dubs   Lord Radice
Lord Geddes   Lord Renton of Mount Harry
Lord Grenfell (Chairman)   Lord Scott of Foscote
Lord Hannay of Chiswick   Lord Shutt of Greetland
Baroness Harris of Richmond   Lord Williamson of Horton
Baroness Maddock   Lord Woolmer of Leeds

The Members of the Sub-Committee which conducted the inquiry are listed in Appendix 1.

Information about the Committee

The reports and evidence of the Committee are published by and available from The Stationery Office. For information freely available on the web, our homepage is:

http://www.parliament.uk/parliamentary_committees/lords_eu_select_committee.cfm

There you will find many of our publications, along with press notices, details of membership and forthcoming meetings, and other information about the ongoing work of the Committee and its Sub-Committees, each of which has its own homepage.

General Information

General information about the House of Lords and its Committees, including guidance to witnesses, details of current inquiries and forthcoming meetings is on the internet at http://www.parliament.uk/about_lords/about_lords.cfm

Contacts for the European Union Committee

Contact details for individual Sub-Committees are given on the website.

General correspondence should be addressed to the Clerk of the European Union Committee, Committee Office, House of Lords, London, SW1A 0PW.
The telephone number for general enquiries is 020 7219 5791.
The Committee's email address is euclords@parliament.uk.

CONTENTS

Oral Evidence

Written Evidence

NOTE: Pages of the report are numbered in bold type; pages of evidence are numbered in ordinary type. References in the text of the report are as follows:
(Q) refers to a question in oral evidence
(p) refers to a page of written evidence

ABSTRACT

There have been considerable improvements in the management of European Union development aid in recent years. This report considers how successful the reform programme that was started in the late 1990's has been, and what more needs to be done. It also considers the place of EU aid within the EU's Common Foreign and Security Policy (CFSP) and in the draft Constitution, and how it might be affected by Enlargement.

The reform programme has had a positive impact on aid effectiveness and it should lead to further improvements as long as the Commission retains its current self-critical approach. But in addition to keeping up the momentum and fully implementing existing reforms, there is scope for changes in several areas that would make EU aid still more effective. In particular:

- The organization structure should be changed so that aid policy and programming for all aid recipient developing countries are brought together under a single Commissioner.
- The EU should for aid purposes treat all developing countries, both the African, Caribbean and Pacific states (ACP) and non-ACP countries, on a common basis. This would mean applying common criteria in allocating aid by country, and the principles of political dialogue and conditionality that currently apply to the EU's aid to the ACP countries should be extended to the non-ACP countries. This should be the case whether or not aid currently going through the European Development Fund is brought within the EU Budget.
- Whilst there is a sound case for the EU providing significant help to the countries on its borders, the proportion of EU grant assistance going to the poorest countries needs to be increased. This may mean resisting pressures from the new Member States whose interests are likely to be more in helping their immediate neighbours than in helping poorer countries elsewhere in the world.
- There should be a separate chapter in the EU budget devoted to aid to developing countries to ensure that development assistance remains focused on poverty.

EU aid is playing a valuable and distinctive role in helping to achieve the Millennium Development Goals. Although the Government should continue to press for further improvements in effectiveness, it would not be desirable for the level of EU aid, or the United Kingdom's share of its financing, to be cut back.

EU aid can also help in the achievement of the EU's CFSP objectives. In this context, aid should be seen as a policy instrument with its own policy objectives rather than as subservient to the CFSP.

EU Development Aid in Transition

CHAPTER 1: OUR INQUIRY

1. EU aid[1] has undergone substantial changes over the past few years, aimed at improving its effectiveness. Considerable progress has been made.

2. These changes were reviewed in 2002 by the House of Commons International Development Select Committee. Its general conclusion was that, whilst in many respects the changes were to be welcomed, there remained a great deal more to do in terms of implementation.[2]

3. The principal purpose of this inquiry has been to take stock of the reform programme as it now appears two years further on, and to identify what more needs to be done.

4. The Committee has taken the opportunity to consider the following issues currently under discussion in Brussels and other capitals:

    - The reform programme. How far has it succeeded?

    - Future organisational change;

    - What future for the aid relationship between the EU and the Africa, Caribbean and Pacific (ACP)[3] states?

    - The issue of "Budgetisation"—should aid to the ACP countries be brought within the EU Budget?

    - Development aid and the Common Foreign and Security Policy[4]—How far should they be linked?;

    - The draft Constitutional Treaty;

    - Enlargement—opportunities and risks; and

    - The case for EU aid.

5. Our Report is concerned with EU aid to developing countries. It does not cover EU Pre-accession aid which still applies to current candidate countries (Bulgaria, Romania and Turkey) but is being phased out in the 10 new Member States. Nor did the scope of this inquiry extend to EU humanitarian assistance and the agency that manages it, European Community Humanitarian Office (ECHO).

---

[1] In this report, "EU aid" refers to external assistance managed by the European Commission under the Treaties.

[2] The effectiveness of the Reforms of European Development Assistance [2nd Report Session 2001-02 HC 417].

[3] The ACP countries are the 48 countries from sub-saharan Africa, 16 Caribbean countries and 16 countries located in the Pacific Ocean.

[4] CFSP.

CHAPTER 2: EU AID IN A WORLD CONTEXT

6. In 2002, global Overseas Development Assistance (ODA) amounted to $57 billion. The European Union, taking Member States' bilateral programmes and EU aid together, accounted for roughly half of this. Aid managed by the Commission is considerably larger than that managed by any single Member State. In 2003, ODA managed by the Commission amounted to an estimated €6 billion.[5]

7. The World Bank estimates that in 1999 nearly 1.2 billion people in the world lived on less than 1 US dollar per day[6], representing 23 per cent of the population of the developing countries. A large majority of the very poor are in sub-Saharan Africa and in South Asia. In recent decades, the incidence of extreme poverty has been falling, but because of rising population, the absolute numbers have not changed very much. There has been considerable progress in bringing down poverty in East Asia and, over the past decade, in South Asia. In Africa, progress has been much more limited, and the absolute number of very poor has been on the rise.

8. In 2000, world leaders agreed on the Millennium Development Goals[7] up to the year 2015. Those include:

    - halving the proportion of people in extreme poverty;

    - achieving universal primary education; and

    - reducing child mortality by two thirds.

9. To help the developing countries reach these goals, the World Bank estimates that ODA *inter alia* needs to reach $100 billion per year, compared with $57 billion in 2002.[8] The donor countries have to date committed themselves to increases which might raise the total to $75 billion in 2006—with over half the increase coming from the EU and from Member States.

10. Whether these goals are met will depend primarily on the efforts of the developing countries themselves. In the case of Africa, the chances of meeting them look rather unpromising for a variety of reasons—including the current HIV/AIDS pandemic. Critically, countries need stability and good governance, and economic policies that will foster economic growth—since without economic growth, poverty reduction on a sustained basis is impossible. The external environment will be important too—especially the trade policies of the developed countries; a successful conclusion of the WTO round; and the quantity and quality of external aid. It is generally agreed that the quantity of aid is likely to lag behind what is required. It is therefore all the more important that its quality should be maximised.

11. Aid is most effective when it both supports economic growth and is focused on poverty reduction. Achieving effectiveness is a challenge for all donors. The obstacles to success in recipient countries are formidable, given the weak institutional structures and the unfavourable policy environment within

---

[5] See Box 2.

[6] At 1985 international prices adjusted for purchasing power parity.

[7] MDGs.

[8] See World Bank: "Goals for Development: History, Prospect and Costs" available at http://econ.worldbank.org/files/13269_wps3019.pdf.

which donors often have to work. Nonetheless, there have been a number of aid "success stories" over the years, and the policy and institutional environment in many countries is now more favourable than it was. There is little doubt that EU aid is achieving better results than it has in the past, but is capable of achieving even better results in the future.

EU Aid in Outline

12. EU aid is complicated. One part is funded from the EU Budget and is subject to the same parliamentary and other procedures to which other Budget programmes are subject.

13. Aid via the EU Budget is provided mainly to the non-ACP countries. It includes aid to the countries of the former Soviet Union, Asia, Latin America, the Middle East and the North African countries, and humanitarian aid. It also currently includes Pre-Accession aid to candidate countries under a separate financial heading. The amounts are decided annually within the framework set by the Financial Perspective[9].

14. Aid to the ACP countries is funded directly by Member States for the Commission to manage on their behalf and until now has been subject to quite different procedures. This aid is channelled through the European Development Fund (EDF) under the Cotonou Agreement.[10] The amounts are negotiated between the Member States and the ACP countries on a voluntary basis every five years. The amounts channelled to ACP countries through the EDF are more, *per capita* in the recipient country, than through the EU Budget to non-ACP countries.

15. The budgetary burden as it affects DfID[11] is greater in respect of EU aid via the Budget than via the EDF. This is because, under the normal Whitehall attribution rules, DfID is required to attribute to its own budget 18 per cent (the United Kingdom's share, following EU enlargement, of total EU Budget spending) of whatever is spent on development by the EU through the Budget. By contrast, DfID is funding only 12.7 per cent of the current EDF. Taking the EDF and Budget aid together, DfID spending through the EU was about £1 billion in 2003.[12]

---

[9] The Financial Perspective is an inter-institutional agreement negotiated every 7 years between the Commission, the Member States in the Council and the European Parliament. It establishes the maximum amount of EU expenditure in this period and the composition of that expenditure. The current financial perspective ends in 2006. Negotiations are ongoing with regard to the next financial perspective 2007–13.

[10] The Cotonou Agreement was signed in June 2000 between the EU and the ACP countries after the expiry of the Lome Conventions that had previously formed the basis of EU-ACP Relations. Having been ratified by all ACP Member States, it came into force from April 2003. It is valid for a period of 20 years and will be reviewed every 5 years.

[11] Department for International Development.

[12] Attribution to DfID includes EU ODA and Official Aid (see Box 2).

BOX 1
Organisation Structure

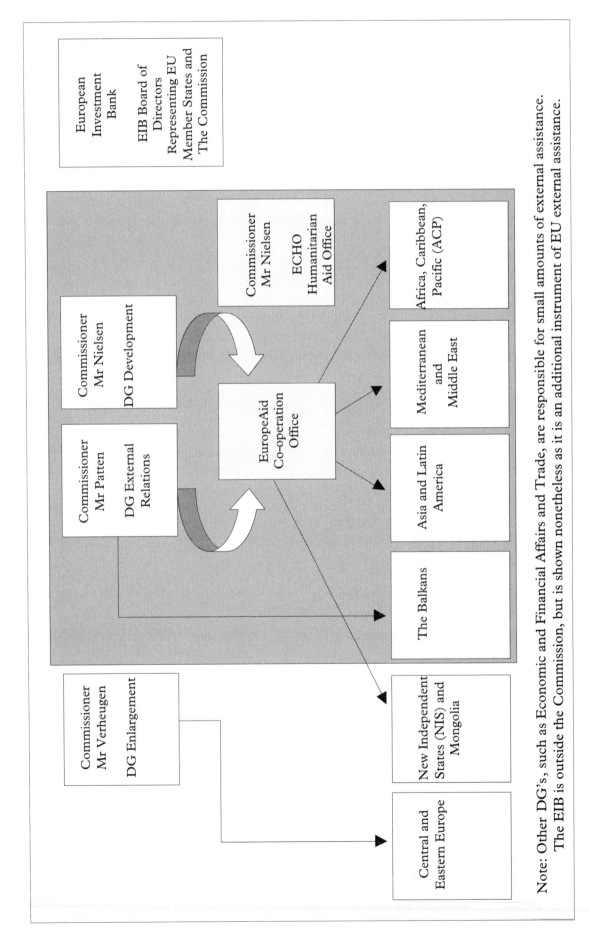

Note: Other DG's, such as Economic and Financial Affairs and Trade, are responsible for small amounts of external assistance. The EIB is outside the Commission, but is shown nonetheless as it is an additional instrument of EU external assistance.

16. Box One shows the current organizational structure for EU aid in Brussels. Key features are:

- the separation of policy and programming as between the ACP countries (in DG Development under Commissioner Nielson), the non-ACP countries (in DG External Relations under Commissioner Patten), and the candidate countries for EU accession (in DG Enlargement under Commissioner Verheugen);

- the separation of policy and programming from implementation (in a separate agency, EuropeAid). EuropeAid is supervised by a Board consisting of five Commissioners,[13] with Commissioner Patten in the chair;

- humanitarian aid is managed by a separate agency, ECHO.

---

[13] External Relations, Development, Enlargement, External Trade, Economic and Monetary Affairs.

BOX 2

EU Development Assistance

	Euros Billion		
	2001	2002	2003
A. Managed by EuropeAid	5.4	5.3	5.6
- of which: ODA	5.0	4.9	5.2
Official Aid	0.4	0.4	0.4
B. Managed by other DGs	2.3	2.6	3.1
- of which: ODA	0.9	1.0	0.8
Official Aid	1.4	1.6	2.3
C. Total EU Development			
Assistance (A +B)	7.7	7.9	8.7
- of which: ODA	5.9	5.9	6.0
Official Aid	1.8	2.0	2.7
D. Financed by: EDF	2.1	1.9	2.4
Budget	5.6	6.0	6.3

Note: Overseas Development Assistance (ODA) is assistance to developing countries (so-called Part 1 countries) as defined by the OECD. Official aid is assistance to countries in transition (Part 2 countries), primarily Russia and the countries of central and eastern Europe.

As shown in the table above, EuropeAid manages the bulk of the EU's ODA. The small amount of Official Aid it manages largely consists of aid to Russia, the Ukraine and Belarus.

Several DGs other than EuropeAid are also responsible for managing EU aid. The largest portion coming under other DGs has been the Official Aid provided to the pre-Accession states (1.6 billion euros in 2002) which is managed by DG Enlargement. The next largest is humanitarian aid (474 million euros in 2002) which is the responsibility of ECHO.

The figures all relate to payments (as opposed to commitments). The figures for 2001 and 2002 have been taken from the Commission's Annual Reports on EC Development Policy and the Implementation of External Assistance. The figures for 2003 are provisional estimates and are based on data given in the Commission's Progress Report as at December 2003 "Reform of the Management of EU External Assistance."

17. Box 2 gives a breakdown of EU aid for the past three years according to who manages it, the split between aid to developing countries (ODA) and aid to countries in transition (Official Aid), and the source of funding. Box 3 shows EU ODA by region and the extent to which it is directed at low income countries.

BOX 3

EU ODA By Region and Income Level 2002

EU ODA By Region		
	Million Euros	Percent
Europe	1,074	18.1
Africa	2,367	40.0
Americas	408	6.9
Asia	1,091	18.4
Oceania	36	0.6
LDCs[14] unspecified	568	9.6
Multilateral aid	376	6.3
Total	5,920	100

Source: Commission Annual Report on EC Development Policy and Implementation of External Assistance.

EU ODA Poverty Focus

Percent Share of EU ODA to Low Income Countries

2000	2001	2002
38	42	42

Note: Low Income Countries are countries with per capita income in 1998 of less than $ 760.

Source: Organisation for Economic Co-operation and Development (OECD), Development Assistance Committee (DAC) on-line data base.

18.   Three key features are:

- provisional figures for 2003 suggest a significant increase in total development assistance over 2002 but most of the increase is in Official Aid (i.e. to countries in transition, not to developing countries);

- the largest concentration of ODA in Africa, more than twice the amount in Asia;

- less than half of ODA going to low income countries (whereas DfID have agreed a Public Service Agreement target with the Treasury that the percentage should rise to 70 per cent).

---

[14] Less Developed Countries.

CHAPTER 3: THE REFORM PROGRAMME—HOW FAR HAS IT SUCCEEDED?

Commission Reforms

19. Mr Marc Franco, Deputy Director-General, EuropeAid, told us that for a variety of historical reasons the EU's external assistance by the mid-1990's "was in a mess...We lacked policy; we had inadequate procedures; and we were understaffed".[15] It was to address these and other weaknesses that the Commission, starting in the late 1990's, introduced a number of reform measures. The main measures can be summarised as follows:

- In November 2000, the European Council adopted for the first time a general statement on development policy. This emphasised the primacy of poverty reduction and cross-cutting issues such as gender, the environment and governance. It also specified six sectors on which the EU should concentrate with its aid—trade and development, regional cooperation, macroeconomic support and access to social services, transport, food security and sustainable rural development.

- EuropeAid was established in January 2001 to undertake implementation—that is to say, project identification and appraisal, contracting, disbursement of funds, monitoring and ex post evaluation—on behalf of both DG External Relations and DG Development. Previously, implementation had been carried out separately.

- Programming has been strengthened with the introduction of Country Strategy Papers (CSPs) covering the five years to 2007. CSPs have been prepared for 140 countries in consultation with national governments, other donors and with representatives of civil society. These CSPs provide a framework for EU aid and Member States' aid for each country, as well as for the EU's relations with the particular country more generally.

- Governance and human rights are now important elements in CSPs, especially in countries where these are serious issues. For aid under the Cotonou agreement to ACP countries, good governance and adherence to good practice on human rights feature as standard conditions in aid agreements. They have also started to feature in aid agreements to other countries.

- Although policy and programming remain in the separate DGs, the two Commissioners for External Relations and Development sit alongside each other on the EuropeAid Board as Chairman and Chief Executive along with the three other Commissioners with external responsibilities[16], and a range of measures (such as the setting up of Quality Support Groups) have been introduced aimed at ensuring consistency, information-sharing and best practice between the two DGs.

- New accounting systems have been brought in to help EuropeAid keep better track of commitments, contracts and payments.

---

[15] Q223.

[16] Trade, Enlargement, Economic and Monetary Affairs.

- Activity Based Budgeting[17] is being introduced this year.

- Responsibility for project management has been substantially devolved to EU delegations overseas. By the end of 2003, "deconcentration"—as the devolution process is known—had been achieved in some 60 countries. The "deconcentration" process in respect of country programmes should be completed by mid-2004, with regional programmes following soon after.

- Staff numbers have been substantially increased, especially on the accounting side in delegation offices.

- Monitoring and evaluation capacities have been strengthened. A separate evaluation service has been established to undertake in-depth evaluations of strategies, themes and sectors; and a Results-Oriented Monitoring (ROM) system has been introduced to allow a rapid appreciation of a project's or programme's performance.

- Contracting and tendering procedures have been harmonised across all the programmes. These are incorporated in the new Financial Regulations covering the Budget aid and aid through the EDF, which came into force in 2003.

- Both the Commission and their overseas Delegations are working more closely with other donors, particularly Member States but also with other donors such as the World Bank—to try to harmonise procedures, and to agree on joint approaches and consistency in their country programmes.

- Under the Cotonou Agreement, conditionality has been strengthened, particularly with regard to governance issues such as human rights and corruption.

- The Commission has improved its reporting to Member States and other stake-holders by instituting annual reports on its aid activities.

Progress So Far

20. What have all these measures achieved? From the standpoint of aid management, all of our witnesses had positive things to say, albeit with different emphases; and some were more positive than others.

21. In the view of the Director of the Overseas Development Institute; Mr Maxwell "the quality is better than it was... The efficiency of delivery is improving markedly". Bringing implementation together in EuropeAid has contributed to this improved efficiency.[18] This was echoed by Mr Frisch, former Director General of Development at the Commission.[19] The Secretary of State told us that the "reform process has made reasonable progress but still has some way to go."[20]

22. Mr Richard Manning, Chairman of the Development Assistance Committee (DAC) of the OECD, referred us to the DAC's Peer Review of EU

---

[17] Activity Based Budgeting has been introduced across the spectrum of EU activities in order to ensure that resources are distributed in a manner that is consistent with pre-defined political priorities and objectives.

[18] Q2, Q10, Q27.

[19] Q150.

[20] Q281.

assistance carried out in 2002. Whilst recognizing that more needed to be done, that Review had generally commended the Commission on the changes made. The DAC had concluded that the "EU has made substantial progress since January 2001 with organizational and management reforms...Of particular note are improvements to accountability at all levels, the introduction of the Country Strategy Paper process, the speedy and efficient delivery of humanitarian aid, the clarification of the links between relief and development, improved evaluation systems, and progress in the decision-making process with Member States and "deconcentration" of authority to field offices".[21] Mr Manning suggested to us that in the period since 2002 there has been further progress in a number of areas. He cited in particular the harmonisation of regulations and procedures with "deconcentration" which, he felt, "has sharpened the performance of Commission operators in the field" and made the Commission a "more effective player in the local donor club".[22]

Commission's Annual Report on EU Development Policy

23.   Mr Maxwell told us that the Commission has "made a serious effort to improve the management of European aid and to improve the degree of transparency". The publication of a detailed annual report has "greatly improved accountability and transparency", and the EU development programme is now "no less transparent and no less accountable" than the United Kingdom bilateral aid programme. **The Committee was impressed by the comprehensiveness of the Commission's latest Annual Report covering aid activities in 2002.**[23]

Country Strategy Papers

24.   We were told by Ms Hilditch, Coordinator for the ActionAid Alliance, that Country Strategy Papers represented a "qualitative leap in terms of quality control of the (aid) process".[24] She also told us that the tendering process for NGOs has greatly improved, and the Commission's "response time" has been cut from 18 months in 2001 to 9 months now.[25] Dr Mackie, Programme Coordinator at the European Centre of Development Policy Management, said that the Commission has "done a lot to improve (evaluation) over the last five years and been willing to learn a lot from some of the more rigorous evaluation systems".[26]

The Development Policy Statement

25.   Witnesses generally welcomed the 2000 Development Policy Statement.[27] It provided helpful guidance to the Commission on how it should be spending its aid money, with a welcome emphasis on poverty reduction.

---

21   Press release—DAC Aid Peer Review of the European Community, 6 June 2002.

22   Q127, Q134, Q137.

23   COM (2003) 527 Final. Adopted on 3/9/2003.

24   Q95.

25   Q106.

26   Q51.

27   Statement by the Council and the Commission on the European Communities Development Policy, 10/11/2000 "Doc 13458/00".

Real Improvements?

26. Firm evidence of improvement in terms of implementation and results was less easy to come by. The Commission has recently written that "the impact on speed and quality will become clearer in the medium term".[28] This is not unreasonable given the fact that the impact of organizational changes is never immediate, and the fact that with development assistance there is usually a considerable lag between programming, the start of a project and its completion.

27. Yet there are some quantitative and qualitative pointers to improvements:

- The large portfolio of old commitments that were never likely to be spent has been substantially cleaned up. Commitments made prior to 1995 and not spent have been reduced by €1.65 billion over the past four years. Expressed in terms of the number of years for a commitment to be spent, the ratio has been reduced from 4.6 to 3.5 in the case of budget aid, and from 5.5 to 4 in the case of the EDF.[29]

- According to an internal Commission evaluation, "deconcentration" has already resulted in improvements in both the speed and quality of aid.[30] Mr Manning expressed a similar view.[31] The Secretary of State gave us the example of Kenya where, as a result of "deconcentration", the time taken to pay invoices has been reduced from 50 days to 8 days.[32]

- In 2002, under the new ROM system, an impressive 743 project reports were prepared, covering projects with a total value of €6.1 billion. These reports showed that, on average, project and programme performance was good (on a 4 scale rating from "very good", " good", "some problems" to "major problems"); and, again on average, that projects were progressing according to plan or better. Projects were marked for sustainability, impact, effectiveness, efficiency and relevance. On all counts, average ratings were "on track"—i.e. projects and programmes performing well—though performance varied between regions with Asia, Latin America and Southern Mediterranean and the Middle East doing significantly better than the ACP and the Balkans.[33]

- We were given examples of programme improvement, as in Burkina Faso where the Commission had adopted a "simpler and more focused, sector programme approach" and was "promoting the use of conditionality and results indicators....which is viewed by many as a model for use elsewhere".[34] We were also told that the Commission has been the leader amongst donors in developing budgetary support as an aid instrument.[35] Other donors such as the World Bank which in recent years pulled back

[28] Reform of the Management of EU External Assistance—Progress Report as at December 2003.

[29] Ibid.

[30] Ibid.

[31] Q134.

[32] Q281.

[33] EC Annual Report 2003.

[34] Q136.

[35] Q224.

from infrastructure financing were looking to the Commission for advice in this area.[36]

- We were told by Mr Robert Reynders, Member, European Court of Auditors, that recent audit reports in respect of a random 45 aid transactions had shown "fairly good" results; that audits carried out in six aid recipient countries had shown that the EU's aid "systems were well constructed" and there were few criticisms to be made in terms of legality and regularity; and more generally, from an audit point of view, "the whole administrative reform is going in the right direction".[37]

28. In summary, there are a number of indications that in terms of both organizational effectiveness and results, the reform process has had a positive impact. In particular we applaud the focus on governance and Human Rights. **It is our view that, taken overall, significant improvements in aid management and organizational effectiveness have been achieved, and the Commission is to be commended for its efforts.**

Outstanding Challenges

29. **There is, however, more to be done if the EU's aid is to match the best. Mainly, this is a matter of intensifying and carrying to completion the reforms that are currently in train.**

30. We were impressed by the frankness with which Commission officials were willing to discuss the problems and challenges that still have to be dealt with. As Mr Franco told us, "there is still a lot of work to do".[38] Likewise, the Commission's recent progress report to the GAERC[39] sets out clearly what further has to be done to make EU aid fully effective.[40]

31. From this progress report and from the evidence we took, we noted in particular the following:

- The allocation of aid by country and region does not match up with the primacy given to poverty reduction in the 2000 development policy statement. The percentage of EU ODA going to low-income countries was only 42 per cent in 2002. The main reason for this is that the Commission, with the support of Member States, wishes to spend substantial sums on the "near abroad"—that is to say, the Balkans and around the Mediterranean where for political reasons the aim is to support broad-based development and political stability on the EU's borders.

- There is insufficient progress as yet with the three "C's" (Coordination, Complementarity and Coherence) established in the legal provisions for development cooperation of the Maastricht Treaty (1993). Although Brussels and delegations in the field are working more closely with other donors, they have some way to go in terms of bringing about a **coordinated** approach in individual countries. Country Strategy Papers are shared with other Member States but in most countries they have yet

---

[36] Q223.

[37] Q179.

[38] Q223.

[39] General Affairs and External Relations Council. See Footnote 28.

[40] See footnote 9.

to achieve a clear division of responsibilities between the Commission and Member States. This means continued duplication of effort on the part of donors and imposes an excessive burden on local administrations. But if there is to be more coordination by the Commission, Member States have to agree to be coordinated: this has not always been the case.[41] Donors need to agree on the broad aid and development strategy for the country concerned; they also need to agree a division of responsibilities, with individual donors taking lead responsibility for particular sectors. Which donor takes the lead in different sectors or for being the lead coordinator overall will differ from country to country depending on relative size of programme and their respective expertises. However, we would expect the Commission to be playing a prominent role in many countries. **We regard it as essential that faster progress is made in achieving coordination between the various aid programmes in aid-receiving countries.**

- Lack of coordination inevitably means that the objective of making the Commission's and Member States' aid **complementary** is also not met. But this is exacerbated by the fact that, notwithstanding the Commission's aim to focus more, in many countries its aid is still rather widely spread.

- As for **coherence** between the EU's development and other policies, there is still a wide gap between the principle and the actuality. This is less because of process since the mechanisms for achieving coherence exist (e.g. regular meetings of the relevant Commissioners and the fact that development now comes under the GAERC), but **more a failure of policy-making. The prime examples are failure to reform the Common Agricultural Policy (CAP) and the failed world trade negotiations** (though the reasons for the latter go well beyond the actions of the EU). The efforts under-way to get these negotiations restarted and the attempt to link development policy into the Common Foreign and Security Policy (see below) may be seen as a move in the right direction.

- Whilst the introduction of Country Strategy Papers (CSPs) is a great advance, country strategies are in need of periodic up dating and review—as it is the Commission's intention to do at the half-stage of their implementation—and any changes made quickly operational.

- Even after the rationalisation and harmonisation of regulations and procedures, these still appear too complicated and tend to slow down aid delivery. One witness pointed out that the EU's procedures are bound to be slower moving than those of bilateral donors because of its obligations to tender internationally and to be totally transparent.[42] Nonetheless, further efforts are required in this area.

- Relative to the size of aid programme, staffing levels are still inadequate especially in the "deconcentrated" delegation offices. There remains a particular lack of people with development expertise, as opposed to people with general administrative training. It was suggested to us that

---

[41] Q85.
[42] Q224.

the hiring of more local people could help to deal with this problem, and in a cost effective way.[43]

- While good progress has been made with developing performance indicators and in monitoring and evaluation, there remains more to do to bring these up to the standard of the best donors.[44] We agree with the Secretary of State that their programmes, and reporting thereon, should be more closely linked to the achievement of the MDG's.[45]

- The EU Budget continues to lack clarity and transparency.[46]

32.   On this last point, the Commission's Communication on the future Financial Perspective[47] (dated 17 February 2004), has proposed a very significant simplification of the External Actions part of the budget. In place of the existing 100 or so instruments, it is proposed these be reduced to just six:

- Economic Cooperation and Development (incorporating the EDF);

- Peace and Security;

- Humanitarian Aid;

- Pre-Accession Aid;

- A new Neighbourhood instrument for cross-border cooperation;

- Macro Financial Assistance.

33.   **In general terms, we think a simplification on these lines is to be greatly welcomed.** We return to the proposal for a Peace and Security instrument later in this report, and also to the idea of incorporating the EDF within Economic Cooperation and Development. But we whole-heartedly support the idea of a single instrument for development in place of the multiplicity of regulations at present which make for confusion, misunderstanding and difficulty in ensuring that aid is tailored to recipient countries' overall needs. We suggest that serious consideration should be give to wrapping Macro Financial Assistance into the Economic Cooperation instrument since such assistance is usually part and parcel of the EU aid programme in any particular country: there seems no good reason to separate it out under a different instrument.

34.   **We agree that for political and strategic reasons the "near abroad" countries need help and that the Commission is well placed to provide this support on behalf of Member States. However, we have sympathy with the Secretary of State's view that a larger proportion of EU ODA should go to low income countries.[48] We make three suggestions:**

- **The Commission and Member States should consider the scope for increasing the volume of loans to these countries from the European Investment Bank (EIB)[49] so as to free up grant**

---

[43] Q9, Q137, Q138.

[44] Q51, Q52, Q224.

[45] Millenium Development Goals Q281.

[46] Q50.

[47] COM (2004) 101 Final 17/2/2004.

[48] Q277.

[49] See Appendix 5.

assistance for the low income countries. If the EIB is to play a larger role in these countries in place of EU grant aid, it may need to extend its reach beyond its traditional emphasis on private investment and public infrastructure and utilities to investment in the social sectors.

- The Commission should concentrate grant assistance to these countries on governance and on poverty reduction.

- The Commission should review the 2000 development policy statement so as to ensure, in the words of DfID's and the FCO's written submission to the Committee, "its continued relevance and to clarify its role in guiding the future direction of EU aid" [50], so that it encompasses the objective of assisting the "near abroad" as well as poorer countries.

35. Where the reforms need to be fully "bedded in", the Commission seems to recognize what needs to be done. **We urge the Commission to take all necessary steps to bring the reform programme to full fruition so that EU aid can be made still more effective.**

---

[50] DfID/FCO Memorandum p.122.

CHAPTER 4: FUTURE ORGANISATIONAL CHANGES

36. One area of the reform programme where change is needed is in relation to the organisational structure.

37. Whilst welcoming the bringing together of implementation in a single agency, EuropeAid, several of our witnesses argued that the current structure remains far from satisfactory. Mr Maxwell, for example, said that—owing to the separation of implementation from policy and programming—the current arrangement is an "unsatisfactory compromise".[51] Ms Gavas, Policy Officer, BOND, described the "gap between policy and implementation" as "very serious".[52]

38. A different criticism came from former Director General Development Mr Frisch. He argued that the separation of policy and programming from implementation is working reasonably well (though he felt that identification of projects should be included in the programming function and not left to EuropeAid). What was not working so well was the separation of programming and policy in External Relations and Development: much would be gained, he argued, from bringing these together.[53]

39. There are several possible organisational models for consideration. First, of course, is continuing with the status quo—favoured by those who believe there has been enough organizational change in recent years already. Second, all aspects of development assistance—including policy, programming and implementation—could be brought together in a single DG under a single Commissioner. This is the model generally favoured by the NGO community and is favoured by the Secretary of State.[54] Third, policy and programming could come together in a single DG, but EuropeAid would maintain its separate status.

40. A separate question is where responsibility should lie for the Commission's overall political relations with third countries. At present it lies with both DG External Relations and DG Development. On the one hand, it was suggested to us that there are considerable benefits from the point of view of coherence in having the same country desks responsible for aid policy and the EU's political relations with particular developing countries. This is the model in several Member States. On the other hand, this model gives development policy a less distinct focus and it is likely that the DG or DGs will continue to be staffed by generalists rather than by people with development expertise.

41. An alternative model analogous to the DfID/FCO split in the United Kingdom would be for an external relations DG with country desks to cover political relations in cooperation with a separate development DG focussing entirely upon Development assistance. This is the model favoured by the Secretary of State.[55] If in due course an EU Foreign Minister is appointed with overall responsibility for all external functions, one of his/her tasks would be to ensure that the development and political sides really do work together in a consistent manner.

---

[51] Q10.

[52] Q107.

[53] Q150.

[54] Q292.

[55] QQ292–294.

42. The Commission will soon have 10 more Commissioners and jobs will need to be found for each of them. We very much hope that this factor will not materially interfere with the need to put in place a structure that is fit for purpose.

43. **We are of the opinion that continuing with the present organisational structure would be a mistake. Even though change would involve some disruption, we see considerable benefit in unifying the policy and programming functions in a single development DG under a development commissioner. Whether there should continue to be a separate implementation agency we find it more difficult to say. On balance, we feel that EuropeAid is working well as a separate agency, and that it would be best to leave it as it is. At the same time, it should be more closely linked than it is at present to the policy and programming functions.**

44. **We urge the outgoing Commission to prepare a blue-print for a revised structure for the incoming Commission—taking into account above all the need for efficiency and effectiveness, but also the move towards a strengthened CFSP** (see below).

CHAPTER 5: WHAT FUTURE FOR THE EU/ACP AID RELATIONSHIP?

45.   For historical reasons the funding of the ACP countries is quite different from the funding for other developing countries. ACP countries, most of which are very poor, have received much more aid from the EU on a *per capita* basis than have other very poor countries such as India and Bangladesh. They have also received better treatment in terms of trade policy, though their preferential status in recent years has been eroded.

46.   The Cotonou Agreement, which governs the EU's relationship with the ACP, only came into effect in 2003 and is supposed to last until 2020. Yet questions are increasingly being asked as to whether the special EU/ACP relationship has a future. Mr Maxwell from the Overseas Development Institute, for example, in his evidence said that he was becoming an "ACP sceptic" both because of the erosion of trade preferences (which is expected to continue) and because of the huge differences in aid allocations compared with other poor countries. He also noted that the ACP grouping is far from homogeneous in its interests as was shown in the Doha trade negotiations.[56] Dr Mackie from the European Centre for Development Policy Management raised similar questions.[57]

47.   The ACP countries would like the benefits they receive from this special relationship to continue. They argue that many of their members have small and highly vulnerable economies and therefore require special treatment; and as the Secretary of State emphasised, they are mostly very poor countries.[58] They also benefit from a greater degree of predictability of EDF money than there is with EU budgetary aid. Member States for their part value the inclusion in Cotonou of conditionality relating to human rights and governance which enables aid to be cut off if the conditions are not met[59]. Moreover, the relationship is not just about aid and trade. There is also a political dimension to the Cotonou Agreement, involving more consultation than is normally the case with aid programmes and at least in theory a measure of "reciprocal accountability" which the ACP countries and the development NGO's say they value. Mr Maxwell suggested that this aspect of the relationship was a model worth extending to other aid recipient countries.[60]

48.   Whether the ACP has a future as a grouping is less a choice for the EU than for the ACP. Some of the African ACP countries are showing signs of wanting to build a new relationship with the EU through the recently formed African Union which includes a number of non-ACP countries. In any case, the EU cannot unilaterally walk away from the EU/ACP relationship. But it could reduce the size of the EDF at its next replenishment, causing the relationship to wither; or by budgetising all EU aid (see below) and applying more equitable criteria in its country allocations. From Britain's point of view, although the ACP does include many countries in which we have a strong interest historically and which deserve substantial assistance, the

---

[56] Q21.

[57] Q70.

[58] Q279, Q302.

[59] Article 96.

[60] Q21.

skewing of EU aid in favour of these countries at the expense particularly of the Asian sub-continent, where we also have a strong historical interest seems increasingly hard to justify.

49. **We recommend the following approach. In the EDF's "mid-term review", which is due later this year, the government should put its EU partners on notice that it will be looking for the Commission to develop a new strategy that will treat all developing countries that wish to have a partnership relationship with the EU on a common basis. This would not necessarily mean that all ACP countries would receive less aid than at present: there may be good reasons for some of them to continue to receive preferential treatment. But there would at least be common criteria for allocating aid across the globe. In addition, other elements that are particularly valued in the EU/ACP relationship should remain and be extended to other countries: political dialogue and "reciprocal accountability", conditionality in relation to human rights and governance; and the greater predictability of aid flows.**

CHAPTER 6: BUDGETISATION

50. The question of whether the EDF should be budgetised has been a recurring one over the years. The Commission has proposed this on several occasions, and has recently done so once again: in November 2003 the Commission published a Communication requesting budgetisation.[61]

51. Member States' positions on budgetisation have tended to depend on whether they would have to pay more or less. In the United Kingdom's case, budgetisation would mean paying more.

52. The Secretary of State said he remained to be persuaded of the case for budgetisation partly because of the extra cost it would involve for DfID, but partly also because he was worried that it would lead to less EU aid going to the poorest countries.[62]

53. Most of our witnesses, however, favoured budgetisation. They argued budgetisation would bring greater coherence to EU aid; would increase parliamentary scrutiny; would greatly simplify aid procedures by allowing full harmonisation across the EU programme; would enable country aid allocations to be made on a fairer basis; would put an end to the difficulties involved in using budget and EDF funds for regional programmes including ACP and non-ACP countries.[63] It was suggested to us by Mr Schmidt, Deputy Director in Commissioner Neilson's Cabinet, that budgetisation would enable a stronger poverty focus for the Commission's programmes because "we would be giving priority to the size…. and needs of countries".[64]

54. There certainly is a risk, as the Secretary of State pointed out, that budgetisation would result in less aid being spent on poor countries because there would no longer be the ring-fencing provided by the EDF.[65] Furthermore, more of the "external" budget might be spent on peace-keeping and other non-developmental activities. At the same time, it has to be recognised that without peace, there cannot be development. It was suggested to us that the risks of too much money being spent on peacekeeping might be reduced by adding a separate development chapter to the budget, distinguishing aid for development and poverty reduction from other spending on "external actions".[66] This, as explained earlier in this report, is what the Commission has now proposed. Another witness suggested that, to prevent money intended for development from being raided, it would help to have a substantially larger sum set aside in the EU Budget specifically to support the CFSP.[67] As indicated earlier, the draft Financial Perspective proposed a separate "Peace and Security" budget. Apart from helping to protect the spending on poverty reduction, moves such as these would also help to make the budget and budget-making more transparent. But it was also pointed out to us that if Member States and the

---

[61] COM (2003) 590 Final 8/10/2003.

[62] Q280.

[63] Q26, Q224.

[64] Q163.

[65] QQ279–280.

[66] Q26, Q82.

[67] Q151.

Parliament really want the EU's aid money to go to the poorest, they can ensure that this happens whether or not there is budgetisation.[68]

55. **If it were not for the extra cost to the United Kingdom, the advantages of budgetisation in our view would clearly outweigh any disadvantages. We believe the government should weigh these carefully, including the extra cost, before reaching a decision on the current Commission proposal. Whether or not budgetisation goes ahead, we believe there is a strong case for a separate chapter in the budget for development assistance to maintain the poverty focus currently found within the EDF.**

---

[68] Q86.

CHAPTER 7: DEVELOPMENT AND CFSP—HOW FAR SHOULD THEY BE LINKED?

56. The EU has been providing development assistance to third countries for decades. The Common Foreign and Security Policy (CFSP) was only developed after the Maastricht Treaty of 1992. There is great concern amongst the development community that poverty reduction will in the future be seen as an objective to be pursued in a security context rather than as something to be pursued *per se*.[69] This concern was summed up by Dr Mackie saying that, with the proposed strengthening of the EU's foreign policy role, "development (aid) will become a tool of foreign policy".[70] This perception has been confirmed by Javier Solana's recent strategy paper, "A Secure Europe in a Better World",[71] which has been approved by the European Council. This speaks of external assistance as supporting a future security strategy. The Strategy argues that "security is a precondition of development and that new threats require a range of interventions. The Strategy links the foreign policy, development, and security agendas in response to the 'new' security threats: terrorism, proliferation of WMD, failed states and organised crime." The draft Constitutional Treaty reinforces the point. It proposes the creation of a European Foreign Minister able to use all instruments, including development and humanitarian aid, in pursuit of the EU's foreign policy objectives.[72]

57. The development community already perceives a down-grading of development policy with the abolition in 2002 of the separate Development Council, with development matters now taken twice a year in the GAERC.[73] We were told by the International Aids/HIV Alliance that in their view there was already "evidence of increased influence of foreign policy objectives in the allocations of EU funding" at the expense of aid to the poorest countries.[74]

58. It is clear that neither development nor CFSP can be entirely divorced from the other. Mr Childs[75] described this as "an intimate link between political objectives, such as securing stability and peace, and development objectives."[76] For the EU to achieve its objectives of peace, stability and poverty reduction in Africa, it is essential to "deploy all the instruments at our disposal", including humanitarian, development and military aid. The Secretary of State said he supported the use of aid money for the African "Peace Facility" since bringing peace to war-torn countries was an absolute prerequisite of development.[77]

59. In our view the key questions are on what terms will there be collaboration between development and foreign policy, and whether development policy

---

[69] Q55, Q114.

[70] Q35.

[71] Endorsed at the December 2003 European Council. Available on http://ue.eu.int/pressData/en/reports/78367.pdf.

[72] Document CIG 50/03.

[73] Q119.

[74] International Aids/HIV Alliance written submission.

[75] Head, Cabinet, DG External Relations.

[76] Q231, Q264.

[77] Q276.

will be subservient to foreign policy interests? Mr Maxwell did not think there were too many principles at stake provided it is clear that "development policy focuses on development and not on fighting terrorism".[78]

60.   We agree with Mr Manning from OECD that the development community must recognize that development and security are linked: without development there will be no security, and vice versa. In helping to address security issues, it is vital for EU aid to "be very serious about building sustainable institutions....(and) avoid gesture politics". We also agree with his statement that "reducing poverty in the world is...very much in the interests of the Community". He cautioned that development aid is for the longer term, whilst foreign policy issues tend to be dealt with on a shorter term basis.[79] Our witnesses from the NGO community said that, in theory, the proposed Foreign Minister could provide greater coherence between development and foreign policy; but there was a real danger the Minister would devote most of his/her time to short-term foreign policy issues and not enough time to development.[80]

61.   We accept that EU external assistance can have a wider purpose than pure poverty reduction—especially in the "near abroad". In particular, it can help to build institutions and support economic development which in turn will help to create stability. But the Commission must not lose sight of its commitment to the Millennium Development Goals—which, if achieved, will over the longer term make Europe more secure.

62.   In the latter context, it is perhaps surprising that Mr Solana's paper referred to above, whilst indicating that external assistance should be used to support the security strategy, did not include poverty reduction as one of the EU's strategic objectives.

63.   There is an inevitable overlap between the EU's aid in support of development and assistance that may be motivated more by the desire to secure peace and stability. We are not talking here about military assistance but, rather, aid in support of, for example, security sector reform, police training, de-mining, destroying small arms and light weapons, peace-keeping and post-conflict resolution. These can all contribute to achieving the Millennium Development Goals, are justified under the International Development Act,[81] and could in principle be funded from the EDF or from the chapter of the Budget dealing with development.

64.   It has been suggested to us, however, that there is a case for having a separate budget for assistance of this nature. The advantage of this would be that it would provide a useful budget discipline for "peace and security" type spending, and ensure that such spending is linked to clear objectives; and it would protect the more traditional spending on development with its intended focus on poverty programmes from being raided at short notice for "peace and security" projects.

65.   **We see merit in the idea of a "Peace and Security" budget, as proposed in the draft Financial Perspective, which would be the responsibility of the External Relations DG and Commissioner.**

---

[78] Q11.

[79] Q131.

[80] Q116, Q117.

[81] International Development Act 2002.

66.   **We believe it is essential that development policy is not downgraded and made subservient to the CFSP. While fully accepting that a successful development policy will bolster the EU's foreign policy objectives, we would prefer to see development described as an important element in its foreign policy—rather than as an instrument of it.**

CHAPTER 8: THE DRAFT CONSTITUTIONAL TREATY

67. The issue of the link between development and the CSFP also arises in the context of the draft Treaty. The draft, as presented by the Convention on the Future of Europe, was generally welcomed by the development community. The draft provides that:

    - poverty eradication is to be an objective of the Union's relations with the wider world (III–193 and III–218);

    - development objectives are to be taken into account in implementing policies which are likely to affect developing countries (otherwise known as the 'coherence principle') (Article III-218);

    - humanitarian aid is given a separate legal basis (Article III-223);

    - the joint competence between humanitarian aid and development is confirmed (Article III-220);

    - and aid to third countries which are not 'developing countries' is provided for in a separate article (Article III-221).

68. There remains some concern, however, that development policy and poverty reduction will not be given a sufficiently high profile in whatever Treaty is finally agreed. This concern is clearly shared by some development Ministries. On 1 May 2003 the then Secretary of State, along with six other like-minded development Ministers, submitted a joint paper to the Convention on the Future of Europe[82] arguing that development policy should be given a strong and independent place in a new Treaty. We were told that Commissioner Nielson would have welcomed stronger language than exists in the current draft.[83] For our part, we feel that there is unnecessary opacity in the existing language on development, and the absence of any clarity as to the relationship between development and foreign policy. The Secretary of State, however, told us that he was broadly content with the draft language, though he too would have liked to see the relationship between development and foreign policy clarified.[84]

69. BOND are concerned that legal experts in the IGC have proposed to remove the distinction between development aid and aid provided under Article III–221 which clarified the remit of Article 181a EU Treaty (post-Nice) to make it apply EU aid to all third countries. They believe this would make Article III–221 redundant, by negating the differentiation between aid to developing countries and aid to non-developing countries, and thereby dilute the commitment to the MDG's.[85]

70. **We share BOND's concern in this regard, as we understand does the government. We recommend:**

    a. **that the current differentiation between developing and non-developing countries in the Treaty is retained by using the wording in the latest version of the Treaty[86];**

---

[82] http://europa.eu.int/futurum/documents/other/oth010503_en.pdf.

[83] Q161.

[84] Q273.

[85] BOND letter to the Prime Minister dated 15 October 2003 p.

[86] Document CIG 50/03.

b. and that development cooperation and development policy, whilst in support of CFSP, do have distinct and autonomous objectives.

CHAPTER 9: ENLARGEMENT: OPPORTUNITIES AND RISKS

71. There are opportunities and risks for EU aid arising out of Enlargement.[87] The main opportunities are:

- Although the new members are unlikely to contribute to the EDF, they will be contributing to budgetised aid through their general contributions to the EU budget. Consequently, budgetised aid should increase;

- There will be considerable savings when Pre-Accession Aid (Chapter 7) to the new members comes to an end. This will be offset elsewhere in the EU budget, especially by additional expenditure on agricultural, structural and cohesion funds. It is to be hoped that some of the savings made in Chapter 7 of the EU budget by the accession of 10 new Member States can be re-allocated for spending on the aid budget (Chapter 4 of the EU Budget);

- Some of the new members have been recipients of aid in the past. Their experience in undertaking successful economic transition may be useful for the Commission's programmes elsewhere. The Hungarian Government told us: "the exchange of our experiences and technical know-how gained during the period of political and economic transition would greatly contribute to the political stability in the region and would promote good governance."[88] and

- The present enlargement should permit a refocus for EU development aid on the poorest countries, though there will continue to be a requirement to provide economic assistance to some new neighbours.

72. The main risks are:

- The commitment by most of the new members to development cooperation is relatively low, and they have limited development constituencies. There may therefore be a further dilution of the EU's development effort;[89]

- The new Member States' principal concerns on the external front are likely to be about security and stability issues in their neighbouring countries. This could put further pressure on the EU to spend aid money on the "near abroad" rather than on the poorest countries. DfID are worried on this account.[90] The Hungarian government told us that it would be interested in forming a "development partnership with countries that are important to its foreign and security policy and foreign trade relations that are well known to Hungarian social and economic actors and where its international development cooperation efforts are duly received;"[91] and

- The European Investment Bank will focus even more on lending within the Union. We were told by Mr Peter Sedgwick, Vice President at the EIB that "Around 90 per cent of our lending is within the EU. That

---

[87] Q63, Q91.
[88] Hungary written evidence p.
[89] Q155.
[90] DfID written evidence p.
[91] Hungary written evidence p.

percentage will go up to around 95 per cent on 1 May, when the acceding countries become members of the Union."[92]

73. The NGO, Saferworld, told us that "the increase over the last decade of amounts of EU aid to middle-income countries in Central Eastern Europe and South Eastern Europe and the Mediterranean at the expense of the poorest countries is not desirable. The process of enlargement has no doubt contributed to this trend, in order to facilitate the accession of new members this May. Whilst increased stability in the region is most welcome, this should not be at the expense of efforts to support development and peace within the EU's wider external relations."[93]

74. This gets to the heart of the problem: the EU and its new members rightly want to secure development and stability in the near-abroad, but at the same time the EU is committed to poverty reduction and the Millennium Development Goals.

75. We have expressed the view earlier in this report that aid allocations need to be rebalanced in favour of the poor countries. **We recommend that the Government works with other like-minded Member States to ensure that enlargement does not lead to a disproportionate share of EU aid going to the "near-abroad", and that the Commission takes full advantage of the benefits that enlargement may be able to bring to development cooperation.**

---

[92] Q195.

[93] Saferworld submission p.

CHAPTER 10: THE CASE FOR EU AID

76. Finally, we have addressed the question of whether EU aid provides added value as compared with national aid programmes. Senior politicians in both of the main United Kingdom political parties have on various occasions cast doubt on whether the United Kingdom is getting adequate value for money by channelling its aid—or at any rate such a large proportion of the DfID budget—through the EU, and have threatened "repatriation" of this money unless the quality improves. In a recent speech, the Leader of the Opposition described a "compelling case for increasing national control over overseas aid and development".[94]

77. Most of our witnesses were loath to rate the quality of EU aid relative to British aid. We were told that in a few respects EU aid was now amongst the leaders. However, the underlying view seemed to be that, while the quality of EU aid was improving quite fast and was likely to go on improving, it was still on average somewhat inferior to that of British aid. Mr Maxwell, from the Overseas Development Institute, was the clearest of our witnesses on this matter when he told us the quality of EU aid is "not as high the British" but better than that of a number of other Member States.[95] DfID are also clearly of this view.

78. Even though EU aid quality remains less than it might be, and its country allocation likewise less than satisfactory, our witnesses pointed to a number of advantages that it has over bilateral aid:

- The EU has an advantage over the bilaterals in some countries in being better able to handle sensitive political issues because it is seen as more neutral. In the same vein, it is easier for the Commission to impose conditions without this appearing "neo-colonial";

- In some regions, such as the Balkans, the Member States have been more than happy for the Commission to take the lead as the principal European donor;

- The EU has particular experience and expertise in certain sectors— particularly humanitarian assistance where it is able to put together large packages of aid, regional integration and transport;

- The EU has more experience and expertise than the bilaterals in dealing with middle income countries, in particular the experiences gained in institution building and cohesion policy through the process of eastern enlargement;

- The EU, acting on behalf of all the Member States, is in a good position to argue the case for good performance on governance and human rights, and include this in aid agreements.

- In principle, though this is not yet proven, there should be economies of scale in procurement and administration—because the EU programme is much larger than most bilateral programmes;

- It should be possible to secure greater coherence between aid and other instruments in which the EU has competence, particularly in trade and

---

[94] Speech by The Rt Hon Michael Howard QC MP, Berlin, 12 February 2004.

[95] Q27.

agriculture; and if the EU is to have a larger foreign policy role, its external assistance programme can be used in support of it;

- As mentioned earlier in this report, there are advantages for recipient countries in dealing with a coordinated group of donors, and for the donors there is value in having their aid coordinated in a single aid strategy. The EU can provide this coordination. (One country, India, has decided that it is drastically reducing the number of bilateral donors it is willing to accept aid from. In future, it will accept aid on a government to government basis only from the US, Japan, the United Kingdom, Germany and Russia. Consequently, for the smaller donors within the EU, aid through multilateral channels such as the EU becomes their only way of assisting India); and

- The existence of a substantial EU aid programme is a mark of the EU's maturity and solidarity, and of its seriousness as a group of states in trying to assist the achievement of the MDG's.

79. In addition, to the extent that the quality of EU aid is better than that of some Member States' aid, the quality of EU aid taken as a whole may be enhanced. (It is noticeable that several of the southern Member States, which have rather undeveloped aid programmes, are happy to put a much larger proportion of their aid through the EU than other countries such as the United Kingdom).

80. Whether the United Kingdom would do better to "repatriate" its aid, assuming it was politically possible, is thus more complicated than simply whether DfID is able to spend the same money more effectively. If we had been conducting this inquiry ten years ago, we might very well have argued in favour of such a course—given the very poor quality of EU aid at that time and the pressures on the United Kingdom aid budget at that time. Today, in view of the improving quality of the EU programme, the much larger United Kingdom bilateral aid budget and all the other considerations noted above, our view is that the existence of a substantial EU aid programme is in Britain's interest.

81. In practice, of course, the options for reducing our contributions to the EU aid budget are not very great—barring a general move in this direction by other Member States which seems unlikely. The main practical opportunity for reduction would be at the next replenishment of the EDF in 2007 (unless by then the EDF has been budgetised). However, our share of the current EDF is already well below our share of the budget, so—although our contributions are voluntary and could in theory be reduced to zero—the scope in political terms for a further reduction is limited. As regards budget aid, the United Kingdom will go on paying our "normal" share of whatever is agreed in the next Financial Perspective which will also take effect in 2007. The Government might argue for a reduced external chapter, but ours would only be a voice amongst many. We recognise, moreover, that the size of the EU aid budget, including the issue of budgetisation, will be decided partly by wider consideration in the negotiations on the EU's future financing.

82. **We conclude that the benefits of EU aid outweigh the possible advantages of "repatriating" it to national aid budgets which is of doubtful practicality. Until EU Development Aid's quality and speed of delivery further improves, the Government and other Member States should be wary of any large increases. But we think it would be**

neither desirable nor feasible for EU aid to be cut back. The Government can take some credit for helping to bring about the changes that have been achieved so far. The Government should continue to give priority to supporting the reform programme and ensuring that it produces its full potential. It is inevitable that there will be pressure for the EU aid Budget to be expanded in the future; any increase should be directly linked to further improvements in quality and focussed on the most poor. With continuing vigilance, understanding and (on occasion) pressure from the United Kingdom and like-minded governments, EU aid can improve further.

CHAPTER 11: CONCLUSIONS AND RECOMMENDATIONS

83. The Committee was impressed by the comprehensiveness of the latest Annual Report covering aid activities in 2002[96] (para 23).

84. It is our view that, taken overall, significant improvements in aid management and organizational effectiveness have been achieved, and the Commission is to be commended for its efforts (para 28).

85. There is, however, more to be done if the EU's aid is to match the best. Mainly, this is a matter of intensifying and carrying to completion the reforms that are currently in train (para 29).

86. We regard it as essential that faster progress is made in achieving coordination across the EU between the various aid programmes in aid-receiving countries (para 31, second bullet point).

87. Coherence is lacking between the EU's development and other policies; this is a failure of policy making. Prime examples are failure to reform the Common Agricultural Policy and the failed world trade negotiations (para 31, fourth bullet point).

88. In general terms, we think a simplification of the External Actions part of the Budget in the Future Financial Perspective is to be greatly welcomed (para 33).

89. We agree that for political and strategic reasons the "near abroad" countries need help and that the Commission is well placed to provide this support on behalf of Member States. However, we have sympathy with the Secretary of States view that a larger proportion of EU ODA should go to low income countries.[97] We would make three suggestions:

    - The Commission and Member States should consider the scope for increasing the volume of loans to these countries from the European Investment Bank so as to free up grant assistance for the low income countries. If the EIB is to play a larger role in these countries in place of EU grant aid, it may need to extend its reach beyond its traditional emphasis on private investment and public infrastructure and utilities to investment in the social sectors.

    - The Commission should concentrate grant assistance to these countries on governance and on poverty reduction.

    - It should review the 2000 development policy statement so as to ensure, in the words of DfID's and the FCO's written submission to the Committee, "its continued relevance and to clarify its role in guiding the future direction of EU aid", so that it encompasses the objective of assisting the "near abroad" as well as poorer countries. [98] (para 34).

90. We urge the Commission to take all necessary steps to bring the reform programme to full fruition so that EU aid can be made still more effective (para 35).

---

[96] COM (2003) 527 Final. Adopted on 3/9/2003.

[97] Q277.

[98] DfID/FCO Memorandum p..

91. We see considerable benefit in unifying the policy and programming functions in a single development DG. On balance, we feel that EuropeAid is working well as a separate agency, and that it would be best to leave it as it is. At the same time, it should be more closely linked than it is at present to the policy and programming functions (para 43).

92. We suggest that the outgoing Commission should prepare a blue-print, or blue-prints, for a revised structure for the incoming Commission—taking into account above all the need for efficiency and effectiveness, but also the move towards a strengthened CFSP (para 44).

93. In the EDF's "mid-term review", which is due later this year, the government should put its EU partners on notice that it will be looking for the Commission to develop a new strategy that will treat all developing countries that wish to have a partnership relationship with the EU on a common basis. This would not necessarily mean that all ACP countries would receive less aid than at present: there may be good reasons for some of them to continue to receive preferential treatment. But there would at least be common criteria for allocating aid across the globe. In addition, other elements that are particularly valued in the EU/ACP relationship should remain and be extended to other countries: political dialogue and "reciprocal accountability", conditionality in relation to human rights and governance; and the greater predictability of aid flows (para 49).

94. If it were not for the extra cost to the United Kingdom, the advantages of budgetisation in our view would clearly outweigh any disadvantages. We believe the government should weigh these carefully, including the extra cost, before reaching a decision on the current Commission proposal. Whether or not budgetisation goes ahead, we believe there is a strong case for a separate chapter in the budget for development assistance to maintain the poverty focus currently aimed at by the EDF (para 55).

95. We see merit in the idea of a "Peace and Security" budget, as proposed in the draft Financial Perspective, which would be the responsibility of the External Relations DG and Commissioner (para 65).

96. We believe it is essential that development policy is not downgraded and made subservient to the CFSP. While fully accepting that a successful development policy will bolster the EU's foreign policy objectives, we would prefer to see development described as an important element in its foreign policy—rather than as an instrument of it (para 66).

97. We share BOND's concerns with the draft Constitutional Treaty, as we understand does the government. We recommend:

    a. that the current differentiation between developing and non-developing countries in the Treaty is retained by using the wording in the latest version of the Treaty[99];

    b. and that development cooperation and development policy, whilst in support of CFSP, do have distinct and autonomous objectives (para 70).

98. We recommend that the Government works with other like-minded Member States to ensure that enlargement does not lead to a disproportionate share of EU aid going to the "near-abroad", and that the Commission takes full

---

[99] Document CIG 50/03.

advantage of the benefits that enlargement may be able to bring to development cooperation (para 75).

99. We believe the benefits of EU aid outweigh the possible advantages of "repatriating" it to national aid budgets. Until its quality and speed of delivery further improves, the Government and other Member States should be wary of any large increases. But we think it would be neither desirable nor feasible for EU aid to be cut back. The Government should continue to give priority to supporting the reform programme and ensuring that it produces its full potential. The Government can take some credit for helping to bring about the changes that have been achieved so far. It is inevitable that there will be pressure for the EU aid Budget to be expanded in the future; any increase should be directly linked to further improvements in quality and focussed on the most poor. With continuing vigilance, understanding and (on occasion) pressure from the United Kingdom and like-minded governments, EU aid can improve further (para 82).

100. We make this Report to the House for debate.

APPENDIX 1: SUB-COMMITTEE C (FOREIGN AFFAIRS, DEFENCE AND DEVELOPMENT POLICY)

Sub-Committee C

The members of the Sub-Committee which conducted this inquiry were:

Lord Bowness (Chairman from November 2003)
†Lord Harrison
†Baroness Hilton of Eggardon
Lord Inge
‡Lord Jopling
§Lord King of Bridgwater
§Lord Lea of Crondall
Lord Maclennan of Rogart
Lord Morris of Aberavon
§Baroness Northover
Baroness Park of Monmouth
Lord Powell of Bayswater
§Lord Tomlinson
†Lord Watson of Richmond
†Lord Williams of Elvel
†Lord Williamson of Horton

The Sub-Committee records its gratitude to Sir Tim Lankester KCB for his services as Specialist Adviser.

‡ Chairman of the Sub-Committee until November 2003

† Member of the Sub-Committee until November 2003

§ Member of the Sub-Committee from November 2003

APPENDIX 2: CALL FOR EVIDENCE

The Sub-Committee on Foreign Policy, Defence and Development (Sub-Committee C) of the European Union Select Committee is launching an inquiry into EU Development Policy and External Assistance.

The Sub-Committee would be interested in receiving views on the following questions:

(1) Evaluating the reform of EU development assistance

- 'European Development Policy'

(a) To what extent has the joint Declaration agreed by the Development Council in November 2000, which set out the main objectives of EU development assistance, had an impact on the allocation of aid?

(b) To what extent have poverty reduction and the agreed cross-cutting issues, including the environment, gender, human rights and good governance, been incorporated into country programmes?

(c) Has the intention to make EU aid, to a greater extent than before, conditional on performance as well as need, been brought into effect?

- Coherence and Consistency

(d) Has there been progress in bringing about more coherence and consistency within the EU's aid programmes?

(e) Has the agreement on broad development objectives and the introduction of Country Strategy Papers helped?

(f) How much progress has been made in bringing about greater coherence between development and other policies affecting third countries?

- Commission

(g) How successful in terms of improved efficiency and effectiveness has been the new organisational structure for EU aid introduced in 2000? Is there a case for further rationalisation?

(h) Are the quality, skills and number of staff now commensurate with the size of the overall programme?

(i) How much progress has there been in simplifying financial procedures so as to speed up disbursements without taking undue risks?

(j) What progress has there been in making the budget more transparent, bringing allocations into line with clear objectives and in achieving better reporting?

- Governance

(k) Has the abolition of the Development Council resulted in a down-grading of input and oversight by Development Ministers? Or by putting development aid within the ambit of the General Affairs and External Relations Council, has development been given greater political prominence and ensured greater coherence with other international policies?

(2) Looking ahead to 2004 and beyond

(i) Development and Foreign Policy

EU assistance and CFSP

(a) There has always been a strong political/foreign policy element in EU aid. This has increased over the past decade with increased aid to Central and Eastern Europe, the Balkans and the Mediterranean countries, and with the greater emphasis on governance and conflict prevention. Is this desirable?

(b) Has the relatively large amount of aid that continues to go to middle income countries been at the expense of aid to the Low Income and the very poorest countries?

(c) Should development aid be used as an instrument of foreign policy as is suggested in the High Commissioners 'Security Strategy' presented to the European Council at Thessaloniki in 2003, or should it be seen as an autonomous policy with its own objectives and rationale?

(d) Whilst good governance, political stability and conflict prevention are necessary for development, will the new emphasis on these objectives mean a down-grading of other development objectives, particularly poverty reduction?

Aid to the 'near abroad' and other middle income countries

(e) Should financial assistance to the near abroad come under the remit of EU development aid?

(f) Whilst recognizing that the EU will for political reasons want to continue to assist a number of such countries, can the assistance be provided in ways that could free up scarce grant money for the Low Income countries – e.g. by placing more emphasis on technical assistance and loans from the EIB?

(g) To what extent has aid to the middle income countries tackled poverty issues in those countries?

(h) How realistic is DfID's Public Service Agreement target to increase the proportion of EU Overseas Development Assistance to Low Income countries to 70 per cent by 2006?

Development in the Constitutional Treaty

(i) Is the new Treaty being negotiated able to ensure that development assistance is provided for the poorest and that humanitarian assistance is adequately protected?

(ii) Enlargement

(a) How will Enlargement affect EU aid policy, e.g. country allocation, relative emphasis on development versus political issues, and quantity of aid?

(iii) Does the ACP grouping have a future?

(a) Although the Cotonou Agreement was only signed in 2000 and is supposed to run to 2020, questions are being increasingly asked whether the ACP grouping of countries continues to make sense as a

Partnership for the EU. What is the particular benefit for the EU or for the ACP countries themselves of continuing on this basis?

(b) Is it right that the ACP countries benefit disproportionately from EU aid compared with Low Income countries such as Bangladesh and India?

(c) Would it not be better for the EU to treat countries on a regional basis and/or on the basis of their development status?

(d) How effective have been the joint consultative arrangements with recipient country Ministers and Parliamentarians under the Lome and Cotonou Agreements? Should these be carried over into other aid Partnerships?

(iv) EDF and Budget

(a) The Maastricht Treaty requires Member States and the Commission to produce complementary policies and to avoid duplication. To what extent has this been achieved with EU and Member States' bilateral aid?

(b) Does the EU provide a contribution in its aid-giving that adds value to Member States bilateral programmes?

(c) Formal negotiations on the new Financial Perspectives begin in 2004, and the mid-term review of EDF 9 in 2004 will lead on to the negotiation of EDF 10 in 2005. Given the pros and cons of using the EU as a channel for aid, what should be United Kingdom's approach on both these issues?

(d) The issue of whether the EDF should be budgetised is also likely to come into play. Would this be a good idea from the United Kingdom's standpoint?

APPENDIX 3: LIST OF WITNESSES

The following witnesses gave evidence. Those marked ⋆ gave oral evidence.

Mr Giampiero Alhadeff, Secretary General, Solidar, Brussels⋆

Mr Nick Banner, Member of Cabinet, Office of Chris Patten, European Commission, Brussels⋆

Ms Barbara Brandtner, Member of Office, Office of Chris Patten, European Commission, Brussels⋆

Charity Finance Directors' Group

Mr Patrick Child, Head of Cabinet, Office of Chris Patten, European Commission, Brussels⋆

Mr Olivier Consolo, Director, Concord, Brussels⋆

Mr Dominique de Crayencour, Director Institutional Affairs and Brussels Office, European Investment Bank, Brussels⋆

Dr Anna Dickson, Department of Politics, University of Durham, and Dr Peter Clegg, University of the West of England, Faculty of Humanities, Languages and Social Sciences, Bristol

Embassy of the Federal Democratic Republic of Ethiopia

Foreign and Commonwealth Office[†]

Mr Marc Franco, Director General, EuropeAid Cooperation Office, Brussels⋆

Mr Dieter Frisch, former Director-General for Development⋆

Ms Mikaela Gavas, EU Policy Officer, BOND⋆

Global Witness

Ms Louise Hilditch, Co-ordinator, ActionAid Alliance⋆

Department for International Development⋆[†]

Jamaican Mission to the European Communities, Brussels

Dr James Mackie, Programme Co-Ordinator, European Centre for Development Policy Management, Netherlands⋆

Mr Richard Manning, Chair, Development Assistance Committee, Organisation for Economic Co-operation and Development, Paris⋆

Mr Simon Maxwell, Director, Overseas Development Institute⋆

Mr Carlos Montes, Director, Development Strategies⋆

Embassy of Portugal

Mr Robert Reynders, European Court of Auditors, Brussels⋆

Saferworld

Mr Kristian Schmidt, Acting Head of Cabinet, European Commission, Brussels⋆

Mr Peter Sedgwick, Vice President, European Investment Bank⋆

Stop Aids Alliance

Ms Francesca Villiani, Development and Humanitarian Aid Officer, Solidar, Brussels*

WaterAid

† Combined written evidence

APPENDIX 4: GLOSSARY OF ACRONYMS AND TECHNICAL TERMS

ACP	African, Caribbean and Pacific states
BOND	British Overseas Non-Governmental Organisation for Development
CAP	Common Agricultural Policy
CFSP	Common Foreign and Security Policy
CSP	Country Strategy Paper
DAC	Development Assistance Committee
DfID	Department for International Development
DG	Director General
ECHO	European Community Humanitarian Office
EDF	European Development Fund
EIB	European Investment Bank
EU	European Union
FCO	Foreign and Commonwealth Office
GAERC	General Affairs and External Relations Council
IGC	Inter-Governmental Conference
LDGs	Less Developed Countries
MDGs	Millennium Development Goals
NGO	Non-Governmental Organisation
ODA	Overseas Development Assistance
OECD	Organisation for Economic Co-operation and Development
RELEX	External Relations
ROM	Results-Oriented Monitoring
WMD	Weapons of Mass Destruction
WTO	World Trade Organisation

APPENDIX 5: EUROPEAN INVESTMENT BANK

The EIB's shareholders are the EU Member States and the Commission. It provides loans, risk capital and guarantees in support of private and public investment in the Member States and in developing countries. Over 90 per cent of its loans are to Member States. It currently lends and provides other forms of financing to developing countries in a total amount of about €3.5 billion per annum. For its lending to Member States, the EIB is funded by borrowings on the capital markets (its so-called "own resources"). For its lending to developing countries, it also relies on "own resources"; but in addition, it receives loans and guarantees from the Member States and interest subsidies from the Commission.

APPENDIX 6: REPORTS

Recent Reports from the Select Committee

Review of Scrutiny of European Legislations (1st Report session 2002–03, HL Paper 15)

Annual Report 2003 (44th Report session 2002–03, HL Paper 19)

The Draft Constitutional Treaty (41st Report session 2002–03, HL Paper 169)

Session 2003–2004 Reports prepared by Sub-Committee C

Current Developments in European Foreign Policy (4th Report session 2003-04, HL Paper 28)

Session 2002–2003 Reports prepared by Sub-Committee C

EU Russia Relations (3rd Report session 2002–03, HL Paper 29)

EU—Effective in a Crisis? (7th Report session 2002–03, HL Paper 53)

The Future of Europe: Convention Working Group—Reports on Defence and External Action (15th Report session 2002–03, HL Paper 80)

Evidence by the Minister for Europe, Foreign and Commonwealth Office on European Security and Defence Policy Scrutiny, the General Affairs and External Relations Council of 18–19 March 2003 and the Current State of Common Foreign and Security Policy (19th Report session 2002–03, HL Paper 94)

The Future of Europe: Constitutional Treaty—Draft Articles on External Action (23rd Report session 2002–03, HL Paper 107)

A Fractured Partnership? Relations Between the European Union and the United States of America (30th Report session 2002–03, HL Paper 134)

Current Developments in European Foreign Policy (37th Report session 2002–03, HL Paper 152)

MINUTES OF EVIDENCE

TAKEN BEFORE THE EUROPEAN UNION COMMITTEE (SUB-COMMITTEE C)

THURSDAY 16 OCTOBER 2003

Present:

Bowness, L.	Morris of Aberavon, L.
Harrison, L.	Park of Monmouth, B.
Hilton of Eggardon, B.	Powell of Bayswater, L.
Jopling, L. (Chairman)	Williams of Elvel, L.

Memorandum by Mr Simon Maxwell, Overseas Development Institute

BATTLES WON? BATTLES LOST, BATTLES STILL TO FIGHT? NOTES FROM THE FIRST FIVE
ODI MEETINGS ON EUROPEAN DEVELOPMENT CO-OPERATION

Five of ODI's eight meetings on the future of European development co-operation have now taken place. The full programme, and summaries of all the meetings, can be found on the ODI website and EUFORIC[1]. Six key messages have emerged from the debate so far.

— **First, those who want development and humanitarian aid to be independent of CFSP, or on an equal footing to it, have battles still to fight.** Gisela Stuart emphasised that CFSP had featured much more prominently than development in the Convention discussions, and said that most EU countries viewed development co-operation as a tool of foreign policy. Carlos Montes agreed, saying that most Member States saw aid as a form of soft power to be deployed in pursuit of European values. The draft Constitution has a chapter on development co-operation which emphasises poverty reduction[2], and these aspects were praised by Baroness Amos, who also said it would be necessary to preserve them in the IGC. However, the Constitution appears to give the new EU Minister for Foreign Affairs (a Vice-President of the Commission) responsibility for co-ordination. Joanna Macrae saw some erosion in the draft Constitution of the commitment to neutrality and impartiality in humanitarian action, with the risk that humanitarian aid would be instrumentalised for foreign policy purposes. Martin Griffths, on the other hand, argued that the EU should become more active in the field of "humanitarian diplomacy", and wanted greater involvement in the politicial sphere.

— **Second, the ACP faces a major challenge.** It still has defenders—for example, Glenys Kinnock pointed to a strong sense of solidarity, purpose and identity in EU-ACP relations, and said the Association was strong. The Cotonou Agreement had a life of 20 years. However, as Adrian Hewitt pointed out, there is also recognition that the benefits to the ACP of its special relationship are being eroded, for example as a result of trade liberalisation, but also by virtue of new trade arrangements (eg EBA), new trade alliances and new regional economic partnership agreements. Even aid had become more conditional over successive renegotiations of the Convention. The EU was actively pursuing relationships with other regional groupings, some of which (like the African Union) cut across ACP boundaries. As discussed in one meeting, the key strength of the ACP arrangement may lie in the political relationship and the network of joint institutions (eg the joint Council of Ministers and the joint parliamentary assembly): there is potential here for genuine partnership and reciprocal accountability.

— **Third, the opportunity has to be taken next year to restructure the Commission, with a single Commissioner for development and a reorganised internal structure.** This point was made forcefully by Baroness Amos. Others also argued for less micro-management of the Commission by Member States and the Parliament: Carlos Montes, for example, argued that they should concentrate on strategic issues.

— **Fourth, enlargement will make little difference economically, at least to aid flows, but may well do so politically.** Victor Bulmer-Thomas made this point, noting that the accession countries will together have 10 votes out of 25 on the EU Council. Their aid programmes are small, and likely to remain so, but they will contribute a special concern for security and development in Eastern Europe.

— **Fifth, the battle to preserve the special status of the EDF has been lost, but there's still a battle to fight on poverty orientation.** There seems to be a consensus that the EDF will be "budgetised" when the new Financial Perspectives come into force in 2006: Glenys Kinnock made this point, welcoming the move because it would increase parliamentary scrutiny of aid programmes, but arguing for ring-fencing of aid for ACP countries. The question will be whether poverty orientation "sticks". As Gareth Thomas pointed out, the Mediterranean area currently receives $98 per capita, compared to $US 0.50 in Asia: he wanted to see more emphasis on poverty reduction, though he also recognised the special expertise and opportunity for the EC in middle income countries. Some believe that the poverty orientation should be reviewed. For example, Carlos Montes argued that the EU had a legitimate role in Eastern Europe, the Balkans and the FSU.

---

[1] See *http://www.odi.org.uk/speeches/edc 2010/edc 2010.html* and *http://www/eadi.org/edc2010*.
[2] Ch IV in Title 5.

— **Sixth, the collapse of the Cancun talks raises important questions about the commitment of the big players, including the EU, to multilateralism.** The US has already indicated its preference for "competitive liberalisation" and for bilateral agreements. Some think the EU may go the same way.

Future meetings will deal with trade, the CFSP and the policies of EU reform. Full details on the website.

15 October 2003

Examination of Witness

MR SIMON MAXWELL, Director, Overseas Development Institute, examined.

Chairman

1. Mr Maxwell, good morning. Thank you very much for coming. As you know, the Committee is conducting an inquiry under our remit with regard to EU development aid. I wonder if you could begin by telling us about the Overseas Development Institute and what is the involvement of it with the European Union, and also say what you might have learnt from the initiative which is titled "EU Development Co-operation 2010: What Scenarios for the Future?" If you could begin by filling in the background it would be helpful.

(*Mr Maxwell*) We describe ODI as Britain's leading independent think-tank on international development and humanitarian issues. We have about 55 researchers, many of whom are engaged on different aspects of European development policy. I have brought some copies of the ODI annual report in case anybody would like to know more. As you say, we are engaged in a process of thinking about European development co-operation and there are two sets of issues that we are grappling with, both of which I suspect might be of interest to the Committee. The first is about what position should one take on a series of European issues. The second, equally important, is how does one's voice become heard in a European context, because for those of us in the United Kingdom to have a view about Europe is no guarantee that that view will be shared anywhere else in Europe or that anything will happen as a result of us holding that view. On the first set of issues, clearly there is a great deal on the European agenda just now. The Intergovernmental Conference has just started, there are elections next year which will lead to the constitution of a new Commission, there are trade negotiations under way, the financial perspectives discussion for the next round will start and there is a series of reviews connected to the Cotonou Convention about to come up. One of the reasons why I think this particular Committee has a strong comparative advantage is that you bring together the development and the foreign affairs sides in a way that committees in the House of Commons do not for example, it seems to me that some of the most interesting questions are at that interface of the CFSP and the security and defence policy and the development side. On the process issue, we decided to take this question up by trying to put together a coalition of partners across Europe, because, as I say, we do not think that our voice on its own will carry sufficient weight. We are working with a group through the European Association of Development Institutes that has 150 members around all the countries of Europe. We are calling our project "European Development Co-operation to 2010", 2010 being an arbitrary date between now

and 2015, when the millennium development goals are intended to be achieved. We have listed the issues and then have tried to apply the technique of scenario planning which we have pinched, if you like, from industry. BP, for example, is well known for its work on scenario planning. We have asked what are the main drivers of change that might influence all these decisions I have listed? Can we classify them in some way and can we then generate some alternative imaginings of the future of what Europe might be like in 2010? The two key drivers we have identified are: first, whether Europe will work together or as a set of individual nation states with separate interests, so the degree of commitment to Europe; and, second, the degree of commitment to poverty reduction. Will European international development policy be guided by the millennium development goals or will other concerns, like security and terrorism, take their place on the agenda? If we have two drivers and we put them on two axes we have four possible scenarios which are described in more detail in the background paper of which I will also provide some copies. We couched our whole discussion in very neutral terms so as not to frighten the horses. I would like to give you the non-sanitised version. There are four options for Europe and this is a slightly pro-European reading of the options but let me make it anyway. If we are in the quadrant which has a greater commitment to European co-operation and a greater commitment to the millennium development goals we can think about that as progress. If we have the commitment to poverty reduction but not the commitment to Europe that will tend to compress Europe's role in this arena. If we have the quadrant where there is a greater commitment to Europe but no commitment to poverty reduction that will be a real step backwards, and if we are in the fourth quadrant, which is no commitment to poverty and no commitment to Europe, we think that people will begin to secede. We have called the four scenarios "progression", "compression", "regression" and "secession". We are organising a series of meetings, five so far with three to go. I have produced a two-page note on the main conclusions which I would be happy to submit to the Committee as part of this evidence. Similar meetings are happening around Europe with all the results being posted to a central website. We will produce some briefing papers in the new year summarising where we have got to.

Lord Williams of Elvel

2. Mr Maxwell, could you talk about your experience on the accountability question? Do you find the EU institutions helpful, open? Can you understand what they are doing very freely or could all that be improved?

Lord Williams of Elvel *contd.*]

A. If you had asked me that question five years ago, I would have said not transparent, opaque and very often difficult to work with. The new Commission has made a serious effort to improve the management of European aid and to improve the degree of transparency. They now publish an annual report. The second one is about to come out and I have a draft of it here. It provides in exhaustive detail, 350 pages I think, an account of what the European Union is doing in terms of international development, with statistical tables and accounts of innovations and measures to improve efficiency. That has greatly improved the accountability and the transparency. The Parliament remains strongly interested in European development co-operation and provides another measure of accountability. In the European context, the Court of Auditors has always been a strong institution holding the Commission to account, particularly in terms of the annual budget. If I compare the European Union's development programme with that of the United Kingdom, I would say that it is no less transparent and no less accountable. One issue that has been very much of concern to the NGOs is the abolition of the Development Council, which brought together development ministers. I am perhaps less informed about how that works but less worried than many, because it seems to me that there are other opportunities for development ministers to meet as a sub-council of the General Affairs Council which brings foreign affairs ministers together. I do not think there is a major issue at the moment about accountability and transparency of the European Union development programme.

3. But can the average layman like me pick up an annual report with all those statistics and 300-and-something-or-other pages and say, "Yes, I would really like to know how much the EU is spending on Guinea and how that is working"? Can I do that without too much trouble?

A. If you have the patience, sir, the information is there. There are certainly financial tables and chapters summarising what has happened at regional level. I do not think there is a country by country analysis, but it would not be too difficult to find. If you did have further questions, then I guess as a British citizen you would be entitled to work through your Member of the European Parliament and have questions asked either in Strasbourg or in Brussels.

Lord Morris of Aberavon

4. On the issue of transparency how confident are you and, coming back to Lord Williams' question, can one trace where the money is going to ensure it has gone to the right place and not got lost on the way?

A. The allocation of money by Europe is normally approved through committees on which Governments are represented, so there is, for example, an EDF Committee, on which the British Government is represented, which allocates European development fund money, and commitments are made as a result of project cycle papers being presented to the Committee. In the past,

the European Union has had a very significant problem with making large commitments and not spending them. The overhang problem has been famously large and is something that all the commissioners have spoken about in the last few years. The Commission claims to be reducing that problem very significantly and the figure that they cite in the annual report is that they have reduced the overhang from an average of 4.7 times the annual budget to an average of 3.8 times the annual budget. The 3.8 still sounds a relatively large number. I suppose that if you approve a project for five years then in the first year you would only spend 20 per cent so you would expect to have a significant overhang. I do not know whether there is a target for the overhang. The individual programmes and projects are then subject to normal monitoring and the Commission does spend money on evaluation of projects and whole country programmes, and the whole package is examined by the Court of Auditors. As with many things in Europe, it is important to make sure that one looks at what is written on paper and then checks it against practice. An obvious benchmark is to compare it against British practice. I suspect that there is rather more accountability at the level of project approvals than there is in the United Kingdom. It is probably true to say that evaluation is not as strong as it is in some of the large bilateral donors. Do we have a counterpart to the Court of Auditors? We do. It is the National Audit Office and they have done a couple of reports recently on DfID. It is broadly comparable.

5. My concern is whether the money has been properly spent. You say that it will be subject to normal monitoring in the role of the Court of Auditors and our procedures. What confidence is there that if the European Union allocates money to Guinea or whatever the money has been spent properly and somebody comes back with a report to say, "Yes, there have been three things spent there. The proposal was X amount for this, Y amount for that". How do you know whether the money has been properly spent and has not greased somebody's palm? Do you know?

A. Of course, I am not going to sit here and claim to have studied every project in every country. The question is, are the procedures in place to do that?

6. What are the procedures that are in?

A. The projects are checked and the accounts are checked. The very important question you have put your finger on is, are these projects any good?

7. Exactly.

A. There is a conventional wisdom about European aid that it is not as good as the best projects in the best bilaterals. To take a random example of a good bilateral, DfID, project for project, technical input for technical input, the conventional wisdom is that the British project will be better than the European project. There is a quality issue about European aid and that has been referred to several times by ministers in our meeting series. Both Baroness Amos and Gareth Thomas spoke in our series and both made a point about quality. It is pretty difficult to assess the impact of an aid

Lord Morris of Aberavon *contd.*]

programme because there are so many other things going on in most societies and the chains of causality are very long. The European Union reports in the latest annual report that they have introduced an impact monitoring and measurement system. I do not think there are many results from that yet. It will be very important, I think, to keep your question in mind when those results begin to come out. Quality is an issue and it does need to be improved. We need to ask why quality is not as good as it might be and that is something I could also voice an opinion on if you wish.

Lord Powell of Bayswater

8. Transparency and accountability used to be a problem in the award of contracts by the Commission financed under EU development assistance. Certainly in the eighties there were deep and dark suspicions as to why most contracts seemed to end up in the hands of French contractors and a number with Italian contractors. Is that an area which has been cleaned up in your experience?

A. I cannot give you a definitive opinion. It is not something I have heard spoken of as much as I did in the 1980s, so I suspect that it has been cleaned up but I cannot be sure. Certainly the procedures, again on paper, would be entirely clear and you would like them.

9. There was particular murkiness, if I remember, about food aid and the provision of contracts given for that and the quality of the food which resulted.

A. Food aid has shrunk very significantly as a share of European aid. Perhaps I may answer the question about why is there a quality problem? Quite a bit of that has to do with staffing issues. People always say about the European Commission that the total staff is less than the number of dustbin men in Frankfurt or something. It is clearly true that the European Commission has been very seriously understaffed ever since it started running the development programme. DfID has just reorganised its policy division and it now has a policy division with something like 200 professional staff and a budget of around £300 million to spend on thinking about what development programmes should be doing and about the interface between policy and project design. The European Commission has nothing like that and is very seriously handicapped by the fact that it does not have sufficient professional staff. That carries through right the way down the line. They are at the moment de-concentrating out to the field, moving responsibilities and accountabilities from Brussels out to delegations. As part of that exercise, they have recruited large numbers of accountants and people to worry about contract allocations in developing countries, to the extent that almost all the delegations where de-concentration has taken place have had to move, because they have recruited so many people that they cannot squeeze them into the office. I would be happier if they had also recruited lots of economists, social development advisers, political scientists and education specialists, because the programme needs those too.

Chairman

10. What do you think is the difference in terms of transparency and accountability between European Development Fund projects and budgetised aid?

A. The procedures are very similar. They have been through a big exercise to try and harmonise procedures, again described in the annual report. As you will remember, when the current Commission took office, there was what many of us considered to be a very awkward division of responsibilities between the commissions. Chris Patten was the *primus inter pares* and External Affairs Commissioner. Paul Nielsen was the Development Commissioner. Chris Patten retained all the desks that dealt with those countries that were not members of the Africa Caribbean Pacific Group, the ACP, and so the system was divided between a planning unit under Nielsen, and also dealing with ACP countries, and then a whole set of desks under Patten, dealing with non-ACP countries with different procedures, different histories, different degrees of transparency and so on. That was recognised by everybody to be an unfortunate political compromise. It reflected on something I hope we can come back to, about the relationship between foreign affairs and international development. The Commission tried to square the circle by creating an independent implementation agency called EuropeAid. The idea was that the Patten directorate and the Nielsen directorate would carry out the policy and the planning and prepare the country strategy papers for countries, and EuropeAid would then take responsibility for implementation. It is an unsatisfactory compromise and it is a priority, I think, to try and have that arrangement changed after the next Commission takes office next year. In the meantime, EuropeAid has been quite successful at trying to harmonise procedures across these different spending units and they have reduced the number of different protocols from 70-something down to seven; the precise numbers are in the annual report. I do think that has made some contribution to improving efficiency. There are other issues about the balance between funding to the ACP and other countries which lie at the heart of the dilemmas we are struggling with.

Baroness Park of Monmouth

11. Do you have concerns when you look at the plans in the Convention and the Treaty for a single foreign minister who would have very many more responsibilities? Do you have a fear that that might mean that decisions are made much more on foreign policy grounds than on grounds of need?

A. Many people do, and I share those concerns. It is an important question. There are issues about double hatting to do with the relationship between the Council and the Commission that I think are not my territory. The general question of what should be the relationship between international development and foreign policy and humanitarian policy is problematic. Many observers believe that foreign policy should dominate. The text of the Convention at some points hints in that direction: Europe has

Baroness Park of Monmouth *contd.*]

strategic interests in the world, these should be pursued, and it has values which should be promoted in the world. When you come to the development section of the Convention, there is a statement of principles. I have it here. It is title five, chapter one, paragraph two and it lists some of the priorities, including common values, fundamental interests and security, independence and integrity of the Union, and poverty reduction and sustainable economic development. Those are at a general level. When we come to the aid programme, which is a little further down in chapter four, section one, development co-operation, poverty reduction is stressed. The question is a pragmatic one of how the balance between these various priorities is going to play out in practice. On paper, there is protection of a development programme which is poverty focused, but in practice the European Foreign Affairs Minister, if that is the title eventually selected, will be a vice-president of the Commission and is likely to be the *primus inter pares* once more of those engaged in external action. Now, I am not one of those who believes that you can completely separate international development policy from foreign policy. In preparation for this discussion, I went back and had a look at the United Kingdom action plan for Africa that was produced after the Kananaskis G8 summit last year. It is quite clear that in order for Britain to achieve its objectives in Africa, which are about peace, stability and poverty reduction, it will be necessary to deploy all the instruments we have at our disposal. In Sierra Leone for example, that includes development aid, humanitarian aid, and also military assistance. I do not think we should be embarrassed or ashamed about that. The question is really about the terms on which the collaboration takes place. Will it be a collaboration which is subservient to foreign policy interests or will it be conducted on an equal basis? Those in the development community worry very much that the driving forces for foreign policy will be security, terrorism, migration, global diseases that might affect our own countries and so on, and that poverty reduction will be ignored. DfID has produced institutional strategy papers about the European Union, in a series of papers summarising policy towards different institutions including many UN agencies. They have done two or three on the EU. Because they are DfID, they do not deal with the foreign policy question. When they are tasked with that, they say, "Of course we have the International Development Act and we have our own responsibilities and we liaise very closely with the Foreign Office, but it is not our job to write the Foreign Office policy." The critical question for Europe and the future is: is the British model the right one in which we have the FCO and the DfID side by side or would we be better following what is the most common European model in which we have a senior minister responsible for foreign affairs who also has responsibility for development policy? I do not think there are too many principles at stake in that argument except that we want to be sure the development policy focuses on development and not just on fighting terrorism.

Lord Harrison

12. Mr Maxwell made the point that the best bilaterals were the best examples from the EU, to which he seemed to attribute the fact that DfID, for example, had 200 personnel as opposed to the smaller number in the European Commission. I wanted to know what you thought the remedy was for that, because one remedy would simply be to pump up the number of civil servants in Brussels; or is the remedy more along the lines of meshing the two groups of people to some degree or having secondment? The second point you made was that in one particular case more accountants have been appointed as opposed to economists and so on. Was this in reaction to the criticism the Commission has had over the years in terms of the spending and application of moneys? If that is a wrong balance, what should be the better balance?

A. Let me deal with the second question first, if I may, which is are more accountants a response to the criticism. In part, they are. It is also an attempt to manage deconcentration. The European Union has always been very French in its approach to administration, which is to say very centralised. I am always struck by the fact that they have delegation offices in very many countries but the French translation of 'delegue' is really representative, rather than somebody who is empowered to act. The delegations were very much in that position. The decisions were all made through committees in Brussels on which Member States were represented. Everything had to go back to Brussels for decision. The local offices were largely in charge of implementation. That is not what other donors do and it is not a sensible way to behave in a world with very good communications and rapidly changing conditions on the ground. The Commission was strongly encouraged, therefore, to deconcentrate. It was worried about deconcentrating because of not having the capacity or the accountability in the field. It made the decision that in order to manage deconcentration successfully—and they have deconcentrated some dozens of offices, 21 in 2001, 26 in 2002, and 30 in 2003, a large scale deconcentration—they needed to be sure that they were entrusting the money to a system that would not let them down in the field. Whether you need that many accountants is a technical question. My main hope is that they are not all European. I carried out an evaluation of European aid to Ethiopia some years ago and we discovered in Ethiopia there was not a single Ethiopian employee above the rank of secretary and that, for the price of one 25 year old European civil servant out-posted from Brussels, it would have been possible to hire 20 Ethiopians of university professor standard. Clearly, it is important to have a deconcentration process which also involves some recruitment of local staff. I think they are very cautious because they have been criticised so much. I think they are worried about scandal. The wider question is a very interesting one: why do we need a European aid programme? What are we trying to do here? Why not just do it through national, bilateral agencies? There are some interesting answers to that. Of course, it is partly an expression of solidarity, working together and so on, but that is

Lord Harrison *contd.*]

really not enough. There is a general case for multilateral aid: economies of scale, more efficient procurement, more coherent political response, better integration of instruments. If that is the rationale, we could give the money to the UN or to the World Bank and not necessarily have a new programme. We need to demonstrate that the advantages of multilateral aid really exist in the European context. There are some other reasons for having a European programme and some other comparative advantages one might cite. Those have been discussed in our meetings series, not least by Gareth Thomas, the Parliamentary Under Secretary of State in DfID. There is an issue of voice. There are some political aspects to the relationship Europe has with developing countries which are better than anything any of the bilaterals do, through joint parliamentary assemblies, joint councils of ministers, and they are part of the accountability mechanism. There are issues of trying to work together in international meetings. The Monterrey meeting on financing for development was an example where Europe worked together and was able to deliver a commitment to increase aid to 0.39 per cent of GNP. Of course, there are the claimed advantages of being able to work closely on issues such as trade policy, which link aid and trade. There is a final set of arguments, which is I think becoming less relevant than it used to be, although that may change when the accession countries join, which is that although the European aid programme may not be as good as the best of the bilaterals it is probably better than the worst. Not to name any particular countries, countries which have very small aid programmes, have very little experience of working in developing countries and do not have the technical resources might well find that the quality of the aid programme improves if they pass it through Europe. Some of them do pass very substantial shares through Europe. For example, Italy passes 38 per cent of its aid programme through Europe. Greece puts 47 per cent of its aid programme through Europe. Of course, there are some big bilaterals which also put large shares through Europe and the United Kingdom has traditionally been one of them. It is part of the conventional wisdom that the average quality of British aid is reduced by the fact that we put a share so large through Europe. The main reason for that has to do with which countries the money goes to, which is something I hope we will come to before the end of this session.

Baroness Hilton of Eggardon

13. Could I pick up an expression that you have used twice, which is conventional wisdom. When you say "conventional wisdom", do you mean United Kingdom conventional wisdom and therefore an assumption perhaps that our aid is better on that basis than other people's; or are you talking about conventional wisdom in the whole of Europe and our aid is better than European aid?

A. Those who hold the conventional wisdom will differ issue by issue, I suspect. You would have to remind me when I used the expression. The statement that European aid has been variable in quality is probably held pretty universally across the Union. The statement that it ought to be used entirely for poverty reduction is certainly not held universally across Europe. The statement that it is improving is probably held universally across the Union.

14. When I chaired the Environment Committee, we looked at TACIS and PHARE and found many of the things that you are talking about. The lack of staff in Brussels was certainly one of them. Also, they used very defensive systems for monitoring and evaluation, that it was all right protecting their backs and protecting themselves from allegations of fraud, waste and so on. It seems to me what you are saying about sending all these accountants out there is a continuation of that defensiveness. They had these enormous paper systems which did not mean anything at all. It was just people ticking boxes in Russia or somewhere, but no one was actually looking at the projects that the money was being spent on. Given that, do you think that things have improved over the last five years since I was involved in looking at this particular topic?

A. There have been a number of independent reviews of the Commission. For example, there was a peer review by the Development Assistance Committee of the OECD in 2002. The DAC organises regular peer reviews by other donors. They organise reviews of each other's work. The EU was reviewed in 2002 and had a relatively favourable report on the extent to which quality was improving. There are a number of references in the new annual report to impact monitoring that has been introduced. The big issue which remains with European aid is the question of who is getting the money. The Union has devoted a disproportionate share of its resources to what are called the ring of friends, which largely means eastern Europe and the Mediterranean. That distorts very significantly the share of the aid programme which is directed to poverty reduction. By 2006, the United Kingdom expects to spend 90 per cent of its bilateral resources on the poorest countries. Europe is still struggling along at just under 50 per cent and the reason for that is the money that is going to countries like the Balkans, Morocco and so on. There are many examples. That is a very interesting political question because it is entirely legitimate for the European governments to say, "We care about the Balkans and we pretty much care about North Africa as well." I have been puzzling over this one. I have come to the conclusion that it is an issue about the volume of aid. At the Monterrey financing for development conference last year, the argument was very clear. We have an international commitment to the millennium development goals expressed in the millennium declaration at the UN. The British Government is very strongly behind those. We have carried out an exercise led by former President Zedillo of Mexico, to estimate the cost of reaching the goals and that exercise indicates we need to double aid. At Monterrey countries committed to providing additional money. The European Union committed to providing 0.39 per cent of GNP by 2006. That is fine, but if you then spend that money on countries which are not in the poorest category, the money is not available to the countries which most need it in

Baroness Hilton of Eggardon contd.]

order to reach the millennium development goals. The conclusion that I have come to is that it is perfectly legitimate to provide money to the Balkans, North Africa and anywhere else you like, provided you are not asking the poor in India, Bangladesh or Ethiopia to act as the providers of that money by taking money out of their aid pot and putting it into those other countries. We need to have a clear commitment from the donors that the 0.39 figure will be for the poorest countries and that anything for other countries will be additional. In 2002, we passed in the United Kingdom an International Development Act, which permits the British Government to target its money entirely for poverty reduction and sustainable development. This is not quite of the level of the Pergau Dam, but I think there is an interesting question to be asked about whether or not providing money for non-poor countries genuinely meets the requirement of the International Development Act. The Act is quite carefully worded and says that the aid must be for the purposes of poverty reduction, so provided you could show that money going to middle income countries was being used to target the poor in those countries, then it would probably meet the test. It is a question that nobody has quite asked and would be worth investigating. I would be the last person to want to see DfID taken to court on this issue because I think DfID itself is very strong on the need to have a stronger focus on poverty reduction. There are ambiguities at the edge however. When Gareth Thomas spoke at ODI—his speech is on our website—he did say that the EU has a comparative advantage in middle income countries. Clearly, the British Government wants to see money being spent in those countries.

15. I wondered whether you thought the House of Commons reports on EU development aid had any effect and, by implication, whether whatever we say will also ultimately have any effect on EU development aid?

A. First of all, the reports that have been produced on Europe by both Houses have been serious, substantive, strategic and interesting. The International Development Committee has done a number of very useful reports on Europe. But this comes back to the process point I was raising at the beginning of our discussion. Wonderful reports; who is listening? The first people to listen and the people to whom the reports are largely addressed are the British Government. It would be difficult for me to say whether or not British Government policy has changed significantly as a result of the reports. I think they have been genuinely rather supportive of British positions, so there has not been a great divide between the committees and the Government. Having the British Government on our side is the least of our problems here. The question is how are we going to get the rest of Europe on our side, and indeed the rest of the world, because many of these issues require an input from the developing world. As we have thought about this as researchers and as a think tank, I have developed three models of how policy change could work across Europe and across the world. The first is what I call the Microsoft model, which is you have a single, hegemonic policy.

In every country you go to, you switch it on, so to speak, there is the same policy and it is all written in Seattle in the United States. Clearly, that is not where we are and not where we are going to be. The second model I call McDonalds. Every time you walk through the front door, it looks roughly the same but every branch is a franchise and is independently managed. We might get to that position but we are not there yet. The third model is inspired by airline alliances. Airlines very often are independently owned and work independently, but they collaborate. They will advertise together. They will perhaps move your baggage without you knowing about it from one airline to another and, at the extreme, they will have code sharing where you have very clearly linked flights. That works because there is a very high degree of trust between the parties and a great deal of information exchange. What we are trying to develop with our project is what I call "policy code sharing", which is trying to get people across Europe to work with the same high degree of trust and the same visible level of co-ordination. We as researchers are doing policy code sharing. The question worth asking is whether the parliaments of the Member States should not also be trying to do some policy code sharing. A few years ago, a House of Commons committee took the interesting initiative of setting up a regular meeting of chairs of select committees. I think they meet now once a year and try to co-ordinate their activities and involve also the European Parliament. It would be very interesting to have a similar exercise involving the upper Houses of Parliaments across Europe. There is more even than that that could be done. Why not have joint select committee inquiries, the French, the German and the British upper Houses, inquiring together into European aid? Why not go one step further and have the French, the Germans, the British and the Kenyan select committees all examining European aid together? It does seem to me that there is a great deal that could be done if we were to think about ways of collaborating more. I also think DfID should have a dedicated junior minister, whose only job is to pursue the British aid agenda in Europe. This is, after all, over 20 per cent of our aid programme and sometimes over 30 per cent. It is, by comparison with other elements, understaffed and certainly politically somewhat under-resourced.

Lord Morris of Aberavon

16. How do you ensure what you have termed poverty reduction money from Europe does not go to Balkan type problems? Is this war being won or lost? You talk about poverty reduction money going to countries like India. You talk about money going to problems in Balkan type situations and obviously the proportion of one would vary. The greater the money that goes to the Balkan type problems, I suspect means less going to poverty reduction in India. What are the proportions? Is more money going to Balkan type problems and less to Indian type problems or the reverse?

A. The share of aid is going to the poorest countries, which I said was about 50 per cent in the case of Europe, has crept up a little. It was 43 per

Lord Morris of Aberavon *contd.*]

cent; it is now 50 per cent. The disparities are still huge between what different countries receive. I looked up the figures from the latest annual report yesterday which are for 2002. Just as an example, India received 14 million euros in new commitments. Bangladesh received 32 million in new commitments. Morocco received 124 million. Romania received 696 million euros in new commitments. There is a huge discrepancy between what the poorest countries, especially in Asia, are getting and what the ring of friends are receiving. The European defence of this will be that that is okay because the amount of money available for poor countries has not gone down, it is just that we have put new money into the ring of friends. From the logic I followed earlier about Monterrey, I now realise that that is an invalid argument because, certainly from the point of view of individual Member States which are paying for this, the aid budget is fixed. Britain's aid budget which is targeted at the poorest is being diverted, if you like, and we could reach significantly more poor people if we were to repatriate the money and spend it bilaterally. I do not necessarily think we should do that, but I do think we should be providing aid over and above the 0.39 in order to reach the ring of friends.

Chairman

17. Perhaps I could return to the Development Act which you talked about a few moments ago and ask whether you believe it covers budgetised aid. Surely there is a powerful argument to suggest that it does not because budgetised aid is only attributed to DfID and DfID does not make appropriations in the same way as it does for the European Development Fund. Is that not right?

A. That sounds entirely plausible, but I am afraid I do not know whether attribution monies would be covered by the International Development Act. If they are not, they probably ought to be.

18. If you would like to ponder on that question and have second thoughts, I am sure the Committee would be glad to receive a note from you.

A. I will do that.

Baroness Park of Monmouth

19. Do you think it is possible that some of the money that is going into, say, Romania and Bulgaria, while they are waiting to come in, is going so that the EU can bring them up to the standard of the *acquis*? Therefore, that diversion of funds may have a limited life and may only go on for the next three or four years; or do you think it is a long term thing?

A. As countries join the European Union they become ineligible for money funded from international development budgets and they become eligible for other forms of support, including regional funds, structural funds, the CAP and so on. So yes, in due course, there will be savings. On the other hand, there are plenty of countries in the ring of friends who are not candidate members and some who might be candidate members but are not going to become members for quite some time. Perhaps

Turkey might be one of those. There is, given the strategic priorities of the European Member States, probably a very large demand for money in the Middle East, North Africa and central Asia.

Lord Williams of Elvel

20. I want to ask a question on aid delivery. Are we satisfied that the EU have a handle on possible fraud in the payments that are made to whoever for the purposes of development? I remember the famous alliance of progress which was pretty well abandoned because the amounts going out from the United States and Latin America more or less coincided to the amounts going to illegal bank accounts in Zurich.

A. I am not competent to give you a detailed answer. My impression is they are much better than they used to be and that the number of scandals has decreased. I cannot give you chapter and verse. The Court of Auditors, I imagine, would be the place to acquire that information. I would be happy to check back with the last couple of auditors' reports to see whether we can find anything for you.

Lord Bowness

21. You have talked about the ring of friends in eastern Europe and the Mediterranean. Could I turn to the ACP grouping? Do you think that the benefit which they receive is equally disproportionate compared with India, Bangladesh and other countries? Do you think there is a better way of doing it? Should countries be treated regionally or alternatively on the basis of their development needs and status? Perhaps you could give some indication of whether the disproportionate element for ACP is greater than the ring of friends.

A. With one exception I am becoming an ACP sceptic: The ACP, which now has 77 countries, has been a very central part of the European development co-operation from the beginning. It has had three dimensions, an aid, a trade and a political dimension. When Britain joined, the decision was made not to bring in some of our former colonies, particularly in south Asia, so it is still very much an Africa, Caribbean and Pacific group. On the trade side, the value of the preferences given to the ACP is rapidly eroding and that is because trade generally is becoming much more liberal and because initiatives like the everything but arms initiative apply not only to ACP countries but also to least developed countries which are not members of the ACP, which is a significant number. As trade liberalisation proceeds, the trade benefit of being a member of the ACP will further erode. Furthermore, the trade interests of ACP countries are not as homogenous as they once might have been. What we saw at Cancun was a number of different groupings of developing countries, some of them regional, some of them not, acting on particular topics. There has been a bit of a debate in our meetings series about the question of whether or not the ACP were significant players in Cancun. Some people who were there think they were; others think they were not. We had one ODI staff member on the Malawi delegation, Sheila Page.

Lord Bowness *contd.*]

Malawi is a member of the ACP. Her view was that the ACP had not been the most important avenue for Africa's interests to be pursued. The aid arrangements are becoming increasingly more difficult and hard to justify, given the kinds of figures I gave you earlier for India and Bangladesh, compared to some of the countries in the ACP. I do not think I cited Mauretania, but Mauretania received 15 times more than India received last year, for example. Mauretania is a very small country and very needy, but India has most of the world's poor. What remains very strong and worth defending is the political relationship between Europe and the ACP, expressed in a number of joint institutions like the Joint Parliamentary Assembly and the Joint Council of Ministers and also in some sort of reciprocal accountability. This is the exception I talked about when we talked earlier about accountability, I was thinking very much of accountability to United Kingdom taxpayers. There is also an accountability of donors to recipient countries which needs to be taken into account. In work we have done at ODI on partnership, we have talked about trying to have a partnership between the donor and the recipient which is not the same as the partnership between the rider and the horse. We want something more equal than that. The way to move towards a more equal partnership is through a political relationship and then some kind of procedure for recourse if you do not agree and, for arbitration if there are disputes between the parties, just as a couple of plumbers would do if they were working together in a partnership. They would have rules which govern the relationship. Britain, in its first White Paper in 1997, trumpeted the notion of partnership as being the guiding principle for our aid with developing countries but there was very little in the way of a reciprocal relationship. Since then, DfID has begun to be quite innovative and they now have something that looks a bit like a contract with Rwanda, Ethiopia and I think Tanzania, in which there is independent review of the aid relationship and some procedure for deciding disputes. The model of how to do that, I think, is the ACP relationship and the Cotonou Convention does have in it some quite specific procedures if the European countries disagree with what is happening in the ACP countries. You cannot just cut off aid. You have to go through some sort of process. In the document that I am going to leave for you, we have a box which summarises what that procedure is. I am all in favour. I think it is impossible to have a genuine relationship without some kind of reciprocal accountability. Your question is: is that enough to justify preserving the ACP relationship. My own view is that the EU has rapidly been developing relationships with other regions, the Barcelona process, the ASEM process, the Cairo process. Why not have a relationship which is rather more coherent across the whole range of developing countries which builds in the advantages of the ACP political relationship? As I have discussed this with people, one colleague has made the suggestion that perhaps the Commonwealth might be a model. The Commonwealth does not quite do its business in the same way, but there are clear parallels between the relationship that a group of rich countries—Canada, us, Australia—have with a group of developing countries, that could be replicated with the developing world. Perhaps we can then build on the ACP relationship and draw in other countries. I have suggested, for example, that some of the larger developing countries who are not members of the ACP should be invited to attend as observers and should perhaps be given speaking rights. Perhaps the agenda of ACP meetings could be structured so as to have some items on it of interest to a wider group of developing countries. This is a baby and bath water problem, not to throw out all the advantages of the ACP, while recognising that some of its core elements have been significantly eroded.

Baroness Park of Monmouth

22. Would you not say that NEPAD fits that, the contract on governance between the aid countries and the countries due to benefit?

A. NEPAD, and the African Union, is a good example of why the ACP is becoming more difficult to sustain, because of course South Africa is not formally a member of the ACP, and NEPAD also includes a number of North African countries not members of the ACP. The African Union includes all those countries too, so the African Union cuts across the ACP. If we have a relationship with the African Union, it is hard to have a relationship on the same topics with a sub-group of that called the ACP. On the contract question, there is an implicit contract. It is not a very clear contract. There is no treaty between Europe and the African Union, for example. What has been put in place is a peer review process, rather like the DAC process I described, whereby African countries will review each other's performance. When I last looked at this some months ago, it was making very slow progress. Not many countries are willing to offer themselves to that review and not many are willing to criticise their neighbours—including a few obvious cases we might think of. There is an implicit contract. You govern yourselves properly and we will provide more aid. As with the British White Paper of 1997, the question arises, "who decides?"

Lord Powell of Bayswater

23. Do you not think there might be some quite difficult political problems about de-privileging the ACP countries? When you said earlier why do we have a European aid policy, the real answer is that in 1957 France and, to a degree, Belgium came into the European Community with dependent territories and they wished to spread the load of the financial obligations they assumed towards those territories. The ACP grew out of that privileged relationship. You said rather tactfully that it was decided not to include India and Pakistan. The answer was it was vetoed by the existing members of the Community at the time we joined Europe. They were not allowed to be brought into the ACP. We were allowed to bring in some of the smaller African and Caribbean Commonwealth countries but not these south Asian countries. Do you think there is any reason to believe that the same considerations would not be used now?

Lord Powell of Bayswater *contd.*]

France clearly sees a strong advantage in having a privileged group, the ACP group, within which the francophobe countries are extraordinarily privileged and would be very resistant to any attempt to bring others to their level or to create what I think is an excellent suggestion of having a Commonwealth type institution which extended to all developing countries.

A. If you believe that the ACP privileges are quite rapidly being eroded on matters of substance *vis-à-vis* trade and to some extent aid, what is left is a shell which even those enthusiastic proponents in 1957 might find less useful.

24. It does not sound as if they are being that eroded if Mauretania is getting 15 times as much aid as India.

A. That is true. It was a slightly low year for India, I think. There is also a general problem that large countries tend to be under-aided and small countries tend to be over-aided. The point you raise is a very interesting one. The question we are asking is: is it worth battling to preserve the ACP. When I raise this question, people say to me, "What a ridiculous question. We have just signed the Cotonou Convention for 20 years. It was only ratified earlier this year. The question is not remotely on the agenda". There is an issue, however, about how much political capital, time and money rich countries will want to invest in what are increasingly seen to be rather irrelevant institutions. The Joint Council of Ministers, for example, does not attract very many ministers from Europe and the Parliamentary Assembly I am not familiar with in detail, but I doubt it has the influence it would hope for.

Chairman

25. What do you say to those who are critical of bringing into policy reciprocal political relationships, who question it and say, "Does this not just make the EU a soft touch for aid?"?

A. I say it depends how you write the rules. In the old days under Lome I, II, III and IV, European aid was largely contractual, which meant that once the EDF had been agreed it was divvied up and countries knew what they were going to get. There was a sense that that was a useful thing to do because it removed uncertainty in aid flows. On the other hand, it also meant that the EU found itself supporting some very unsavoury regimes and was not able to do much about it. Idi Amin, for a while, was a case in point. Because all this was contractual, you could not cut off aid. You need to have an aid relationship where, if there is a gross derogation on one side or the other, something can be done about it. If Idi Amin or someone like him were to come to power again in Uganda, one would want to be able to say, "We are no longer going to support this regime." The question that arises out of the discussion of reciprocal accountability is whether that decision can be taken by one party alone without consultation and without recourse or whether there should be some due process in making the decision. The argument for reciprocal accountability is to say, "Yes, this is an issue. We have defined in our contract of relationship that there will be good governance"—indeed, that is what the Cotonou Convention says—"and if those requirements are not met we will enter a process. If you do not like it, there is a procedure." I think it involved the Joint Parliamentary Assembly or the Joint Council of Ministers. It is not done arbitrarily but follows some kind of due process. I think that is right. You should not give aid to baddies; nor should you be allowed arbitrarily to suspend aid without consultation.

Lord Morris of Aberavon

26. We have already had a preliminary canter on some aspects of this. Could you clarify the relationship between European Union aid giving and bilateral aid? Are they completely independent, interdependent, or is it value added? Secondly, what governs the contribution that we make for bilateral aid and what we give to the European aid programme. From what you said earlier, there is a pretty traumatic effect if large areas of the world which are extremely poor get less and comparatively prosperous countries get more.

A. Europe has always had two ways of providing aid. The first is through category four of the budget, the external action section of the budget. The second is through the European Development Fund, which is directed to ACP countries, now under the Cotonou Convention. At present, about three-quarters of external aid is financed from the budget and one-quarter from the European Development Fund. I will address budgetisation first, if I may. Many people believe that it would be sensible to budgetise all European aid, for all European aid to be within the budget. Glenys Kinnock, when she spoke at our meetings series on this topic, made that point and gave in support the argument that it would increase parliamentary scrutiny because the budget is subject to the codecision procedure with the Commission, whereas the EDF is fixed by treaty and the money allocated by the Council. The only role Parliament has is in signing off the accounts. Budgetisation would enable more coherence to be brought to the totality of spending. It would increase parliamentary scrutiny and it would simplify arrangements. There are two arguments that have been made against it. The first is that the poorest countries would lose, which is why Glenys Kinnock argued for ring fencing money for the poorest countries. That relates to the argument I was making earlier on about the 0.39. The other is that some countries would have to pay more as a result of that change. For example, the United Kingdom of course pays a standard percentage of all attributed costs and that figure is currently 14.3 per cent. At the time of the last renegotiation of EDF, it negotiated for itself a lower contribution to the EDF and that figure is 12.7 per cent. Budgetisation would mean that Britain would have to pay a larger contribution to European external assistance, although given that the aid budget is growing I am not sure that that should be a major blockage. Budgetisation is probably quite a good idea, in my view, provided that we can retain the same kind of poverty orientation that is found in the British International Development Act and not see greater

Lord Morris of Aberavon *contd.*]

diversion of money to the countries which are not among the poorest, unless we are able to increase aid sufficiently to make that possible.

27. How do you ensure that?

A. You could do it legislatively. As they already do have budget lines for certain things, you could have a budget line not for forestry or de-mining, but called "poorest countries", which could be a very large budget line. It is perfectly possible to earmark money within the European budget for the poorest countries. The trick is to make sure that the budget is growing fast enough if that is what we decide to do and that there is enough money to meet both the poorest countries' needs and those of the Balkans, for example. There is a much more difficult question, which is what share of British aid is it sensible to be putting through the European Union in the first place. We know that some political parties, if not all at some stage, have threatened to repatriate British aid. Clare Short at a certain point said, "If it does not improve I want my money back." That is a political decision which researchers can inform, by looking at the relative advantages of European aid in terms of efficiency, in terms of its distribution and in terms of the quality of aid programmes. In earlier discussion, I think I have said that the quality is better than it was, though probably not as high as the best of British aid. The efficiency of delivery is improving markedly. That provides a case. The further case for European aid is of course around acting together, solidarity, simplification and the advantages of multilateral aid.

28. Is the bottom line, assuming that there is a constancy in the total provisioning, that the more we give, whatever mechanism we design, as our contribution to European aid the less we give bilaterally?

A. *Mutatis mutandis*, yes. With a fixed aid budget that must be the case.

Lord Powell of Bayswater

29. As I understand it, the only bit of aid we give through Europe which could be repatriated would be the EDF contribution. We could not repatriate the budget contribution because you cannot say you are not going to contribute to this part of the budget or that part. It is not an option.

A. It is not, but the financial perspectives discussion is one in which it is possible to agree the total size of category four expenditure. The financial perspectives take place every seven years and are due to start over the next year or so, ready for the new arrangement which will start in 2007, if I am not mistaken. It would be possible for Britain to go in and bat very strongly for a much smaller category four.

30. You could not just on that basis get your money back. Really you are just talking about the EDF contribution.

A. If you say so.

Lord Harrison

31. Instead of "get your money back", how about "give your money away"? Let us look at this problem not in terms of repatriating the quantum that is already there. Is there not an argument for giving more to the Commission? That was what lay behind my question to you when you talked about the 200 staff beavering away here in London on behalf of DfID and the paucity of numbers in Brussels. Is there not a logical argument to be made there that we would have all these other benefits that you have talked about but we would also save on duplication, sharpen up what we intend to do and provide the poverty reduction aim well preserved, brought to the fore and so on? Is that not a route that we could go down?

A. Say you are in Hilary Benn's, shoes, with an aid budget to spend there are various ways you can spend it. You can spend it bilaterally. You can spend it through the UN. You can give it to the World Bank. You can give it to the EU. In a rational world, the question you would ask is which of those disbursement options at the margin is going to give you the greatest return in terms of poverty reduction. You would then make that judgment based not only on where the money that you gave was going to be spent but what it was going to be spent on and how well it was going to be spent. I know that DfID is currently going through an exercise looking at the allocation of its multilateral spend with those sorts of questions in mind, but I have not yet seen the outcome. If you were to make that decision looking only at British bilateral aid and European aid, by far the dominating factor would be where the money was spent because so much more British money goes to the poorest countries than EU money. If you value that criterion above others, you would want to keep the money as far as possible running through the bilateral programme. If you think there are other reasons for having a European aid programme, you would want to put a greater share through Europe, which might be political as much as administrative. It is, like all budget allocation decisions, complicated.

Baroness Park of Monmouth

32. Would you not say that one of the problems is how much it costs to administer things? On that basis, the UN would cost a great deal. The EU probably would cost a fair amount. Does that bring it back to having more money to spend on the object because you do not have too much money to spend on the administration?

A. I could not sit here with confidence and tell you that the administrative cost for an equivalent kind of project is greater or lower in any particular case. I would be surprised if the UN were more expensive than the United Kingdom. I would be surprised if the EU were not somewhat more expensive than the United Kingdom. An interesting question here though is that the administrative cost depends on what you spend it on. By far the easiest way to spend money is to give a single cheque in the form of balance of payments or budget support, which does not require any agronomists or education specialists.

Baroness Park of Monmouth *contd.*]

It just requires a few macro-economists working in the Ministry of Finance. In the case of the European Union, at a stage when it was very badly under-resourced in terms of technical skill, the cliché I used was that they should cut their coat according to their cloth. If you do not have a lot of people, you need to find ways of disbursing aid which are not people intensive. Sometimes the best way is balance of payments support, but there are also one or two sectors in which the EU is specialised, like transport, for example, where they have expertise, they are pretty good at building roads and many bilateral donors do not do that any more, including the United Kingdom. The pressure on the EU, though, is always to do more. Somehow or other, the EU has to be seen to be present in every country and in every sector. The result is that it is very thinly spread and there is probably a case for greater concentration. They published an important strategy document in 2000, I think, which was designed to narrow down the programme. They identified six areas they were going to specialise in: trade, regional development, macro-economics, transport, food security and rural development and institutional development. That is a rather eclectic list and they have not done terribly well at concentrating within that list. Cut your coat according to your cloth is not a bad maxim for an administration under stress.

Baroness Park of Monmouth

33. DfID has suggested that EU development assistance receives comparatively little interest from the NGO community. Do you agree with that and, if so, what has been the effect of that lack of interest?

A. Interestingly enough, I am not sure that I do agree. I think there is a serious problem with the academic community which I will come to in a second. The NGO community is patchy but there is a co-ordinating organisation of NGOs called BOND, the British Overseas NGOs for Development, and they have a European team of three people which has done sterling work in, for example, stimulating debate about the Convention. BOND is the British platform for a European coalition of NGOs called CONCORD which is represented in Brussels and is again very active. That is on European issues generally. On certain topics, for example, trade, of course the NGOs are extremely active in the United Kingdom. ActionAid prided themselves on having representatives on eight separate delegations at Cancun. CAFOD are very active, so are Oxfam with their excellent trade report. There is less debate on EU issues generally. It is not something that has been top of the agenda for many NGOs, they are always making choices about what to campaign on, and they have found education or HIV or trade more attractive than the reform of the European Commission. The academic community I am more worried about. I am President of the Development Studies Association of the United Kingdom and Ireland. We have a European Study Group but it is relatively small and there are not more than four or five academics in the United Kingdom who are working in this territory. That is a pity and if I were the British Government I would be wanting to encourage more research. DfID has put money into a European oriented research window, the acronym for which is EC PREP, but it has not been very successful yet at funding work on the kinds of issues we have been discussing today. I ought to be able to come to you with a much more coherent research based story than I have been able to. We are still too anecdotal. There is more to do.

Chairman

34. I only make one comment myself, Mr Maxwell. You have talked about joint meetings with other parliamentary committees. I think it is a difficult road to go down. My experience of attending meetings of Chairmen of Defence and Foreign Affairs Committees within Europe really does not amount to very much and it is very difficult indeed to focus on a particular issue at those sorts of meetings. I hesitate about that one. Thank you for coming. You have been extremely clear, if I may say so, and I think a great many of the things which you have said to us will appear in our report because I think you have opened our eyes to a lot of things we did not fully understand earlier.

A. I have enjoyed it. Thank you all very much.

Supplementary memorandum by Mr Simon Maxwell, Overseas Development Institute, London

1. At the evidence session on 16 October, I was asked to clarify two points:

   (i) Whether all the monies contributed to EU external assistance programmes were subject to the International Development Act, or whether the Act only applied to contributions voted but not "attributed" (ie and for example, to contributions to the EDF, but not attributed contributions to the budget); and

   (ii) Sources of information about the audit trail of European external assistance, especially with regard to fraud.

2. On the first question, information from DfID is that the International Development Act does indeed only apply to voted expenditure, ie to the EDF but not the budget. Budget expenditure is governed by the European Communities Act of 1972, which does not have the same strong poverty reduction focus. The Committee will recall my evidence that three quarters of external aid is currently financed from the budget, and may wish to consider whether or not it might be possible to extend the provisions and principles of the

International Development Act to external action under the budget. This will become more urgent if the EDF is budgetised, as seems likely to be the case.

3. On the second question, I can provide information about sources, but cannot claim to have undertaken a detailed review. The main sources are:

(i) The Commission's annual report on external assistance, the second edition of which, covering the budget year 2002, has just been published;

(ii) Reports published by the Evaluation Service of EuropeAid;

(iii) Reports published by the Court of Auditors;

(iv) Other EU reports; and

(v) External reviews, for example by the Development Assistance Committee of the OECD.

4. The Annual Report on external assistance is a valuable source on both current programmes and the continuing reform process. For example, the 2001 Report describes the new results-orientated approach; the 2002 Report contains information about deconcentration and improvements to financial management. The Reports are available on the EU website:

(http://europa.eu.int/comm/europeaid/reports/aidco__2001__big__annual__report__en.pdf).

5. Evaluation Reports since 1997 are also available on the EU website (http://europa.eu.int/comm/ europaid/evaluation/index.htm). 187 of these are listed, covering all geographical regions of the world, and also a number of sectors (eg gender, food aid) and special topics (eg drugs, humanitarian assistance). The full list is attached.[3] (not printed) An important question for the Committee to ask is whether or not the terms of reference of evaluation reports include audit issues.

6. The Court of Auditors reviews the work of EU institutions, including EU aid to non-Member States. It produces annual reports, special annual reports, special reports and opinions. Some 245 of these are listed on the website (http://www.eca.eu.int).

7. The Court of Auditors' report on the 6, 7 and 8 EDF (EC Official Journal of 28 November 2002, pp. 289–313) reported on the accounts of the Commission. This assessment was largely document-based and did not include on-the-spot research. The report stated that "payments for the financial year are, taken as a whole, legal and regular. However, because it did not carry out on-the-spot audits and because it cannot rely on the results of the audits initiated by the Commission, the Court is not in a position to provide assurance regarding the reality of work, supplies and services underlying the payments at the level of local beneficiaries." (p. 301).

8. Other reports supply more detail. For example, a report on the execution of infrastructure work financed by the EDF (EC Official Journal, C 181, of 31 July 2003, pp. 1–28) concluded that: "in overall terms the works financed by the EDF made a significant and relevant contribution to national infrastructure development strategies. [. . . But] studies were not subject to quality control, and as a result too many contracts were based on faulty or unrealistic terms and conditions. [. . .] Unfortunately, the organisation of the central departments [. . .] did not allow them to build up sectoral expertise that could be applied to the advantage of all works contracts financed by the EDF, and thus robbed the Commission's involvement of some of its added value." (pp. 15–16).

9. With regard to other EU initiatives, and specifically on fraud investigations, the Union's anti-fraud office (OLAF) publishes annual reports with a comprehensive overview, indicating the number of investigations and an estimate of the sums involved. OLAF, however, deals exclusively with activities financed via the EU budget, ie the EDF is not covered by its reports. Other institutions involved in development assistance in the broad sense, such as the European Investment Bank (EIB), the European Bank for Reconstruction and Development (EBRD) and the Humanitarian Office (ECHO) have their own evaluation units and report regularly on their activities. The European Parliament also plays an active role.

10. Finally, an external assessment is provided by the peer review process on the Development Assistance Committee (DAC) of the OECD. A DAC Review of EU aid, carried out by Canada and Norway, was published in June 2002. A summary is attached.[4] (not printed) Among other points, the report concluded that: "of particular note are improvements to accountability at all levels, the introduction of the CSP process, the speedy and efficient delivery of humanitarian aid, the clarification of the links between relief and development, improved evaluation systems, and progress in the decision-making process with Member States, and with 'deconcentration' of authority to field offices".

---

[3] Not printed.
[4] Not printed.

THURSDAY 23 OCTOBER 2003

Present:

Harrison, L.   Morris of Aberavon, L.
Hilton of Eggardon, B.   Park of Monmouth, B.
Inge, L.   Powell of Bayswater, L.
Jopling, L. (Chairman)   Williams of Elvel, L.
Maclennan of Rogart, L.

Examination of Witnesses

DR JAMES MACKIE PhD, Programme Co-ordinator, European Centre for Development Policy Management and MR CARLOS MONTES, Director, Development Strategies, examined.

Chairman

35. Good morning, Dr Mackie and Mr Montes. Thank you for coming; we very much appreciate it. The Committee is conducting an inquiry on European Union foreign policy, defence and development but with particular interest in international development assistance. We are in the early stages of our inquiry and perhaps I can begin. Dr Mackie, in the briefing note which we have received, you have raised four major changes to the EU next year which you have highlighted as meriting attention. For the record, I repeat them: changes to the European Union's institutional structure; key financial decisions; global trade negotiations; a more proactive stance by African leaders. May I ask you to put those in order of urgency? What would you like to come out of those four points you have raised. What would you like to come out of them, but what in practical terms do you think is the likely outcome?

(*Dr Mackie*) Good morning everybody. Thank you for the question and thank you for inviting me. Yes, that is quite an all-encompassing question. The major change, the one which would have the most impact, would be the institutional changes. That can have a long-running effect which we will not necessarily see immediately. The point at the moment is to look at the IGC and how that is developing. The major challenge there is increasing the level of coherence between different areas of policy. So we have this whole debate about the "double-hatted" foreign minister that you are probably well aware of and it is quite difficult to see where that is going. The challenge there is to try to achieve greater levels of coherence. The difficulties are split between the Council and the Commission in the foreign policy area and if they can be overcome, that will be quite important. For development, that then means: what is the relationship between development and foreign policy? If you strengthen the foreign policy side, in the European Union structure development has always been the stronger traditionally as the older policy area and the foreign policy area is much newer, that will therefore mean a certain shift in relationships. Many people in the development sector are worried about whether development will then become a tool of foreign policy. That is an area really worth watching. I personally do not believe you can hide your head in the sand and avoid this relationship. It is becoming more and more of an

issue and it is a question of finding the right balance between foreign policy and development policy, ensuring that neither becomes instrumentalised by the other, allowing enough space for the development policy to develop and the programmes to develop in a professional manner and an effective manner, but at the same time recognising that impactful development can have an important impact on things like stability in countries and therefore security issues and so on. The financial questions are also important. They relate partly back to this first point: will the changes taking place make it easier to use development funds for foreign policy objectives? There are several worries in that area. One can imagine ways of protecting the development funds. The big change here, particularly for the African Caribbean Pacific (ACP) group of countries is whether or not the EDF will be budgetised, whether it will be brought into the European Union budget and what that will do to the security of the fund. It has always been one of the big principles of Cotonou and Lomé that the funds are reasonably secure for the countries and that is now being very seriously challenged; the French Government in particular has shifted its position on this quite markedly. The debate would run rather differently this time than it has in previous years. This is coinciding with the debate on the financial perspectives, the next six-seven-year framework for the EU budget, and it is therefore an opportunity to marry the two and it is a good opportunity to bring the EDF into the budget. I personally am not reassured yet that a solution has been found to protect the EDF funds sufficiently for the ACP countries, but it is still quite early days on that. I would probably put the two institutional changes first and then the financial issues second, as the two most important. After that I would say that the changes taking place are very encouraging, particularly in Africa with the African Union (AU). That gives much more of a solid framework to deal with from the European Union's point of view and I would see that as strengthening the position of many poor African countries if the whole construction of the AU, particularly since the Maputo summit with the new commissioners etcetera, goes forward in the way it has been progressing over the last year or so. Personally I think it is much too early to say how successful that can be, but it has a lot of potential in my view.

Chairman contd.]

36. You put a good deal of emphasis on foreign policy objectives. Do you think that DfID are mistaken in asking the European Union to switch aid effort over to the poorest countries?

(Dr Mackie) No, not at all; no. This is something which was recommended in the EU Treaty and has been a major feature of the development policy statement from November 2000. It is not just DfID pushing for that. There are other Member States pushing for that. In terms of focusing work and focusing resources, this focus on poverty eradication is very important to me. I would not disagree with DfID on that.

37. Mr Montes, as Dr Mackie has said, it was a rather broad opener. Is there anything at this stage you would like to add? Let me say to both our witnesses that if either of you wants to chip in at any time, please feel free. Is there anything you would like to add at this stage?

(Mr Montes) Just very briefly. Thank you for inviting us. My background is a bit different because most of the work I have done is official work for the Commission on evaluations generally and more recently high level reviews on Tacis and enlargement. Taking that into account, and the work is in the public domain, I would say that I agree that the most important thing is institutional change. This offers risks, but also many opportunities, particularly having more coherent and effective policy action by the European Union and good governance both in foreign policy and development. This is something new for the development community and the foreign policy community and in that sense this meeting is particularly interesting because in my view this is where the European Union assistance and foreign policy is going to be five years from now, in the integration of these two areas. On the areas of financial perspectives, trade issues and the stand of African leaders, in my view there is little room for manoeuvre. In the details of how these institutional changes take place, because it is not just an issue of the merging of foreign policy and aid policy but whether there are separate aid agencies for implementation or whether that is going to be part of the EU foreign service, in those details, the issue of whether development suffers or not is going to be determined.

Chairman: We will move on, because we will come later to a good many of the issues you raised, like enlargement, like the future of the ACP, like budgetising EDF.

Lord Morris of Aberavon

38. In November 2000, the joint declaration on European Development Policy, was agreed and it set out the main objectives for development assistance. What impact has it had? May I follow that on, that in the post-Iraq situation, if Europe agrees to provide aid, it seems the British allocation, our own aid, is going to be less to other countries, given that we are now pledged to give aid to Iraq. Is that likely to occur so far as the European aid is concerned?

(Mr Montes) The European Development Policy statement was something which was appreciated by most donors and particularly by the United Kingdom because of its poverty focus. As always, the policy part is easier to carry out than the implementation part. You have the first constraint which is the financial perspective. This seven-year budget is the one which determines the regional allocations to each area and that obviously was not affected by that development policy. The EDF allocation (2000–05) was also not affected by the development policy statement. Then you have the country strategy review mid term, so you are supposed to try to re-allocate a bit of the budgets to countries depending upon performance. That process is difficult because in a way it presupposes the reform of the entire organisation and that obviously takes time and probably we will discuss that later. There is much more progress in the planning and strategy and policy area. In terms of allocations themselves, progress has not happened yet, but there is greater poverty focus at that strategy level. On the issue of the United Kingdom programme, I better leave that to an expert on United Kingdom aid. I have an opinion, but it would not necessarily be the most informed one.

39. It is not the United Kingdom that I am concerned about, but whether there is going to be an effect on the policy of allocating aid to countries from the European Union in the same way as I suspect and understand it is going to happen as regards the United Kingdom.

(Mr Montes) The European Union already focuses quite a lot on foreign policy and broad issues and this is a result of a consensus within Member States. I understand the allocation to Iraq is very limited—about €100 million—and therefore will not have a direct impact on the allocations to poor countries.

40. Only small.

(Mr Montes) Yes; only small.

(Dr Mackie) There has not yet been much debate in the European institutions about finding large amounts of resources for Iraq and it would depend on the position of different Member States. The British Government is obviously in a particular position on that one and the others are more reluctant. I would expect that debate to follow in due course. The way the EU budget works, the money would probably have to come from the reserves at first within the budget. It would not affect the EDF because they could not remove money from there, out of the bulk of least developed countries (LDCs), so those funds at least would probably not be affected by Iraq. Funds to other countries like India, Asia and Latin American groups, might see a reduction. That is possible. That looks similar to the sort of debate I understand is taking place here in London with DfID. As I understood it, the money was primarily going to come from middle income country budgets and not from the least developed countries. It is rather early to say on that. Coming back to your first question, the development policy statement did have this major focus on poverty eradication, but it also laid out six priority areas. In terms of finances, the bulk of finances traditionally—and it is still the case—a large proportion of the EU budget funds and also the EDF go on infrastructure projects. That was one of the areas identified as a priority area for the Commission, particularly transport, as an area where

Lord Morris of Aberavon *contd.*]

the Community had a certain specific value added, a certain expertise. Looking at allocations since that date, that continues to dominate, even though, in the country strategy process that Mr Montes was referring to, there has been an attempt to shift away from that a bit. A very important part is still in that area. I would agree that it is still a bit early to say three years on where there has been major impact.

Lord Williams of Elvel

41. Could you tell us what the legal status of the European Development Policy is? It is a declaration, but is it binding on anybody, or is it just a pious attempt to allocate something or other and nobody pays much attention?

(*Dr Mackie*) It is a decision of the Council and the Commission, so from that point of view it is a declared policy for the European Community funds. It also indicates to the Member States the areas where priority is given in the EC and encourages Member States to deploy their funds in a complementary fashion. That is reinforced by the Treaty and goes back to the Maastricht Treaty where there is a commitment to growing complementarity and co-ordination between Member States and the Commission. The policy itself is not binding on the Member States, as I understand it, but the Treaty behind the policy does encourage this complementarity. Efforts have been made to move in that direction and that goes back to Maastricht, which is ten years ago. Efforts have been made to try to move towards greater complementarity. At first it was extremely slow and successive development directors-general—DGVIII—complained bitterly at one point about the reluctance of Member States to fall in and be more willing to discuss co-ordination and complementarity. Over the last few years, we are seeing greater emphasis on co-ordination, particularly between Member States and the EC, particularly at the field level. In visiting delegations and talking to heads of missions and so on you do get a sense of much greater levels of discussion. I would say it is still very dependent on personalities, but there is certainly progress in the last three years.

(*Mr Montes*) Translating overall policies into implementation of assistance programmes always takes quite a while. The general direction is there, but the actual implementation requires the reform of the European Commission as would happen in any organisation.

Lord Inge

42. In 2000 the European Commission introduced a new organisational structure for aid. Do you think that has been effective and what recommendations would either of you make to improve the efficiency of that organisation, particularly given what has been said about the gap between policy and the effectiveness of implementation. Could you touch on that as well? You might have to do it in words of one syllable because I do not really understand it.

(*Mr Montes*) I shall be very short. In principle the fact that Europe Aid manages aid for all regions contributes to coherence and that is positive. Before

you had separate agencies or directorates. However, there is still division between External Relations DG, Development DG and Europe Aid. There is need for the next wave of reforms and these will happen with the new organisational structure.

43. Are they planned?

(*Mr Montes*) This is part of the new Constitution. One possibility is that an EU foreign service, which is postulated in that new Constitution, will run this foreign policy and development policy together and in a way that would give this coherence. The alternative is to have a separate agency just for the implementation of aid, which means again that there will be a separation between the people who actually implement the policies and the foreign service. The second point is deconcentration, as they call it, which is the fact that they are now running their operations much more through their delegations and taking decisions at a local level which in principle is obviously a good idea. It is a complex process and requires many resources. These are early days.

44. When you talk about resources, are you talking about the bureaucracy rather than what is being produced?

(*Mr Montes*) What I mean is that it requires a lot of effort to make sure that auditing capacities, technical capacities are transferred to the local delegations and this is a difficult process. That is why it needs resources. In general the issue is that changes of behaviour which require this sort of reform are more difficult than changes of rules, so even if you change the rules real reform is still difficult. Operationally people will agree that the impact has still been limited.

(*Dr Mackie*) Below the surface there are many improvements in the way the actual nitty-gritty of management of aid is carried out in the Commission. Within Europe Aid, within this new agency, a lot of harmonisation of procedures, a lot of simplification, greater clarity in procedures too. There is real movement there which a lot of people will recognise and note. From that point of view, it has been a good step forward. I would agree with Mr Montes that there are still one or two areas of reorganisation which are not yet decided upon and which would be useful, particularly the way things are split at the moment: the implementation is in Europe Aid, but the policy desks, the country desks, are split in Development DG and External Relations DG. That means that you have a slightly different ethos, a slightly different culture in these two DGs and that has worked against getting a real standardisation of the implementation or the way policy is carried through. That is certainly one change that I would hope to see in this period next year when we will get some changes, but we do not know whether that change will be among them. Then there is also still some dissatisfaction and many staff will complain, officials will complain, that the actual point of split between the policy and the implementation from one DG to Europe Aid is still not as satisfactory as it should be and there is a greater need for integration there. It is certainly much better than the first phase. The first reorganisation was the Common Service which was set up. There were an awful lot of complaints and it was clear to everybody that it was

Lord Inge *contd.*]

not working. There has been an improvement on that. Yes, there is improvement, but there are one or two things there. Those are not agreed yet. There are areas people are aware need to be improved and I would hope that there is enough awareness of them so that people take advantage of the changes coming out of the IGC and the new Commission and the new structures which are likely to be with new Commissioners and actually carry them through.

45. May I ask one question of fact and one general question? In terms of fact, if you deliver X packet of aid to country Y, does that then hand it over to someone in country Y, or do you have a team there to look after it? How does that work?
(*Dr Mackie*) That is what Mr Montes was referring to, this devolution of authority.

46. That is what I am talking about. Is the authority devolved to a team which you would have in country? That is what I am trying to get clear.
(*Dr Mackie*) Yes, that is right. There is a process[1] currently going on. It is in three phases over three years of delegations.

47. That is what I wanted to clarify. My other question is: how is the evaluation of the success of the aid you have delivered done?
(*Dr Mackie*) Mr Montes probably knows more than I as he works closely with the evaluation department.
(*Mr Montes*) Performance assessment is always difficult within government and I am not referring here just to the Commission but to the aid development system in general. You can imagine if here within the United Kingdom it is difficult to assess the performance of schools or education, what it is like when things are being delivered 5,000 miles from London. Obviously this is an area which is crucial. External inspection of programmes, not just of EU but other donors, is essential for improvement, but it is an area which donors in general find difficult. The fact that civil society or the public in general pay little attention to these programmes makes it difficult too. In that sense the integration with foreign policy and security might be of interest, because once issues which are more linked to the public, such as organised crime, border controls in nearby countries, come into the minds of the public, I imagine there will be more of a requirement that these programmes are inspected more rigorously.

48. So you say there is a problem.
(*Mr Montes*) I have not said that.

Chairman

49. We have heard a number of criticisms of the general transparency of the European aid effort. To what extent do you both think that is justified? To what extent and how would you like to see the level of transparency improved?
(*Dr Mackie*) It is not as justified as is often felt. In fact the Commission has a lot of people looking over

its shoulder a lot of the time with Member States. Other bilateral donors do not have that sort of committee of Member States breathing down their necks. I exaggerate, but there is a lot of discussion there with Member States. I also feel that the Commission at times reacts to that and says "We want to work out our ideas first before we have to debate them with outside parties". I would say that it is usually pretty easy to get information out of the Commission on what is going on internally in terms of discussion. You do not necessarily get the final result, but I would say it is a fairly open organisation in terms of getting information. I think people often find it difficult because they do not deal with it on a regular basis and a lot of people who have to deal with the Commission are not in Brussels. They deal with it from capitals around Europe or abroad and then it becomes a much more opaque organisation. The culture of the organisation is much harder to follow and certainly when I first started dealing with the Commission it was here in London and I found it incredibly opaque. When I moved to Brussels and started dealing with it much more regularly, I began to realise that in fact it was easily as open as the Department for International Development here and it was as straightforward in terms of getting information out. That is a personal experience and I am not saying that everybody has exactly the same one. I do think this question of familiarity does make a difference.

50. Forgive me, but you did not answer my question about how it might be improved. You say it is very opaque, that it looks opaque in the capital cities. How do you think that could be improved?
(*Mr Montes*) I have a suggestion. The issue of the complexity of European Union institutions and the fact that they are criticised probably also means that in general it becomes more difficult for the organisation itself to be transparent. This issue of transparency and external inspections and learning is essential for aid implementation because an organisation does not improve without this. The element I would mention here is that in looking at the programmes and how they operate I would agree that Member States, and in other cases the European Parliament micro-manage quite a lot of the activities of the European Commission, introducing new budget lines, new programmes and all that, which contribute to the opacity, the lack of transparency of some of these programmes. In my view the Member States are not actually achieving much by doing this. It is not that the policies which the Member States support are going to be implemented through such a complex process but it contributes to the Commission being slower. This is very difficult but a way out of this problem is to exchange some of this micro-management for a system by which clear targets or objectives are set at the beginning and then these are inspected more rigorously by Member States and independent agencies; in that way to have an institution which behaves with more effectiveness.

Lord Williams of Elvel

51. A quick question on evaluation. Do you think that the European Union systems of evaluation are as efficient, more efficient, less efficient than Member

---

[1] This process of devolution of authority from Brussels HQ to the EC Delegations in developing countries is taking place over three years (2001–03) at a rate of about 25 Delegations per year.

Lord Williams of Elvel *contd.*]

States individually? Take the United Kingdom for instance.

(*Mr Montes*) I have to declare an interest here because I have been doing lots of evaluations for the European Union.

(*Dr Mackie*) Different Member States have very different standards in evaluation. Britain is probably among the better ones. I would cite some of the Scandinavian countries as being very good too at that level, with some good traditions, good methodology, etcetera. I would say that the Commission does not have a bad evaluation system. They have done a lot to improve it in the last five years and been willing to learn a lot from some of the more rigorous evaluation systems and in particular in the northern European countries. I would not really like to give a direct answer to the question.

(*Mr Montes*) Having now collected myself, I would say that in general aid programmes are not evaluated sufficiently. If you compare Spain with Denmark you will see a difference. Actually DfID does not have an independent evaluation function either in the sense for example that the World Bank has a separate agency which undertakes evaluation reporting directly to the executive directors from its member countries. It is complex, but the only way to make progress is by having a system of peer review. This means it is not only you as DfID who evaluates the programme or you as the Commission who evaluates the programmes but a collection of Member States and maybe even people from outside the development community, from foreign policy, then when you are looking at whether you are really supporting good governance you are better able to make a judgment.

Chairman

52. Are you saying that you would like to see DfID have an external evaluation? I ask you both that question.

(*Mr Montes*) As an evaluator I would ideally want things to be done outside the organisation and even more—I am talking in principle rather than of the practicalities of this—I would like not only development specialists but people from foreign policy and from other areas of government, carry out joined up evaluations. Evaluations are seen—and this is the difficulty—normally as a way to foster criticism rather than as a way to learn and improve. This creates enormous political difficulties. Only by bringing along more teams and having evaluations of this type would we avoid the problem.

53. Would you say that it would be better to have independent evaluation in all Member States, not just DfID?

(*Mr Montes*) Yes. I am even saying that because it is not just an issue of one Member State, because aid is about helping development of a third country. To get that result many other donors are involved and joint reviews would be useful. If we are reviewing a DfID programme or a Commission programme, I would like to have many donors looking at that programme, many outside organisations. In principle transparency improves effectiveness.

54. Dr Mackie, do you go with that?

(*Dr Mackie*) I would hesitate to advocate purely independent evaluation agencies. There is a lot to be said for an evaluation methodology—and I do not do as much evaluation work as Mr Montes—with more direct discussion between those being evaluated and those doing the evaluation. A level of integration is useful. Probably the most useful evaluation system we have at the moment is the peer review system from the OECD and certainly the European Commission takes that review extremely seriously. That after all is precisely what you are saying, a review by peers where it is people, professionals and the same type of organisation but from another Member State, looking at the internal work. I am not sure that the World Bank inspection panel is more efficient than, say, the evaluation unit in Europe.

(*Mr Montes*) We are talking about the World Bank evaluation office which reports to their directors which have a political dimension. Obviously there are two types of evaluations. One can be an internal evaluation but when you are trying to learn big lessons it is useful to have more external opinions.

Lord Inge: Just a comment. Let me say first of all that this has been very educational for me. What strikes me in all this is that what you are trying to do is deliver aid to a country and we are getting more and more bureaucracy evaluating the delivery of that aid. It is a comment and I do not know how to solve it, but it seems a problem to me.

Lord Maclennan of Rogart

55. We have been talking about instrumentalities and I should like to take you back to your first answer and subsequent answers, in which you pointed to growing complementarity between the functions of the Union in the sphere of foreign policy and development aid, and ask whether you see this growing coherence of which you have spoken, as a desirable objective both because the effectiveness of aid does depend to some extent upon foreign policy considerations and because aid is a useful tool to underline foreign policy points. Concerns have been expressed that the latter might skew the pure objectives, if I might put it that way, of aid giving, but it seems to me that the two are so closely linked that it is artificial to separate them in a way. I must ask you a specific point, which suggests that perhaps the balance has been altering and that is flowing from the High Commissioners' security strategy, which was presented to the Council at Thessaloniki in the summer. It might be thought that the foreign policy objectives were taking over a higher salience than the older, more established development objectives. Do you think that is true, desirable, is there something to be concerned about?

(*Dr Mackie*) It is certainly something to watch, but it is a trend which has been going on for quite a number of years. Development policy has been something which the Commission has been dealing with for many more years than foreign policy. This purity you are talking about was something that people were proud of in the Commission and when you talked about European Community development policy, one of the advantages was precisely quoted as being the fact that it was free from

Lord Maclennan of Rogart *contd.*]

political considerations in a way that bilateral aid from Britain or Germany or some Member State was not in the past. That has been shifting a little over the last ten years and is going to continue to shift, particularly with the effort made in this inter-governmental conference to try to get more coherence between the foreign policy activities. People are concerned about it and there are some people who get a bit protective and say there are dangers here. I think it is a nettle which has to be grasped. I would agree with you when you say that there is greater awareness now of the impact one has on the other, of the fact that development is not possible if you have continuous conflict in the place. Stability issues, security issues become a factor which is important for development. Likewise, with more development our experience certainly here in Europe is that you get more stability or you can get more stability; it is perhaps not a direct relationship. So the two can help each other. The paper presented by Mr Solana in Thessaloniki puts the emphasis more on the needs of the security policy and how it is important to have an integrated approach in policy terms and not just look at security in terms of hard military security, but also in terms of external policies, in terms of trade, in terms of development, poverty; it recognises very clearly that poverty is an issue. It tends to see it from the security angle and some people reading that are therefore afraid that not enough credence is given to the development side. I think this is a matter for debate. It is something that the foreign policy and the security community and the development community need to discuss and get the balance right.

56. It is not a theoretical debate if the giving of aid becomes increasingly conditional upon the fulfilment of certain political criteria of good governance, of human rights, of democracy, of the abstinence from cross-border wars, the diminution of unnecessary defence expenditure or whatever. If conditions like that are attached for foreign policy reasons and/or the attainment of development aid goals, it seems in a sense artificial to distinguish.

(*Mr Montes*) And in practice most donors already use their aid programmes in part to satisfy foreign policy, commercial and security objectives. There is a list in the paper I distributed and that is beyond doubt. Now the issue is how we define foreign policy to include these development concerns and try to balance all the objectives, which is obviously a difficult exercise.

57. Is it your impression that the different rate of institutional attachment to these issues, the more recent involvement of the foreign policy instrumentalities and intergovernmental activity creates some sort of rivalry between institutions? Is that a risk we have to watch?

(*Mr Montes*) Within the European Union, the assumption is already that foreign policy, security and commercial objectives and the promotion of European values are the main objectives of the overall aid programme. So this is already a fact. The new Member States are probably only going to reinforce that trend. We might like or not like that trend, but this is something it is difficult to avoid

because this is the view of the majority of Member States.

58. It seems to me that what you have described as a kind of converging course is healthy, and I think you are saying it is healthy, but is there any reluctance within the older established development aid sectors of the Commission to accept these good governance issues as having significant relevance to the effectiveness of their job?

(*Dr Mackie*) I would not say that. I would say that there is a reluctance to accept that development funds could start being used for hard security work. The good governance issue is widely accepted. There is a strong recognition throughout DG Development and Europe Aid that good governance is an important issue and needs to be tackled head on and this is something into which a good deal of effort is going. Guidelines have been formulated and a good deal of discussion, training of staff and so on. May I come back to one of the other points? The insistence on the poverty eradication goal we were talking about right at the start is in a sense a sort of defence for the development policy establishment, that if they insist on the primacy of that, that is in a sense a protection against the impinging issues coming in from foreign policy, so it is all the more important to go on insisting on that and saying this is a prime focus. That does not mean we do not relate to other issues, but at the end of the day the thing the development funds have to tackle is the issue of poverty. I see having that strong position on that side as entirely compatible with engaging in debate with these other sectors, trade, foreign policy, combined work, etcetera.

(*Mr Montes*) A comparative advantage of the European Union might be in this area of good governance for a number of reasons. In fact Commissioner Patten in a recent article in a foreign policy magazine suggests that part of the aid programme to Mediterranean countries should be used exclusively to reward good governance in these countries as a way to attain not only development but peace and stability.

Baroness Park of Monmouth

59. So far we have been talking about whether the EU itself should move in a more political direction or a purely developmental direction. Are we not forgetting the other side of the equation? You mentioned that there is a more proactive stance by African leaders. When we were discussing Barcelona the countries concerned were saying "Wait a moment. You are making decisions for us. You are not consulting us enough about what we want". Do you not see a certain problem in the new relationship with the African Union, which is very much saying we are for good governance and peer review and asserting its rights. Do you see that might be a risk to the straightforward programmes of help under Cotonou for instance? There is a danger that if the EU concentrates as much as it seems to be doing on developing a relationship with the African Union, they may be producing a situation where the money will not be allowed by those countries to go into what we really feel is needed. I see that we are giving them

Baroness Park of Monmouth *contd.*]

some money; indeed a £10 million grant for the AU's work on peace and security. I should be very interested to know what that was—and to provide the institutional development of the AU commission. You may well remember that about 18 months ago the G8 countries thought they were dealing with something in NEPAD which was going to be able to do something about good governance, only to be told at the end of the year that in fact it was only a part of the African Union and that the African Union had not yet reached its policy decisions. Briefly my question is: are we allowing enough for the fact that the other end of the equation may, in my view I am afraid, distort and misuse a lot of our wish to help those countries, because it is not going to help the people at the bottom, it is going to help the leaders at the top.

(*Mr Montes*) That is why this focus on good governance, meaning more democratic accountability and focus on corruption as a principle to be considered when offering aid, is important because it precisely avoids aid programmes being managed just by governments, even when governments do not have really democratic representation.

60. That is encouraging.

(*Dr Mackie*) I would disagree with you. I do not actually think that there is the danger that you see in the strengthening of the AU. I suppose I go back to a fairly basic principle arising out of my experience in the non government sector that ownership of any project is fundamental to its success and that to the extent that you come in from outside as donors, if you are not able to relate to an institution or a person on the ground who says "Yes, this is the project we want to do and this is the sort of help we need", if you do not have that sort of debate, your project is much, much less likely to succeed. That is a fundamental issue to me. Writ large, that is what I would see in the AU.

61. Rather than Cotonou.

(*Dr Mackie*) Rather than Cotonou. The ACP group is a group which has formed round Cotonou, or around Lomé originally of course. It has not formed around itself, around the interests and need of the countries. It is formed around the need of those countries to relate to Europe, whereas the AU is formed around the needs of Africa, the needs of the African nations, the African people, etcetera. You may dispute how strong the link between the establishment at the top, the leadership and the people at the bottom, the ordinary African citizen is, but my perception is that there is a much greater sense of ownership by the AU, by African people than there is of NEPAD and that is why, in a sense, I personally was not too worried by the difficulties with NEPAD, because I did not feel it was grounded in ordinary African aspirations as strongly as the AU can be.

62. The point Thabo Mbeki made to the G8 in December last year was precisely that NEPAD was part of the AU, but a junior part, only a part of a much larger political organisation which had its own commission, its own parliament, its own humanitarian organisation and everything else. I had understood that NEPAD was part of the AU. It cannot be dealt with on its own, it is part of the AU.

(*Dr Mackie*) You are entirely correct. Originally when it was started it was seen as something separate and this raised a lot of concerns and people started saying there was a duplication, whom should they deal with, which was the programme, etcetera? The solution to that has been made absolutely clear and Thabo Mbeki and others have been insisting for a year or so now that NEPAD is a programme of the AU and they have been taking more concrete steps towards that. That has strengthened NEPAD as a programme to breathe dynamism into the development effort, because it gives it that sort of stronger legitimacy that the AU has and which NEPAD did not have. You are right, this does raise questions for the ACP as a group, but I would say that if you looked at the ACP traditionally the Caribbean and the Pacific have always been better organised amongst themselves, smaller groups of countries, much more homogeneous perhaps and so on and not such a difficult task as for Africa. Some of the instability of the group has been caused by the difficulty of the African nations to get together. The OAU predates the AU and is not to be forgotten, but it did not have quite the same development goals, certainly when it started, though those were added on later. In the formation of the AU they have also sought to correct many of the problems they had with the OAU, which was seen as very bureaucratic, never getting anywhere and that is one of the things which the outgoing group of interim commissioners, for the first year of the AU were very keen on: they had to change that image. It is a bit early to say with the new commissioners and new president, but I would hope that was something which would be retained. The one commissioner who has transferred from the old interim status to the new permanent status has that message very clearly in his mind: they have to be a very much more dynamic organisation, get rid of the bureaucracy, work in a much more forceful sort of way.

Lord Powell of Bayswater

63. Just as a tail piece to that and to help us, could you point us at some specific examples where European aid has led to significantly improved governance and reduced corruption?

(*Dr Mackie*) Not off the cuff, but I will keep that in mind and get back to you.

(*Mr Montes*) I have some. In Uganda. Looking more to the future and this idea of good governance, I have to make the distinction between the Commission itself and the European Union, meaning Member States, Commission and the entire apparatus, and there is a spending of €10 billion a year, so you would expect examples could be found. The one I am mentioning is interesting because it is really looking towards the future in Uganda. We carried out a country strategy evaluation there with someone from the United Kingdom Government as well. The World Bank and IMF had a mandate to look particularly at economic issues and therefore the fact that the Ugandan Government was supporting the conflict in the Congo with enormous

Lord Powell of Bayswater *contd.*]

cost and poverty implications and lives, was not something they could explicitly take into account. However, the diplomats of the Member States, particularly Germany, began discussing how important this issue was or the issue of development in general in Uganda and how nothing could be done, talking initially in Kampala with like-minded ambassadors and then integrating later the Commission and some discussions with the World Bank. They made representations and had discussions in Washington and out of all these discussions came an agreement that these political factors, including defence spending by the Ugandan Government, should be taken more into account in the design of IMF/World Bank programmes. Of course this had an impact. Of course the final solution of the Ugandan role in the conflict did not stop there, but that is an example of how the power the European Union aid programme brings can lead to positive results.

Chairman: If either of you in the immediate future can think of other examples, it would be very helpful. The relative silence which followed Lord Powell's question was rather significant. If you could fill in that silence over the next few weeks, the Committee would be very grateful.

Lord Maclennan of Rogart

64. Just for clarification, if you have examples where specific conditions have been attached to deal with the issues of good governance, that would also be of some interest.

(*Mr Montes*) To respond very briefly to the Chairman, the silence would similarly have happened for programmes of other countries. The role of aid is not immediate. It is very difficult and I have been looking at aid for 20 years and I have just come back from Bolivia where we did an analysis of public administration reforms and looked at the situation of Bolivia now. The fact that the Commission among other donors can stay in a country in conflict longer than other donors as well as come back, as in the case of the Republic of Congo, faster than other donors, is another attribute which can be given to EU aid.

Baroness Hilton of Eggardon

65. Can we go back to the objectives of development aid, which we have been talking about as good governance, but DfID has specifically made poverty reduction the main focus of development aid in this country. Dr Mackie, you seem to be very comfortable with the present situation where in a way aid is supporting trade, economics, politics, whatever, rather than poverty reduction directly. The current situation in Europe is that half the aid actually goes not to the poorest countries, it goes to countries with which there are old colonial links. It does seem to me that if politics are going to drive aid in future, even the provisions in the new treaty for development aid are not going to be addressing the most disadvantaged, the poorest. Are you comfortable that our policies are going to be in tune with European policies on this front, or is there going

to be a widening split between what we want to do with development aid and what the rest of Europe wants to do?

(*Dr Mackie*) I am comfortable with the fact that in the development sector you cannot afford to ignore these other policy areas and you have to work with that. I am not necessarily comfortable with the fact that you use the funds which are intended for development for those purposes. It depends a bit how much they will have a development impact before you can take decisions like that. The ACP group, which still gets a large proportion of the EC aid, does include three quarters if not four fifths of the least developed countries (LDCs) in the world. What you do not have of course is the large numbers of poor people in countries like India or Indonesia and so on. The Commission should be looking at greater orientation towards trying to focus our money more towards poverty—I would not dispute that at all. I do think the effort is already fairly good in terms of the ACP. I do not like the suggestion that the ACP is just about countries with old colonial links; certainly it did grow out of that but it is an important group in terms of the countries it covers. It is a perfectly legitimate group for an aid programme to be oriented to those countries, certainly the poorer ones amongst them. That is very important.

66. We do not seem to have been as successful in relation to our old parts of the empire, like Bangladesh for instance, which is perhaps the poorest and most disadvantaged country and is going to have enormous problems in future with global warming and sea levels rising and so on. Do you think Europe is really aware of some of our old colonial links?

(*Dr Mackie*) I must admit that I tend to work more on the ACP countries than the other aid programmes of the EU. Some of the aid programmes to a number of Asian countries are quite important too. I would not be able to tell you off hand what the level to Bangladesh is, but certainly a lot of funds are going further east to eastern Asia, Sri Lanka and so on.

(*Mr Montes*) It is true that Bangladesh receives relatively little aid for their level of poverty. An argument to be considered is that aid to governments of poor countries is not identical to aid to the poor. When you are giving money to governments which might not be very democratic or are very corrupt, that does not translate into giving aid to the poor. This is just a general argument, but a number of the countries favoured by donors go to these sorts of countries. Just by having a large proportion of the aid programme going to governments of poor countries is not in itself a positive thing. We need to look behind to find the impact of that aid, how democratic those countries are, how much corruption reduces the impact of that aid.

Lord Harrison

67. In asking you how enlargement will affect EU aid policy, I wondered whether you could divide your answer first of all into those recipient countries which will benefit and those which will lose out. Secondly, in terms of the existing 15 EU donor countries, will they have access to a bigger budget or to bigger

Lord Harrison *contd.*]

bureaucracy. Thirdly, how will the ten new countries coming in fare as poachers turned gamekeepers?

(*Mr Montes*) We did this 200-page study for the Commission on enlargement, but I shall be very brief. We went to all the ten new Member States and talked to the people in the development co-operation agencies. One of the conclusions of that is that there is no constituency for development in these countries, as might be expected. The commitment of these governments to development co-operation is generally low. They focus much more on regional stability, governance and security issues. As a result, I think that the tendency you have already observed and which has been much commented on, is that in general the budget of the ACP has not grown as much in the past or in general for poor countries, but is increasing for the "near abroad". I think that it is reasonable to expect that this tendency will continue. So increases from the EU budget for poor countries is not going to happen. That is the first aspect, the one we looked at in more detail. What was your second point?

68. On the recipients first of all and then on the existing 15 EU donor countries. Would they get a bigger budget or will there be an increase in bureaucracy in terms of their helping third countries. Perhaps it does not affect them at all?

(*Mr Montes*) What is happening is that the aid budget of the Community, the one managed by the Commission, will increase a bit and then we will have to see. There will be no contributions to the EDF from these ten new Member States because they are relatively poor; they will not be contributing. In that sense, what was expected from the Monterrey targets was how to increase the quantity of aid and that raises more difficulties again because the new members will probably not be able to contribute. I do not know whether that answers your question.

(*Dr Mackie*) I see the impact as less on the budget and more on the policy side. When we had the last wave of new members to the Union we got in a number of countries which had very strong development co-operation policies, countries like Finland and Austria, and they brought in more money. This time they are not going to bring in that much more money, apart from the fact that they will have to contribute to the budget according to GNP. On the policy side we really are not very clear what the impact will be with ten new votes in the Council of Ministers from countries which do not have that much tradition in development policy terms. Certainly some of the existing Member States, which have evolved strong, clear development policies, are wary that the new members will water down the strength of some of those policies and the level of commitment. The worry is more in that policy area.

69. Will it not be of interest to the 15 existing EU countries to have sitting on the inside, at the table, someone who was recently a recipient country, who might say you might need to rethink how you deal with third countries. Is there not going to be some interesting interplay there?

(*Dr Mackie*) Certainly reference has been made quite a lot—and I do not know whether you found this when you were visiting those countries—to the fact that they do have experience of transition economies, etcetera, which would be valuable experience to gain. Going further back in their history, some of them have experience of technical assistance programmes to some of the more Communist countries in Africa etcetera. There is some knowledge and some experience there. Yes, that is a valid point to make.

Lord Powell of Bayswater

70. Just to come back for a moment to the question of the ACP grouping, does it have a future, or is it not really outdated and irrelevant now? Does it not lead to a significant distortion of the EC's aid giving priorities? What does the ACP bring to the party these days? Are the institutional structures between the EU and ACP actually of any value? I speak as someone who is probably the only person in this room who has attended EU/ACP ministerial meetings because no British minister could be persuaded to go to them. I do not recall them being very edifying occasions.

(*Dr Mackie*) This is a common problem. You are certainly right to point to the fact that there are many question marks about the future of the ACP. There is a good deal of tension with the group and certainly the trade negotiations, which is an area I do not know much about, are splitting up the interests and that is one major tension. The interests in the Pacific and in the Caribbean areas for dealing with the regional blocs around them is also quite important. Yes, but that is not a decision for a European state. It is a decision for ACP countries to take and to decide whether having that group helps them in their negotiations with the Community. I would go back to this positive development, certainly on the African side, of strengthening their own regional institution, the AU and if that really takes off and works well, then that puts the African nations in a much stronger position and at one point they may decide it is actually more important to have an agreement between the AU and the EU than doing it through the ACP for positive proactive reasons.

71. Surely it does benefit the ACP to have this arrangement; I can quite see that. *Per capita* they get far more aid than is probably justified under a more fair-minded allocation of European aid across all deserving recipients. So they are not going to be the ones saying they will give this up. No country would want to give up aid. Surely the initiative must come from the European side which says "We cannot any longer justify this imbalance in our aid programme and we want to find some different way of allocating our aid on the basis of regional groups equally or certain levels of development".

(*Dr Mackie*) There has been a shift gradually. You referred to the fact that EDF is not increasing as steadily as aid levels elsewhere, so the EU is already *de facto* doing that. It has already introduced into Cotonou the ability to claw back funds. We distribute them and cut the security of the funds as it were. So those steps are already being taken.

72. But if you look at the *per capita* aid being given to Mauritania and that given to Bangladesh, you would say that it was hardly a sensible distribution of the Community's resources.

Lord Powell of Bayswater *contd.*]

(*Mr Montes*) It is right that a more functional grouping rather than an historical allocation of money would make more sense. Working with the Commission I am aware of the emotions on the ACP grouping and they tell me that it is there to stay. Linked to that is the fact that the issue of having this ACP group introduces some distortions. When you are in the World Bank or in DfID of course you always look at countries in which you have a special interest, but you also look at the world as a whole. In the Commission, you have a particular set of procedures and rules for every region and there has been some harmonisation, but still people think differently in every region. I am told that the Commission is going to try to work on a more common basis for all regulations which give the rules on how policies and aid are implemented. Eventually the ideal would be to have just one regulation for all aid to different regions.

Chairman

73. We have mentioned Bangladesh once or twice this morning and I have been looking at the papers which Mr Montes most kindly distributed to us, which will appear as part of our evidence (not printed). I notice that you give Bangladesh a corruption ranking of 102, which is the highest of all the countries you list. Is the lack of aid which in fact goes to Bangladesh, a function of that very high corruption rating in your view?

(*Mr Montes*) That table is just an indication of how major donors and governance issues are related and indicators of democracy taken from Freedom House and corruption from Transparency International. In the case of Bangladesh, I think the point which was being made in the European Union, and this applies in general for countries in that region of Asia, was that they receive relatively less than ACP countries. That is more due to historical reasons than to the use of performance indicators which would say we will not allocate as much money to Bangladesh as, let us say, to a country like Senegal which has better governance indicators. At the moment, these governance indicators have not been used much. They are in fact being used by the World Bank and there is a lot of work on the issue of "Governance Matters", trying to find indicators. That table was just meant to say that if we were concerned about democracy and corruption, a number of countries receive large amounts of money from the major donors which are in that list.

Lord Powell of Bayswater

74. I should like to move on to this question of what real comparative advantage European aid brings to recipients over and above what Member States bilateral programmes bring. I am not talking about the allocation. I can quite see the European case for wanting to have a European aid programme and having it as an adjunct to foreign policy. I am talking about the advantage to the recipient not to the donors.

(*Mr Montes*) The difference between beneficiaries and recipients is essential because a lot of things we have been mentioning, including the near abroad, control of borders, organised crime, is more clearly for the benefit of Member States. I mentioned in a talk I gave about a month ago, and I had to think hard on this, that one element, is that European Union aid gives an additional option in the aid menu that it is available to recipient countries. There is only one large donor in the world which is the US (and the World Bank is closely linked). I am not saying this is a positive argument. I am just saying that from the recipient's point of view, the fact that there are two large donors gives some flexibility. Flexibility can be used correctly or incorrectly, but it gives you an option. The World Bank will come with one set of conditions, then the Commission on the implementation of a health programme, let us say, will come with a different set of conditions. That is one general argument.

75. My question is really more in terms of the effectiveness of the implementation of the aid coming from the EU. What is the comparative advantage there? Why is it better to have an EU aid programme than sub-contract the implementation of the aid back to member governments? You could have an EU aid programme and say Britain has the biggest aid giving structure in Kenya, so ask the British to administer European aid to Kenya. France is obviously much bigger in some of the West African countries so France could do it there, and Germany and so on. What would be the real problem?

(*Mr Montes*) I am not here at all to say this is clearly the comparative advantage of the European Union because that is a political issue. In principle, what I can say is that bilateral aid is also subject to commercial pressures. Let us say when Spain is providing aid to the Dominican Republic you would imagine that there are considerations which are taken into that discussion which are not necessarily present with the same intensity—and this obviously will depend on the country—when the European Commission is providing aid to that country. That applies to many cases. To me, more interesting, because I think it is the big issue, is this link with governance. After working for 20 years in development, I really do not see how aid can be effective, neither for the World Bank, nor for DfID, if they do not take into account that the money they give to these countries has to be given to governments who have some degree of democracy, some degree of corruption controls. The question of aid effectiveness, although it is true it applies particularly on the instruments of the European Union, applies to all donors.

76. I see that point, but let us just say we have $100 of aid to Ethiopia. What is it that makes the European Union a better administrator or implementor of that aid than, say, Germany or France or the United Kingdom?

(*Mr Montes*) I lived in Ethiopia for a year. In principle, when the United Kingdom Ambassador is received in Ethiopia, he will be received with much less "attention" than the EC, not ambassador but head of delegation (he would become an ambassador presumably with the common EU foreign service five years from now). When this new ambassador comes and if he happens to control both foreign policy,

Lord Powell of Bayswater *contd.*]

which means some sort of agreement from 15 Member States, and the aid policy of €10 billion that he controls directly, I think the influence of this person saying he would like Ethiopia to consider the issue of the freedom of the press or that the issue of human rights is particularly important for the delivery of EU programmes, means that the EU will be taken very seriously. So I see that there is a comparative advantage in that.

77. I have understood that point. I am still trying to get at this issue of the terms of the administration of an aid programme, the actual implementation, the administration on the ground. Does the EU have advantages which Member States do not? If so, could you explain them to me?
(*Mr Montes*) If we just go directly to implementation, of course it has been found in most evaluation reports that the Commission has technical weaknesses and accountability weaknesses in its programmes, but when you compare, for example, the amount of resources that the Commission can put into Bolivia, the number of staff, compared, let us say again, to the United Kingdom Government, it means you have 20 staff who can look at how to make aid more effective compared with three or four or even fewer because of this issue of reducing aid to middle income countries. (Bolivia is a poor country, but its aid budget is still being reduced). You have this idea which is not just a question of the Commission *per se* but the fact that if you have four or five Member States working together on an aid programme, it will be more effective than the implementation by one Member State on its own. That is the argument.

78. So the Commission can afford a bigger bureaucracy in each country than Member States could.
(*Mr Montes*) In part that and ideally it could work with other Member States.

Lord Morris of Aberavon

79. With the development of European foreign policy and ambassadors and people of that kind which you envisage, will European aid then be a means of buying influence?
(*Mr Montes*) This is an issue under the Constitution and not only the composition of the foreign service is yet to be decided but also whether there is a separate aid agency or not.

80. Leave the mechanism. Whatever it is, will it be a means of buying influence?
(*Mr Montes*) Foreign aid is always used by donors to achieve foreign policy, commercial and security interests as well. This obviously means that the risks will become larger, as well as the opportunities I have mentioned. It is up to the Member State to find ways to balance these objectives.

Lord Powell of Bayswater

81. My next question is about budgetisation of the EDF. Dr Mackie, if you were the British Government, which way would you jump on this? Would you go for budgetisation of the EDF or do

you think it would be better to leave things as they are?
(*Dr Mackie*) It would depend where I sat in the British Government. If I were in the Treasury, I would certainly say no, because of the big increase, given that the United Kingdom got a fairly small share from the negotiation of the last EDF. Trying to look at it dispassionately, the question I would want to see answered is: what influence would budgetisation have on the ACP themselves and particularly their big fear that the security of the funds is in danger?

82. Because they are not contractual.
(*Dr Mackie*) Because they are not contractual; that is right, and because once in the budget, they work on an annual basis. Of course, if you discuss this with the Commission, what they will tell you is that this would still be guaranteed through the regulation which provides for a certain level of commitments over a certain number of years. I would remain concerned, but it is still possible within the EU budget to do internal transfers of funds, and we all know that this happens half way through the year in September/October. They do look at where money is being spent and where it is not being spent. That does not mean that the overall allocation necessarily gets eaten into, but if that happens several years running, then the funds would drift over. I am not convinced with the proposal coming from the Commission that that security is provided for. There is one other way you could tackle this and that is to look at the financial perspectives and see whether it would be possible to establish an extra chapter to the financial perspectives. At the moment the external relations come out of chapter four, but would it be possible to have a development chapter? In this case you would have in the development chapter, the EDF funds, for Asia and Latin America development purposes, and the old chapter four would then be constrained to other foreign relations. That might provide a more watertight arrangement for the development funds. That is a major undertaking and convincing the EU Member States to change the financial perspective and add an extra chapter would be a huge task.

83. Turning the question round, do you not feel the EDF system might be applied more widely rather than budgetisation, not just to ACP but to many others, which in a sense is what you are suggesting?
(*Dr Mackie*) Some people I have talked to in Brussels actually say that. It is not the budgetisation of the EDF but the "EDF-isation" of the budget in certain respects which would be very good.

84. That is a very interesting idea.
(*Dr Mackie*) May I come back to your earlier question? You were asking what the advantage of the EU was to the ACP country. Traditionally, apart from the political one you mentioned, it was the question of joint management. That has got into contortions and has become quite ponderous, but the principle is quite a positive one for an ACP country and it is valued as such by ACP officials and the national authorising officers, etcetera. They do see that as an important issue. Then the other point, which is not immediately the EC budget but the framework which the European Union provides for

Lord Powell of Bayswater *contd.*]

the co-ordination of aid, could be a big advantage for co-ordination of aid between Member States to that country, could be a major advantage to the ACP country of whatever recipient country we are talking about, if that were really taken much further. Certainly in places where you start to see that happening, that does simplify, rationalise systems, it does help with avoiding duplication, perhaps reduce the different procedures required in each case, etcetera.

85. Are you suggesting that the Commission should have powers over how we allocate the remainder of our bilateral aid budget, the bit which does not go directly through the EU? Are you saying that the Commission should have the right to say how we spend our aid in Kenya or Ethiopia or wherever?

(*Dr Mackie*) I am not sure it is a question of powers; it is more a question of the Member States taking more seriously the point about complementarity. It is there in the Treaty; it is something governments have been very reluctant to get into. More effort could be made in that direction.

86. Government might argue that they have a right to say how they spend their tax payers' money.

(*Dr Mackie*) Yes.

(*Mr Montes*) Briefly, on the issue of budgetisation, people talk a lot about ring-fenced funds, but if Member States really care about the protection of aid to poor countries, they need to exercise their powers within EDF or in the budget. In the budget they do have a right to allocate more resources to poor countries. The question is not whether it is inside the budget or outside the budget—and it is not very clear what is more effective and what is less effective—it is how you make EC aid more effective.

Chairman

87. I want to ask one last question which is probably more to Dr Mackie than to Mr Montes. In the United Kingdom we have been told that academic interest in development assistance seems to be at a very low level. Do you believe that is true? If you do, do you think anything could be done to inspire greater interest?

(*Dr Mackie*) I would find that very hard to answer. I am not sufficiently in the British academic system any longer. My sense from outside Britain is that there is actually quite a lot of interest in development in academic circles in Britain and that some of the British universities have quite high quality work in that area. I do not get the sense that you get much more attention in some of the other Member States of the Union than you do in Britain in fact. I quite accept that you may be worried about that, but sitting in Brussels you do not get the picture that there is much less academic interest in development in the United Kingdom than it is elsewhere in the Union.

(*Mr Montes*) The quality of the aid programme and discussion would benefit in general from a greater understanding in Member States governments as well as among academics on these very technical issues of aid implementation. So more resources in this area in general, not necessarily just for the academics. The merging of foreign policy and development might make these issues of more interest for academic study.

Chairman: We will close the session there. You have both been very helpful to us indeed and thank you for coming, particularly for coming a long way. We appreciate that and it has been very helpful to us. Thank you so much.

THURSDAY 30 OCTOBER 2003

Present:

Bowness, L.   Maclennan of Rogart, L.
Harrison, L.   Morris of Aberavon, L.
Hilton of Eggardon, B. (Chairman)   Williams of Elvel, L.
Inge, L.   Williamson of Horton, L.

Examination of Witnesses

Ms MIKAELA GAVAS (EU Policy Officer, BOND) AND Ms LOUISE HILDITCH (Co-ordinator, ActionAid Alliance), examined.

Chairman

88. Good morning and welcome. May I start by asking you about the Development Policy that was established by the European Council in 2000. Most of what we will be talking to you about is what has been happening in the last two or three years rather than anything historical. How do you think that they are actually managing to spread across European Union programmes all with different diverse aspects of good government, environment and gender, which are now supposed to permeate, are they not, everything that the EU does? Do you think that has actually happened, or not?

(*Ms Gavas*) In terms of the poverty focus of the European Union, there have been pretty strong commitments to poverty reduction and mainstream cross-cutting issues with the Development Policy, but unfortunately we feel the practice fails to meet the policy plans. The Commission is, however, aware of this and, for example, in relation to gender they have just published a report, which is on the website, called *Gender Equality and Gender Co-operation*, in which they highlight some of the problems related to main-streaming the cross-cutting issues. I was speaking to One World Action, which is a BOND member. They are just about to publish a report specifically on gender called *Closing the Gap*. This looks at how successful the delegations have been in main-streaming gender. Some of the conclusions they came up with were that gender equality has been put forward as a priority and that it is in most country strategy papers. However, there is little analysis of what this actually means in practice and, where there is uncertainty about how to implement the gender policy, it is usually dropped. Other issues are the lack of financial resources and human resources. Within the Commission, there is one person only dealing with gender. There is also a severe lack of expertise in some of the cross-cutting issues. In relation to governance, the Commission has just published a communication on governance in developing countries. I am afraid I have not had a chance to actually look at this in depth, but hopefully it will bring out some of the principles of governance that can be applied to all programmes.

89. What about the environment?

(*Ms Gavas*) I think the same applies to the environment. I have talked to FERN, which is a network of environmental agencies. They have done projects looking at how environmental issues have been main-streamed in country strategy papers. Again, the same problems come up: lack of human resources, lack of financial resources, and lack of expertise.

90. Can I ask you what you understand by the concept of governance, which seems to be one of those hoorah words that perhaps does not have much behind it. Do you have a clear definition of what good governance means?

(*Ms Gavas*) I think it relates to the promotion of human rights. It is about building the capacity of governments and institutions to exercise good governance and promote human rights. It is about partnership as well, I think, and ensuring the effective participation of all stakeholders in policy formulation.

91. We are very keen that it is poverty that should be addressed specifically. Do you think that there are prospects for a switch of EU aid from the "near abroad", as it is called, to the poorest countries?

(*Ms Gavas*) With enlargement, the prospects become less likely. The development policy frameworks of the new Member States are very much focussed on regional stability and global security; hence, a consistent focus on the "near abroad". I do not think the trend will change. There is a very severe lack of development experience and very low official development assistance budgets.

(*Ms Hilditch*) I do not think it is necessarily the case that there will not be a change, but if current trends continue and no action is taken to address the situation, then it would be more likely that more resources increasingly will go to the new frontier countries and fewer resources will go to traditional development countries who are on the DAC's No.1 list of developing countries. There are opportunities. It is part of our *acquis communautaire* that all of the accession countries have to have development policy budgets; they also have to meet the Monterrey commitments . They are already being measured, as are the existing Member States, on how well they are meeting the Monterrey commitments. There are opportunities, and political opportunities, to encourage the new Member States to be more development-minded, but that will probably not be their top priority.

92. But there is more flexibility in the system?

(*Ms Hilditch*) Yes, and it is a legal obligation.

Lord Maclennan of Rogart

93. I would like to return to the issue of governance and get from you, if you can give it, some indication of how the Union seeks to ensure that its objectives are met in practice. Are moneys made conditional upon the delivery of human rights or some evidence of the elimination of corruption? Does this get discussed with the recipient countries prior to the agreement and, if undertakings are given, how are they followed up practically and monitored to see whether the money given has been frittered away or somehow got into the wrong hands? I do not have a picture of how these objectives are realised or even of how the Commission would seek to realise these objectives.

(*Ms Hilditch*) When you are talking about the EU, one thing that is quite tricky is that you always have to talk about two systems in relation to development. There are the ACP countries governed by the Cotonou Agreement and those countries governed by bilateral agreements in the Asian and Latin-American regulations. Taking first those countries governed by the Cotonou Agreement, as you know, within the partnership agreements there are clauses relating to fundamental freedoms, governance, respect for human rights—political causes, which are new to the Cotonou Agreement that did not exist in the Lomé Convention in the sense that they can be a reason for starting to discuss suspension of the provisions of the agreement. If there are human rights abuses or lousy governance or endemic corruption and nothing is happening as it should, then the EC can start discussing with the ACP countries about: what do they think about suspending aid—be it Togo or Haiti or Liberia where aid is suspended or under discussion. There are some opportunities there. The other thing is that the EC aid now is all linked to the PRSP process, obviously supposedly country-owned, obviously led by the external agents. Within that, there is a vast number of conditionalities, as you may know, both political and economic. If all donors agree that aid can only be disbursed once PRSP has been agreed, then that is another guarantee, if you like, in terms of guaranteeing that the money would be spent correctly and on most things that would have an impact on poverty eradication. In other countries, there is not quite the same situation. Although there are human rights clauses in all of the bilateral agreements, and so all bilateral agreements and regional agreements between countries in the whole world always include a human rights clause, because the same partnership concept does not exist, I think it is not managed by DG Development in the same way. In any case, it is DG RELEX that is the lead Commission department responsible for this discussion, but more or less the policies apply across the board if it is a policy on governance in developing countries, on the participation of civil society, on protection of the environment or gender. All those policies that come from DG Development apply also to all countries in Asia and Latin-America. As for the possibility for monitoring, there is not quite such an easy way in as there is in the framework of the Cotonou Agreement from the point of view of an external observer.

94. Why is it less effective in the case of the EU?

(*Ms Hilditch*) I think that is because it is not a partnership agreement in the same way that it does not involve a group of countries on one side and a group of countries on the other. It is not within the framework of an agreement. For example, unilaterally the EU cannot decide to suspend aid to an ACP country; it can only enter into discussions between the two partners about whether they think they should do this, and then they take the decision to do it or not, whereas with other countries it is more of a classical kind of arrangement whereby they are called development partners and there are lots of discussions and negotiations. In terms of monitoring and following the objectives, there may be as many opportunities for dialogue as there are in the framework of the Cotonou Agreement.

Lord Inge

95. Can we go from policy to quality? Do you think there has been any improvement in the quality of the aid provided by the EU over recent years? Secondly, how does it compare, for example, with the World Bank aid and DfID's aid and things like that? If there are areas where it has improved, are there any particular areas where you think it is bad?

(*Ms Hilditch*) You want good examples and bad examples. When we were preparing for this session, basically we were looking at what had happened post the adoption of the Development Policy statement in 2000. We were trying to see what impact there had been. One thing about the Development Policy statement is that it is all things for all people because the six priority areas they agreed more or less allowed them to carry on doing everything that they were doing before. What has been positive, I think, is that since then a raft of country strategy papers have been agreed under the Cotonou Agreement. Those are all now strategy papers. At the same time, there have also been new strategies agreed with some other countries as well. There has been an opportunity on paper to improve the quality. There has not been so much implementation yet because at the time when the statement was agreed, and as you know programmes go for a long time before they are eventually closed, they were still implementing old stuff before starting with the new stuff. I think certainly they have made a qualitative leap, in terms of quality control of the process that they enter into with a country to design a country strategy paper and in their own in-house process of making sure different points of view are taken into account. The end product of the country strategy paper is that there is a better document than it may have been before. On the implementation side, it is not clear that so much has changed. If you take, for example, this year's budget report, the Commission, when it looked at this, decided that it would like to do lots of budget support. That was a way of spending lots of money with very few personnel. Mostly the onus is on the ministry of finance in the country concerned. They are trying increasingly to do that, but what they do not yet have in place are their indicators for judging whether or not their budget support has been a success. They have a headline indicator, which is: the budget support should lead to increased outcomes in the education and health sectors. But they do not yet have any specific indicators about

Lord Inge *contd.*]

how they would measure, for example, primary enrolment rates, primary completion rates, numbers of people who live within five kilometres of a primary health centre. They are still developing those kinds of indicators now and they are not yet measuring for those. Quality control in terms of the actual quality of the products and development is not measurable. The only way you can measure that is to go and do studies yourself, and some NGOs do a lot of that, and they also do a lot of their own evaluation. That is the only way of measuring it at the moment. They do not have any statistical measures in place at the moment. They are supposed to be coming on stream in the mid-term review of the Cotonou Agreement countries, which takes place next year.

96. You are saying that the aid itself is the right sort of aid and it is the right sort of quality, but you are not able to measure it properly? Is that what you are telling me?

(*Ms Hilditch*) The theory is that it is the right sort of aid.

97. So the quality is all right?

(*Ms Hilditch*) Yes. Also, the process that they went through was a good process to get to the country strategy paper. Now they are coming to the implementation. They have moved to do the implementation before they have actually agreed what all the outcome indicators will be. They still have not agreed, apart from headline indicators, how they intend to measure effectiveness.

98. In other words, the quality might not be quite what they want?

(*Ms Hilditch*) Yes, that is it exactly.

99. How does that compare to the World Bank and to DfID?

(*Ms Hilditch*) I have never worked on United Kingdom aid policy and so it would be quite hard for me to say how it compares with DfID, apart from saying in general terms that the Commission implements the European Union policies not European Commission policies. In theory, they are the same policies. In theory, it is not as though the Commission have a policy on governance and then the United Kingdom has another one. In theory, they have one policy, which is the European Union policy on governance. There could be differences in implementation but there should not be any differences on policy approaches. In terms of the World Bank, it is a slightly different animal; they are facing it much more at a macroeconomic level and, also, it operates through loans rather than grants. Again, it is hard to compare. A final point I want to make is that, especially in relation to budget support, it is very hard to see your impact as opposed to anybody else's. The whole point of doing donor co-ordination and harmonisation is that you pool your resources much more and that you cannot see what the impact is of, say, the German development finance, or what the impact is of the United Kingdom finance or EC finance because all that is going into the same pot and they are all being measured by the same indicators. In that sense, it is quite hard. One other point that Mikaela has already raised in relation to EU and DfID quality is that DfID has many more resources and probably has more

support institutionally within the United Kingdom political context. DG Development always feels itself a little bit under siege *vis-à-vis* its other colleagues in other departments.

100. The final question is: in terms of trying to keep up with policy and at the same time trying to speed up aid, has trying to speed up the aid affected the quality or not?

(*Ms Hilditch*) The Commission thinks it has made really good progress in speeding up the aid, and it has made some progress. It has not actually speeded up that much. In that sense, you could say that it has not impacted on the quality. On the contrary, you will know that now they have just started to spend the EDF9 money. Because the Cotonou Agreement has finally been ratified, they are starting to spend EDF9 money. The concept of partnership for those employees means that both national authorising officers and heads of delegations in the country need to sign for every single payment order, no matter how small. In fact, that has brought disbursement grants to a halt, and they are going to be looking at that next year in the review of the Cotonou Agreement. I was looking at some documentation they produced; they regularly produce this financial trends paper every year where they look at how well they are doing at spending old commitments and how well they are doing at a series of indicators. One indicator that I picked up was that in 2002 they were saying that it was still 41 per cent of all commitments made in the last quarter, and so it still goes to show that there is quite a lag between what they decide to do and what they actually do, and that was not even looking at the payments side.

(*Ms Gavas*) Perhaps I could give an example of some of the inconsistencies between policy and implementation. With regard to the communication on non-state actors that was published by the Commission, this was supposed to be a horizontal policy. However, it is in contradiction to the Asian and Latin-American regulation, which does not refer to any participation of civil society whatsoever. There is an inconsistency there. This also has to do with the responsibilities of both DG Development and DG RELEX.

Lord Harrison

101. Could I ask Louise Hilditch: when you said earlier that because of the paucity of personnel within the Commission there was, as it were, an offloading of the money to the finance treasury departments of individual countries, some people might see that as a good thing: you get the money to the country as quickly as possible. Is it a good thing in so far as it, as it were, cuts out bureaucracy, or is there a lack of planning and foresight because of the lack of personnel in Brussels in the first place?

(*Ms Hilditch*) Our professional view would be that in principle budget support is a good thing. If you just look at it on paper, obviously it is far better for countries to get all of their money on budget. If they are always going to the treasury, the treasury needs to know over a three-year period how much money they are going to be getting from donors and to be able to plan accordingly. If you do not do budget

Lord Harrison *contd.*]

support, if you either do projects or even sectoral programmes—education, health or transport—sometimes the money goes directly to the ministry of transport or the ministry of health, and it is very hard for the ministry of finance even to know that that money has come in and is being spent in some way. It is much more challenging for governments to manage various bits of programmes and project support is, first of all, very difficult to keep track of in the country. We did some research in Ghana where we found in the education sector that Ghana entertained 54 donor missions in one year—that was more than one a week—whereas obviously if the money had all been going just into the education sector or just into the budget, there could have been only one donor mission representing all the donors; there could have been one audit, which would be the national audit; there could be one set of accounts. You have more of the money on budget when it is budget support, and so the national parliament in the country concerned can see what money is coming in, whereas with a lot of programmes and projects, the money is often in a separate budget, which never goes to the parliament and is not publicly scrutinised. In principle, budget support is a very good idea. The only problem is that in practice it is untested. It is a new development approach.

Lord Williams of Elvel

102. You touched on evaluation. Could you speak a little more about that, whether you think EuropeAid is effective and will there be improvements? Is everything going according to plan? Are accounting arrangements for EU projects properly set up and properly audited?

(*Ms Hilditch*) One positive thing that has come about subsequent to reforms in the Development Policy statement is the appearance of an Evaluation Unit that reports directly to the Director General of EuropeAid. It has a strategy for several years. In its strategy, it is supposed to evaluate about 140 countries. It tries to do geographic evaluation, and so country by country. It also tries to do schematic evaluations: evaluation of aid to the health sector; evaluation of aid to the transport sector. It also tries to do evaluation by type of instrument: for example by budget support or by various types of direct aid to NGOs. It also does those kinds of evaluations. One problem is that it has a fantastic amount to evaluate and so each country or each type of evaluation does not happen that frequently. I think they plan to do five or six country evaluations a year out of 140 countries. They do not really look at each country that often in order to be able to evaluate the aid. This is for the official evaluation process. There are other evaluation processes, for example in an annual review which would take place in the country and in Brussels. There are also mid-term reviews now under Cotonou and a rolling programme, which is an opportunity to reallocate resources, to take resources away if they have not been spent. In that sense, there are more and more systematic evaluations than there were before, but there are not very many. One weakness that we identified is that there do not seem to be any joint evaluations. The Commission set this

up on the basis of best practice but probably all other donors in those countries are doing similar evaluations of projects which they are also funding. It is probable that resources could be used more effectively if they tried to do joint evaluations and to account for the expenditure to the Court of Auditors and to the public, though not necessarily by the Danish Government's evaluation or by the British Government's evaluation, rather than everybody trying to do their own evaluations all the time. In terms of accounting and audit, historically the Commission has always come in for a lot of criticism for poor accounting and audit procedures. I honestly do not think that they are out of the woods yet. As NGOs, we do not devote a lot of time ourselves to looking directly into accounting and audit procedures. We monitor the Court of Auditors' reports. The Court of Auditors' reports are really on the implementation of the budget, and the European Parliament also does this, but they are also on the EDF spending which, as you know, is a part of the EU budget. If their diagnosis is that there has been some improvement but they are not there yet, particularly in terms of audit, that they have not managed to sort out adequate systems and systems that can be employed in delegations, that would be important because, as you know, they are deconcentrating or devolving a lot of power and responsibility to all their delegations. Before they can do that really effectively, they need to have audit and accounting systems established which, according to them, they are in the process of establishing, but they are not there yet. The most recent Court of Auditors' reports were not totally positive and rosy about the Commission's accounting audit procedures.

103. To go back to evaluation procedures for the moment, you did mention that national governments have their own methods and the EU has its own methods. Is there a standard practice right across the EU on how to conduct an evaluation of an aid project or does everybody have their own ideas?

(*Ms Hilditch*) Yes, there is a community of practitioners, one could say—people who specialise in evaluation. They meet regularly and develop new thinking regularly. That includes: academics, NGOs staff, staff appointed by various governments and by the European Commission. There is an informal community of established best practice. Also, at the level of the DAC, there are government-to-government discussions about what the best practice is in an evaluation. The Commission certainly has its methodology, a step-by-step methodology. The delegations themselves are responsible for doing projects and programme evaluation and so they all need to be uniform, even though they are all conducted by different people in different countries. They also employ firms, again with expertise, which gives guidance—and those firms carry out the evaluation, the Commission does not do them in-house—to those firms that carry them out, and they also have to follow the Commission's methodology for carrying out an evaluation.

104. Have there ever been any cases, to your knowledge, where, say, a national government has evaluated a project and said, "This is a good project" or "That was a good project that has worked", and

Lord Williams of Elvel *contd.*]

the EU has evaluated the same project and said, "Actually, it is not much good", or *vice versa*? Can you think of any project where the evaluation of the national government and that of the EU has varied substantially?

(*Ms Hilditch*) I cannot think of any but I have never tried to look for any. That does not mean they do not exist. They are a fairly closed shop, are they not? If they are both financing the same project, it is in their interests to reach a similar conclusion. I imagine that there could be cases but I have never discovered any.

Chairman

105. When we looked at European aid to Ukraine on the environment about five years ago, the evaluation consisted of just tick boxes, which were completed by the people out there and they sent back in hundreds to Brussels who put them all in a file and somebody made some sort of evaluation. Has evaluation improved since then? Is there any independence in the system? Is anybody really looking at these projects?

(*Ms Hilditch*) I think it is much better now. Also, there is perhaps much more political attention paid to evaluation than five years ago. For example, I can think of an evaluation that was done two years ago of aid for education to ACP countries that was really delayed because the Commission violently disagreed with the conclusions of the evaluation, which had been conducted by independent evaluators. When the evaluation came out, it was discussed in the Development Committee of the European Parliament and taken up by NGOs. It depends what use in a participatory system what you tell us can be made of the learning as well as what use the Commission itself can make of it. We certainly follow evaluations in areas and countries where we are working and try to use those to persuade the Commission to use them to inform their work. Improvements have been made since self-certification, the tick the box thing. I have not seen any of those. They do have to publish them on the website.

106. That does sound rather better. Would you like to go on to talk about evolution of NGO funding arrangements since 2000? I think BOND gave evidence, did it not, to the House of Commons International Development Committee and made comments about lack of transparency, slow turnaround and all those other bureaucratic problems. Have things become better since then?

(*Ms Hilditch*) I think that it has changed by 50 per cent. In terms of the comments that you raised about the lack of transparency, that has become much more transparent since the 2001 inquiry. They have introduced a call for tender system. With the call for tender, any and every NGO can apply if it meets the minimum criteria, as a result of which the line is hugely oversubscribed now and 80 per cent of projects are rejected, even though there is nothing technically wrong with them; there just is not enough money. In that sense, it is still a lottery because that still means that many good projects with no problems do have to be rejected. I think, in terms of

transparency, it has been a great leap forward that they have introduced a system of call for tender. They have also managed to cut the response time. In 2001, that was 18 months and now it is down to nine months. Nevertheless, problems remain. On the positive side, you can say that the Commission is aware of that. They have set up a working group, the Joint NGO, European Commission, Member State Working Group to look at the problems of that particular line of EU/NGO co-financing to try to find some solutions. They held a big meeting last week of Commission, Member States and NGOs to discuss what should be done about the line. They are planning on getting their thinking in order in terms of the next financial perspective, which will be the next big opportunity when they rationalise budget lines and try to reorganise the way in which they work. They are looking for a solution being in place, which they have to put on the table by next year. There are various options on the table. One is to have more programme funding, programme funding for larger NGOs and project funding for smaller NGOs. Another possibility raised is that the project has to have a capacity-building element; that is, looking more at the capacity of the NGOs applying and seeing what work they are doing as well. We are not really out of the woods yet. The line is still oversubscribed; it is all 100 per cent used. It is not a very big line and it has been cut again this year in the budget in the First Reading of the budget; 5 per cent of it has been put in reserve, which means it cannot be spent automatically and the Commission needs to ask permission later in the year from the budgetary authorities to spend it. There are some problems with it, both technical and political.

107. Do you think in other respects things have changed for the better with the splitting of policy from implementation and the devolvement of more responsibility to local delegations? How do you feel about those?

(*Ms Gavas*) From our perspective, the reforms have actually marginalised development to a great extent. The administration, DG Development, has been severely cut down in size, as well as in terms of policy making and implementation. The removal of the implementation and moving it to EuropeAid has brought about a gap between policy and implementation that is very serious. The Commissioner for Development's portfolio has reduced in size. The implementation of development co-operation now comes under the chairmanship of the Commissioner for External Relations. With the cutting down in size of DG Development, the gap between policy and implementation, the gap between countries that DG Development is responsible for, the ACP countries and the rest in DG RELEX has marginalised development in the Commission set-up.

108. That is disappointing. What about the delegation of responsibility to delegations? Is that part of the same problem? Theoretically, that should put it closer to the countries, which should actually help, should it not?

Chairman *contd.*]

(*Ms Gavas*) Deconcentration has been a lot slower than first anticipated. I think 21 delegations were devolved in 2001 and 26 have been included in the second wave; of these, 23 have begun to work in a deconcentrated way. The rest will follow in 2004, which are mainly the ACP countries. Most of the problems around deconcentration have either been related to the capacity of the delegations themselves—human resources and financial resources—and certainly logistical problems as well as political situations on the ground.

109. I gather it has mostly consisted of sending out accountants. Is that right?

(*Ms Hilditch*) Not for the contract management, but you know the Commission has an A, B, C, D grade division of staff. In order to deconcentrate non-budgetary responsibilities, that is a job that is mainly done by B grade officials, we call that contract management. Basically, a lot of development is around contract management and accounting and audit, especially from an enlargement point of view. They have had to recruit and it has taken them a long time to recruit sufficient numbers of that level of staff. They have not been able to recruit. They do not have the resources with sufficient staff who are specialists in the various sectors. At one time, we were campaigning for sectoral staff to be devolved as well; for example education specialists, health specialists. That is not really happening, or not happening enough, even at a regional level. For example, they have one education specialist who services perhaps five countries. They are much more concerned, which I think reflects slightly the nature of the political debate in the EU and a succession of financial scandals, with the accounting side of it and that is where they are recruiting.

110. It is self-protective rather than devolving responsibility?

(*Ms Hilditch*) Yes, but then again if they are mainly getting into budget support, they really need economists and accountants.

Lord Bowness

111. If I may follow your question, Chairman, because we had evidence earlier in the month on this very point about staff in the decentralised office and there was an implicit criticism that there were not enough local staff recruited. That had implications both for cost, because they were cheaper than the staff being sent out, and also it put the projects further away from the people in the country. Would you support more local recruitment in the delegations?

(*Ms Gavas*) I think it is something perhaps we would support. We have supported the idea of a civil society liaison officer in each delegation. This is something that will be put in place by the Commission. Local staff would fulfil those positions.

(*Ms Hilditch*) They do have some local staff in delegations but they could have a lot more and that would probably improve the quality and be less expensive. They could have more local staff than they do but they always have some in every delegation.

112. The evidence we were given by a previous witness was that in theory they simply do not have employees above the rank of secretary.

(*Ms Hilditch*) I do think it should be encouraged. This is an inefficient way of organising the resources that exist.

113. The question I would like to ask both witnesses is whether they are in favour of bringing all the development assistance under a single Commissioner? Do you favour EuropeAid continuing, as I understand it, with autonomous status? Should you bring it together under that single Commissioner in one Directorate General?

(*Ms Gavas*) The ideal situation would be an independent Development Commissioner and a Directorate General for Development responsible for elaboration of development policies and aid programmes in all recipient countries, whether they be ACP or not. This would guarantee an institutional focus on development within the Commission. Then DG Development would be responsible for defining development policy and the strategic planning and co-ordination, for devising sectoral policies across the regions. It could also oversee the implementation of aid programmes by EuropeAid, which could become its operational arm, and then of course, it could support the delegations in the field by drawing up the country strategy papers. That would be the ideal situation.

114. Following on from your answer, may I ask whether our witnesses share the fears that some people have expressed about the proposals in the Draft Constitution for the Foreign Minister to have the double-hatted position and what effect that might have on development aid? Is that something you have a view about?

(*Ms Gavas*) We are very concerned about some of the proposals in the draft constitution, particularly the provision that the Foreign Minister would be able to use all instruments of the European Union, and that includes development co-operation and humanitarian assistance. I think the debate there will be around the Commission proposals. There are two proposals on the table for the Commission. There is the 15 + 10 model, which would allow an inner cabinet of commissioners and 15 commissioners with a vote and attendance at the outer circle. That is a very risky model for development. It is unlikely that we will get a Development Commissioner within that cabinet. The other model, which is the 25 model, 25 commissioners each with a vote, is perhaps less risky. There will still be a need for an inner cabinet that makes the decisions. In both scenarios, it is very unlikely that there will be a strong Development Commissioner. We will probably see a sub-commissioner or a junior person for development.

Lord Williamson of Horton

115. May I follow up on the same point? The key issue, surely, is that there are a substantial number of people in the delegations of the European Commission. They will fall, under the current proposals, under the Minister for Foreign Affairs, who is half in the Commission and half in the Council. We know the details. The real boss of the

Lord Williamson of Horton contd.]

people to whom we are devolving, deconcentrating, whatever the word is, responsibility for development aid is going to be the Minister for Foreign Affairs. Experience does show that they will tend to look rather a lot to the boss although they may have some responsibility to someone else as well. It needs quite a bit of careful attention, does it not?

(Ms Gavas) We feel there is a severe lack of clarity in the Constitution of the actual role of the Foreign Minister and for what he will be responsible, but the trend seems to be that he will be overall responsible for development co-operation, humanitarian assistance, the whole external relations framework, including the delegations.

(Ms Hilditch) Is there not a parallel with how the United Kingdom permanent representation to the European Union is established? That is made up of civil servants from different specialists in different departments, but for the time that they are working in Brussels I think they are all seconded to the Foreign Office. At the moment, the debate around the Constitution is all of that—it is black or it is white—but maybe there are other solutions that one could think of that would be administratively efficient but respect the fact that, at the end of the day, the development specialists have different priorities in terms of the main focus of poverty eradication than perhaps the foreign policy staff have.

Lord Maclennan of Rogart

116. As for the role of the proposed Minister for Foreign Policy, would you not see some potential advantage if he were responsible for the ultimate use of these instrumentalities of aid, as part of foreign policy, in giving a higher profile to the development issues within the Union, because it is a higher profile position even than that of a regular commissioner in prospect?

(Ms Gavas) I agree, as long as we can distinguish between the objectives of foreign policy and the objectives of development policy and understand that development policy is for the long term in its objectives and perhaps more strategic, whereas foreign policy is shorter term; that distinction needs to be made. In terms of overall coherence, I think it could provide coherence for the external relations of the European Commission. I believe it will be very much up to the discretion of the Foreign Minister to decide how those policies will be implemented.

117. Could it perhaps give greater impact to the matters we were talking about earlier, good governance, human rights and some of the political obstacles to aid being effective, which might be more easily tackled by such a minister straddling these areas?

(Ms Gavas) I think that as long as there is a distinction between the two policy areas and that is ingrained in whatever structure there is, that could provide for more coherence.

(Ms Hilditch) It is unlikely to be to our benefit from a development perspective to have a Foreign Minister in the new EU set up overall responsible for development policy, because the person in that post would be under a vast amount of political pressure,

competing political pressures, from Member States with different foreign policy objectives which were trying to get those heard. Also, they will be focusing on much more high profile type issues. At the end of the day, development is not a very high profile or glamorous activity. We see quite often in the EU annual budget process that every year there is a new crisis and every year the funds to support the new crisis come from that expenditure, and that includes development. Basically, the budget comes from the development spending. It is the same thing: the fact that the Development Council has been abolished does not mean that Foreign Affairs Ministers will be sitting around talking about something in Namibia; they will not be. They will be talking about Iraq. The situation would be the same: the Foreign Minister would be aware of his obligations to be responsible for development but I do not know in practice how much time he would really have to devote to development issues. Every development policy to some extent is the instrument of the government which is giving it. Everybody gives their aid for various reasons. There are various reasons for which people pick one country and not another. At the end of the day, to say that the Foreign Minister has at his or her disposal all the instruments, including development policy and humanitarian aid policy, goes against best practice and the experience of what makes effective development and humanitarian aid policy.

118. May I interrupt you for a moment? You mentioned two or three countries, for example I think you said Haiti, Togo and one other, where aid has been discontinued and development has been blocked, essentially for political reasons. We have seen that corruption in Bangladesh is so bad and Bangladesh is the absolute bottom of the league of countries that are helped by the EU; if those political problems were tackled more effectively, then maybe there could be a restoration of aid in those areas? It seems to me that talking of the long-term aid objective for Togo without tackling the problem that is blocking the aid is an artificial distinction. I want to see how you view that.

(Ms Hilditch) That is right, but it does not need a Foreign Minister of the European Union in order to be able to sort that problem out. You could, for example, delegate responsibility for specific country cases to different groups of national level, high profile, political figures, who could then intervene to try to find a solution. Basically, you could use political and diplomatic pressure on the government to change its ways. Ultimately, all change, including that kind of momentous political change for the end of corruption, does come from within. It is not the European Union Foreign Minister who is going to be able to bring a political solution to Haiti; it is basically the people in Haiti, with outside support, who will do that, with political and diplomatic pressure at the right time. I do not think that having a Foreign Minister ultimately responsible would necessarily help because in practice I do not think he or she would have the time.

Chairman: Lord Harrison, I think quite a lot of your questions have been pre-empted.

Lord Harrison

119. I think they have. I wanted to ask about the clash of the foreign policy consideration with the development objective. It was a very interesting response: one is short term and the other is long term. I thought you were quite realistic in saying that this is going to happen. Countries inevitably, even in their own individual aid giving, are going to be influenced by their own foreign policy considerations. If that is the case, and you talk a bit about some of the remedies or the ways to ensure that there is some measure of coherence between the two, what else might be done, other than what you have said, to ensure that the foreign policy considerations do not entirely eliminate what many of us would regard as the best, dispassionate approach to poverty reduction or whatever?

(*Ms Gavas*) I think there needs to be a very strong fundamental legal basis in the constitution and for development co-operation. There was until a couple of weeks ago a very clear development chapter with poverty eradication as a central aim, as well as a humanitarian aid chapter. Unfortunately, a couple of weeks ago the IGC legal experts removed an extremely important reference within that chapter, a reference to economic, financial and technical assistance applying to countries other than developing countries. This undermines the legal basis of development in the constitution. There is no distinction between official aid and official development assistance right now. We would hope that would be remedied, and we have been pushing the United Kingdom Government to do something about this. There needs to be a distinction between the notion of values and the notion of strategic interests. What has happened is that the notion of values has been replaced by strategic interests, and that is evident throughout the Constitution. The fact that humanitarian aid is a tool for foreign policy but it is also part of the solidarity clause is a very serious concern. That being so, if we can achieve that fundamental legal basis for most development co-operation and humanitarian assistance, as an independently neutral policy, I think it will help to resolve some of the problems with development policy and foreign policy.

(*Ms Hilditch*) I have nothing to add.

Chairman: You said something about how the Charter has been changed. I was not aware of that. I do not know whether you could provide us with a note about that. It was news to me. I did not entirely grasp what it meant. It would be very useful if you could send an explanatory note on that.

Lord Williamson of Horton

120. I have two completely different questions. The first is this. Obviously, we are trying to concentrate aid more on the poorest countries. That is our clear objective. We do have the residual effect of past agreements, basically the Cotonou Agreement, and so on. Do you yourselves feel that we can, as it were, just keep going on these two tracks: that is to say, most of our aid will go to the poorest but we will continue special arrangements for the ACP, or in the medium term do you think we are going to have to change what we are doing with the ACP?

(*Ms Hilditch*) The beauty of the ACP arrangements, even though there is no obvious connection between all the countries that are included within it, is the nature of the agreement itself because it is a comprehensive agreement and it covers aid, trade and political dialogue and because it is more partnership based than most aid arrangements between groups of countries, more based on negotiation and also based somewhat on predictability as well in terms of funding and also in terms of participation of other actors, apart from the two governments which are non-state actors; they are a party to the agreement. That includes trade unions, churches, NGOs, local authorities. In that sense, it is more comprehensive and these are all quite valuable elements of the agreement that it would be worth hanging on to in some shape or form, even if one decided that there is no logical reason to continue with them actually in the ACP discussion. It is a question of a choice for ACP. Maybe the ACP themselves will decide one day that they have more to gain by approaching their relationship with the European Union in a different way, but I see it as being much more a choice for ACP countries rather than a choice for the European Union side.

121. That is a very good point. I have worked with the ACP quite a lot in Brussels. I attach a lot of importance to the various factors that you have mentioned, such as partnership in countries which are the poorest. I agree with you. I become enraged when people say that the ACP policy is inconsistent with our policy towards the poorest. The next point I have is quite a different one and it relates to the budgetisation of all EU aid. We have this curious system now under which we have the European Development Fund and also quite a lot of elements of aid in the normal budget, although these are not all labelled like that. What do you feel yourself? Do you feel that it should all go under the classical method on to the European Union budget, thus changing the treatment of the European Development Fund, or in any other way do you feel that the way it is treated as a financial matter should be altered?

(*Ms Hilditch*) We feel that the EDF, should be part of the EU budget. It would be a good idea to budgetise it, although there are risks associated with doing that. I think it is better to put it in the budget and to address the risk than to keep it out of the budget because you think the risks are too great. From an accounting and audit point of view, it is clearly not appropriate to have such a large sum of money treated as a separate fund and the only oversight of it is exercised by the Member States, whereas it would be more usual for national budgetary spending to be audited by national parliaments. I think in that sense it is quite inappropriate that it is not part of the budget, but there are risks associated with that. As you know, there is a historic, very large underspend of the money, but how can you hang on to the money in an annualised budget process? If the money has not been spent in ten years, in an annualised or even a three-year budget process, you would not be able to keep the money in your department, but you would have to give it back to the pot. There are quite a large number of issues that need to be addressed

Lord Williamson of Horton *contd.*]

around the underspend, the fact that disbursement is quite slow, but at the end of the day I think it would be fairer and give a better opportunity to ACP countries were it to be part of the budget process, albeit I think within the next financial perspective one would want to see a kind of development category. The external affairs category, in our experience, which we have had since 1999 has been quite unsatisfactory because it includes all external spending and it is very hard to separate. All those categories of spending in Category 4 are legitimate, but it is just that within the one budget, there is all the money that goes to the Balkans, there is all the money that goes to MEDA, there is all the money that goes to Tacis and there is all the money that goes to the poor, so it would be better to have a development category and say that in the development category, we put the money to the developing countries and to try to manage it that way and have some flexibility around the fact that development is not a very long-term activity and you cannot expect the money to be spent in the year in which you sign the agreements, for example.

122. It would change the amount paid by the different countries. We have to realise that, if you change the system, some countries would pay more, such as Britain, and some would pay less. There is an important point there.

(*Ms Hilditch*) Yes. When it was discussed in the informal council last week, all the countries who would pay less were in favour and all the countries who would pay more were against and then Germany asked for more time because they had not worked out what it would mean for them.

(*Ms Gavas*) Once again the ideal scenario would be in the Constitution to have a strong legal basis for development and to have a separate development chapter in the budget, separate from the foreign policy, and then budgetise it. That would be the perfect scenario and, in that way, you would be able to ring-fence the funds for the ACP.

Chairman

123. Well, I have a final question about the clash between bilateral aid and that which is distributed through the EU. How do you think the British Government should be addressing that problem for DfID when a large part of their budget actually goes into the EU pot and may not be, therefore, directed to the sort of objectives perhaps which the Government favours? Do you think that is a problem or do you think that the two different methods of delivering aid are actually addressing the same objectives?

(*Ms Hilditch*) I think it would be better to see it as an opportunity because the idea is that the aid of the Member States and the aid managed by the European Commission are supposed to be complementary rather than competing and it is a fact that that is what the Commission uses to justify its large investment actually in the transport sector, that all of the other donors have pulled out of transport, so they are the only ones left in it, so that is one thing to this, that maybe DfID does one thing

best and maybe the Commission does another thing best and the Swedes do another thing better. I think it would help if donors, instead of acting as EU16, they would just act as a donor and try to have more of a division of labour and really look at where their competencies lie in and what they are best at. It is not necessarily a problem for DfID that so much of its money is allocated directly to the European Union. I guess what is more a problem is if all of DfID's money goes to Category 4 of the budget because that is not a development category, but the external spending category, and the Commission spends money out of that category that the Member States have asked it to spend on a number of different programmes and countries, including all of those countries which were official aid recipients, not ODA recipients. So I think that could be a challenge for DfID, but it is perhaps something we need to discuss more with the Foreign Office and the Treasury, the fact that because it is money which is going into Category 4, which is not a development-only category, it brings the percentage down, if you like, but it is all legitimate spending which Member States ask the European Commission to spend on their behalf, but I can imagine that that would be frustrating for DfID if it was not all spent on development.

124. Did you want to add anything to that, Ms Gavas?

(*Ms Gavas*) No, thank you.

125. Is there anything else which you wish to say to us which you have not had an opportunity to say, maybe we have not covered all the ground that you wanted to cover?

(*Ms Hilditch*) I wanted to mention one thing on coherence, which we did touch on, but not in any great depth. I am going to leave the report behind so as to publicise our report which is around policy and coherence in developing countries. We talked a lot about coherence between foreign policy and development policy in this session, but we are also talking a lot in Brussels about coherence between development in trade policy, development in agricultural policy, development in fisheries policy and development in consumer protection and public health policy. It is quite a high-profile discussion at the moment about how to improve that, such that the effects of one policy are not negated by another policy which the European Union might have, so I think it is an important thing to bear in mind, that it is another thing that the Commission is aware is an issue and it has not really got to grips with what it should do about it and I think it is something that the United Kingdom Government is much stronger on and the European Union could learn from the United Kingdom in terms of policy coherence.

126. Yes, because there used to be clashes between the structural funds and the environmental ambitions and terrible things happened in Spain, so have they got all of that sorted out better?

Chairman *contd.*]

(*Ms Hilditch*) Yes, I think they are better on internal coherence, but I am sure it will increase again with the accession countries.

Chairman: Well, thank you very much indeed. It has been very interesting and very helpful indeed.

Memorandum by British Overseas NGOs for Development (BOND) and Charity Finance Directors' Group (CFDG) joint submission to the Call for Evidence on EU International Development Assistance

SUMMARY

The summary has been set out according to the sections set out by the inquiry, to provide brief answers to the questions BOND and CFDG have identified as being of particular importance. Full answers to the specific questions raised by the inquiry, with evidence, follow in the main text.

1. *Evaluating the reform of EU development assistance*

European Development Policy

The main objective of EC development assistance, the reduction and eventual elimination of poverty, has not led to a significant increase in targeting spend in low income countries, despite continuing efforts from agencies including DfID, BOND and CONCORD (the network of European NGOs for Development). Spending in middle income countries in Eastern Europe, Central Asia and the Middle East is disproportionately high, The annual budget process for 2004 has continued this trend, with the MEDA programme receiving a 34.7 per cent increase on 2003 allocations.

The incorporation of the agreed cost-cutting issues into EC development assistance has been, at best, patchy. The prevalence of such issues, including gender, disability and decentralised co-operation, within the EC's Country Strategy Papers (CSPs) and National Indicative Programmes is limited. As a result, thematic lines continue to be an essential part of the Commission's development portfolio, to ensure the cross-cutting issues are a protected area of development assistance.

The more recent CSPs have shown a definite improvement in reviewing the performance basis of EC assistance. Indicators and targets have been set in these papers. It is too soon, however, to see the impact that these indicators and targets will have in the actual future allocation of assistance. Indicators set also vary in quality.

Coherence and Consistency

Institutional divisions with the EC continue to cause problems in the coherence and consistency of EU aid policy and programming. The split between Directorate General for Development and External Relations is a major cause of this. However, the split between these DGs' responsibilities and EuropeAid's involvement in contract issuing, monitoring etc, coupled with the ongoing, non-uniform deconcentration process, is also a key factor in this lack of coherent overview.

In addition, over-reliance on global structures such as the Millennium Development Goals, leaves gaps in coverage. The MDGs are mainly focused on quantity of delivery, not quality and sustainability. It is crucial that the EC continues to support sustainable programmes. In addition, major gaps in the MDGs, such as reproductive health, must continue to be filled by the EC.

Commission

The reforms made have been too focused on the administrative and structural aspects of Commission development assistance. Two major problems remain, the gap between policy and implementation (DG DEV and AIDCO) and the gap between the treatment of the ACP and other developing countries, due to the split between DGs DEV and RELEX and the non-budgetisation of EDF funding.

Until these, and other issues such as the lack of incorporation of cross-cutting issues into CSPs, are resolved, it would be dangerous to attempt further restructuring or rationalisation. More positively, deconcentration is leading to increased programmatic co-operation and dialogue between the EC and implementing NGOs. This is still not possible at the Brussels level, due to the lack of staff, particularly in EuropeAid.

Outweighing this positive side is the absolute necessity of a review of the EC's financial procedures. The new Standard Contract is excessively administratively burdensome, and will have a drastic effect on the efficiency of EC development assistance. Actors in receipt of EC financing for development are likely to have to take on additional administrative staff to cope with the new demands made on them. These include separate bank accounts for each EC financed action (some agencies will therefore have to set up nine or 10 new accounts each year), new procurement rules, bank guarantees and project audits. These issues are dealt with in detail in the main text from paragraph 1.i.1 on. One of the foreseen impacts of this burden is that development programmes will lose some of the essential flexibility and innovation necessary for success and impact. Continuous contract amendments and budget changes will slow dispersal of aid, even to those actors which have in the past shown high capacity to spend and complete contracts with positive impacts (for example, the NGO Cofinancing budget line B7–6000).

Governance

The abolition of the Development Council has already led to increased discussion of development within the context of wider external affairs policies and procedures. This is unacceptable as development is not a tool of a common foreign and security policy (perhaps the primary current issue of the EC's external affairs agenda), but a separate area of policy.

2. *Looking ahead to 2004 and beyond*

Development and Foreign Policy

Many Member States have integrated development assistance programmes into foreign ministries. This has generally led to the downgrading of development at a policy level, for example through loss of cabinet-equivalent representation. Separate development agencies, such as the United Kingdom's Department for International Development, tend to be more successful in delivering quality programmes.

The ideal solution within the context of the EC, would be a separate Development Commissioner and a single Development Directorate General with responsibility for development policies, programming and implementation (alongside delegations and with EuropeAid as its operational arm) in all recipient countries. This should be separate from spending to support the development and implementation of the Common Foreign and Security Policy, which could well include financial assistance in the near abroad.

Enlargement

Enlargement is likely to reinforce the trend of decline in the share of EC ODA going to LDCs. In terms of foreign policy, the new Member States are primarily focused on neighbouring countries. While some of these countries (eg Afghanistan) are undoubtedly among the poorest in the world, there is no doubt that, as regions, the ACP countries, South Asia and parts of Latin America, contain the vast majority of the world's poor. Spending must be concentrated there.

EDF and Budget

There is a significant European dimension to EU development assistance which argues that there is an added value to separating its development spending from that of Member States. In terms of the complex issue of EDF budgetisation, this issue is dealt with in the attached BOND paper.

1. *Evaluating the reform of EU development assistance*

— "European Development Policy"

(a) *To what extent has the joint Declaration agreed by the Development Council in November 2000, which set out the main objectives of EC development assistance, had an impact on the allocation of aid?*

1.a.1 The United Kingdom DfID's Briefing Paper on the Poverty Focus of EC Development Assistance (August 2002) states that in 2000 the EC was allocating 62 per cent of its spend on middle or high income countries. DfID has stated one of its main goals is "an increase in the share of EC aid that is spent in low-income countries to 70 per cent by 2006". However the 2004 EC budget shows Asia, with two thirds of the world's poor, is not receiving the necessary increase from the External Relations budget. In the 2003 geographical envelope, Asia received €563 million. In 2004 this will be €591 million. This €28 million (4.9 per cent) increase is more than accounted for by the increase of €59 million in the rehabilitation budget for Afghanistan. Therefore the budget reflects an actual reduction in aid to other Asian countries.

1.a.2 By contrast, the budgets for the MEDA (Middle East) and TACIS (Eastern Europe and Central Asia) programmes have both increased dramatically. TACIS from €391.5 million in 2003 to €425.9 million (8.8 per cent increase) in 2004; and MEDA from €732.5 million in 2003 to €986.8 million (34.7 per cent increase) in 2004. A large amount (€160 million) of the MEDA increase is for Iraq's reconstruction and rehabilitation, which it could be argued is more of a foreign policy objective.

1.a.3 These increases can be ascribed to a number of reasons including the growth of budgetised EC development spending in addition to the ex-colony-focused European Development Fund, EU border state and regional security, the accession of new Member States, continuing insecurity in the Middle East, and more recently, the "war on terror". These may be good reasons for financial support to third countries from the perspective of a Common Foreign and Security Policy (CFSP). However, they are not primarily poverty-focused and therefore do not support the EU's move towards increasing the poverty focus of its aid spending. Spending to achieve CFSP objectives must be administratively and programmatically separated from development spending, to ensure more effective allocation of aid on the basis of development policy.

1.a.4 There has been some progress in the concentration of thematic line spending on the low income countries. For example, under the 2001 call for proposals of the NGO cofinancing line (b7–6000), 55.2 per cent of the value of contracts awarded was for projects in low income countries; 29.23 per cent for lower middle income countries; 8.79 per cent for upper middle income countries; 0.5 per cent for a single DAC list Part II country; and 6.2 per cent for other regional contracts. For the 2003 call, the corresponding percentages of contracts awarded (contract value figures not yet available) are low income—60 per cent; lower middle income—27 per cent; upper middle income 11 per cent and other 2 per cent. This is moving towards DfID's target of 70 per cent in low-income countries. However, this gain was mainly at the expense of a reduction in regional contracts, some of which were in lower-income regions. Taking these regional figures out, the low income figures were 59 per cent in 2001 and 61 per cent in 2003, a less dramatic increase and still short of DfID's target. By contrast, the percentage for upper middle income and Part II countries has risen, from 9.3 per cent to 11 per cent.

1.a.5 Overall in budgetary terms therefore, it is difficult to argue that the EC has shown a marked movement towards increased poverty focused targeting of aid spending. As a first step, the EU must follow the lead of Member States such as the United Kingdom Government in focusing its aid primarily on the poorest countries, whilst recognising that real poverty exists in middle-income countries and working in effective ways to tackle this poverty.

(b) *To what extent have poverty reduction and the agreed cross-cutting issues, including the environment, gender, human rights and good governance, been incorporated into country programmes?*

1.b.1 From the NGO perspective, to date the Commission has had little success in its mainstreaming strategy. A recent study by Aprodev[3] and One World Action on mainstreaming of gender in EU policy finds that mainstreaming is "more an idea than a reality".[4] Save the Children's recent study "Invisible Children: Towards integration of children's rights in EU and Member States development co-operation policy" comes to the same conclusion regarding children's rights.

1.b.2 These studies find that mainstreaming is only successful when it is accompanied by specific, targeted measures that identify clearly the area to be mainstreamed, for example gender, the environment or human rights. Such a double-track approach would need to be reinforced with clear instruments in support of implementing mainstreaming and earmarked funds in the geographical lines. These could then be filtered out over a set period.

1.b.3 It is clear that in the absence of specific guidelines and training on the way these issues should be addressed under the national envelopes, delegations and desk officers will continue to attach a low priority to them. It is also disappointing to see how little attention is given to the exchange of good practices with other donors and especially Member States regarding mainstreaming.

1.b.4 Aprodev's analysis on the way gender issues are taken into account in 40 CSPs shows that some efforts have been made to meet external coherence. For example, reference is increasingly made to governments' international commitments in existing or forthcoming national gender policy plans. More gender aspects are taken up in the country analysis and in social sector-specific approaches. Yet there remains a lack of translation into EC response strategies or National Indicative Programmes. The sector-based analysis done demonstrates the low interest attached to gender in most NIPs. For example, even though transport was a major concern for over 50 per cent of the CSPs studied (22 out of 40), and rural development for 25 per cent of them, only 5 per cent NIPs explicitly mention gender in relation to either sector.

1.b.5 Further, in relation to decentralised co-operation, an objective of EU-ACP cooperation since Lomé IV, the concept is not mentioned in 17 of the 40 CSPs, only in reference to past aid or the current budget line B7–6002 in a further 13 cases, and is part of the NIP for only six countries.

1.b.6 NGOs have also found that other key cross-cutting issues are not included in country strategies or policies. For example, there is little mention of disability, while there is no doubt that disabled people are amongst the poorest of the poor in most environments.

---

[3] APRODEV is the association of the 17 major development and humanitarian aid organisations in Europe, which work closely together with the World Council of Churches.

[4] *"Assessing Gender Mainstreaming in European Community Development Cooperation"*, Aprodev and One World Action October 2002.

1.b.7 There is evidence that the situation is improving, with the latest Country Strategy Papers more likely to adopt the agreed cross-cutting issues and include participation of civil society (again a key part of the Cotonou agreement and further elaborated in the Communication on Non-State Actors) in both the analytical and operational sections.

1.b.8 However, considering the inconsistent results so far, BOND continues to support the existence of separate thematic lines even where, as with Food Aid and Food Security, these are deconcentrated. These lines play a key catalytic role and support innovative actions, exchanges of experience and research in essential sectors of development co-operation. Until mainstreaming is able to provide these same advantages, further rationalisation could well lead to increased marginalisation of some of the priority cross-cutting issues.

(c) *Has the intention to make EC aid, to a greater extent than before, conditional on performance as well as need, been brought into effect?*

1.c.1 Certainly the will to do this is reflected in the newer ACP Country Strategy Papers. According to Aprodev research into the published Country Strategy Papers, the results-orientated approach is better reflected in terms of indicators and targets being set. However the quality of these targets remain inconsistent. In Uganda, monitoring and evaluation in education and health are well co-ordinated through bi-annual sector reviews that monitor targets, set new targets and judges whether progress against agreed undertaking is satisfactory. In the case of Lesotho, where 50 per cent of EC aid will be provided in the form of macro-economic support, the parameters for the review process are very general (eg reduction of unemployment, increase of the rate of vaccinated children and school enrolment) and certainly not sufficient to really assess the impact on poverty.

— Coherence and Consistency

(d) *Has there been progress in bringing about more coherence and consistency within the EC's aid programmes?*

1.d.1 There continues to be institutional divisions within the EC which cause significant problems to the coherence and consistency of aid programmes. These revolve around the split of development aid regional policy and programming between the EC's Directorate Generals for Development (ACP) and for External Relations (ALA, MEDA, TACIS etc), with EuropeAid undertaking the contract issuing and management process. The non-uniform deconcentration of many of the budget lines has complicated many issues further, leading to different interpretations of EU policy and contract procedure, from different sources.

1.d.2 In addition, there has recently been an effective weakening of democratic control of the European Parliament over EC aid. Already constrained by the fact that the EDF is outside parliamentary control (although it is acknowledged that moves to change this are apparent), decisions over strategic aid priorities are being made without reference to the Parliament. The proliferation of new initiatives includes the ACP Water Fund (announced in May 2003 with a €1 billion EDF allocation), President Prodi's pledge of €1 billion in support of the fight against HIV/AIDS, Malaria and Tuberculosis at the G8 and the announcement of a €250 million fund for returning migrants. These figures have been announced without any concrete commitment to allocate additional funds and with a lack of transparency regarding the origin of the funds. This lack of transparency leads to a perception that the money will not actually be forthcoming, or will be at the cost of other, lower profile expenditure. It also runs counter to the acknowleged need for long term, predictable aid flows that enable developing countries to plan effectively.

(e) *Has the agreement on broad development objectives and the introduction of Country Strategy Papers helped?*

1.e.1 From the point of view of NGOs, it is a positive step for the EU to have clear, defined objectives for its aid spending, provided these remain developmental in character. However, this is only the case if the programming, monitoring and review of these objectives are critical and open. As an example, the 2001 European Commission Development Report cites supporting the Millennium Development Goals (MDGs) as a key means to achieve the EU's development objectives, and therefore to judge the effectiveness of EC aid spend. However, the MDGs focus primarily on numbers. While quantity is important, it is possible that the rush to meet the goals could lead to an over-focus on numbers, to the exclusion of the poorest of the poor, who are generally more difficult and more expensive to reach. It must also be noted that key development sectors, such as reproductive health, are missing from the MDGs. This is an area in which the EC must continue to provide development support.

1.e.2 Within countries and regions, civil society can assist in monitoring whether these objectives are being met in a consistent manner, or if development is proceeding on an ad-hoc basis, depending on geographical, political, social or economic conditions. The periodic development of Country Strategy Papers can serve as a means for including civil society in the development of the EU's country aid programmes. The inclusion of a given country's civil society in its development planning is an essential part of achieving sustainable and successful development.

1.e.3 In terms of performance against the country strategy papers, the Cotonou Agreement provides that a mid-term review be undertaken in 2004 of the country strategy papers in respect of the individual 77 ACP States and the Regional Strategy Papers. This should provide a clearer idea as to the progress and focus of the CSPs.

— Commission

(g) *How successful in terms of improved efficiency and effectiveness has been the new organisational structure for EC aid introduced in 2000? Is there a case for further rationalisation?*

1.g.1 The reform has not been underpinned by a clear vision on the political objectives of EU external assistance. The focus of the reform has been perhaps too much on the administrative and technical aspects. Thus, while poverty reduction is said to be the central goal, this is not consistently translated in budget allocations to the poorest regions nor in new management tools to address the goal. Furthermore, the development perspective has been sidelined through the:

— Cutting down of the administration of development cooperation (DG DEV) and a serious reduction in the involvement of the DG in policy making and implementation.

— Removing implementation of development cooperation to EuropeAid under the leadership of the Commissioner for External Relations.

— Reducing the scope of the portfolio of the Commissioner for Development to a General Director (or CEO) for implementation of development cooperation under the chairmanship of the Commissioner for External Relations.

— Expanding the portfolio for the Commissioner for External Relations to policy-making and implementation of development cooperation.

— Re-arrangement of the delegations in developing countries to be directly accountable to the Commissioner for External Relations, as opposed to the Commissioner for Development Cooperation.

1.g.2 Two major problems prevail: The gap between policy and implementation (DG DEV and AIDCO); and the gap between the treatment of the ACP and the rest of developing countries due to the Cotonou/EDF splits and the split between DG DEV and DG RELEX.

1.g.3 Given the current lack of incorporation of cross-cutting "thematic" issues into geographical envelopes and the continuing policy-level confusion caused by the split of regional policy and programming into two DGs, a period of consolidation of previous changes is necessary, before further changes are made. Further, the process of deconcentration has not yet been completed, either in terms of building delegation capacity, or in terms of moving actual tasks from the centre. Until it is clear where all responsibilities lie, and how the new division of labour is working, further rationalisation might be precipitate.

1.g.4 In addition, whilst the introduction of a new standard contract for all EC-funded actions initially led to some efficiency gains and increased coherence, NGOs are now debating the efficacy and necessity of some of the newer changes, in particular the new Standard Contract. The principles agreed at the recent Palermo conference between Member States, the EC and NGOs, included that co-operation between the EC and NGOs should be based around developmental and poverty reduction objectives and that contract monitoring should be based on programme learning (eg donors learning from NGO innovation and scaling up project approaches to a larger scale).

1.g.5 However, the new Standard Contract is excessively administratively burdensome, when compared to other donors contractual procedures, and places the majority of reporting effort on detailed accounting, not on programme learning. This is neither efficient, nor effective. NGOs are absolutely aware that financial accountability is important, in order to ensure that aid money is not wasted. However, it is equally if not more important to be sure that the money is spent effectively and sustainably. NGOs would prefer to be using their capacities to report to the EC on this basis, not on the almost exclusive basis of financial auditing.

1.g.6 Deconcentration of many of the development functions to delegations, over a period of years, has further complicated many of the above issues. Some delegations have been unable to properly manage the "Project Cycle". Inadequate number and quality of human resources in delegations have led to financial problems within NGO's structures, as they are systematically required to pre-finance operations in order to guarantee the project's progress and outputs. Several NGOs have experienced long delays regarding the disbursement of intermediate and final tranches, slowing down or at times paralysing the project. When the NGO reserves are limited, NGOs are required to seek private funding mechanisms, representing additional costs through bank loans, when available. This can produce a very negative impact upon direct beneficiaries ie national governments, ministries, regional authorities and in particular with populations. In addition, delegations often have different interpretations of contractual procedures and regulations. Therefore NGOs can often receive two or even three different answers to the same procedural question, in different regions or between delegations and Brussels. This is a serious issue, as it could open NGOs up to future legal action and could lead to the cancelling of development contracts and the loss of development resources.

1.g.7 On a positive note, the process of deconcentration has led to more direct contact between the EC (through the delegations) and NGOs and projects. Monitoring visits have been more frequent and generally useful, both through developing an increased output/outcome-based relationship between the EC and NGOs, but also through mutual learning. This should be encouraged, as it will lead to improved programming of EC aid, increased development understanding within the EC's staff, and the ability to learn between the EC's programmes of NGO support, and its own multilateral support of government programmes.

(h) *Are the quality, skills and number of staff now commensurate with the size of the overall programme?*

1.h.1 There is no doubt that the general feeling is that the Commission, especially DG Development, is woefully understaffed. Certainly the experience of NGOs is that the staffing at the delegation level remains very varied. Some delegations already have the capacity to take on more of a role in development contracts (in terms of staffing, technical and administrative skills). However, others do not (often according to the delegations themselves), see paragraph 1.g.6. At the same time, decision-making and control remain firmly rooted in Brussels, as this is a deconcentration procedure, not decentralisation.

1.h.2 The problem is more enhanced within the EDF Framework, where the National Contracting Authorities frequently have weak institutional capacity.

(i) *How much progress has there been in simplifying financial procedures so as to speed up disbursements without taking undue risks?*

1.i.1 The introduction of a standard contract by the Commission for funding across the EU in 1998 brought simplicity and improved some administrative inefficiencies. However, the inclusion in that standard contract for provision of the end loading of payments has caused enormous financial difficulties for many charities, which far outweigh any risks of non-delivery.

End loading of payments

1.i.2 These payment procedures are outlined in Article 15 of the new General Conditions for EC-financed grant contracts for external actions. They allow the EC to retain 20 per cent of funding from year one, and a minimum of 10 per cent of the entire contract value, until the contract with the organisation is complete. The payment of each tranche is withheld until each completion report is accepted. Once accepted payment should be received within 60 days, however every time the completion report is questioned this 60 day wait for payment starts again, thus producing more delays with payments, while the programme continues, using the NGOs or other donor funds.

1.i.3 The cumulative effect of end loading of payments is damaging, particularly as voluntary organisations lack the financial capacity that private companies possess. One organisation currently has three funding contacts with the EU, which has resulted in it pre-financing 380,000 Euros worth of projects. This amount is much bigger than its unrestricted reserves. This cash flow has effectively put a barrier on any new applications the organisation wants to undertake, not for programme capacity reasons, but because its reserves are not big enough. In fact they are in the unusual situation of having to receive money from another grant making body to cover their debts.

1.i.4 Organisations can respond either by being in possession of substantial unrestricted reserves, or by taking out bank loans. However, the very nature of voluntary organisations means that they can find it very hard to secure a bank loan. According to member-research by the Charity Finance Directors' Group, many banks do not understand the idea of restricted funds, and are unwilling to give loans unless the organisation has no money in reserves at all.

1.i.5 This process also goes against the stated aims of other policies for charities; the costs are more than just financial. It has a disproportionate effect on long-term programmes. For example a five-year programme will feel the effects far more than a one-year programme because these involve less pre-financing. This has ruptured the emergency to redevelopment continuum in projects based in places such as Afghanistan. The process also has severe implications for southern partner organisations. It damages partnership working, through the creation of an unreal financial risk for both partners.

1.i.6 Cash flow problems caused by delays in the release of planned tranches can create a bottleneck at the partner level and the problems experienced by northern charities are passed on to their southern partners. In some ways these problems are felt more acutely because all of their funds are designated. They do not have the unrestricted reserves to compensate for cash flow problems, and many will be tempted to divert designated grants. This can have unhealthy implications for financial controls and monitoring systems for the organisation. Another implication would be in terms of statutory compliance for partners in the countries they are based. In India the government permits tax exemption for charities' as long as 80 per cent of the annual income is expended in the financial year. End loading of payments challenges this, as "income" for the first year of a project may not be received until three or four years later. Southern charities could therefore be left with large unjustified balances at the end of the financial year and be required to a pay tax on the total income.

Bank guarantees

1.i.7 The requirement of a bank guarantee for projects involving EC pre-financing of more than €1 million adds to the already impractical and financially costly process of engaging with EC funding. In order to get projects underway and receive advance payments for these projects, charities have to provide up to €1 million as a cash deposit to banks in order to obtain a guarantee that the amounts budgeted for will be provided, and work can still continue on projects, whatever happens to the agency in that three, four or five year period.

1.i.8 Current discussions in Brussels between the EC and representatives of the charity community may lead to the bank guarantee requirement being waived in relation to budget lines that are specifically targeted at charities. The problem is likely to remain, however, in relation to charity bids for big bilateral funding money (European Development Fund etc), which is often dispersed via tenders.

1.i.9 The huge amounts needed in cash to secure a deposit mean that it is near impossible for charities to acquire one in their home countries. The same is true of banks in the field. Although these banks are more eager to provide for these organisations the amounts they are being asked to guarantee are beyond their means. One organisation tried to secure one from a Bosnian bank, but the amount required would have equalled 5 per cent of the bank's capital.

Project bank accounts and audits

1.i.10 Finally, project-specific bank accounts and annual project audits have also been included in the new General Conditions. These are costly, inefficient, administratively burdensome and, in the case of bank accounts, actually go against standard healthy financial practice. Specific bank accounts are now required to receive funds for each contract held with the EC. This means that if an NGO has five contracts funded in a year, they have to open five new bank accounts, one for each action. This goes against standard procedures to reduce numbers of bank accounts. Some banks have already stated they will start to charge to open more than a certain number of accounts, to prevent this practice. This sort of bank charge is not an efficient use of development resources, whether they are from the NGO or the EC's funds.

1.i.11 In addition, project-specific audits are now requested annually for all projects over €750,000. Again, this is an unnecessary expense, as general audits of the organisation, followed by annual detailed financial reports, have been sufficient to meet the needs of the Commission for decades. The question can be raised as to why these audits are essential now? At the very least, the need for an annual financial report to accompany payment requests should be abandoned if such a financial audit is to be produced.

Contract amendments

1.i.12 All changes to planned programmes, including changes to spending between budget headings of more than 15 per cent, must now be incorporated into a full contract amendment, involving a submission of the changes, discussion within the Commission and, if approved, three new copies of the contract, with the amendments included, being drawn up. As this is only applied on a per cent basis, and not a value basis, this has led to huge numbers of contract amendments being drawn up by NGOs each year.

Procurement rules

1.i.13 The EC's Procurement Rule of Origin is becoming far more complex and burdensome to deal with. In some cases, NGOs have been forced to ask suppliers for a breakdown of components of equipment, where this is not clear. In effect, this means NGOs having to get written authorisation from the EC each time they buy equipment of non-European origin. Given that much of the equipment and supplies NGOs buy is sourced as close to the beneficiary population of the project as possible (in line with poverty-focused, sustainability theories of development work), this creates a further wholly unnecessary administrative burden.

Application process

1.i.14 In addition, the application process of the EC for the thematic budget lines, are overly complicated and reduce the chances of effective EC interaction and direct funding of southern NGOs, an aim of the decentralised cooperation budget line, the Non-State Actor communication, and the Cotonou agreement.

Summary

1.i.15 In summary, while it is recognised that the creation of a Standard Contract was undeniably a positive step in rationalising and increasing transparency in EC funding, the new Standard Contract is far too administratively burdensome. The measures introduced go far beyond ensuring financial probity, and into the realms of administrative inefficiency. Appropriate spending of development aid is absolutely a cause to which NGOs are committed. However, the balance between accountability and administrative efficiency must be maintained. Far from making procedures more efficient, the new Standard Contract has merely made them more consistent in their inefficiency and costliness.

1.i.16 The increasing complexity of development procedures within the Commission risks threatening the very innovation, ingenuity and flexibility that make civil society development programmes so effective a conduit of EC aid.

(j) *What progress has there been in making the budget more transparent, bringing allocations into line with clear objectives and in achieving better reporting?*

1.j.1 The new Activity Based Budget format used for the 2004 budget is definitely a step in the right direction. However, the split needs to be refined, so that development spending is not split according to the structure of the EC (ie along ACP v Asia and LA lines) but according to purpose of expenditure. Therefore, all development spending must come under the development heading. Spending for CFSP priorities should come under External Relations.

— Governance

(k) *Has the abolition of the Development Council resulted in a down-grading of input and oversight by Development Ministers? Or by putting development aid within the ambit of the General Affairs and External Relations Council, has development been given greater political prominence and ensured greater coherence with other international policies?*

1.k.1 The abolition of the Development Council has minimised the level of political representation in discussions on development, and hence the political impact of decisions and could leave development cooperation dependent on other EU external affairs policies. This subsuming of the development agenda within the external affairs agenda reduces the status of development cooperation and extends a trend already seen in the Commission and Member States. The predominance of EU external relations which are governed by event-driven short-term agenda could limit the importance attached to the reality of development co-operation, which is based on the long-term.

2. *Looking ahead to 2004 and beyond*

I. DEVELOPMENT AND FOREIGN POLICY

EU assistance and CFSP

(c) *Should development aid be used as an instrument of foreign policy as is suggested in the High Commissioners "Security Strategy" presented to the European Council at Thessaloniki in 2003, or should it be seen as an autonomous policy with its own objectives and rationale?*

2.i.c.1 Many MS have integrated development assistance programmes into foreign ministries. On a policy level, this has generally led to the downgrading of development. Development concerns have usually not been given much weight in broader discussions on issues such as migration. Changes in the status of development cooperation often come with changes in the political affiliation of governments. This leads to the question as to whether development cooperation gets downgraded because there is no minister to defend it or because the government as a whole does not support it.

2.i.c.2 Separate development agencies tend to have been the most successful in delivering quality programmes, as is the case with the United Kingdom Department for International Development, although there is a problem in maintaining links between the development organisation and other government organisations.

2.i.c.3 The ideal situation for EU development cooperation would be an independent Development Commissioner and a Development Directorate General. The Development Directorate General and Commissioner should have responsibility for the elaboration of development policies and aid programmes in all recipient countries, be they ACP countries or not. This would guarantee the maintenance within the Commission of an institutional focus for development. DG Development would be responsible for:

1. defining development policy;

2. strategic planning and coordination;

3. devising sectoral policies applicable across regions; and

4. it could also oversee the implementation of aid programmes by EuropeAid, which woud become its operational arm.

2.i.c.4 It could support EC field delegations in the design of country support strategies, assist them in the conduct of political dialogue and provide guidance on governance conditionality and aid suspension.

Aid to the "near abroad" and other middle income countries

(e) *Should financial assistance to the near abroad come under the remit of EC development aid?*

2.i.e.1 BOND supports the need for a well resourced policy towards neighbouring countries but the significant increase reflected in these regions in the 2004 budget set against a marginal increase in development spending (in the ALA and ACP regions) raises the question of how the EU intends to meet its international poverty eradication commitments in the short to medium term. There is now consensus internationally that aid to the poorest countries needs to increase massively to meet the 2015 development targets. There is scant evidence of such an increase in the 2004 budget following its first Budget Committee reading.

2.i.e.2 One possible way to avoid this confusing situation in future would be to separate funding for the near-abroad from development spending in other regions. This is complicated, as there is already an argument over the splits between EDF and budgetised spending, and between DGs Development and Relex. However, BOND believes that there must be a differentiation made between CFSP spending and Development policy spending. It is entirely possible that spending on the near abroad would count as the former.

Development in the Constitutional Treaty

(i) *Is the new Treaty being negotiated able to ensure that development assistance is provided for the poorest and that humanitarian assistance is adequately protected?*

2.i.i.1 See BOND's Parliamentary Briefing on International Development and the EU Constitutional Treaty, attached.

II. ENLARGEMENT

(a) *How will Enlargement affect EU aid policy, eg country allocation, relative emphasis on development versus political issues, and quantity of aid?*

2.ii.a.1 Government commitment in Accession Countries to development cooperation is low. Development policy frameworks focus on regional stability and global security rather than on poverty reduction. The new Member States have a consistent focus on the neighbouring countries which are difficult areas (Chechnya or Afghanistan). In terms of the institutional model in the new Member States, aid coordination is integrated into the Ministry of Foreign Affairs. Furthermore, there is a lack of relevant experience in the development field and limited financial resources devoted to ODA due to overall budgetary constraints.

2.ii.a.2 The share of EC ODA to LDCs has been declining over the last 40 years although the absolute volumes have increased. This trend is unlikely to change much after enlargement as it is consistent with the development policies pursued by new Member States. Given the limited staff resources of new MS in development, they will concentrate their resources on regions where their commercial, security and historical interests are stronger. The influence and voting of new MS (25 per cent of the vote) will reinforce existing trends towards a focus on the near abroad. It may also reduce the focus on issues related to aid to LDCs. There is a strong need for capacity to be strengthened in policy formulation and aid implementation.

IV. EDF AND BUDGET

(b) *Does the EC provide a contribution in its aid-giving that adds value to Member States bilateral programmes?*

2.iv.b.1 The added value of EU aid includes the collaboration of EU NGOs on projects (consortia); raising the development education and contribution of EU citizens as a whole; funding of the European body of development NGOs, CONCORD, which increases development NGO coherence, capacity and cooperation; increased engagement of European civil society on EU development policy; the contribution to international development by countries without the necessary structures or institutions to follow professionalised aid policies.

(d) *The issue of whether the EDF should be budgetised is also likely to come into play. Would this be a good idea from the United Kingdom's standpoint?*

2.iv.d.1 See BOND's draft response paper to the Commission Communication on EDF Budgetisation, attached.

Budgetising the European Development Fund

A BOND response to the Commission Communication

BOND welcomes the Commission's initiative to launch a debate regarding budgetisation of the EDF through the publication of a Communication on this subject. The Commission's proposals for the incorporation of the EDF into the EU budget raises a number of concerns regarding the protection of funds and the fundamental principles underpinning the EU-ACP relationship. This paper explores some of those concerns and suggests that the key outcome should be a strengthened focus on poverty eradication as well as the safeguarding of the fundamental, innovative elements of the Cotonou Agreement.

BACKGROUND

On 8 October 2003, the European Commission issued a Communication *Towards the full integration of cooperation with the ACP countries in the EU budget* (COM(2003)(590). The Commission puts forward its case for the incorporation of aid to ACP countries from the European Development Fund into the European Community budget (see appendix for main arguments). EC development assistance currently comes from two distinct sources:

— The annual European Community (EC) Budget which covers cooperation with developing countries in all geographic regions and countries with economies in transition (Category 4: External Actions).

— The European Development Fund (EDF) which covers cooperation with ACP countries under the Cotonou Agreement.

Different administrative rules and decision-making structures apply to these. Funds from the EU budget are administered in accordance with existing EU financial regulations. Funds from the EDF are administered in accordance with rules laid out in the Cotonou Agreement, which is the general framework for EU/ACP cooperation, and specifically in the EDF Regulations adopted by the Council. The EDF is inter-governmental and voluntary in its funding and managed by the European Commission, with the European Parliament granting the discharge.

THE CONTEXT

European Community aid appears increasingly dwarfed by other agendas, such as trade, foreign and security policies and the changing balances of power within the EU institutions. This has serious consequences for Community aid programming. The proposal to transfer EU development assistance funds for the ACP countries from the EDF into the EC budget must be understood in that context. The foreign policy imperative of funding investment in Europe's "near abroad", middle-income countries on the Mediterranean and Eastern borders, has diverted scarce development resources away from low-income developing countries in the South. This trend is mirrored by the move of EU Member States' own national, bilateral official development assistance towards increased "selectivity" and "conditionality". BOND has serious concerns about the potential for Community aid resources to lose their proper focus, namely tackling poverty.

BOND POSITION ON EDF BUDGETISATION

EDF budgetisation raises concerns regarding the legal mechanisms and guarantees that would need to be put in place in the budget to ensure that EDF funds would be protected for the mainly low-income ACP countries in the budget cycle and to ensure that these funds do not get diverted to foreign policy initiatives. The EU cooperation budget under Heading 4 "External Actions" includes several non-poverty related budget lines, such as cooperation with industrialised countries, migration, the Common Foreign and Security Policy. The distribution of funds under Heading 4 is also strongly influenced by EU commitments in favour of highly political crises that are in the spotlight (Afghanistan, Iraq). It would need to be absolutely clear that the EDF element of the budget could not be reallocated, even in years when disbursement rates are low, to other category 4 priorities.

BOND welcomes authoritative parliamentary scrutiny over all EU expenditure and believes that this is an important point of principle to keep in mind during these discussions. Budgetisation, under the right conditions, could increase the profile of the ACP in the political debates of the Union and improve the consistency and coherence of EU external policy as well as the control mechanisms on spending regarding the EDF. The following points aim to demonstrate that these outcomes are by no means a foregone conclusion and more clarity on how the EDF would be safeguarded for ACP countries is required.

MARGINALISATION AND MODERNISATION

1. *"Modernisation" should not result in weakening the strong focus and content of the Cotonou Agreement or the EDF and rendering it similar to other less ambitious agreements.*

The Commission argues that EDF budgetisation will be a measure to ensure that cooperation with the ACP will not be marginalised and relations will be modernised. However, EDF budgetisation will not necessarily solve the issue of marginalisation. The problem lies with the institutional architecture of the EU which is effectively sidelining the development perspective. There has been a serious cutting down of the administration for development cooperation (DG DEV) in the Commission and a serious reduction in the involvement of the DG in policy making which is limited to the ACP countries.

Cooperation with the ACP is the most advanced form of cooperation between the EU and developing countries and sets an important example for cooperation between the EU and other regions. Cooperation with other regions is not as advanced in terms of specificity of development objectives, namely poverty eradication, quality of partnership, ownership and participation and in terms of institutions (i.e the ACP-EU Joint Parliamentary Assembly, ACP-EU Joint Council of Ministers, ACP Secretariat...). Furthermore, under agreements with non-ACP regions and countries, non-development related activities are being funded within these programmes related to migration and the anti-terrorism clauses and actions in third countries to support EU security issues. At present, the EDF offers the most secure and viable long-term structure for development cooperation although concerns have recently been expressed by the European Parliament and NGOs regarding the undertaking to use the EDF, including programmable aid, for military peace keeping activities of the African Union which do not fall within the Official Development Assistance DAC criteria. The fact that the Peace Facility was created in response to an initiative and request from the Africa Union and not from the ACP group and that it is not legally possible to raise part of the funds from the EU-Mediterranean cooperation instrument (MEDA) represents a major concern regarding present and future governance of the EDF.

Aid Quantity and Quality

2. *A binding commitment should be made to maintain the level of resources for ACP countries and poverty focus of the EDF.*

How will the Commission ensure that the strong focus of the EDF on low-income countries (which is weak in the EC budget) is maintained following budgetisation? How will funds for the mainly low-income ACP countries be protected or ringfenced in the budget cycle? Within the EU budget there is flexibility in shifting commitments from one region to another. How will the Budgetary Authority protect the EDF once it is included in the budget? The EU budget is skewed towards middle-income countries, while low-income countries such as India and Bangladesh receive only token amounts. Attempts in the past by the European Commission to allocate more funds to low income countries have been thwarted in favour of other regions, and in particular, the "near abroad" and countries under the spotlight. Budgetisation would make the funds earmarked for ACP countries more vulnerable to capture by other Union foreign policy objectives unless they were specifically earmarked for the ACP. This should be the subject of an inter-institutional agreement prior to the eventual budgetisation of the EDF.

The above trend is likely to be exacerbated by the enlargement of 10 countries from Central and Eastern Europe, which might have little interest in development co-operation with Africa, and perhaps even less of an interest in the Caribbean and Pacific regions. In the period 1999–2001, only 5 per cent of Czech ODA and 0.5 per cent of Slovak ODA was directed to Africa.[5] Given that the accession countries have subscribed to the *"acquis communautaire"*, and co-operation with the ACP countries through the EDF, they have accepted the need to contribute to the EDF but their commitment will be highly influenced by the attitude and commitment of the current EU Member States towards aid to the ACP.

The principle of annuality and the present re-allocation procedures of the EC budget through transfers represents a real challenge in this respect as there is a serious risk that the disbursement rate will become a more important factor than the quality of actions supported in the management of EC aid to the ACP. Increasing disbursement will require political will and additional human resources if this large sum of money is to be disbursed efficiently.

The consequences of EDF budgetisation should be fully integrated into any discussion regarding the future level of the EU's own resources. The incorporation of the EDF into the EC budget, will necessitate an equivalent increase in Member State contribution to the EU's own resources. A binding commitment is needed from the budgetary authority for the entire period of the new Multi-annual Financial Framework to maintain the present level of EDF funding.

[5] Development Strategies IDC, *"The Consequences of Enlargement for Development Policy,"* September 2003.

PARTNERSHIP, OWNERSHIP AND PARTICIPATION

3. *The fundamental innovative principles of partnership, ownership and participation enshrined in the Cotonou Agreement should be safeguarded as fundamental elements of any strategy aimed at poverty eradication.*

How will the Cotonou Agreement's fundamental principles of equality between partners and ownership of a country's development strategy by the country itself be preserved in the event of budgetisation? In its Communication the Commission heralds the principles of ownership and partnership of the Cotonou Agreement. However, the Communication does not examine the impact of EDF budgetisation on the joint ACP-EU institutions and on ACP-EU political dialogue. On the basis of these principles, discussions with the ACP countries need to be held on the desirability of EDF budgetisation, possible conditions and potential scenarios. How will the EC ensure that the political commitments to the Cotonou Agreement are well reflected in the way the budgetised resources are managed and allocated? Current experience with other agreements shows clearly that the responsibility of the partner governments in aid management and allocation is substantially lower than under the EDF. What consequences will the budgetisation of the EDF have on ownership and partnership?

Furthermore, how will the principle of the participation of non-state actors in political decision-making through dialogue with governments on EU aid be enhanced in situations where government responsibility of aid management is weakened? Generally, civil society participation in EC development policy is strongest under the Cotonou Agreement in which it has been granted a legal basis and an extremely important benchmark of civil society participation is through the Country Strategy Paper process and the Mid-Term Reviews.

FOCUSING ON POVERTY REDUCTION IN THE FINANCIAL PERSPECTIVES

Creating a sub-heading for EC development co-operation

The most effective way of tackling the problems of the lack of democratic control, lack of visibility, lack of coherence between regions and budget lines and ensuring a single approach to funding development co-operation in line with the EU's Barcelona and Monterrey commitments is at the level of the Financial Perspectives, the negotiations on the new Multi-annual Financial Framework. One way in which this might be achieved would be through the creation of two sub-headings within Heading 4 (External Actions): one for EC development co-operation to all developing countries and another sub-heading for security and foreign policy related issues, such as the Common Foreign and Security Policy. Separation between the two sub-headings would be based on the OECD definition of Official Development Assistance (ODA) and its classification of developing countries. The advantages of this structure are numerous:

1. It would ensure visibility of the Union's external assistance and make it easier to monitor financial contributions and their use.

2. It would be clearly in line with EU commitments from Monterrey and Barcelona (harmonisation, increasing the level of funding available).

3. It would give the European Parliament a role in controlling all development resources, enhancing accountability and transparency.

4. Since sub-headings are largely subject to the same procedures as headings the budgetary authorities would be consulted before transfers of resources between priorities could be carried out.

5. It would allow the Commission to operate with one single system and one set of procedures for all EU external assistance to developing countries.

6. It would ensure and strengthen coherence between the EU's development policy and other external policies thereby reconciling with the aims of the new EU Constitutional Treaty.

If a solution to the annuality of the EU budget can be found then a balance between sound management, flexibility and speedy disbursement versus predictability, quality and multi-annuality could be found.

Such a structure would not only improve ACP-EU co-operation and keep it at the forefront of international co-operation, but would also base the allocation of European development assistance on firmer and more objective grounds. It would ensure that decisions about policy priorities are fully informed by related resource requirements and enable accurate comparisons with other donors. This could then be followed up by a more rational organisational structure in the Commission. There may be other structures that could achieve this outcome equally well and BOND welcomes the opportunity to contribute to ongoing discussions in this area.

RECOMMENDATIONS REGARDING THE COMMISSION'S PROPOSALS

In the current discussion on the future of EC Development and Foreign Affairs policies and awaiting further information from the Commission on the conditions and practicalities of EDF budgetisation, BOND would make the following recommendations:

— The new EU Treaty sets the objective of poverty eradication as the overarching aim of EU co-operation with developing countries.

— The new EU Treaty reflects the principles of ownership, partnership and participation as fundamental elements of any strategy aimed at poverty eradication.

— The new EU Treaty includes the principles of coherence of all Union policies that have an impact on development.

— On the basis of the OECD definition of Official Development Assistance (ODA) and classification of developing countries, the EU establishes a clear, transparent and consistent framework for its Development Policy Area in the EU budget that includes all EU aid instruments to all developing countries. A separate sub-heading for Development Co-operation should be created within Heading 4 in the Financial Perspectives.

— Allocation criteria for the EC development co-operation budget, including but not limited to ACP countries reflecting a poverty focus, are agreed by the Budget Authority and the Commission, and a monitoring mechanism is established on allocation and disbursement.

— The principles on partnership in the Cotonou Agreement are not watered down in the review of the Agreement.

— A process of negotiation is launched with the ACP, both at governmental and civil society levels, on the impact and desirability of EDF budgetisation.

— The opinion of the Joint Parliamentary Assembly is respected. Although the JPA could not have a formal role *vis-à-vis* the EC Budget similar to that of the European Parliament, it could no doubt serve as a useful additional sounding board from which MEPs could draw inspiration in their budget scrutiny work.

— Legal guarantees are given in the new Financial Perspectives that the resources for ACP countries will not diminish during the period covered by the Cotonou Agreement (until 2020).

— Funds are protected for the ACP countries in the budget cycle beyond the $N+3$ formula, decommitted funds must be used in support of the Cotonou Agreement objectives.

— A transitional period is introduced following incorporation of the EDF into the next financial perspective that ensures that the backlog as incorporated into the current spending period, will not be lost even if it remains unspent more than three years after allocation.

APPENDIX

THE COMMISSION COMMUNICATION

The Commission sets out a number of arguments in its Communication outlining the benefits of EDF budgetisation:

a. *Efficiency*

One set of administrative rules and decision-making structures will reduce the administrative burden on Commission staff and on recipient countries, which presently receive resources from the Community according to different rules. Budgetisation would entail:

— Unified procedures.

— Coherent management and the facilitation of devolved management by ACP Delegations.

— Rationalisation of comitology between the Commission and the Member States.

— Simplification of reporting and accounting requirements.

— The removal of duplication in financial decisions, legal commitments, payments.

b. *Effectiveness*

Annual discussions on the budget by the Council and the European Parliament have become the main forum for debate on the substance of development policy, the political priorities of the Union and their resource implications. Budgetisation would improve the effectiveness of EC aid to ACP countries through:

— Budgetary discipline.

— Yearly assessments and yearly authorisation by the Council and the European Parliament.

— The rapid availability of funds without the need to wait for ratification of a financial protocol by 25 Member States and two thirds of the ACP.

— Faster response to evolving needs and priorities and more flexible reallocation mechanisms.

— Regularised patterns of commitments.

— Easily identifiable build-up of unspent funds.

— The facilitation of regional co-operation between ACP and non-ACP developing countries which would increase synergy.

— Long-term planning in the financial perspectives.

c. *Transparency*

One budget including all external aid expenditures will provide a more accurate and global picture of external assistance and development policy in terms of size and geographical repartition. Budgetisation would lead to:

— Budgetary unity and universality.

— An overall commitment to poverty eradication easier to track.

— Coherent and comparable presentation of budgets.

— Consistent decision-making.

d. *Legitimacy*

Despite its political importance and financial scale, the EDF is currently the only expenditure that is not subject to authorisation by the European Parliament, yet the Treaty specifies the co-decision procedure for development policy. European Parliamentary scrutiny would:

— Strengthen public legitimacy of the EU's external assistance.

— Strengthen the legitimacy of co-operation with ACP partners.

BOND PARLIAMENTARY BRIEFING PAPER

INTERNATIONAL DEVELOPMENT AND THE EU CONSTITUTIONAL TREATY

Civil society, international development and the future of Europe

On 8 September the United Kingdom Government will publish a White Paper setting out its position on the forthcoming negotiation of a new Constitutional Treaty of the European Union.

A broad-based civil society movement is concerned that the negotiation of a new EU Treaty risks not only marginalising Europe's commitment to development, but subordinating development instruments to a narrowly defined foreign policy agenda.

This briefing paper outlines the concerns of development advocates regarding the up-coming EU Intergovernmental Conference; asks Members of Parliament to engage in the process and calls on the United Kingdom Government to back a pro-poor, pro-human rights agenda for EU external relations.

Key Messages to the United Kingdom Government

— Development must not be subordinated to EU foreign, security or commercial policy agendas. EC aid is not a "tool" or "instrument" for projecting Europe's self-interest.

— The autonomy, neutrality and impartiality of EC humanitarian aid must be safeguarded. It does not constitute an "instrument" for EU security policy in a "war on terror".

— EC aid should be founded on a commitment to democratic ownership and partnership of development co-operation; and allocation re-targeted at OECD-defined low-income and Least Developed Countries and people living in poverty in Middle Income Countries.

What is at stake in the EU Treaty negotiation? EC aid and foreign policy

The Inter-Governmental Conference (IGC) negotiation of a new EU Treaty will agree proposals that directly impact on how the European Union defines its global role and identity. Legal EU Treaty changes will translate into policy and institutional reforms which impact in developing countries.

Positive proposals from the Convention on the Future of Europe for the IGC include the placing of sustainable development, human rights and poverty eradication amongst the strategic objectives for EU external policy.

Yet development advocates have serious concerns about other components of the draft EU Constitution which could, in effect, subordinate development policies, institutions and instruments (including aid resources) to foreign and security policy objectives. Throughout the Convention development co-operation was discussed as an "instrument" and "tool" of EU external relations. A qualitative differentiation between the "tools" of development and those of foreign policy has been acutely absent.

The proposals for "all EC instruments", including aid, to be at the disposal of a new EU Foreign Affairs Minister would entail an increased politicisation of development co-operation. Another article in the draft Constitution concerning Common Security and Defence Policy proposes the use of humanitarian aid in the fight against terrorism.[6] This reflects the broader trend for "politicised humanitarianism" amongst EU Member States and other donors.

Background: Europe's role in international development

As the world's largest donor block, European Union aid policy matters. Collectively it has trade or aid relations with all developing countries and can influence the practice of other donors. Annual European Community aid consists of over seven billion euros pooled by the EU Member States and managed by the European Commission. Thus it is essential that the new EU Constitutional Treaty establish a progressive legal, policy and institutional framework for EU policies that impact on developing countries.

Effective European Community development programmes could galvanise an enlarged EU behind huge resources and progressive, autonomous policies for poverty reduction. Member States and the European Commission adopted their first formal EU development policy statement in 2000, which placed poverty eradication at its heart. According to the Laeken declaration of 2001, Member States have committed the EU: "to seek to set globalisation within a moral framework, in other words to anchor it in solidarity and sustainable development."[7] However, the reality of EC policies and aid programmes is far removed from the commitments to tackling poverty. Enlargement will include countries with little or no history of involvement in international development. Broader institutional changes, such as the division of responsibility for EC aid between the Development Commissioner and an External Relations Commissioner and the abolition of biannual Council meetings devoted to development issues, threaten to effectively marginalise the political voice for development. Mainstreaming development is a key objective; but subordinating development is a key concern.

KEY DEVELOPMENT CONCERNS IN THE DRAFT EU CONSTITUTION

1. Whilst development co-operation has been accorded its own article, articles on the Common Foreign and Security Policy and the Common Security and Defence Policy imply that all EU instruments, including development co-operation and humanitarian aid, are at the service of a new EU Foreign Affairs Minister.[8] This approach would appear to undermine the United Kingdom Government's commitment to the Millennium Development Goals and the United Kingdom International Development Act, which insists that development policy maintain and operate on the basis of its own developmental principles, objectives, institutions and instruments.

2. The chapter on development co-operation (Article III–218) is unclear about geographical coverage: there is no reference to all developing countries. This could perpetuate the confusion regarding the application of various EU policies relating to third countries and division in Commission responsibility for EC aid to developing countries in various regions. The Organisation for Economic Co-operation and Development (OECD) provides a practical definition of developing countries (DAC list of developing countries) which could be included in the article.

3. The development chapter has not taken on board the fundamental principle of partnership in development co-operation. Despite on-going criticisms of EC aid effectiveness, the Cotonou Partnership Agreement signed between the EU and African, Caribbean and Pacific states constitutes an innovative framework for development co-operation that puts partnership, mutual accountability, civil society participation and democratic ownership at its heart. These principles should be incorporated as legal commitments in the new Treaty for EC aid to all regions.

4. The chapter on humanitarian aid should commit to the principle of independence. This concept is central to the existing humanitarian aid regulation and institutional framework of ECHO (European Community Humanitarian Office) but is dropped in Article III–223. Its omission could entail dangerous

---

[6] Article 111/205, Draft Constitution.

[7] On 15 December 2001 the European Council approved the "Laeken Declaration on the Future of the European Union", which included a decision to set up a broad-based Convention to pave the way for an open, transparent reform of the EU.

[8] "... may propose the use of both national resources and Union instruments" (Article I–40.4).

linkages between aid provision and politicised or military intervention which would constitute a threat to the independence and thus the safety of humanitarian aid workers, as well as the populations affected by political crises.

5. We strongly oppose the creation of a European Voluntary Humanitarian Aid Corps in Article III–223.5. Humanitarian response is for experienced, trained professionals, not for volunteers, especially in dangerous crises.

The negotiation of a new Constitution of the European Union provides an opportunity to strengthen and safeguard the political voice for development in EU external relations.

United Kingdom Members of Parliament are called upon to lobby the Government with the following questions and demands to ensure that EC development co-operation is defined in terms of poverty reduction, human rights and sustainable development.

How can MPs and Lords help?

PROPOSALS FOR PARLIAMENTARY QUESTIONS AND POLICY RECOMMENDATIONS

1. Will the United Kingdom Government ensure that the new EU Constitutional Treaty strengthens the political voice for development by ensuring that Union's relations with developing countries are guided by the 2000 EU Development Policy Statement and commitments by all EU Member States and the European Commission to implementing the Millennium Development Goals; and the EC aid will not become subordinate to the Common Foreign and Security Policy or European Security and Defence Policy?

2. Will the United Kingdom Government call on the EU Constitutional Treaty negotiation to clarify the geographical coverage of EC aid by inserting a commitment to "all developing countries" with the aim of ensuring that all developing countries as defined by the OECD Development Assistance Committee receive a fair and equal treatment by the EU, proportionate to their development needs?

3. How will the United Kingdom Government ensure that the fundamental principles of partnership and democratic ownership in aid, as embodied by the Cotonou Partnership Agreement between the EU and African, Caribbean and Pacific states, become incorporated as legal commitments for EC aid to all regions in the EU Constitutional Treaty?

4. Will the United Kingdom Government ensure that the Constitutional Treaty enshrines the principles of independence, neutrality and impartiality for EC humanitarian assistance as contained in the current EC regulation but absent in the draft Constitution; thereby preventing a politicisation of humanitarian aid?

5. Will the United Kingdom Government call under the IGC and broader EU policy debates for EU development policy and practice to be represented, developed, implemented and scrutinised by a Commissioner for Development, a Service or Directorate for Development, a re-activated Development Council and a European Parliamentary Committee?

12 January 2004

Further submission of evidence from BOND

LETTER FROM THE BRITISH OVERSEAS NGOs FOR DEVELOPMENT (BOND) TO THE PRIME MINISTER

I am writing to you on behalf of the undersigned organisations (not printed) with a sense of great urgency and concern regarding articles in the draft Constitutional Treaty for the European Union relating to international development.

We strongly welcomed the inclusion of two separate chapters on *development co-operation* and *humanitarian aid* for these policy areas, providing a legal basis in the Treaty. We, like the United Kingdom Government, also welcomed the commitment to poverty eradication as the primary objective of European Union development policy.

However, on 6 October, we were extremely disappointed to see that the legal basis for development co-operation was removed by the IGC Secretariat. Deleting any reference in the Treaty to *developing countries* could potentially undermine the future of Europe's international development programme, as EU funds could be disproportionately used to assist richer countries at the expense of the world's poorest countries. This would thwart the contribution that EC aid could and should make to the eradication of poverty, and the achievement of the Millennium Development Goals to which the Member States have committed themselves.

Tackling this anomaly presents a key opportunity for improving the poverty focus and effectiveness of European Community aid, which is a key objective for the United Kingdom Government, and consistent with DFID's latest Public Service and Delivery Agreement.

Please find enclosed BOND's Parliamentary Briefing Paper on the IGC, outlining our key concerns regarding the draft Constitutional Treaty. I hope that you share these concerns and look forward to receiving your response.

15 October 2003

BOND's PARLIAMENTARY BRIEFING PAPER ON THE IGC

AMENDMENTS TO ARTICLE III-221

Legal experts from the IGC Secretariat in the Council have proposed several modifications to the Draft Treaty elaborated by the Convention on the Future of Europe. Those changes should theoretically be only technical, however one of them is political and it relates to article III-221, on economic, financial and technical co-operation.

On 6 October, the fundamental legal basis for development co-operation in the Treaty was effectively removed as a result of legal amendments proposed by the IGC Secretariat. The amendments propose the deletion of the application of the article on economic, financial and technical co-operation (art III-221) to countries "*other than developing countries*". The removal of the reference to "non-developing countries" as beneficiaries of this article could render the article on development co-operation superfluous, creating an unclear legal framework for relations with developing countries. It creates a fundamental ambiguity about the scope of the two sections on development co-operation and economic, financial and technical co-operation. It undermines the differentiation between EC development co-operation (ie Official Development Assistance) and EC Economic, Financial or Technical assistance (ie Official Aid) to other third countries; such as Pre-Accession aid.

ARGUMENTS OF IGC SECRETARIAT LEGAL EXPERTS ON ARTICLE III-221

1. *IGC Secretariat Argument 1:*

Article III-211 has originally been introduced in the Nice Treaty (article 181a). The Nice article did not exclude developing countries, article III-221 (as proposed by the Convention) should reflect article 181a. The proposal is therefore to remove "*Other than developing countries*" from III-221.

Response to this argument:

Article III-211, as proposed by the Convention does not constitute a change from the *acquis communautaire*, it only clarifies former article 181a. The fact that the scope of the Nice Treaty article is ill-defined created confusion on the scope of the development co-operation chapter. The Convention has therefore included "other than developing countries" in article III-221 with the only aim to clarify the scope of section 1 (development co-operation) and section 2 (economic, financial and technical co-operation). A legal expert from the Commission confirmed that article 181a from Nice has been introduced for non-developing countries. Macro economic aid to non-developing countries was not possible before 181a, that is why they introduced this article in Nice.

2. *IGC Secretariat Argument 2:*

Article III-221 could bring a second legal base for developing countries to receive macro-economic support if "*other than developing countries*" was removed.

Response to this argument:

There is no dispute on including article III-221 in the constitution, however the aim of this legal base must be specified. The only macro-economic support falling under article the Nice Treaty article 181a (now article III-221 in the draft Constitution) has been delivered to Serbia and Montenegro. Any other macro-economic support was provided under the legal base for development. Therefore article III-221 should either specify a region (eg accession countries, non-developing countries or even neighbouring countries). Macro-economic is part of development policy in almost all developing countries, it therefore does not need a specific legal base.

3. *IGC Secretariat Argument 3:*

The fact that article III-221 explicitly states that it will not prejudice articles on development by carrying out economic, financial and technical co-operation ensures the integrity of the development section.

Response to this argument:

The beginning of article III-221 strengthens the view that it is specifically targeting non-developing countries.

LETTER FROM THE MINISTER FOR EUROPE, FOREIGN AND COMMONWEALTH OFFICE (IN RESPONSE) TO BOND

Thank you for your letters to myself and the Foreign Secretary of 2 October on participatory democracy and the draft EU Constitutional Treaty, and to the Prime Minister of 15 October on development and humanitarian aid. I am replying as Minister for Europe.

In your letters of 2 October you noted that the IGC offers us an opportunity to create a Union which reflects citizens' concerns and aspirations. I strongly agree. Through the IGC we have the chance to make the Treaties, and the EU, more coherent and easier to understand. We need a clearer statement of what the EU does, why it does it and how. Its legal structure should be made easier to understand. Europe's citizens should know what powers national governments have conferred on the EU, and what powers they have kept for themselves. I believe that the draft Constitutional Treaty provides a good basis for realising these aims. I hope that it will lead to a better organised Union, which is more effective in delivering practical benefits to its citizens.

You raise some specific points in relation to values and rights and the draft Treaty provisions on participatory democracy. As you know, the Charter of Fundamental Rights sets down rights, freedoms and principles applicable at EU level. It draws existing fundamental liberties together and makes them more visible to the citizen. The EU should respect these, whenever it acts. On participatory democracy, we believe the provisions in draft article I-46, which allow for an "open, transparent and regular dialogue with representative associations and civil society", clearly recognise the importance of the role of civil society in the EU.

Your letter underlined the importance of coherence between policy objectives and implementation in the EU. I agree that this is of central importance. Our support for a full-time Chair of the European Council is based on the need to ensure greater coherence and delivery on the strategic priorities which Member States have chosen. I believe that this will be essential to EU effectiveness at 25 and more members.

In your letter of 15 October you expressed your concern at the possibility that the reference to "developing countries" in Article III-221 might have been removed from the draft Treaty. As you know, the Government believes that humanitarian aid is an important international issue. We welcome the fact that a separate chapter on humanitarian aid was secured in the draft Treaty resulting from the Convention on the Future of Europe and believe that this will provide a clear basis for the EU's efforts in this field.

I would like to reassure you that the United Kingdom has worked to protect the language in Article III-221 in the IGC, and that it is included in the current draft Treaty. We believe it important that the final Treaty should reflect the progress made in the Convention, both on development policy and on humanitarian aid.

10 November 2003

THURSDAY 13 NOVEMBER 2003

Present:

Bowness, L.	Morris of Aberavon, L.
Harrison, L.	Watson of Richmond, L.
Inge, L.	Williams of Elvel, L.
Jopling, L. (Chairman)	Williamson of Horton, L.

Examination of Witness

MR RICHARD MANNING, Chair of the Development Assistance Committee, Organisation for Economic Co-operation and Development, examined.

Chairman

127. Mr Manning, good morning, and thank you so much for coming. I know you have come from Paris to share your wisdom with us. As you know, we embarked upon this exercise a few weeks back, and this Committee will continue its inquiry into the European Union's development aid programme into the next session of Parliament. This will be our last meeting during this particular session as the House rises next week for prorogation and the Queen's Speech in two weeks' time. Let me begin. OECD's Development Assistance Committee, of which you are the Chairman, I know you reviewed these matters in 1998 and 2002. I wonder if you could open by just reminding us of the main findings and in which areas you believe the European Union has made progress since 1998, where you think the problems are and what are the areas where you have found most concern? Then tell us how you think they have responded to your report of 2002 and what you believe they ought to do as a result of your two reviews. We would appreciate your being as frank as possible with us in how you see the whole system, and particularly we are looking for what are the main problems?

(*Mr Manning*) Thank you very much, my Lord Chairman. I should explain to the Committee that, as you may know, I became Chair of the OECD Development Assistance Committee only in June this year, and hence I was not the Chair at the time of the review which took place in mid 2002. Obviously, I have had a careful look at the documents but I speak with that degree of distance. I think the first thing to say about the review is that the 2002 review was significantly more positive than the 1998 review, and the reviewers, who were Norway and Canada, gave the European Commission some credit for a number of actions taken between the two dates, notably in terms of producing more of an overall statement of policy on what it was seeking to achieve, and some aspects of the improved management. An interesting indicator, I think, is that in the two years previous to the review the actual disbursements of European aid rose very sharply, they rose by 13 per cent between 1999 and 2000 and then by 21 per cent, in real terms, between 2000 and 2001. So the review had some evidence that the attempts by the Commission to deal with some of the well-known problems about slow disbursement, excessive backlogs, and the rest of it, had shown some fruit. Against that background, the recommendations fell into five areas. The first was

around strengthening the European Community's comparative advantage in promoting development. There I think the Committee put some weight on the fact that the European Community is a unique aid donor, in that not only does it provide significant amounts of assistance but it is also responsible for trade, agriculture and other policies that have a significant impact on developing countries. So there is considerable interest about what are described usually as coherence issues, how far European Community policies, as a whole, if you like, promoted development or improved the environment within which developing countries have to operate. The second area of interest was around promoting the sustainability of poverty reduction, and there I think that the most crucial issue is put very briefly as bringing ODA allocations into better alignment with the principal aim of poverty reduction. As you know, the Union produced a Development Policy Statement in 2000, which stated that the central aim of its development policy was to do something serious about poverty in the world, and the review noted that the allocation of European Community aid did not appear to be fully consistent with that objective. There are also comments about the sectoral allocation, about deepening the dialogue with partner countries and pursuing what was regarded as promising developments in relation to post-conflict assistance. The third area, coming back a little bit to the first one was in relation to not only the coherence of broad policies but coherence within the development sector itself. The review felt that the introduction of Country Strategy Papers for all significant recipients of Community assistance was good, but it commented that the analytical capacity and resources were lacking, both in the field and in Brussels. They wanted to see stronger linkages and feedback, I think feedback is the more important here, between the various quality control systems: audit, of course, evaluation, the Quality Support Group, which to my mind is a rather good Commission innovation, a group, as it were, peer-reviewing within the Commission of new activities. The fourth area was strengthening the focus on results and effectiveness, and this had to do with an important issue, which is still on the agenda, of structural responsibilities within the overall RELEX family, further simplification of procedures, strengthening the capacity of impact assessment, which I think is important. You could argue that in 2002 we had some evidence that work on efficiency of European aid had progressed, but it was less clear

Chairman *contd.*]

whether we had enough information on effectiveness of European aid. For which reason the Commission was encouraged to develop what is called here a strategic role for evaluation, with more of the evaluations about the results of Commission activity. Also it contained a recommendation, under this heading of 'Strengthening the European Community's contribution to discussions in the DAC on aid effectiveness', and there I can clearly report to the Committee that I have seen a much stronger engagement by the European Commission in DAC discussions. The European Commission is a founder member of the DAC. At times, it has not punched its weight in the DAC, if I can put it like that. The evidence over the last couple of years is that it is making a serious effort to do exactly that. A fifth and final area was improving implementation, with a view to enhancing country ownership, and here there is much talk of the prospects of further delegating authority to the field. There again I can certainly report to the Committee, first of all, that the deconcentration process, as it is called, has gone a lot further since 2001-02. Secondly, my own visits, in my former capacity in DfID and a visit I have just paid to the Pacific in my new capacity, do suggest that deconcentration, where it has happened, has both increased significantly the speed at which decisions get taken on boring but important matters like contracting, and so on, but, very importantly, I think, has given a sense to field staff that they genuinely do have more responsibility. To my mind, I think that has sharpened the performance of Commission operators in the field, so I think it is an area of progress. The review raised questions about whether the Commission could staff adequately these country offices with appropriate personnel, and it talked also about improving personnel management for development staff. Of course, this is a fairly common issue in many members of the DAC. How do you create and sustain a cadre of people who have enough understanding of development issues, particularly in systems where these are integrated into wider foreign ministries or other government departments, and the Commission is no exception to that. I hope that is helpful as an overview of the last review.

Lord Williams of Elvel

128. You did mention, Mr Manning, one of the recommendations of the 2002 report as being the European Community should improve its "contribution to DAC discussions on aid effectiveness". What does this mean precisely?

A. Let me give you a concrete example. The DAC has spent quite a lot of time, in the last couple of years, looking at what we can do to harmonise our procedures from the point of view of making aid easier to manage, partly from a donor perspective but most importantly from a recipient perspective. At the moment you can easily have a situation where six different donors are operating in a particular sector in a particular country, in a way which is not very coherent or joined-up, where they are pursuing different objectives. Even where they are pursuing the same objectives you tend to have different monitoring systems, different accounting systems and a lot of duplication of effort. The DAC has made it its business to try to put much more emphasis on doing these things in a more efficient way, and the Commission has played an important role in these discussions. The Commission has decided that it would focus particularly on delivering some results on the ground in a limited number of countries. There is certainly evidence that there has been a lot of engagement between the people in EuropeAid, who are managing the process centrally, and people in the field in the countries concerned. We have embarked on a new push on this, following an important meeting that took place in Rome earlier in the year. We set ourselves a number of targets which we are trying to achieve over the next year or two, and the Commission is taking the lead in one or two areas in putting those into place on the ground. I think I am right in saying, for example, that the Commission will lead work which will take place in Nicaragua, on this point.

129. We are talking not just about improving delivery, we are talking also about improving evaluation procedures, are we, and what else are we talking about?

A. We are talking about the whole project cycle, if you like, from the point of view of how you identify what you are going to do. The general model, if you like, which we are trying to promote and within which the European Commission, I think, is playing a very positive role, is one where, first of all, we make a reality of recipient country ownership. In other words, instead of donors coming and doing their things in countries, it is much more a question of how we can help particular individual developing countries put in place policies that they wish to pursue, obviously policies that are sound and sustainable, and then find a much more joined-up way of donors supporting that process. The Commission has been an important player in this. A nice example, which was drawn to my attention by the Asian Development Bank the other day: in Bangladesh, a wide group of donors have now constructed together a support programme for the whole of primary education in Bangladesh, of course, a very important sector in a very big country. It involves expenditure of $1.8 billion over the next five years, of which the Bangladesh Government is putting up more than a billion. It involves, I think, seven or eight donors, half a dozen of which are putting all their money into a pot, if you like, managed by the Asian Development Bank on behalf of all of them. I am very pleased to see that not only is the United Kingdom a member of that, and Canada is a member of that, but also the European Commission is a member of that. The European Commission is putting substantial amounts of funding, I think it is $100 million, or something like that, into this basket, which is all part of a joined-up attempt by Bangladesh to make a real impact on basic education over the next five years. That is a very good example of the kind of model we are looking for, and I am very pleased to see the European Commission playing a really constructive role within that.

Lord Williams of Elvel *contd.*]

130. Some of our witnesses have been quite critical of the Commission and how it has behaved in the past. You seem to be much more positive and telling us they are doing fine?

A. I do not think any donor that I know of is beyond criticism, and certainly the Commission is not and I do not think the Commission is trying to be. I have noticed a tendency sometimes in the United Kingdom to have little good to say about the Commission. I think it is important to have a balanced view of this. I have perhaps a particular reason for saying that because I was the first ever United Kingdom development specialist in the United Kingdom permanent representation in Brussels when we joined in 1973. I can recall, from being there, that there can always be a feeling in London that "These guys don't really know what they're about and we know it all, and why don't they do it the way we do it?" Of course, there are a lot of good things that the Commission can learn from the way things are done in the United Kingdom, but the United Kingdom is not the only fount of wisdom on these matters, and I think the Commission is right to try to learn from a number of different angles. The Commission has a difficult job to do. It is no surprise that multilateral bodies in general, and the Commission in particular, do tend to be heavy on procedures, people worry about transparency, people worry about fairness, people worry about who is getting the contracts, and so on. The natural reaction is to set up procedures which are often over-elaborate and often do not actually deliver what people want them to deliver, there is a lot of signing of bits of paper and much hierarchy, and the rest of it. I think it is clear the direction in which the Commission needs to move is more in terms of giving people responsibility and holding them accountable, rather than having too many checks in the system before you can actually move. The Commission still has work to do I think on the effectiveness of its delivery. It still has a structure in Brussels which, as I say sometimes, is hard to explain to the average Martian, and of course it does try to deal with a number of multiple objectives, as all donors do, and that is something that does complicate the way in which assistance is delivered. I do think it is right that the Commission should get credit for some of the good work it is doing in many countries, particularly in playing a positive role as a member of the wider development co-operation community, if I can put it like that.

Lord Williamson of Horton

131. We have met before, because everybody in the European Union is recycled a few times, but now we are both in different positions. I would like to ask you a question about policy coherence, and particularly in relation to the potential future developments on the Common Foreign and Security Policy. We know there have been quite a lot of comments and concern from other organisations that the way the Foreign and Security Policy is going, particularly in the draft Constitutional Treaty, could cause some difficulties *vis-à-vis* the interface with development policy. That is the point I want to ask about. I think it does relate to two of your recommendations in 2002, the one on policy coherence and also on the sustainability of poverty reduction, because we all know that sometimes, sometimes when I have been present, the ministers want more poverty reduction but they take a decision which puts money into something else. It is quite common. We know that happens. Would you like to comment on how you think the European Union can best handle the interface between development policy and their increasingly ambitious Common Foreign and Security Policy agenda?

A. To put this in context, we should be clear that most donors are struggling with the same issue. It has been sharpened particularly by 9/11. In the DAC, for example, we are working on a paper at the moment on aid and the security sector, in which we are looking at how we can put into practice the recognition that we all have that without security you will not get development, and quite possibly without development you will not get security, but how we make a reality of this and do so in a sustainable way. I think it is very important for development people to recognise that governments have objectives which go well beyond development. At the same time, I think it is important that, as we adapt government policy and government expenditure to some of these international realities, we do not lose from sight what I suppose the development community has learned over the years, which is that we need to be very serious about sustainability. There is always a danger of the short term and the long term getting at odds with each other. I was recently in Australia and it is very interesting to see that in the last few months Australia has been forced to lead a major intervention by Pacific countries in the Solomon Islands, because essentially of state failure in the Solomon Islands, which led to a situation of extreme insecurity and basically where the Government has had to turn to outside countries to help it. That is an interesting comment on the way we, and not least the United Kingdom, I suppose, and I was partly involved in this, have managed sustainable development in the Solomons over the years. One feels that if we had done a better job on that then we would not have had the security problem that the Australians have just had to deal with. I think that shows that we have got to be very serious about building sustainable institutions, supporting countries in improving their governments, which has become a very central theme for development co-operation. I think it shows us also that while it may well be necessary, and certainly was necessary in this case, for there to be quite a heavy intervention, it is going to be very important to match that with building sustainable systems for the future in the Solomons, and you can apply that to the near abroad for the Community as well. So that, as various very obvious pressures force the Community to look as a community at some of these, foreign policy, migration, crime, all these issues that impact on the periphery of Europe, we need to understand always that if we are going to do that in a sustainable way we have got to avoid gesture politics with European aid and we have got to build systems that will survive. The other part of this, and the point that the review focused on, is how you take account of these realities of Foreign and Security Policy while sustaining the

Lord Williamson of Horton *contd.*]

development policy of the Community, which is about, essentially, reducing poverty in the world, something which I would argue is very much in the interests of the Community and all of us. That is where you get onto these quite hard-edged questions as to whether we have the balance of expenditure right in the European Community between the near abroad, on the one side, and the areas where most of the world's poor live, on the other.

Lord Watson of Richmond

132. On a slightly different angle but as you have raised the impact of security issues on development, I would be interested. Sitting where you are in Paris, is it your perception that, because of the attacks particularly in Iraq, and so on, on people involved in development programmes and aid programmes, that is going to become an issue for people going into this area and wanting to work in this area of their own physical security and the willingness and ability of international organisations to say "It's safe for you to be there, or reasonably safe for you to be there"? Is this going to become a factor?

A. I fear it is, and of course Iraq has a number of special circumstances which make it particularly risky. I think, looking more broadly, the proliferation of light weapons all round the place puts people in a new situation. This is very true in Africa. Talking to a colleague who used to work in the Solomon Islands 20 years ago, when there were not many guns at all, and comparing that with the situation now, makes the point in the Pacific and it is true in many other places. I do think that development workers face very significantly higher risks today than would have been the case 20 years ago, and I do think that effective means of reducing the proliferation of light weapons in developing countries is a very high priority. Of course, not just from the point of view of development workers, much more importantly from the point of view of poor people in those countries, who are usually the victims of the violence that goes on. What we have learned, it has been made very evident in cases like Sierra Leone and elsewhere, is that we simply cannot get sustainable development if we do not get on top of security issues in the country.

133. It is a new dimension, to some extent, is it not?

A. In a way, we were able to take for granted certain things 20 years ago, which we cannot take for granted any more, and we need to be conscious of that.

Lord Morris of Aberavon

134. You mentioned earlier that duplication of effort concerned you. May we move on from that to comparisons. In the peer review which was conducted, how are the EC programmes viewed in comparison with bilateral assistance and other large donors which you mentioned earlier? Secondly, you mentioned also the deconcentration policy has gone much further and increased the speed of decision-making. Perhaps you could illustrate that and give a view as to how successful it has been, and, to take

your own words, the average Martian on the Clapham omnibus, what view would he take?

A. On the first point, the DAC does not run league tables, except in the sense that we do publish annually the statistics on how much aid people give and the terms on which they give it. We have not attempted, and I think it would be more difficult to attempt, to score our members as to how effective they are. Having said that, we are working very hard on better ways of measuring results, and I think this is a crucial issue for the development community generally. What I anticipate over the next three, four years is that, following the decisions, not least the decisions by the European Union announced in Monterrey last year, there will be a very significant increase in international aid over the next three years, despite budget pressures in the European Union. At the moment, total aid internationally, the last year for which we have the figures, which is 2002, was \$57 billion. I would be surprised if that figure does not exceed \$70 billion by 2006, although that depends heavily on decisions in Europe and indeed in North America. The way I see it is that we will have a serious job to explain to taxpayers, parliaments, and so on, whether this increased aid is producing real results in the real world. For that reason, I welcome what is said in the peer review about the importance of evaluation, the importance of results-based management. We have a string of work in the DAC at the moment precisely on that theme. The Commission has been one of the leaders, along with the World Bank, in looking at metrics that you could use to try to show whether we are having an impact. For my money, a particular problem is that it is becoming increasingly hard to say what individual donors have achieved. If you take the Bangladesh example I gave you earlier, how would you say, in that situation, what the European Community have achieved as opposed to what the Canadians have achieved, within this basket funding? Clearly, you cannot. You have got to take a view of what is the total effect of this operation and then probably you can ask the question "Did the European Commission play a positive role within that consortium?" We have to go on evaluating what each donor has done, but also we have to look at the total effectiveness of aid, particularly when it becomes more joined up in support of poverty reduction strategies, and the like. To that extent, we are in a slightly new world. It does not minimise the importance of how institutionally effective is the Commission, and that remains a very crucial question. You have a structure which is quite complex, with RELEX and DG DEV and EuropeAid, and it is going to be interesting to see how that plays in the post-Constitution world and what the new Commission will look like, and there are a lot of important issues around that. I must admit to being unable to place the European Commission as better or worse than some other donor. I think every donor has its own specificities. What you can look at, of course, are the hard-edged questions of how much money does it provide, on which it has now become a very important donor. I think a crucial issue for this Committee is that this is not a marginal player in international development, the European Commission alone is providing more than a tenth of international development assistance

Lord Morris of Aberavon *contd.*]

at the moment, or round about that figure, so it is significant. Where is it going, what can we learn from evaluations, and all the rest of it? As you pursue your inquiry, I think probably you would want to get feedback from the Commission's own evaluation services and their own results-based operations, to say, "What can we say, with the independent advice that's available?" On deconcentration, as I say, my experience, which I confess is limited, does suggest to me that where it has happened, and it has happened now in most of the world, it has led to quite hard-edged and monitorable improvements in the speed of taking certain kinds of decisions. I think that has led, as I say, to the Commission being a more effective player in the local donor club. The Commission has been widely reviled, as I am sure you know, for being about the slowest donor to deliver anything, and enough people have told me that from a developing country perspective for me to believe it. I do think that the present Commission management has worked quite hard on that and I do think deconcentration is beginning to help.

135. What does it mean, in practice?
A. What it means, in practice, is that it takes an awfully long time for decisions to be taken, and that, particularly with developing countries, you can be waiting for the Commission to come to the table, and that has to do with the amount of things that have to be cleared in Brussels and the way in which clearance in Brussels takes place. I am not sure how far this has progressed, but I would be very keen to see the management committees, on which the European Member States sit and which look at these decisions, become much less transaction conscious and, instead of looking at individual operations all the time, look much more at strategy and let the Commission get on with delivering the one agreed strategy. I think there is still work to do to try to make that happen.

136. Going back to my original point, it seems that it is very difficult to grapple with a problem globally as to which is better in whatever circumstances. Having accepted all the caveats you have entered, is there not in some countries a view that can be taken, maybe the smaller countries, and Bangladesh may be a bad example because of the sheer size of it, are there some countries where one is manifestly more effective than the other, bilateral, as opposed to European, or an individual donor?
A. I am sure that one can find examples. The peer review looked at two programmes specifically. They looked at the Bangladesh programme, as it happened, before the operation I am talking about, and they looked at the programme in Burkina Faso, and they observed quite a number of differences between the two. I can certainly leave for the Clerks—they are in the public domain anyway—the conclusions of these two reviews. The main findings of the Burkina one were that the EC was an important and influential donor by virtue of its large volume of aid and its close association with other EU Member States. That deconcentration was widely applauded. "It will be a special challenge," it says, "to EC leadership to implement this ambitious reform efficiently in the short timeframe allotted." Deconcentration had not quite happened when this took place, so it is pre rather than post. Aid

modalities: the programme "is being restructured around a simpler and more focused, sector programme approach," with a strong emphasis on budget support. On Procedures: "The most commonly cited issue for EC aid was the heaviness of its procedures. Deconcentration will help move the locus of procedural decision-making to the field, but not simplify the procedures themselves." Which is an interesting point. "Although some consolidation and simplification of procedure has been carried out, it is still not clear if reform has been taken far enough . . ." Country ownership: it gave a reasonably positive mark. Sustainability: it had questions about how sustainable anybody's activities were in Burkina. Results orientation: "The Delegation is applauded by its partners for the work it is promoting in the use of conditionality and results indicators to promote a poverty-based contractual relationship between donors and recipients. This is viewed by many as a model for use elsewhere." On Bangladesh, it concluded that they thought well of the new Country Strategy for 2002-06. They thought they had worked quite hard on complementarity with the Members States, but it still was not entirely clear what that meant, in practice. That there was a useful focus on trade and political dimensions along with development co-operation. "As was true in Burkina Faso, partner perceptions are widespread concerning the slowness and perplexity of EC implementation procedures. Many felt that EC efforts on the ground were too "control" and process oriented, and created the impression of seeking 'formality over development reality'" which is a nice phrase, I think. They were strongly in favour of more deconcentration. They thought: "The small, professional staff within the Delegation is perceived by partners as professional and hard working. They are also seen as overworked and understandably unable to provide sufficient time to partner co-ordination . . ." The EC was graphically described by one donor as a "timid giant" with large resources, but little visibility. Given appropriate staff, "the EC has the potential" say the Examiners "to play a more important role among donors, especially with the EU Member States and with the multilateral institutions. Enhanced Delegation staff capacity was also applauded as an immediate and visible response to current procedural problems . . ." "Additional use of experienced, Bangladeshi professionals . . . is another cost-effective capacity building opportunity that should be fully explored . . ." Measuring success: they say that "Current attempts by Brussels to carry out project monitoring . . . would seem more effective and less costly if left to the Delegation . . ." They worry about the overall feedback system, and they welcome the channelling of funds through NGOs, which is a significant part of this, but note that donors are considering in Bangladesh what is the proper role of NGOs compared with the Government. Those are some of the highlights from the two field visits that were undertaken.

Lord Inge

137. Mr Manning, one of the impressions I have got, and not just from hearing you speak but others, is that the balance between what I call the

Lord Inge *contd.*]

bureaucracy of giving aid and getting the aid on the ground is a major issue, and you have touched on that yourself. I have got the impression from your earlier remarks, and you have considerable experience of this both in DfID and now in OECD, that you thought some of the Commission's internal reforms, analysing more effectively how that aid is being developed, had improved. However, I have been left with the clear impression, hearing a number of people giving evidence, we still have not got right the balance between what I call the bureaucracy and actually delivering it on the ground. If you were starting with a blank sheet of paper, so that the people on the ground got this aid, and I would have to admit that I am a prisoner of my experience in Bosnia to an extent, and Rwanda, where would you want to put priorities for action, the co-ordination of NGOs, and all those sorts of things, but where would you put priority so the bureaucracy does not destroy what I think is a fundamentally important part of CFSP?

A. I think it is very important to look at two things. First of all, what does your rule book say, and, secondly, how do you apply it? To their credit, the Commission inherited a completely mad system, where each regulation—regulation for Asia and Latin America, regulation in the Mediterranean, and so on—had a different procedure, and it is unbelievable that we had that situation, they have spent a lot of the last four years trying to get a single procedure agreed, which largely I think they have done. What I do not know is whether that procedure itself may be unnecessarily complex for what it is seeking to deliver, and I have some suspicion that may well be the case. I think it comes back to what I was saying earlier about the difficulty that a number of multilaterals have, and I think the Commission has had. After all, there is a lot of worry about misappropriation of funds, and the rest of it. That tends to move you into too much of a control psyche here, rather than a situation which gives people real responsibility which then holds them accountable for their mistakes, and, if I were running it, that would be the main transition I would seek to do. I would be inhibited, because most likely this is controlled by the overall Financial Regulation of the whole Commission, and the development co-operation people have to operate within that framework. Of course, to some extent, Member States send conflicting signals here, Member States send signals they do not want anything very minutely controlled, and also they send signals, as you and I will do, that we want to deliver something. To my mind, there has to be understanding that if you want to get good results then you have to trust people, and that means you have to trust people to make some mistakes. What I would be looking for was to move as far as I could within the scope of the Financial Regulation to give real responsibility to people in the field. I would want to look very carefully at a strong internal audit system so that they could be checked up on on a regular basis, because you need to have the check as well as giving people responsibility. Also I would look very seriously at professional competences within the Commission. The Commission has a lot of very dedicated, what I would call, development generalists. I think the Commission is somewhat

weak, compared with a number of Member States, and certainly compared with the United Kingdom, in having developed a cadre of people who are professional in this, particularly in areas like economics and governance, which are two key areas. The Commission to my mind has been weak in not having enough staff who are professionally-qualified economists, are professional in areas of governance. I think these two are crucial areas for the Commission in what it provides in those two areas. What I do not see in the Commission, which I think is a strength of DfID, is an organisation on the professional side that reports ultimately up to a senior figure in these disciplines. For example, the World Bank has always had a top-rate, international chief economist. The Commission has never had an international figure leading the economic side of what they do. I do not know why but they never have. I think I would be looking at a limited number of moves in the direction of professionalising, and I would combine that with the maximum decentralisation of authority and the maximum simplification of the rule book. A particular lesson we have learned in the DAC is, and this applies not just to the Commission: it applies to the World Bank, it applies to DfID, it applies to everybody, everybody needs procedures, let us make those procedures harmonisable, in other words, procedures that we can put together and make sense of, from the point of view of Bosnia, or Rwanda, or whoever we are dealing with. So that we do not have multiple audit requirements, multiple monitoring requirements, multiple evaluation requirements, we can trust each other and say that if the feasibility study has been done by the Germans we will trust them to have done a decent job rather than have to do it all again ourselves. The Commission needs the same approach.

Lord Harrison

138. Could I follow up that interesting point you made about the lack of a chief economist, as it were, within the umbrella of the EU. Where it exists in the World Bank, can you demonstrate how that has influenced the approach the World Bank has, and therefore if we had a chief economist within the EU how that might change the nature or flow of approach?

A. There is a good question. Probably you have followed the high-profile comings and goings of the World Bank Chief Economists, the latest of whom has just moved to the United Kingdom Treasury. Particularly when Mr Stiglitz was the Chief Economist, there was quite a lot of high-profile discussion as to whether Mr Stiglitz' view of the world was to be preferred to that of the IMF or not. Chief economists bring with them a certain amount of at least ability to debate important development issues, whether you think that Mr Stiglitz was right or wrong, and at least he raised a number of important cross-cutting issues. I think the Commission would be strengthened if it had someone of that kind of stature who was able to look at some of these issues—it is a large amount of expenditure, we are talking $5 billion or $6 billion

Lord Harrison *contd.*]

here—about "How can we make this expenditure as effective as possible?" I think you need somebody who can stand back a bit and tap into the international research, and there is a lot of international research going on in these areas, and bring that to the troops. I think that would be the value of appointments of that sort.

Lord Harrison: That is very interesting. Thank you.

Lord Bowness

139. Mr Manning, could I turn to the ACP group of countries and ask whether you think that the European Union should continue to favour that group, rather than other, maybe poorer countries that are outside that grouping? If you think that preference should stop, has your Committee got any agreement as to what sorts of indicators should be deployed by donors to determine a country's needs, of their people?

A. As you know, there is a lot of history underlying all this, and, in a way, it goes back to the accession negotiations conducted by the British in the early 1970s. The situation that I inherited when I arrived in Brussels in 1973 was that there was a famous protocol, Protocol 22, which defined how the enlarged Community would deal with developing countries. A crucial part of the negotiations had been that basically the French had taken the view that the African commonwealth countries, and the Pacific and Caribbean commonwealth countries were broadly similar in character to the countries who were already associate members of the European Community, like the former French and Dutch territories, but that the Asian commonwealth countries were too big and different in character: India could not be equated with Senegal or Malawi. So an important distinction was made in the negotiations, which created the environment within which the ACP group came together. It did not mandate the ACP group, the ACP group was there because the African, Caribbean and Pacific countries chose to negotiate as a group. That was their choice and they negotiated very effectively, I think, because they had made that choice. Indeed, it became an objective of the renegotiation of the Treaty, which was embarked on by the Labour Government in 1974, to get the Community for the first time to provide assistance to Asian countries, and I well remember the French telling me at the time, "This will never happen." It was an interesting example of the United Kingdom taking a *communautaire* position, that the Community must have some kind of relations with Asia and eventually building a consensus, including ultimately the French, that we should do that. That formed the basis of assistance to the non-associated developing countries, which is still manifest in the ALA regulation, and so on. It did mean that there was different treatment, both in terms of the overall institutional arrangements, which are much more complex for Cotonou and much more non-contractual for the other countries, and of course on the scale of assistance that was provided. Now how does this look today? The ACP group, of course, is very diverse, you have within it

countries like the Bahamas, at one extreme, and very poor countries that have made very little progress, at the other extreme. The large bulk of the ACP remain extremely poor and extremely aid-worthy, and are among the countries with the furthest to go towards the millennium development goals. Certainly that would be true of Africa. Having just come back from the Pacific, one has to bear in mind the vulnerability of these relatively small places in both the Pacific and the Caribbean to shocks of all sorts, whether they are climatic, conflict, commodity prices, and the rest of it. I think it is quite important that the Community remains conscious of the risks run by these very small countries, particularly in the Caribbean and Pacific, how do you organise yourself to deal with that. In terms of your second question, about how far the DAC has any wisdom to offer on how to relate to countries, if you look at the list that the DAC and the World Bank provide of developing countries, we tend to use *per capita* income as a convenient way of analysing countries into groups. Our distinctions tend to be more between the least-developed countries, as recognised by the UN, other low-income countries, lower middle-income countries, higher middle-income countries and high-income countries, and to some extent therefore we would look at what their aid requirements might be with that in mind. I think it is important to draw distinctions also of character between countries. India is a low-income country but India has very different capabilities from a place like Nepal, or Laos, let us say, which are also low-income countries. It is for that reason that I think this least-developed category, that the UN has, probably is a useful category, even though there are some concerns at the margin that it is to your advantage to be a least-developed country because you get access to certain things, and hence one or two countries have sought to redefine themselves as least-developed at the margin. I think it is a useful category in reminding us that there is a group of countries which are both poor but also vulnerable, in terms of institutions, lack of human development, lack of industrialisation, and so on, and are rather different in character from India and Pakistan, which have somewhat different characteristics.

Lord Harrison

140. Mr Manning, I am looking at the questions concerned with comparison with other major international donors, which you have touched upon already, but perhaps you have not said a lot about how well we co-ordinate with them. Secondly, whether there are opportunities to learn from them, in the way that they give aid. Thirdly, you said very interestingly that the European Union, the European Community, is unique as a donor, because it has other policies which may or may not be integrated, and you implied also that this was a complication as well. Could you say just a bit more about that unique position, the 'timid giant' as you described it at one point? Are there real advantages from being unique, or real problems from being unique?

A. In a way, I think all your questions come round to a question which is not addressed as such in the

Lord Harrison *contd.*]

DAC report, at least not in the summary, how far should the Commission be, in a Community of 25, a 26th donor, and how far should it be rather different? This is a long-standing debate within Europe about this issue, and the Commission has sought over the years, I think, to try to mark out some space for itself. We have these things, three Cs, of coherence, complementarity and co-ordination. In some ways it has succeeded, in some ways it has not, is my feeling. Where it has succeeded, I think in a way you could look quite positively at experience, for example, in the Balkans, where the Union has decided that, in practice, the Community will be the major deliverer of European aid to the Balkans. The European Commission, as far as I can see, has set up a rather effective operation called CARDS, which delivers that and on which the feedback certainly I had in DfID was pretty positive. There is an area where the European Union has willed the means and the ends, and the Commission has been allowed to get on with it in an important, high-profile area, where it is clear the Commission is a much larger player than any of the Member States. Another area which is positive, I think, personally, though people have different views on this, is that the Commission has set out six areas on which it proposes to concentrate. It includes, for example, road-building, so if you go to Africa you will see that the Commission is regarded usually as a key donor in the transport sector. Some people say this is wrong because the Community should be doing more on health and education, the social sectors. I tend to say, "Well, why shouldn't it specialise? Somebody needs to deal with transport." The most important thing is, is it dealing with transport effectively, and are these good projects and are they within a sensible sector strategy, and the rest of it? I am not convinced that every donor needs to be doing the same thing, and indeed there is a certain amount of herd behaviour among donors, which I would deprecate. I am quite positive about the Commission staking out a few areas where they say, "Well, we're going to invest heavily in this area, and you guys do something different." The other point is about what is the implication in the field of the fact that it is the Commission who are responsible for international trade and agricultural policies, and what implications that has for the aid programme that they seek to run in countries. For example, if you look at trade capacity-building, should this be a really important area for Community aid because it matches what they are doing under the GSP or the ACP arrangements? If we look at trade facilitation, one of the four Singapore issues in the Doha round, would not this be an area where the Commission could invest very heavily in everything from improving port management to a very important area, helping developing countries meet European standards for food safety, and the like? There are areas that go with being an important trading partner which to my mind are obvious areas of Commission aid specialisation. The Commission is doing a lot already in these directions, but maybe it could become still more an area of focus for the Commission and still less an area of focus for Member States, so we could develop complementarity in that way.

141. A question about, albeit it is a different beast from other major donors, are there things that we could pick up and use and run with?
A. I think the Commission experience is interesting. Clearly, one can always learn from anybody, and the fact that the Commission has managed to make a multinational operation of this kind work, even with the concerns that you and others have expressed about whether it has worked that effectively, is something which is relevant. Where the Commission has been quite cutting-edge I think we should learn from them. For example, the Commission has been very strong in support of poverty reduction and strategy approaches, it has been very strong in willingness to look at how to support countries in a flexible way, including through their budgets, and so on. So there are one or two things that people could learn from the Commission, but I think this is all part of mutual learning within the whole development community. I am not sure that I would pick out particular lessons that we should learn from Europe, as opposed to from anybody else, I think we should look at what is good practice around the whole development community. I suppose there is one area that I would single out where Europe collectively has a huge amount to offer, probably it is in the transition in Eastern and Central Europe, where the success of the transition, and, I think, looking back on the last 13 years or so, one could say that it has been, long term, pretty successful. This owes a huge amount to the fact that all these countries had a very big incentive to get into the European Union, and I think this has had a massive impact in Eastern and Central Europe in just shaping up all the government systems to meet European standards, of one sort or another, and I think that has been a very powerful driving force. I have seen from what Commissioner Verheugen has published recently that many countries still have a long way to go, and that is no surprise, but I suspect if you compare where any of the candidate countries are now with where they were six or seven years ago there will be a huge amount of progress to offer. The question is how transferable is this experience to a situation for countries which are not going to be joining Europe? It is highly transferable to Romania and Bulgaria, it is less obvious it is immediately transferable to Malawi or Burkina, because they do not have the same incentive, if you like, that the candidate countries have, but it has exposed Europe to a lot of knowledge and wisdom about how to run a more effective state. Given that a lot of the problems in developing countries are how to run effective states, one would like to see how far that experience could be transferred. Finally, if I can just put in a plug for my own organisation, clearly the OECD has an important role here as a source of knowledge as to how to do things well within states, and there is increasing interest, I think, within the OECD of how we transfer that experience in a more sustainable way outside the immediate OECD area.

142. Does the EU listen to you? How good are the relations between OECD and the Commission?
A. I think that, eventually, the peer review process has had some results. The mere fact that now we have an annual report from the Commission is a direct

Lord Harrison *contd.*]

result of two or three aid reviews in the nineties, saying "It's unacceptable you don't have one." The peer review process, from one point of view, is a very feeble beast, we cannot tell anybody to do anything, we can encourage them to do things. What I find, as I go around, this was brought home to me in New Zealand the other day, is that when the DAC reaches a conclusion that a country has some more to do in a particular area this can then help people who want to reform in any case within that country to make use of this within their own systems. That has been quite powerful. On Monday I will be conducting the four-yearly review of Ireland, which I think is a country which has learned an awful lot from being a DAC member. It has been very smart in putting into effect ideas that it has had from the peer review process, and has some very good practice from which the rest of us can learn, particularly, I think, in the area of technical assistance. I believe that the Commission is increasingly open to this kind of review and making a reality of it, but it is only going to happen to the extent that Member States also pay some attention to these reviews and say "Well, that's something we really ought to try to move on, collectively." The peer review process, I think, does have some merits over time, but it is not a quick fix for anything and needs to be seen as part of a process of continual reform, which all donors can learn from.

Lord Watson of Richmond

143. Mr Manning, first, I was pleased that you said what you did about Eastern Europe. Somebody described to me, the other day, rather surprisingly, in a surprising turn of phrase, that the *Acquis Communautaire* had emerged as a road-map for development in Eastern Europe, which I thought was an interesting idea. While you are quite right to question the relevance of that experience, for instance, to development in Africa, one can see that being relevant to the development problems faced in areas like the Ukraine and Belarus and the border states, so that is an interesting thing. Also you raised this question of whether the Commission should be seen as, so to speak, the 26th donor. That is very important in terms of public opinion because, as the overall figures get bigger, and you are talking about $70 billion, and so on, it is going to be ever more urgent to answer the question to the public clearly, "Well, what is Europe doing in development?" Part of that answer is, is the Commission's contribution distinctive, or how do we put everything into the pot together? I do not know. For example, of the $70 billion, what would you say the Europe of 26 would be likely to contribute? I am saying 26, in other words, 25 plus the Commission?

A. I am sorry, I can send you figures on this. I sent these figures most recently to the World Bank annual meetings in Dubai in September. We do publish what is the present situation and, I think I am right in saying, the European Union accounts for roughly half of development assistance at the moment, but also we have published a forecast of what we think will be the situation in 2006 if people deliver on their Monterrey commitments. What you will note from that is that the largest increments are going to come

from quite a limited number of countries, the most important would be the United States, assuming they deliver on the Millennium Challenge Account and the announcements they have made about HIV/ AIDS, and so on. The other big ones are, and I may have the order not quite right, basically, the United Kingdom and France, Germany and Italy. You will not get huge amounts of incremental aid out of the Scandinavians and the Dutch because they are already at 0.7, so that will just grow with the growth of their economies. The Japanese, the Australians, New Zealanders, have no announced mid-term plans, as the Europeans have, to increase their aid, so it remains to be seen what they will deliver, but Europe is very central to this, and I think Europe's share will be at least as big in 2006 as it is at the moment. The money the Europeans put in is very important, and hence I agree with you entirely that what we can say about the effectiveness of the total European effort is extremely important.

144. If I may, because in communication terms it is such an important thing. If, by 2006, let us say, the total European contribution had moved above 50 per cent, now just in terms of a statement that more than 50 per cent of the world's development budget is coming from the European Union is going to be a big statement to make. In that context, I wonder whether you feel, from the perspective of DAC, that it is possible to put together a coherent, overall picture for Europe, Member States plus Commission? Are you getting enough information, both from the Member States and the Commission? At the end of the day, I come back to the simple question, people will say "These are huge sums of money. What is Europe actually doing? Is it working, is it effective?" We are up against public opinion. You may have noticed, we have had a very strange debate in the United Kingdom over recent weeks about the IQ of Africans, in effect. The subtext of this debate, which was made explicit once or twice but which is certainly implicit, was that maybe you are just pouring money into a hole, because actually, for all sorts of reasons, there is not the wherewithal to make anything of the aid. That seems to me a pernicious argument, and also it is a self-defeating argument. Therefore, I am very concerned about the ability, in an informed and accurate way, to say, "Right, Europe is putting in half," or more than half, "and this is actually what it's achieving," and that we can get a handle on it?

A. I am sure you are quite right. Yes, we get consistent information from European Union members. There will be a bit more of a challenge in relation to new Member States, some of whom have provided aid in the past, like Poland and the Czech Republic, and are going to do so increasingly in future, so one of the jobs in the DAC is how we relate to those who are not yet members of the DAC but are becoming donor countries. I think the tricky question, and this is one that I have debated with myself a bit over the years, is how far you put a hard edge round European aid in the total scheme of things. What I have found operates, when I was operating on behalf of the United Kingdom, was that when actually you come down to operating in a country you find constellations of donors interested in particular sectors, and the rest of it, and it does not

Lord Watson of Richmond *contd.*]

usually match the map too tightly of the European Union. You find yourself discussing with the Canadians, with the World Bank, with the UN, and if you put a kind of hard edge round the European effort I think you can miss the point, if you are not careful.

145. Is the better approach, therefore, not to look at the totality of funding but, going back to an earlier point you were making, looking at areas of distinctive expertise, so you talk about the Commission and roads, or whatever? If one is answering this overall question about Europe's contribution, that one would answer that as much in terms of distinctive skills, and distinctive transfer of skills perhaps, as one would in terms of totalities of funding?

A. The model I am thinking of increasingly is this, that you have to start at the top level with this, with the totality. What is everybody's, not just Europe's, aid achievement in Tanzania over the last ten years, what can we say about the totality of the aid effort in a few heavily-aided countries? We need some smart evaluation work to tease out this black box between the money we have spent and the inputs we have provided and the outcomes which poor people have received, and that black box, which includes a lot of things, all the delivery agents, the Tanzanian Government, the NGOs, the contractors, and so on, I think needs unpicking quite carefully. I suspect that needs to be done in a few countries at the level of total aid. Then I think you can look within that at what any donor, or group of donors, has contributed within that approach, and you may find the European Union a useful construct or you may not find it a useful construct, depending on the country, so I would be rather opportunistic about that. Then, within that, again there is the important question about what has the Commission done, what does the European Community as opposed to European aid provide, and there I do think that a certain amount of distinctiveness is desirable. As I have tried to illustrate this morning, I think the European Commission does see itself as a constructive player with its counterparts. It does need to work on both its procedures and its professionalism to help it do that. There is a question probably about the actual level of staffing in relation to what it is trying to do in certain countries. Certainly there is a need to invest in the kind of evaluations and systems that will give good feedback to the public on this. I am sure we all have to work, not least in the United Kingdom, on the combination of development, which can be maligned in the way you have just been describing, and Europe, which can be maligned in a number of ways. If you put those two things together, we do have to work quite hard on this.

Lord Watson of Richmond: It is a rather bad combination, yes.

Chairman

146. Mr Manning, perhaps you could tell us how good you think the Commission and the Court of Auditors are at monitoring and evaluating the programmes and the operations, and do you think they could be improved, and, if so, how? How independent are they, and how robust and objective are they?

A. It is a very important question, to which I feel myself a little bit ill equipped to give you a really definitive answer. Let us start with the European Court of Auditors. I have not dealt directly with the European Court of Auditors, though I have read a number of their reports over the years. It is very clear that they are a body which is well able to get to the bottom of important issues, and indeed the sacking of the last Commission owed a lot to their efforts, so they are certainly not to be underestimated as a body which is able to do a sound job of following where the money has gone and what has been well or poorly done. I think that, in general, there is certainly discussion within the audit community, and I am not quite sure where the Court of Auditors comes out on this, between what I could describe as a 'counting the pennies' mentality, in other words, how was the money actually spent, and looking more at the effectiveness of what is done. I think the British National Audit Office has been quite good at maintaining that kind of balance, and particularly holding Government to account on the effectiveness side of this. I may be wrong but I have a slight sense the Court of Auditors is probably stronger on the 'How was the money spent?' side of audit, and possibly could invest a little bit more in "How effective was the total spending?" side, but that is not a judgment in which I have a great deal of confidence, but it is worth thinking about. Secondly, on evaluation, I think it is constructive that under the new structures in Brussels we have a single evaluation service. It is located, perhaps slightly oddly, in EuropeAid, which is the delivery agent, though it does report to the Board of EuropeAid, which does mean that it reports to four Commissioners, which I think is good. DAC wisdom on evaluation is that evaluation units should be fully independent line management. Certainly the most effective ones—one thinks of the World Bank's Operations Evaluation Department— have made a virtue of reporting outside the line management structure, in the World Bank case to the Board, and always being managed by somebody who is never going to work for the organisation again, which I think is a sound policy. I believe there is a case probably for further upgrading the European Commission evaluation effort, for ensuring that it has that kind of strong, professional management by somebody who owes nothing to the Commission and that its reports continue to be made public, which I believe is the case already, and given high profile, and that it is seen to be reporting to the top political level in Brussels. Also I think it is very important to invest in the feedback loop from evaluation into delivery. In DfID and its predecessors, I have seen evaluators get into the trap that they are always evaluating what was done, decisions taken, several years ago, and when they produce their reports the present generation say, "Ah, well, we don't do it like that any more." Therefore, you need a certain amount of kind of real-time evaluation, where people cannot escape, because it is coming back at you too quickly, but also you need some very soundly-based, quite strategic evaluation, which really does provide lessons for the future. Getting the right evaluation programme, investing enough in the professionalism of it, I think is a very

Chairman *contd.*]

important, strategic objective for the Commission, whatever the structure.

Lord Inge

147. This may be a totally unfair question. Could I ask, even though there was disagreement within Europe and France and this country, etc., about Iraq, how much consultation there was about what would be needed in terms of help with Iraq after the military campaign?

A. The only answer I can give you, from my own perspective, is that one of my first activities since becoming Chair in June was to chair a meeting in July of the DAC, at which we had present all the donor countries. We had representatives of the CPA, we had some Iraqi Government people, we had Ambassador Belka, who was running the liaison with donors at the time, and we had some very useful outside consultants, who gave us advice about the future of the oil industry, and things of that kind, and we published our findings. Also we tried to draw lessons from experiences elsewhere, for example, in trust funds, and needs assessment, and so on. I hope we were able to play a constructive role in providing what we described as an offline discussion space for people to talk about "What can we do professionally as a decent job in Iraq, whatever the political circumstances that we're in?" To that extent, I feel that at least we provided some opportunity within the DAC, as we had done a couple of years earlier in Afghanistan, where again we tried to do a 'lessons learned' exercise. So far as I know, I was not at the Madrid conference myself but the DAC was represented there, the needs assessment conducted by the UN, World Bank, IMF, and so on, was a professionally-conducted operation, and I think that process and the budget-setting process in Iraq were brought together, in the end, in a reasonably constructive way. To that extent, I think the bits of the international aid system have done a reasonable job in the rather special circumstances of Iraq.

148. When you go and you deal with the particular project, or aid goes in, do you go back, say, X years later, to see how you have done?

A. Donors vary a little bit in how they do this, but in most donors, and I think this is true of the Commission, there is a double loop. One is performance reporting by the people who did the project, which is usually produced at the end of the project. It has the virtue of being, hopefully, done in time, but it has the downside of being produced by people who have an interest in what they are producing. Then you backstop this with an evaluation capacity, which does not look at every project, it is too heavy to do that, but does look at a sample of projects and enables you to cross-check whether the kinds of things that your completion reporting is telling you are, in fact, realistic. It is very interesting, I think, to go back several years later and see what the long-term results of this are. I think that is an important check on all of this. The difficulty is the one I have given already, that there is then a tendency to say "Well, this is all years ago and we're doing it differently now."

Lord Williamson of Horton: Can I just confirm that the Commission does publish the evaluations it does even though they are unfavourable. I would like just to make that point, because there is a slight tendency, when the Commission publishes an evaluation which is not very favourable, to say they made a great hash of it. The other side of it is they have drawn conclusions from it. We do not get everything right. In Britain we do not always get everything right, do we, my Lord Chairman, not always?

Chairman: Not always. Mr Manning, thank you very much indeed for coming. You have helped us an awful lot. You have very wide experience and it is extremely good of you to share it with us. Thank you.

MONDAY 2 FEBRUARY 2004

Present	Bowness, L (Chairman)	Northover, B
	Lea of Crondall, L	Powell of Bayswater, L
	Maclennan of Rogart, L	Tomlinson, L

Examination of Witness

MR DIETER FRISCH, Transparency International, former Director General for Development, examined.

Q149 *Chairman:* May I welcome Mr Frisch to this meeting of the evidence session. I am sure you have seen that we are, as the EU Foreign Affairs, Defence and Development Policy Sub-Committee of the EU Select Committee of the House of Lords, carrying out an inquiry into European Union development aid and assistance. We are looking for evidence on a number of issues: evaluating the reform of the EU development assistance, which I think that you do not want particularly to speak to us about but, looking ahead to development and foreign policy, thoughts on the Constitutional Treaty, the provisions there and where development aid will be if that is enacted; the effects of enlargement; the future of the ACP grouping; and the European Development Fund and possible budgetisation. We are very grateful indeed that you have come to give evidence to us this afternoon. We have all seen the paper which you kindly let our clerk have, covering the areas that you would like to talk to us about. Perhaps, in the first place, I could ask you if you would like to say something in opening to us, before members of the Committee question you on those areas.

Mr Frisch: Thank you, My Lord Chairman. I think that it is the second time in my life that I am before a Select Committee of the British Parliament. You know that I am no longer in active service but I am still close—living in Brussels and having a lot of contacts—to development policy, which I was dealing with for many years. I have spent almost my whole professional life in the European Commission, in different services, but mainly, for 24 years, on different aspects of development co-operation—which is really the field with which I am familiar and, by the way, where my heart is. During the last 11 years of my service I was Director General of DG Development, which at that time was a large department. In the meantime, things have changed a lot in the Commission in terms of structures. I would like to talk to you as a former Director General. I am also a special adviser to the European Commission. However, my freedom of speech is greater if I just speak as a former Director General. I am a loyal former civil servant, but I prefer to make that qualification. Secondly, I am not here mainly to speak about Transparency International, as I saw in the programme. That is my civil society hat. Since

leaving the Commission a little over 10 years ago, I have been one of the founders of that NGO, which deals with corruption—in particular, trans-border corruption. However, it is not specifically the subject of your inquiry, unless you find, by means of the bridge of good governance, the way through to the fight against corruption—things which are very close to each other. I think that you could consider me still as a kind of insider in the Commission. When I talk to people or lecture, as I do, I normally speak as a practitioner. I have not become an academic; that is not in my make-up. If I have said, and you have picked up, that I would not like to focus too much on the recent reforms in the Commission, it is just for reasons of tact. When one has left 10 years ago, it is very delicate to make a judgment about the reforms which have come about. Either it is not fair to the successors, or they might feel that they have not been very fair to their predecessors. However, if you want to talk about the structures of the Commission, I have precise opinions which I am happy to give. On the other hand, I would rather be questioned on the wider range of things which are on your list, preferably in the second and third part of it than the first. I am open, however. If something really bothers me, I will say so, but I normally speak frankly.

Q150 *Chairman:* Perhaps we may start with the suggestion you have made. You have said that you would like to comment about the Commission's organisational structure. Certainly that is something which is discussed. Can I invite you to comment on that in the context of development aid?

Mr Frisch: Yes, I am ready to say a few words on that. First of all, you will find in the Commission's structures—I do not know how familiar you are with this—a new, large department which they call AidCo—EuropeAid Co-operation Office—which is the implementation department for all external aid. This new structure makes a lot of sense because before, in my time in the Commission, there were too many separate lines of action in the different geographic areas. It was high time that, mainly in the field of procedures, contracting, tendering, and also in the substantive approach, there should be something more coherent. AidCo was certainly a good invention. It was a welcome development from my point of view. The three problems which I still see are as follows. First of all, I would consider that there is an unhealthy geographic split between two parts of the developing world. You have the DG Development. There you have a geographic responsibility for the Lomé-Cotonou countries and South Africa; then you have, strangely, in the Relex DG, the foreign relations department, the similar geographic responsibility for Mediterranean, Latin American, Asian, and indeed some Eastern countries which are not accession countries. In DG Development, upstream of the geographic services, you have a policy directorate; but this policy directorate, which should logically have an influence on the policy in all geographic areas, *de facto* has its influence almost exclusively on the Lomé-Cotonou countries, because the colleagues in DG Relex would find that, "These are people who deal with Africa and the policy they make is for them, not for us". In my view, therefore, there is a lack of a consistent policy framework because of this geographic split. The reason why they are split is explained by history. It is because, in 1985 when Delors formed his first Commission, he had foreseen, as before, two Commissioners—one for foreign relations and one for development co-operation. At the last moment, the second French Commissioner who came in was Claude Cheysson. He had, years before, been our Commissioner; then he was Foreign Minister and then, unexpectedly, he came back. He came back as a Commissioner and insisted, contrary to what Delors had asked of him—he had wanted him to deal with industrial policy or something in relation to the Internal Market—on having something in relation to external competencies. They therefore created a third portfolio. From that time, the split emerged and is now consolidated, so that you have two geographic areas, which normally would belong together with one common upstream development policy department. The second point I would mention is the cut-off point between those who, in their regional framework, do the programming exercise. The allocation of the funds and the programming, country by country, is with DG Development for the ACP countries and with the DG Relex for the other areas. They are responsible for the establishment of the multi-annual indicative programme for each country. That is the cut-off point. Then they hand over to AidCo, but AidCo has the responsibility of identification of the projects and programmes they finance. In practice, that creates problems. Normally, somebody who carries out ambitious programming knows at the end of this exercise what he wants to be done in terms of projects and programmes. If you say that he must stop there and that somebody else should take over and be responsible for the identification then, unless the personal relations are very good, this creates a structural problem. It would be better to be responsible for the programming up to the financing decision. Then you know what you have to do, and then you can hand over for implementation. My third point—which will probably be linked to the discussion you will have about the relationship between foreign policy and development policy—is the closeness of the development policy elements which are in DG Relex to the foreign policy aspects of DG Relex. I personally consider that—for the future structures—you should have a foreign relations directorate general that is comparable to a foreign affairs ministry, and it should not be burdened with financial matters. These should be grouped together in a separate structure. It would be different if they were grouped together. These are the structural remarks I would have on the present Commission's organisation.

Lord Tomlinson: I sometimes find myself confused about the objectives of development aid in the European Union. Wearing your hat at Transparency International and the link with good governance that you referred to, how far do you think some of the programmes that are financed from European Union development aid, and I will give you just three—aid to the Palestinian Authority, where about 52 per cent of the flanking measures in the peace process come from the European Union budget, or the one that you mentioned, the global Mediterranean policy or, more recently, the change in priorities between aid to Latin America and aid to south Asia—represent development policies and how far are they a reflection of a political agenda? And is the political agenda necessarily leading the aid to be efficiently and effectively spent?

Q151 *Lord Powell of Bayswater:* Could I just add to that, because mine is very much a linked question, having heard what Dieter has said? It is pretty obvious to a logical mind that the division should be between a DG Development doing developing countries, and a Relex doing middle-income countries and focusing on foreign policy. What are the actual obstacles? Is it a desire on the part of some Member States to protect at all costs the privileged position of the ACP by keeping them in a sort of separate corral, not polluted by Indians, Bangladeshis and other demands on the aid budget? Or are there other reasons historically why this split has been this way? It is not at all logical to have developing countries strewn across two areas of the Commission. They ought all to be together in one.

Mr Frisch: Beginning with the last remark, I do not see a political objective in that separation. It was an administrative accident in the history of the European Commission. If that third Commissioner had not appeared at a certain moment, no one had seen any reason for splitting. Before 1985, my department was responsible for aid to Asia and Latin

America. Mediterranean countries were always a bit contested. Do they turn towards the North or towards the South? But for some years I was responsible for the Mediterranean countries too. It was a consistent package. In my younger years I was responsible for the policy division. That division was relatively strong and it covered the whole. All the papers on Asia, Latin America, *et cetera*—the first ideas—came out of the same team. Now that the split exists, it will be very difficult to change because everyone has become accustomed to living with it. It is also true that the Commission has very limited power to do foreign policy—because the power is on the side of the Council. It is much more on Solana's side than on the Commission's side. So ask Chris Patten and his colleagues whether they want to abandon the advantage which for them is to have some of the foreign aid in their own department. That brings me to Lord Tomlinson's question. There is, of course, a permanent risk, and the risk is increasing, of turning development assistance into a tool of foreign policy—the Common Foreign and Security Policy. Historically speaking, we did not have that problem. Somewhat contrary to what you say in your document, we were not political because we had no competence for foreign policy until the Maastricht Treaty. Some co-ordination existed before, but in fact only since 1993 did we have a treaty which had as an ambition a common foreign policy. Before that, in our own texts and presentations, we always called it the period of political neutrality—whatever that means. What we did in Menghistu's Ethiopia was not very un-political, but at least we could do it because we had no foreign policy ambitions. Since the Maastricht Treaty and since the world has changed, these political matters at the European level—foreign policy matters—come much more to the fore. They have developed a dynamic which I did not expect. I expected that, given the anteriority of development co-operation and trade policy in the European set-up, it would take a very long time to get on our feet in terms of foreign policy. But that is not true. Retrospectively, in the last 10 years the dynamics are with the foreign policy. I would say that, in terms of motivation, there is an *essoufflement*, some calming down, in the field of development co-operation, and there is a tendency to draw development aid into politics. Last week, the Foreign Affairs Council—there is no longer a Development Ministers' Council because two years ago it was merged with the Foreign Affairs Council—had its annual debate on foreign aid, effectiveness, priorities, et cetera. It is now in the hands of the foreign ministers. From my point of view as a development policy man, it would be better to say clearly that certain things must be done—and I accept that they must be done—for political reasons. That the Palestinian Authority must be supported is a political decision. I do not challenge it, but it is

purely political. That we have to go into Afghanistan, around Afghanistan, to Iraq, are political decisions. Although, coming from me, it may sound strange, I would personally prefer that in the Community budget where you have a special line for a Common Foreign Security Policy—but which has just 50 million or so—a substantive amount be allocated, to make it a line to be used for political, foreign aid operations and, in that way, avoid the field of development aid proper being protected against that. So the reply would be, yes, there are a certain number of operations which are going to certain countries for political reasons, also for economic reasons. If you put a new accent on south-east Asia, it may be for political, but certainly for economic reasons. But who goes to Africa for political or for economic reasons? So you must have a development policy motivation to deal with the really poor countries. It is a mixture, therefore, and I would be in favour of a better separation of these two objectives.[1]

Q152 Lord Maclennan of Rogart: Continuing on some of these themes, Mr Frisch, I wonder if you could exemplify how good governance issues impact upon the distribution of aid in the developing countries, and whether the greater problem is that corruption interrupts the aid programmes, or that it is necessary to use aid as an instrument to draw better government out of democratically backward countries. The final question, which is related, is how do you measure these things and, instrumentally, how do you go about building in an anti-corruption or good governance arm into the work that is done?
Mr Frisch: Thank you for this question. It brings me a little to my activities in the civil society area. I will leave a paper with the secretariat, which I have written on good governance and the fight against corruption. The first thing, if one talks about good governance, is to decide upon a clear definition of it. You have the broad definition, which the UNDP and such organisations use. It is an overarching concept which covers everything, but which is not very operational. You will find an operational definition in the Cotonou Agreement. That is the only text which the European Union has negotiated with Third Countries, where you find the good governance concept clearly and operationally defined. I will not include all of the adjectives set out there, but it is defined as "the transparent and accountable management of all resources"—not "all

---

[1] My plea for a better distinction between foreign policy and development cooperation objectives does of course not mean that I would ask for full autonomy of development cooperation. There must indeed be coherence between the different dimensions of foreign relations: foreign policy proper, security, trade, development cooperation, humanitarian assistance. But coherence does not mean that certain elements (development cooperation or trade) should become tools for others (foreign and security policy). In my understanding coherence has to secure that the different policy elements should complement each other and be mutually reinforcing.

affairs"—"of a country for its economic and social sustainable development". So the focus, if you want an operational concept of good governance, is that you should adopt this one—which is the transparent management of all resources of a country. The other definition is the management of the affairs of a country. I do not know how one tackles this wide concept. If it is concentrated on the management of resources, you are very close to the problem of corruption. Indeed, Article 9 of Cotonou makes the link directly. Having given the definition, it says, "Only serious cases of corruption can be considered as a violation of this principle". That is very interesting, though it is perhaps narrowing it down too much. I gave advice to the Commission on the definition of good governance, but I did not expect them, in the negotiations, to link it directly to corruption. It was to reassure the ACP countries that one would not use this clause for any purpose, and the ACPs were happy to see that only serious cases of corruption could be considered as a violation of that principle. I consider that the fight against corruption is one of the concrete things you can do if you want to prove that you are someone who can claim good governance. It is true that, even if you narrow it down to the sound and transparent management of resources, it is still difficult to say how you measure that. I have listed a few possible approaches in the paper I will give you. Then I put on my Transparency International hat and say that there is certainly one way in which you can check whether governance is good or bad: to see whether there is a real determination by that government to tackle the problem of corruption. There is a checklist where you can ask, "Have they done this or that?"—10 or 12 points where you can check whether there is a serious attempt by this government to counter corruption. If they are seriously tackling corruption, then you can deduce from that that they have a serious concern to manage scarce resources carefully and accountably. That is then very close to good governance, but approaching it from a relatively narrow angle. Colleagues from DG Development tell me that in many of the programmes, they have put good governance as one of the main things to be supported. You cannot put large amounts into good governance. If you look for points of application, however, it is certainly in the area of the fight against corruption, the rules for procurement, and these kinds of things—which are more technical assistance matters rather than investment. I consider that one should give a very high weighting to this aspect in the allocation of resources. The first step, however, is to find a way of measuring good governance. You can use the index which our NGO publishes once a year—the corruption perception index, as we call it—where, to the best of our knowledge, we try to classify countries. This year we listed 133 countries, classified

by giving the "cleanest" 10 points and the worst zero points. This index is frequently used. People put the question, "What is good governance?" Then they come to performance and ask, "What is performance?". Then you jump too easily to the quantitative aspects—although that is another question—and say, "The country which absorbs the most money is the best performer". That leaves me rather unsatisfied.

Q153 *Lord Maclennan of Rogart:* Transparency in the use of resources could exclude entirely other considerations of good governance; for example, single-party states or a denial of human rights, or those sorts of issues. They are not taken into the consideration at all, are they?
Mr Frisch: In the conventions or agreements the European Union has concluded, and is concluding—I recently saw the ones which had just been concluded with Latin America, Central America, and the Andean countries—you will see that you have the good governance concept alongside the human rights, the democratic principles, the rule of law. These are deliberately put alongside each other. As it is defined in the Cotonou Agreement, you do not, under good governance, have to check whether human rights are observed or violated: you have it as an element on its own. In the present text, it even has a higher rank than good governance. In the Cotonou Agreement you have human rights, democratic principles and the rule of law as what the lawyers call "essential elements". In international law, "essential elements" mean that, if there is a violation of such an element, the other party is allowed to take appropriate measures, that is to say, as a last resort to take sanctions. In the Cotonou Agreement, good governance is classified as a "fundamental element". They just wanted to change the language. For a linguist, "fundamental" is not so different from "essential", but it is different for the lawyers. You check these things in parallel. It is relevant when you have to take decisions on aid allocation. Aid allocation, at least since the Cotonou text, is clearly based on criteria of need—that is not new, it is a classical criterion—and performance. Performance is new in the text, as a criterion for aid allocation. The problem is what kind of performance you mean. You can have development performance; you can have political performance—and that could involve looking at democratic principles and at least certain kinds of political and civil human rights—and the economic elements, which are more in the development area. Then you can see the quantitative and the qualitative. There is then the risk which I mentioned earlier—that you switch into the quantitative elements, because they are easier to capture than the qualitative elements.

Q154 *Lord Lea of Crondall:* As an aside, our own Committee is now embracing foreign, security and overseas development under one umbrella. This is a function of the committee structure within the European Union Select Committee of the House of Lords. In the light of the discussion so far, one could say that, whether or not you are in Africa or Asia, there is a growing awareness that, in a crisis, vast sums are spent on the military side, dwarfing what we spend on aid. That is one reason for making the connection. From memory, in the west Balkans, through the countries in the EU, we spend five billion a year on the military and one billion a year on aid. That disparity being lessened of course depends on enough military being there to secure peace for development. That is true in many parts of the world. How would you characterise the new thinking about the relationship with the recipient countries? Are they getting contradictory philosophies coming at them, which give them cause to play one off against the other or cause confusion? Does the EU or a single country come at them with slightly different requirements? I see in your list of points something like Country Strategy Papers. Presumably there can be only one world interface with these countries. You cannot have different people asking them to do different Country Strategy Papers. Would you say that we are talking about integration even wider than the EU in the interface with these countries? Would that help to lessen the arguments about neo-colonialism, interfering in their affairs and in their getting more ownership?

Mr Frisch: You are certainly right that one should avoid what in my days was called conflicting policy advice. As a donor community, you should normally have an approach which is as coherent and consistent as possible. The only one thing about which one must be careful is the argument that we had in my earlier years—that the other side says, "This is a ganging-up of the donors". If you all come with a common, pre-co-ordinated position, then they feel that they are steamrollered. They must play a role in this co-ordination process, therefore. However, it is certainly to be hoped that to start with, within the European Union, one acts as consistently as possible. The Country Strategy Papers are a very good new initiative. It is a part of the reform process. That someone, before we allocate money, has a vision of the situation, and has a strategic view on what should be done in the longer term, is a good thing. What I regret is that these Country Strategy Papers are not the framework for the programming activities of the member countries. It is a paper which is discussed in detail between the Commission and the member countries. Then, once it is established, it is the strategy document for the Commission. I saw the text once and I was a bit shocked. The text is something like, "Member countries in their own policies will be

. . ."—and the word "informed" is used. So it is a very loose reference. There is no obligation, or even a push, for them to take this framework as a common framework. My suggestion would always have been that, as we have programmes at different levels and as there should be no tendency to centralise more at the European level, if we continue to have many programmes—as is the case—at the European level, the member countries' level and, in some countries like Germany, even at the *Länder* level, we should have the ambition to create a common framework, a Country Strategy Paper, discussed with input from all the member countries and the Commission. That should then be accepted as a common framework for everybody. Everybody must not do everything under this framework. On the contrary, if you have a common framework, then you can have a certain division of labour. You cannot have that if you just have loose co-ordination. If you have a common strategy then, for example, if there is something to be done in the field of peacekeeping—and a Country Strategy Paper must comprise such things—then some of our member countries are probably better placed to do that than to ask it of the Commission. It is rather an ideal view, but with a common framework a coherent division of labour could be achieved so that everybody would have a certain role to play. As you have mentioned it, let me add one more point. In this context, there has been a tendency in the European Union—which comes out in Solana's statements and also in Commission statements recently—expressed in the sentence, "Peace is a precondition for development". I accept that. However, if you draw the conclusion from that that you can direct development assistance as much as you want into peacekeeping and peace enforcement, then, if you take it to the extreme, there will be less and less for the longer-term development, and you will invest more and more money in peacekeeping and peace enforcement. For the first time, the Commission decided in December, under what they call a "peace facility", to draw from the European Development Fund of 250 million, to be allocated to the African Union for peacekeeping exercises—which are then to be decided case by case. However, the money has been put aside in a formal decision. This money cannot be counted as development aid in the OECD statistics. It therefore shows that you have moved out of the development aid zone into a political zone which, in OECD terms, is not considered as official development aid. There are certainly good reasons to do that but, as I said earlier, I would very much like to earmark these measures as necessary but as politically motivated measures. Lastly, you can turn the whole thing round, of course, and say that development is a condition for the prevention of conflict. Last year there was an interesting study produced by the World

Bank, where they studied the economic elements in some 60 conflicts during the last 10 to 20 years. They looked into the economic/social conditions of the countries concerned and tried to measure to what degree those conditions had contributed to provoking the conflict. There is a real correlation to be found there, between the level of development and the risk of civil wars and conflict. So when I see "peace is a precondition for development", I say yes, but development, in the longer-term perspective, is a real measure of conflict prevention, and that should not be neglected. It is about short-term and long-term approaches. If you see our ministers' work in the Foreign Affairs Council, look at their agenda. All the items relate to crises which already exist—the near-East, Iraq, *et cetera*. But who has the patience and the long-term view to see what has to be done so that these conflicts—to a certain degree, because you cannot avoid all conflicts—can be avoided? That seems to me to be something which distinguishes the shorter-term approach of foreign policy from the longer-term approach of development co-operation.

Q155 *Baroness Northover:* Picking up on your concern that aid is being used as a sort of foreign policy instrument, I wondered whether you felt that this will become even more difficult with the new countries coming into the EU, and whether there will be a greater battle as a result. I would like also to move to some linked questions. I wondered what role the Millennium Development Goals played in the Country Strategy Papers. Are they central to those Country Strategy Papers? And, if not, why not? Also, in a related way, I wonder how responsive and flexible the EU is in terms of its delivery of aid. Given that, as we have heard, a fifth of the aid from the richer countries is from the EU, what kind of response has there been as far as AIDS is concerned? Given that it is having a catastrophic effect in Africa—and you can see, down the track, how that is gathering in its pace and effect, and in fact will ensure that nobody meets any of those Millennium Development Goals—how responsive has the EU been to that catastrophic situation?

Mr Frisch: As far as the new countries are concerned, we do not know enough, of course, about what they will bring into the Community game. What I fear is that, for the first time, we will have an enlargement process where the newcomers will be competitors rather than countries which bring something additional to the development co-operation basket. We should not forget that, at present, these countries are moving from a state of being aid recipients— which they are still and which they will continue to be. Once they are in, they will benefit from the structural funds. In the establishment—the discussion has just started—of the Financial Perspectives beyond 2006, they will be fighting as

much as possible for funds and resources for their own internal needs. So I do not expect, contrary to all enlargements in the past, a very positive move coming from there. It would surprise me. It is not a criticism of these countries, but their problems are such that they cannot be enthusiastic champions of development co-operation. How could they be? So there is a problem there. As to whether they will bring in a political agenda which would make us move more to political aspects, I do not think so. It is more the larger member countries, who determine the political, foreign policy agenda, which may have the tendency to draw us in that direction. I do not think that it will come from the new countries. Turning to the Millennium Goals, for everyone who works in the development area they are a reference to which everything they propose to do must be connected. In terms of the strategy papers, they try as best as they can to be a contribution to that. One must also say that, knowing the reality in these countries, these Millennium Goals are very ambitious. An organisation like the European Union can only make a modest contribution to that with its aid money. However, it is in the development people's mind. Whether it is in the foreign policy people's mind to the same degree, I do not know. It always comes back to the same question. Are we heading for the development goals—because the Millennium Goals are development goals—or are we using part of our money more for political objectives? And that is not the same. If both the foreign policy and the development policy had a long-term strategic vision, then they would converge. We would not have to make the same distinction. However, it is mainly about the short-term and longer-term considerations, the pure politics, and the development aspects. As to the last point you raised, it was—

Q156 *Baroness Northover:* About AIDS and about how flexible the EU has been in terms of responding to that.

Mr Frisch: In my opinion, the flexibility is quite wide in the European programme. First, the range of things which can be done with the development aid money is very large. There is almost nothing excluded, except the military. In the development area you can dedicate your money to what you think is most important for the country and what the country accepts as being the most important for it. It is of course not for us to impose priorities on them. So the flexibility is there. The aid is managed, and that is a positive element, in five-year programmes; but these programmes are adjustable and adaptable. You can change a programme if the situation changes in that period. I do not see that there is a flexibility problem.

Chairman: Could we go back to what you said about structure? I think what you are saying is that you would go for a single directorate general, responsible for all aid that is motivated by a desire for development. All aspects of aid—programming, policy and implementation. Secondly, you would have a separate directorate general responsible for foreign policy, but you would give them a small foreign policy budget. What would you do about pre-enlargement aid? Where would that be? What would you do about humanitarian aid? Would they be within one or other of those? If you do have a single directorate general for development, how will you protect aid to the poorest countries? That is the first set of questions. Secondly, you talked about the need for the strategy papers to provide a common framework. Is there not a problem of competing with the World Bank and the IMF on this? The World Bank have strategy papers; they are trying to get bilateral donors to be involved and to follow their frameworks. I think that there is a bit of a problem there. Perhaps you could comment on that too?

Q157 *Lord Powell of Bayswater:* Could I add one question which is related directly to those? In the structure which has just been described, what happens about EDF and budgetisation? You and I have been discussing that for 20 years, and I do not think that it is ever going to happen. Is it not perhaps safest to de-budgetise aid to developing countries and put it all in an expanded EDF under this new Development Commissioner? That would get it away from the hands of the EU foreign minister.

Mr Frisch: You have become a revolutionary! I would like to say a word on budgetisation. First of all, however, in terms of the structure my idea would be—you will probably not find the same *discourse* elsewhere in the house—that these would be a joint common service—envisaged in the Constitutional Treaty—a diplomatic and common foreign and security policy department which would not have to spend half of its time dealing with development aid or foreign aid matters but, have a budget at its disposal. Not a small budget, but a comfortable budget for politically necessary foreign aid matters. Then I would like to see another department—we must change the name, because if you call it "development" they will say that we are resurrecting the "DG VIII"—that should be for all foreign aid with a developmental objective. You have borderline cases. You could ask whether the eastern countries—those which are not eligible for accession—would be in that department. Many of them are classified as developing countries. By the OECD definition, the central Asian countries are developing countries and so you should have them there. At present, the Accession countries have a special budget line. You might or might not keep that, but that is a

transitional problem; it is not a basic structural problem. I would not put implementation back into this development department. I raised the matter of the cut-off point, but the implementation agency should continue to exist.

Q158 *Chairman:* You would change the cut-off?

Mr Frisch: I would change the cut-off point between the two, but I would not take implementation back because it would be far too large a structure. Within that structure, I do not see a risk of the poor countries getting less. If you have aid in one hand you can, better than with a competing system, distribute the money according to developmental criteria. As to the question of the World Bank, our co-operation with the World Bank is very good. What bothers me—and bothered me even in my time—is that our co-operation with the World Bank is better than with the member countries of the European Union. That is something which is not normal. Normally, our first step in co-ordination should be with our member countries. The World Bank objectives are not necessarily the same as ours. The World Bank does not raise human rights and democratic matters. So we in fact have political aspects in our development policy, but the aspects we have in the development policy are relevant for development. That is a distinction I also want to make. These human rights, democratic principles, the rule of law, good governance, are political aspects but aspects which are relevant to development policy—whereas the support of Palestine is a purely political matter in my view. A last point—budgetisation. Certainly not, please, Charles, to move all development aid out of the budget! We have this anomaly with the EDF of having one single area of financing of all policies outside the budget. We have a budget of 100 billion euros and about two to three billion are outside the budget. My fight, to which I am really committed, is finally to get rid of this special status—which anyway is no longer a privilege. Those who were in favour of that special status—the French in particular—have come to understand that being outside the budget represents an element of marginalisation of these countries. You think less and less of the African countries. Therefore they must be brought to normality and be treated on an equal footing. I am therefore very much in favour of budgetisation. It raises a problem in some countries, including yours, because the financing key is more favourable for you outside the budget. However, can we really defend that, for one single element of one policy, there is a special status which is financed according to criteria of national interest? When this comes up, I say—and it does not hurt you—"I suggest that, for example, we put the fisheries agreements out of the budget and then it will be 90 per cent financed by the Spanish". If you start using the argument that a policy is financed according to the political interest of each member country, then you are lost forever.

Q159 *Lord Powell of Bayswater:* It is a question of defending the developing countries' interests because, if it goes in the budget, then it can be stolen for foreign policy reasons. If it is put out in the EDF, at least it is there, dedicated to development and to developing countries.

Mr Frisch: The whole discussion is about ring-fencing—putting it in the budget, but finding sufficient guarantees that this does not happen. That is the real problem.[2]

Chairman: I am sorry that we have to bring this to a close. It has been a very interesting conversation and we could have gone on much longer. I am sorry that we have to go. Thank you very much.

---

[2] Time was lacking for a thorough discussion on budgetisation of the EDF. I would therefore like to add the following arguments: We could live with an EDF outside the budget as long as we obtained a better deal for ACP-EU cooperation, mainly in terms

of the financial volume, than we would have got within the budget. That was the case until Lome IV (1990). With the two following replenishments (1995, 2000), the increases in the EDF envelope have levelled off. A separate discussion of the next EDF package alongside—or even worse: after—the negotiations of the financial perspectives 2007-2013 would entail for the ACP incalculable risks of further decline.

As an ad hoc financing key would have to be negotiated, one can imagine what kind of horse-trading this could represent with 25 or more member countries.

With budgetisation, funds would be available without waiting for ratification procedures to be completed in 25 (or more) member countries. This would be an enormous advantage compared to the present situation under which it took almost three years (from June 2000 to April 2003) with 15 Member States to make the money from the Cotonou EDF available. How long would it be with 25? This argument by itself justifies budgetisation.

Technical arguments in favour of budgetisaoin can be found in the Commission communication of 8 October 2003. There are in particular solutions to the problem raised by Lord Powell of Bayswater, notably the inscription of a multiannual financial envelope in a regulation co-decided by the EU Council and Parliament. This would be a genuine protection.

To sum up: budgetisation is politically necessary—putting an end to an anachronism with a post-colonial flavour which has meanwhile contributed to move the ACP into a kind of organisaional and budgetary "apartheid"—and it is technically possible whilst safeguarding the core characteristics of the Contonou Partnership Agreement.

MONDAY 2 FEBRUARY 2004

Present   Bowness, L (Chairman)   Northover, B
                 Lea of Crondall, L   Powell of Bayswater, L
                 Maclennan of Rogart, L   Tomlinson, L

Examination of Witness

MR KRISTIAN SCHMIDT, Deputy Head of Nielson Cabinet, DG Development, European Commission, examined.

Q160 *Chairman:* As I am sure you know, we are part of the European Union Select Committee of the House of Lords—its sub-committee dealing with foreign policy, defence and development. We are carrying out an inquiry into European Union development aid and assistance, looking at various aspects of that, including: evaluating the reform of European Union development assistance; looking ahead to the development of foreign policy; looking at the provisions of the Constitutional Treaty and what that means for development aid, if it is enacted; the effects of enlargement; the future of the ACP grouping; and the European Development Fund and whether or not it should be budgetised. We have had a paper which has been circulated, *Reform of the Management of EU External Assistance Progress Report*. Was that prepared by your department here?
Mr Schmidt: It was prepared jointly by EuropeAid, DG Development and DG Relex, but under the supervision of the joint cabinets of Commissioner Patten and Commissioner Nielson.

Q161 *Chairman:* Perhaps I could start this session by thanking you and saying that we are very grateful to you for giving your time to give evidence. Before it gets forgotten, how do you see the proposals in the draft Constitutional Treaty and how they would affect development aid?
Mr Schmidt: Let me first apologise on behalf of Commissioner Nielson, who is in New Zealand for the moment, but who would have very much liked to receive the Committee and always appreciates the quality of the reports coming out of all of the United Kingdom parliamentary work. He is sorry to have missed this opportunity, therefore. To answer your question, I think that on this particular point Commissioner Nielson did not see a need in the convention for new competences, perhaps contrary to the foreign policy area. In development policy, Commissioner Nielson simply considered that the regime of shared competence that we have at the moment is quite adequate, and that that would be a useful outcome. Indeed, it is what is now in the draft Constitution. I think he considers that there is a case to be made for the added value of certain things being done at the Community level, but clearly there is also a role at the national level. Diversity, the way Member States do development co-operation

differently, is of value to our partner countries—but also, of course, a reflection of the societies that they represent. He would basically have been happy with the provisions in the draft Constitution as they stood and, from our side, we did not try to press for any steps on the balance of Member States and the Community. There are a number of points, however, where one could perhaps have expected a bit more from the Constitution, but that is at a lower level of importance. There are things—like taking steps forward in terms of using common analytical platforms for the programming of development aid—where you could argue that this is perhaps too much detail to put into a constitution, but these are the kinds of things that Commissioner Nielson might have wished for. Otherwise, he would of course have welcomed the adoption of the language on poverty eradication as the ultimate target and goal of our efforts in this area. He certainly would have welcomed the legal base on humanitarian aid, which would make it clear that we were operating on the basis of the principles of neutrality and impartiality in that area.

Q162 *Lord Tomlinson:* Can I ask you two questions, both arising from what you have said? You were quite content with the outcome of the Convention; but, since the Convention, there has been the specific Commission proposal in relation to budgetisation. If that was so crucial in terms of raising a proposal, why did you not raise that in the context of the Convention? There was very substantial deliberation on budgetary and other questions in the context of the Convention. Also, you referred to Commissioner Nielson's commitment to the goal of poverty eradication. That is certainly a goal which I believe the United Kingdom Government would fully share. However, I get the impression that there is a substantial feeling in the United Kingdom that that goal of poverty eradication is somewhat diluted by the political nature of so much of the expenditure from the European Union budget—things like the flanking measures for the Middle East process; the support for the Palestinian Authority; the MEDA programme; a lot of the aid to Latin America—which does not seem to fit in with those objectives and therefore seem to dilute the conviction with which they can be put.

Mr Schmidt: First on budgetisation, the text as it stood would have enabled budgetisation by leaving out the reference to the ACP being separate—which is in the current Maastricht Treaty. That text, in parallel with our proposal for budgetisation, would have enabled the two things to go together. So there was an enabling change in the constitution, enabling budgetisation. The process of budgetising is in any case not something that the EU can decide unilaterally. It is something that we have first to agree on internally, yes, but then it is something to be negotiated with the ACP countries. It therefore seems difficult to put it into a constitution up-front without this negotiating process having taken place. There is absolutely no question, however, of the commitment of the entire college to the proposal for budgetisation We are indeed trying as best we can, as it were, to sell the case with all the Member States, including the United Kingdom, which is one of the Member States which remain to be convinced on this point. I can expand on the merits of budgetisation, if you wish, but that was not your question in the first instance. On poverty eradication, I would say that this is a continuing battle. It is a battle where, in terms of statistics, progress has been made in the last couple of years—certainly since 1999. If you take the figures for what was going to LDCs and low-income countries, it was about 34 per cent in 1999; we are now close to 45 per cent. So, over the years when my Commissioner has been in office, there has been a 10 percentage point increase of the share. But you are right to say that more can be done. It is also a question of whether you recognise that Member States have, as they indeed have, decided that some of the things we do jointly are a good choice. For instance, the Balkans. The fact that the Council has decided jointly that the EU should take care of stability in the Balkans, and therefore in past years allocated quite substantial amounts—it is now going down—has allowed Member States, by complementarity, not to spend significant amounts in official assistance in the Balkans. There is therefore a choice: that Member States have decided that this is an additional responsibility for the Community to undertake. If you look at the ACP countries, however—what we call "the primary poverty focus" in the allocation of funds to the ACP countries, i.e. the amount of funds going to the LCD countries and the low-income countries—it is around 90 per cent. So for that part of what we do there is a very clear poverty focus.

Q163 *Lord Tomlinson:* So poverty focus doing better in the non-budgetised funds than in the budgetised funds?

Mr Schmidt: Absolutely. I can feel the conclusion you would wish to draw from that—which is to say that if you budgetise then you would lose poverty focus. I

would say that the opposite is the case. We are currently discussing extending the country allocation criteria from use for the EDF to the budget environment. This is a political agreement that has been reached between Commissioner Patten and Commissioner Nielson and communicated to Council, endorsed by the Council on Monday last week, saying that they would indeed appreciate that in future the Commission uses the same mechanisms for allocating funds to countries—whether it is the ACP or whether it is the budget part of the geography. We feel that would have a number of advantages. First, it would increase poverty focus, because we would be giving priority to the size of countries, and certainly to the needs of countries— and this is simply calculated on the basis of GNI per capita—and then to country performance, in terms of macro-economic stability, et cetera. If that method of allocating funds up-front were to be extended to the budget environment, we think that would be a way to increase the poverty focus. It would also be a way of saying that we apply the same rules to the ACPs as we do to the non-ACP countries which— and here is the second advantage of that—would give Council, the European Parliament and national parliaments a much clearer idea of how funds are being allocated. For example, for the ninth EDF, everything is calculated by a very elaborate scheme of weights that are applied, and then a distribution is made. This is notified to the ACP countries, and Council and Parliament can all see how it is done. It is much less evident, for the budget part, how priorities are set inside the Commission in terms of proposing funds to be allocated to Pakistan, India, and Bangladesh. By extending these criteria, however, the Parliament and Council would have a clear rationale for having allocated these funds; and then Council could have the budgetary authority, could have their political discussion on whether they agreed with these priorities, change them, give extra weight to the fight against terrorism, migration, what-have-you—but the original proposal from the Commission would be transparent and motivated by objective criteria. This is what we have proposed, and it is what the Council have now said that they would want us to take forward.

Q164 *Lord Powell of Bayswater:* I see the logic of what you are saying, but I suspect that the political reality will, as over the last 30 years, prove that the EDF continues in existence. If that is the realistic judgment, does it not make more sense to transfer responsibility for the non-ACP developing countries to DG VIII, rather than to have this split of some under your direct responsibility in DG VIII and others under Relex? Secondly, a related question: does it still make sense to maintain the ACP grouping? Has it not lost its original logic, which was to do with French decolonisation? Obviously, it cannot be changed overnight, but ought not a forward-looking Commission be planning now for a situation where the ACP grouping as such disappears over a five to 10-year timescale, so that there is a genuine similarity of treatment between all developing countries?

Mr Schmidt: Your last question is the most radical question, so I will start with that one. My Commissioner would certainly see it as a great loss to lose the ACP grouping, as it were. Given the earlier question, I would grant you that there is a need for extending or harmonising some of the approaches. For instance, in the area of resource allocation, there is no reason why you should treat Burkina Faso and Bangladesh differently. Whether you are poor in one country or the other does not really give you more merit in terms of our assistance. That is one aspect. However, there is a heritage to preserve in terms of the nature of the partnership. If you go through the Cotonou Agreement, as I am sure you have done, and look at it, the first side of it might be looking through the UN Charter or a UN resolution; but I can assure you that, on some of the provisions in terms of corruption, on political dialogue, the language in the Cotonou Agreement goes far beyond what Europe collectively could ever hope to achieve in negotiation in the UN Assembly. So there is some trust in the partnership and some long-term investment of dialogue there, which should not be lost.

Q165 *Lord Powell of Bayswater:* The language goes beyond. Does the reality really go beyond?

Mr Schmidt: It does on corruption, yes. Before coming to this job, I was at the UN General Assembly, representing my country of origin. I vividly remember the negotiations on a resolution on corruption. Even to discuss in the UN General Assembly the fact that there is corruption in developing countries is a tall order—even to have it put on the agenda. What was achieved in the Cotonou Agreement—and this I remember equally well, because it was one of the first achievements of my Commissioner early in the year 2000—was to say, "We have a disagreement with the other side on whether you want to discuss corruption, but that is because they want to discuss it not as an essential element, or not under the broad, fuzzy term of 'good governance'". My Commissioner's approach to that was to say, "Good governance can be discussed as part of a political dialogue. We need a discussion like that. There are different models of democracy, but it is part of what we discuss. We can discuss it. But corruption—there is only one word for that, and that is zero tolerance. That has to be linked to the essential elements and must lead immediately to suspension of our assistance". By addressing it in that manner, our

partner countries in the ACP group actually accepted those provisions, not just for suspicion of corruption of EC funds, but also if it was corruption using their own taxpayers' money. This is important to us because, first of all, it is a question of good governance; but it is also, in a situation in which we give budget support, absolutely crucial that we can have full confidence not only in our money being used well but also that the whole budget managed by the ministry of finance is sound. That is a long answer, but my main point is to say that there are a lot of areas where we can harmonise, to make sure that on all the procedures we do not treat the ACP differently. That simply leads to the Commission having doubled systems—added bureaucracy, two sets of financial regulations, two sets of tendering procedures. We have to get rid of all of these things, because they add to the burden of handling this. One thing which we should not get rid of is the quality of the policy dialogue. That has to be maintained.

Q166 *Lord Powell of Bayswater:* How many countries have we actually suspended for corruption? Is it just one? Is it just Togo?

Mr Schmidt: It is on and off. The Côte d'Ivoire is the prime example, where there were funds held back. So we held up while the investigations were ongoing. We held up, fully acknowledged by the Ivory Coast, and then they paid back and co-operation resumed.

Q167 *Baroness Northover:* What has happened with Angola?

Mr Schmidt: I do not want to go into details on that, because I simply do not know enough about that case.

Q168 *Lord Lea of Crondall:* Last summer there was a report by a high-level American group on the problem of development, or lack of it, in Africa. They centred their report around the statistic that only 1 per cent of world capital flows was going to Africa—although Africa has 10 per cent of the world's population, 800 million out of eight billion. I would like you to comment on the following way of presenting the dilemma. If you go down the road of saying, "What does it take to get more private investment into Africa? Let's ask big business", and big business says, "When we go to China or when we go to India these days, they lay out the red carpet and say 'You can have that and that'". It is perhaps not the same agenda as would appear in your EU-negotiated Country Strategy Paper. On the face of it, it certainly would place less emphasis on the degree of ownership which the recipient country would feel it committed to the programme—because it had been involved in writing it and it would get its local authorities, its judiciary and all layers of its society committed to the outcome. Clearly you can get nowhere near the world development goals unless you have 7 per cent of your total economic growth, and that will only come through considerably increasing private capital flows. We are just not getting private capital flows going to Africa, and yet there is this great tension between what it takes—as seen by business—to get the private capital flows into Africa, and the sort of stuff that is typically contained in a Country Strategy Paper. Unless I am wrong, I think that there is a tension there. Would you comment?

Mr Schmidt: Yes. It allows me to complete my answer to the previous question, because I should also have answered on the trade part of Cotonou. You are right to touch upon that. I think that this Commission has made great efforts to ensure greater coherence between those two agendas—trade and development. Everything-but-arms is the most quoted example, but certainly our support for regional liberalisation inside Africa is the second leg of that policy. I fully accept the problem as you have posed it. The problem in Africa is that markets are simply too small to be interesting to foreign investments: small and, of course, unpredictable. This, of course, is where corruption comes in. If you could start by offering to an investor that they do not have to face an environment of corruption, it would already be a big comparative advantage for the average mainstream, honest business. Our policy on this, however, is clearly to say, "The markets are too small and therefore you have to open up among yourselves, and possibly start with that even before thinking about asking for market access *vis-à-vis* our economies and opening up *vis-à-vis* our business". On this point, Commissioner Nielson always uses the example of a potential investor in a soap factory in Uganda. Uganda is not a very big market. The first question that investor would ask him or herself would be, "Can I, from that facility, export to the neighbouring countries?". The answer you will very often get is, "Yes, but at a 15 per cent tariff". So it is a problem for regional trade, but it is also a big brake on foreign direct investments into Africa. Another good example that we looked at were mosquito nets. You would imagine that Africa is a very important market for mosquito nets. Two million people per year die from malaria. This is a low-tech production which could be done locally. A textile industry is present in Africa. We therefore looked at this, as part of our policy on communicable diseases. We found that there had been an attempt in, I believe, Tanzania to set up a production facility for mosquito nets, but the feasibility study ruled it out because the market in the neighbouring countries, although promising, presented a barrier of 17 per cent. So all of Africa imports its mosquito nets from Hong Kong. This is not a normal situation; it is something which has to be addressed. We are pushing as hard as we can on

the Economic Partnership Agreements that are the Cotonou trade track. Commissioners Lamy and Nielson are travelling to the regional organisations to persuade, to push that this regional opening is necessary. You are absolutely right to say that, without this work, our whole approach—which is extra resources from development funds, the Monterey conference, the Doha track on trade and sustainability, Johannesburg—that whole three-legged strategy is missing a very crucial leg. We can only tell our partners, "Cancun was a failure. We hope it will get started. But, until it gets started, the Economic Partnership Agreement is the only show in town, and you should take the short pause in the WTO discussions to make sure that you move forward on regional integration in the meantime". Your remark on the gap between resources available and reaching the Millennium Development Goals is well taken, however. The average African country has $2 to $5 per capita for health expenditure. A minister of health in Uganda has that amount—to build hospitals, train nurses, buy drugs, treat AIDS patients, et cetera. There is no way in which, with that amount of resources, you could halve child mortality by 2015. This is absolutely recognised. Our response to that is not to say, "It's trade, not aid", but to say, "It's trade and aid", and the aid argument is what is coming out of the Monterey conference. As you know, the Commission has a role in trying to bring Member States forward jointly to fulfil that promise.

Q169 *Lord Maclennan of Rogart:* I wonder if I might ask you a couple of questions about the interesting report published in December on the management of external assistance. It is not of course addressed to parliamentarians or the general public. It is a rather inward document in some ways, without exemplifications, or with very few. Consequently, it is quite hard to see how you prioritise the different management objectives. One of them is clearly greater effectiveness and that, it appears, is being advanced by de-concentration of some of the programme delivery. On the other hand, there are references to harmonisation of practices. That in some ways seems to militate against de-concentration. There are also references to sensitivity towards the needs of different countries within a region, and yet an attempt being made to standardise within regions, to some extent, what is being delivered. Reading this document, I find that in some ways it looks as though it is facing two ways on almost every question. I am sure that is only because it does not actually have the examples, which might make it much clearer. I wonder if it would be possible to give us a couple of examples of some these things.

Mr Schmidt: I would be very pleased to do that. Let me start with harmonisation and de-concentration. I understand your point. One of the steps forward we have taken is to have these Country Strategy Papers thoroughly discussed with Member States, and approved as upstream political discussions on what we are supposed to do in a given country. These are of course first discussed at the country level with our delegations, with Member States' embassies being present and commenting, with UN agencies, the World Bank and what-have-you. Then they come for approval in Brussels, they go to the committees and are again discussed by Member States and approved. In theory, this allows us to have a clear— "harmonised" is not the word—a common view, an EU view, on what should be done in, say, Bangladesh. The trouble is that, once this whole process is completed, the actual use of this document is a little bit one-way. It only informs what the Community is supposed to do, not the Member States that were involved in producing the whole document. So having agreed and negotiated this document with the Member States, they still feel, "That was the EU Country Strategy Paper for Bangladesh. I, Member State X, will now go back and write the Country Strategy Paper for my country for Bangladesh". That is where we think there is progress still to be made. It is not harmonisation for the sake of harmonisation. However, if you look at it from the side of Bangladesh, they have gone through this whole discussion. We have said that we have based our Country Strategy Papers on Poverty Reduction Strategy Papers. We have already consulted widely and, as a mainstream donor, have based ourselves on the PRSPs. Bangladesh then has to do the whole thing with a new Member State. All of them are big donors, expect to be taken seriously, and met at the level of the minister of finance. The number of negotiation processes that that country has then to manage, with experts coming to their country, to their capital, having to do the tour— because we donors expect to be received with attention, and almost gratitude—imposes a strain on the resources of our partner countries, with this multitude of processes ongoing. What we are saying—and this is what will be coming out in the Commission's report for the April Council on the implementation of the Monterey commitments- is that we are doing well in terms of increasing the level of ODA; but we have not fulfilled the promises of the last 30 years in terms of what we would call "donor discipline", namely decreasing and harmonising our own demands on the partner countries in terms of what they should do to satisfy our needs for reporting. It is a different aspect of the discussion also on the untying of aid, where we are asking for 16 different tendering procedures, Member State by Member State and the Community.

Q170 *Lord Maclennan of Rogart:* Do you apply different laws to all these different tendering agreements? That is just a point of detail.

Mr Schmidt: No, not the Commission. We have our tendering procedure, yes, certainly—agreed and imposed by the Council—but Member States have their own systems. As part of this Monterey exercise, we have sent out questionnaires asking Member States to tell us whether they would agree for us, at least within the EU, to agree on the same tendering procedures. We talk about ownership. In the countries that are capable of doing so, this should mean that, say, Bangladesh is able to say, "You want us to do the tendering procedures, so let us do it according to one set of rules that you all accept, and you all get the chance to control and get reports upon how it is done"—but not that we give the money to Bangladesh and say, "You will now do the tendering according to this set of rules"; then the next donor comes and says, "...with this set of rules". When Commissioner Nielson is visiting ministers of finance in these partner countries, he always takes a look at their archives to see what kind of administration they have to work with. I am sure that you have also seen it when visiting countries. Following all of these procedures is a burden that they simply cannot sustain. You wonder why there are not more mistakes than there actually are, because it is immensely complex. It is our responsibility as donors to make it simpler.

Q171 *Lord Lea of Crondall:* I was in Bangladesh in September and it was very obvious that, on the one hand, there were too many different people coming to Dacca with slightly different agendas. Their capacity is limited, even though Bangladesh is actually a very big country—125 million people. Imagine what it is like in Niger, if too many different people come in asking them to get into detail about different things. Even so, it is also true—this is a delicate subject, of course—that Bangladesh is number one in the world corruption league, according to Transparency International. There is a certain amount of alibi gamesmanship going on here: that "They would shout 'neo-colonialism', wouldn't they?" if the delivery of the Country Strategy Paper, which they have signed up to, is not really to their taste. I am afraid you have to fight your way through that very difficult political—

Mr Schmidt: I want to be very clear that the Commission is not advocating less control, but actually it would be the other way round. If you have just one set of procedures, with the donor community jointly you could control much better that it is being followed. Let me ask you how much confidence and control you have, for instance, on what goes on in the tendering procedures of a different donor. That may not all be completely clean, but the Commission would not know; a bilateral donor would not know. Yet it is a concern if tendering in that country, be it for another donor's money, is not entirely clean. So the idea of adopting the same procedures is a big step forward in terms of transparency and control.

Q172 Baroness Northover: You have talked quite a bit—or it is implied—about how difficult it is to influence even the countries within the EU, as you try to have this strategy for poverty reduction. I am wondering what links you have across the EU bodies to try to implement what you are doing. For example, you were talking about trade talks. You made the interesting comment that your Commissioner thinks that it is more important, for example for Africa, to open their own markets to each other than necessarily to open our markets to them—which I thought rather went against what we were seeking to do in Cancun, despite what was thrown back at us and maybe it confirms what people were saying there. I also wondered, in the case of AIDS, whether there is anything which is done to put pressure on countries within the EU to ensure that, for example, the production of anti-retroviral drugs, in terms of their availability free or very cheaply, is something that is promoted amongst member countries: whether you can pursue the aims that you are talking about via action in individual countries. Perhaps I can link this to it. You talk about improvements in the emphasis on poverty reduction—although you yourself point out that it still has a long way to go. Do you see that continuing to improve? Will it be adversely affected by the new countries that are coming into the EU? Does it depend very much upon the individual Commissioners who are in charge, or are there structural changes which you would see as being important if this is going to be encouraged to move forward?
Mr Schmidt: First of all, on trade I may have expressed myself a bit—

Q173 Baroness Northover: You put it in interesting terms, shall we say.
Mr Schmidt: What I mean to say is that certainly our policy in Cancun was the one that we declared, which is to go for a balanced but progressive market-opening. Certainly everything-but-arms is the first step towards that, but we were ready to go further than that. The relation between the region and the global dimension is simply a recognition that many of our partner countries themselves are not yet ready for competition in the global economy. We may be convinced that it is for the good of, say, Mozambique to make it into the global competition tomorrow, but they may think that is a tall order. Of course, because it is not just in terms of their market access to our markets. It is also the other way round: it is opening up to quite capable competitors in the region like South Africa. There are all these concerns, therefore, that in our view make it reasonable to argue, "If you think that step is too much in the short term, why not

consider, with our support, starting in your region and ensuring that your economies diversify?". Take an example in West Africa like cotton—an issue which is much talked about. The fact that some countries like Benin or Mali have organised the entire country round a cash export like cotton is an example that countries can make it into the global economy. But the counterpart—and you are seeing that now—is that that country becomes extremely dependent on that cash export, and they are left as not very diversified economies. With the overall reduction in commodity prices, they are clearly less vulnerable if they have also developed regional trade. On this point, Commissioner Nielson usually says that the very high level of smuggling in West Africa is the best indication that there is an enormous potential for regional trade, if only they would open up more. I have not added all the benefits, in terms of regional stability if they trade together. They are also less likely to go to war, et cetera. These are all the added advantages of regional trade. I want to stress, however, that there is no contradiction between advocating regional trade and more open global trade. The Cotonou approach was exactly that the former supports the latter. Briefly on AIDS, I think that this can be considered one of the success stories over the last couple of years. We have been able to put in place a comprehensive, coherent policy within the EU. I am not talking of a success story in terms of actually dealing with the disease. We are still not anywhere near that. On your specific point of addressing the price of drugs and access to drugs, I think that the Commission has been both progressive and successful in applying reasonable pressure on the pharmaceutical industry, but also in obtaining the industry's co-operation in reducing prices. Our approach has been to say that the world is big enough to have a system of tier pricing. So there could be one level of prices for the OECD countries and a different, much lower level of prices in Africa and developing countries, and that these different pricing regimes could live together. We have put in place the enabling instrument by proposing a regulation on preventing re-importation of discounted drugs sold by the industry in Africa back into our economies. Of course, we cannot go out and dictate the prices charged by private companies. What the Commission can do, and has done as much as we could, is to put in place the policy framework so that these companies, should they wish to pursue what we think is the right thing to do in Africa, can do so. I think it is fair to say that, in the discussions in the WTO, Commissioner Lamy has taken a stance that is in full support of developing countries and their right to use the property rights to address the health crisis of those countries. On the poverty focus, the Balkans is an historic event which made us allocate a lot of resources to that region. You saw that affected in the statistics. It is now being phased out. You may ask, "What is next?". Next is a wider Europe, and North Africa, in terms of the perceived security threat from that region. I think the challenge for any Commissioner and any Commission is clearly to keep in mind the advantages of the different instruments. Development aid in countries like Egypt, for instance, has so far not made an enormous impact. It does not seem to matter how much money you spend—unless the policies are more pro-poor and the political dialogue is strong and demanding. This is the case for some of these countries in the Middle East and North Africa. My Commissioner often likes to quote the Beatles' "Money Can't Buy You Love", and it cannot buy you influence. If the policies are not right, no amount of money will work. I think that is the short answer. We have to spend much more time on using foreign policy instruments to ensure that our

aid can be effective. That said, the aid that is spent in that region has improved dramatically over the last couple of years, in terms of giving much more attention to the question of ownership, and making sure that the quality of the programming and conditions have improved in terms of spending the money. My last comment would be to repeat the figures which you probably know from the OECD review. All our efforts in the Balkans, eastern Europe, enlargement, what-have-you, have not been made at the expense of the ACP countries. If you look at it in terms of percentage, of course, then yes, there is a decline, but you cannot make the case that euros have been moved from African countries to Balkan countries. These tasks have been additional and undertaken with the full endorsement of the Council.
Chairman: Thank you very much indeed for your time. I am sorry that we cannot stay with you longer.

MONDAY 2 FEBRUARY 2004

Present	Bowness, L (Chairman)	Northover, B
	Lea of Crondall, L	Powell of Bayswater, L
	Maclennan of Rogart, L	Tomlinson, L

Examination of Witness

MR ROBERT REYNDERS, Member, European Court of Auditors, examined.

Q174 *Chairman:* Mr Reynders, thank you very much for coming to give evidence to the sub-committee. As you know, we are making an inquiry into European development aid and assistance, looking at and evaluating the reforms; looking ahead to the development of aid and foreign policy; also looking at the position of development aid post the Constitutional Treaty, if it happens; the effects of enlargement; the future of the ACP group; and possible budgetisation of the European Development Fund. Clearly we cannot cover all those topics with you in the time that we have. Before we move on to questions, is there anything that you would like to say from your position in the Court of Auditors, and perhaps explaining its role in the whole development aid process?
Mr Reynders: Thank you very much, My Lord Chairman, for this opportunity to explain myself on the subject you have just mentioned. I am also pleased that you have given me the opportunity to make some introductory remarks. It is an honour for me to appear before your Committee. I speak personally, because it has not been possible to discuss these topics with my colleagues. I do not represent the Court and in what I say here I will represent only myself. You also know that I have no professional responsibility for defining development aid policy. As a member of the Court, I am principally involved in the audit of the European Development Funds. As Lord Tomlinson knows, being a member of the Court means that I am involved in the audit of the legality and the regularity of EDF transactions. We always come after everything has happened, but sometimes that is very interesting. I am also responsible for auditing the sound financial management of EDF resources. As a result, you will understand why I told Ms Nelson that I was ready to deal with your questionnaire on two topics: whether the ACP grouping has a future and, secondly, the European Development Funds and the budget. For the previous topics, I think it is better to see Commissioners Patten or Nielson. These persons are much better placed to answer such questions. However, I think that the ACP grouping and EDF and the budget are topics by themselves. I have to confess that, with the short time I had at my disposal, I hesitated to appear before this Committee to answer these important questions. When I told a friend that I was coming here, he spoke to me of Winston Churchill, who said, "There are three things in life that are almost impossible: to climb a wall that is leaning against you; to kiss a girl who is leaning away from you; and to appear before a committee of the House of Lords!" I will stop there. I can either follow the questionnaire or, if you have any other suggestions, I am in your hands.

Q175 *Chairman:* I think that those two topics will be of great interest to the Committee.
Mr Reynders: So does the ACP grouping have a future? The ACP grouping was created 40 years ago. It developed into a partnership between ACP countries and the European Union on an equal footing—that is very important—also with the ownership of development policies. I think that these were the two cornerstones of the story. I think that we may say that it also realised an important *acquis* over the years, surpassing national interests. One interesting aspect of this agreement—or partnership agreement now, Cotonou—is that it is not discussing on a national basis, but there are two blocs surpassing the national interest. Also by using the long-term framework that is there, it is interesting for everyone to have a long-term view based on the many relationships existing between ACP countries and the EU. It is also, in the Cotonou Agreement and previously the Lomé Convention, the only collective political co-operation existing in EU external relations. Its future must be seen in the light of the budgetisation of the EDF. You cannot disconnect these two aspects. There is an excellent document on budgetisation of the Commission. It is the document of 8 October. It is a well-written document—a little *plaidoyer pro domo*, as we say, but at the same time it is one of the better Commission documents that I have read. In this document the Commission clearly takes the viewpoint that budgetisation is a good thing; it has many more advantages than disadvantages. Even if there are some risks, it is also the opinion of the Court and of the Convention that we should budgetise the European Development Funds, and that the best way to do it is from the year 2008 onwards. I will come to that later. Having accepted budgetisation, this immediately has an influence on the future of the ACP formula. I think that the agreement can subsist as a principle, but a lot

of things will have to be modified. It is very clear that there is a political aspect in the ACP grouping, and there is also a financial aspect. The financial aspect is explicit in terms of the financial protocol, which is the first annex to the Cotonou Agreement. You have also the internal agreement; you have the financial regulation specifically for the EDFs. All this can be abolished when you budgetise and can be replaced by regulation—such as the regulations which exist for MEDA, for Latin America, or for Asia. Modalities in the agreement will have to be adapted following the abolition of these specific regulations which I have mentioned, and the creation of a specific regulation for the General Budget where, let us say, the aid for the ACP countries would be included. I think that this is perfectly possible, however. At that time this modified partnership, as far as I can judge, could even be used as an example for other kinds of help—for Latin America, for Asia. Why not create a political platform of discussion and a mutual exchange of information? I think that people cannot see too much of each other, even if there could be a certain waste of money. I think that it is better to meet once too often than once too little—*une fois de trop que trop peu.* That is my personal view on the matter. However, I have never attended a meeting at ministerial level. In the recent past, the partnership made it possible to provide the ACP countries with help of almost two billion euros a year. This was possible thanks to a very flexible EDF framework which provided the ACP countries with two particular benefits. Firstly, it provides predictable allocations of aid, defined in the financial protocol on a five-yearly basis, to individual ACP countries over the multi-annual period of the European Development Fund concerned—always five years, I think. Secondly, delays in commitments or payments do not result in a loss of funds, apart from serious exceptional cases. However, every coin has two sides. This flexible system made it possible for ACP governments to postpone difficult political decisions almost endlessly. This is a creeping danger and it permits both parties not to take up their responsibilities. This is not such a good thing, I believe. Once you budgetise, you limit flexibility and you return to more budgetary orthodoxy. In this case, I believe that this is a good thing. Of course, there is the risk that there is not enough capacity-building in certain ACP countries. When they have endless time to commit credits and to make payments on these commitments, even ACP countries with very little absorption capacity will be able to use the money. If you move to a normal budgetary system, as it will be if you include ACP money in the General Budget, you will diminish flexibility, creating a problem for those African countries which do not have so much absorption capacity. At that moment, both sides need to take up their responsibilities and, if there is not enough absorption capacity, you need

to improve it; you need to give technical assistance; you need to do whatever is in your power to do. Of course, this is theory; but you have to do it. As I see it, there was a *laisser-aller* in this help, and it was considered and presented as a good thing. This *laisser-aller*—which, giving it a positive name, is flexibility—gave too much room to these countries to do nothing to tackle the real problems and to take responsibility. It was therefore easy for everybody. I think that this should come to an end, and I think that budgetisation is a good formula in order to arrive at that situation.

Q176 *Lord Powell of Bayswater:* In the past, the Court of Auditors has been quite critical of aspects of Commission and EU spending. Where does EDF rank in the hierarchy of offenders? Is it towards the bottom? Or is its performance actually quite good?
Mr Reynders: I think that its performance is quite good. The Court gives two declarations of assurance. The Court gives a declaration of assurance regarding the General Budget—a General Budget of let us say 100 billion euros, and an EDF budget, let us say two billion euros. We never gave a positive declaration of assurance for the General Budget, except some specific categories like resources or administrative expenses. Fundamentally, for the two main categories of expenses—agricultural funds and structural funds—it was a negative declaration of assurance, because their error rate was too high. In the years since I have been in the Court it has twice given a positive declaration of assurance regarding the use of EDFs, but there was one very important limitation of scope, namely that, for direct budgetary aid from the EU to the ACP countries, we said that we could not make a judgment. It was not included in our positive statement of assurance because it was impossible for the Court to judge: we had no information about the state of the national budgets. When I took over the ACP sector, I was astonished to see—as I told the CoCoBu, the Budgetary Control Committee, a few weeks ago—that my auditors found that the legality and regularity of the transactions in the EDF framework were relatively high. To find this in African countries was astonishing to me, but the rules of the EDF and its framework have existed for so long that they are applied well. Everybody knows the system, there are many controls, and it works well. Therefore, we gave a positive declaration of assurance. Once you give direct budgetary aid, however, it means that this money no longer passes through the EDF framework; it goes directly to the national budgets of the ACP countries, and is then expended following the rules and procedures of those national budgets. This is a totally different story. You have to know what is the quality of those rules and procedures. This is becoming a very important topic because, in 2002,

direct budgetary aid was about 25 per cent of total ACP aid, and this percentage will increase in the future. It does not mean that I am personally against it. On the contrary: I am in favour of it. It is very important to tackle the real problems in ACP countries. Perhaps we may dream, but I think that we should dream a little. As project financing does the other 75 per cent, it has not really worked in fine over the last 20 years. There were many problems. The rhythm of payments and so on was not right, and the final result, even if the evaluation of the project was fairly good, is that the overall situation in Africa is not good. It is difficult to say what has been the role of EDF financing in the general situation in Africa.

Q177 *Lord Powell of Bayswater:* Does the policy of de-concentration and handing out greater responsibility to Commission delegations cause you any concerns about controls?

Mr Reynders: We are making a special report on the effects of de-concentration. The Court's report will be published in about September/October of this year. The Auditors have already been to some countries to make their audits on the spot, therefore, and I have spent some time in Mali. First of all, the resources are indeed given to the delegations, to speed up the transactions, to improve the quality of the programming and the execution of the aid, and also to increase the robustness of the transactions, of the regulations. The resources are there but it is too early to say if this will work in practice. There may be some teething troubles at the beginning, but we have the impression that it will work. It is too early to say, however. In most of the delegations it started only during 2003, so it is too early for us to say. There are some positive signs. I also know that an evaluation exists, which was published in December last year, about de-concentration. I believe that it was carried out by a team of auditors or evaluators from Relex, DEV and AidCo, with perhaps some input from the private sector. This was more favourable and gave a positive view on the results; but we believe that it is too early to say.

Q178 *Lord Powell of Bayswater:* But you are satisfied that there are adequate internal controls in place for handling this money by Commission delegations?

Mr Reynders: Absolutely. These are in place. The guidelines that have to be applied are in place. Sometimes there is a problem of language. For instance, in Kenya they existed in French and not in English, and vice versa in a French-speaking country. This is a detail, however. I think that the 24 standards of internal control will be in place, but it is also a question of filling the posts. That is a difficulty. In theory, you can say that all of this will be done, but you have to find the qualified people on the spot.

That is a real problem. However, AidCo is aware of that problem and they have to tackle that. It is not an easy one.

Q179 *Lord Lea of Crondall:* I would like to follow up what Lord Powell has been asking. To be a bit provocative, aid fatigue is now partly bound up in the picture—that all the money went into Bokassa's diamonds, et cetera. There have been these Kinnock reforms of management audits going with the money from the beginning, rather than sweeping up at the end—which I think is roughly what the European Court of Auditors does. Can you tell us a little more about how you do control that the money is spent on what it is supposed to be spent on in a typical African country?

Mr Reynders: We, as a Court of Auditors, do two things. We make our annual report and we make special reports. Let me speak first about the annual report. Essentially, we do a lot of work for the declaration of assurance. For the year 2002 we have, in Brussels, taken about 45 transactions at random, to look at the legality and regularity of them. It was essentially at the level of payments—also commitments, but essentially payments. The results were fairly good. Then we went to five or six ACP countries, more or less taken at random. In these countries we took seven or eight transactions—let us say the most important transactions, or in the domains where, after risk analysis, we had a presumption that there was risk. The first sample in Brussels was at random, the second one was risk-based. In each of the six countries we applied the same analysis of legality and regularity to these transactions and, again, it came out with a small error rate. When you look at the transactions, it is a way of looking at the systems. You look not only at the transactions; at the same time you look at the systems through which these transactions flow. We observed that in the six countries the systems were well constructed and we had few criticisms of them. These were observations from the auditors on the spot. What more can you do? I think that the whole administrative reform is going in a good direction. I am instructing my auditors to look much more into the systems, to see not only if the 24 standards of internal control are in place in Brussels but also in these countries. We are looking more and more into the systems and less into the transactions. Looking at the transactions was already, to a certain extent, to see the strength of the systems. However, we should be looking less at transactions and, more and more, to see if the standards of internal control are in place. I will not speak of single audit. It is evident that, as a Court, you cannot do everything. You must therefore look at the internal control systems. You must use the work of other auditors in the internal audit service, or the audit capacities of the DGs concerned, if they are doing their job it means that they are themselves ensuring that the internal control of all the DGs are working well. We are then going in the right direction and, with 10 or 15 auditors, you can do the work to see if it is okay. That is the way we are going. It is like a tanker—you have to move at Commission level. Even in the Court, however, there are auditors who are 50 years old, who for 10 or 12 years have become used to working in transaction-based systems. You now have to say to them, "Go more to a system-based audit".

Q180 Lord Tomlinson: You posed this question of budgetisation to us. Looking at the figures we have already received, if you look at the EDF about 90 per cent of the budget is poverty-focused. You get to the EU budget and only about 45 per cent is poverty-focused—because you get these wider, more confusing political objectives. Are you satisfied that you will be able to measure the cost-effectiveness of aid as clearly for the EDF operations that you do now were they to be budgetised? If you look at the paper *Reform of the Management of EU External Assistance* that has been produced by the Commission, although they make great play of the fact that they are improving the latent commitments—payments are getting closer to commitments—the cumulative figure is still getting bigger each year. The excess of commitments over payments year by year since 1999 has been 2.6 billion, 3.2 billion, and then 0.26 and 0.76. But it has now gone up provisionally in 2003 to two billion again. How will you measure cost-effectiveness in a way that will persuade the European taxpayer that that is an improvement in the efficient use of their resources?
Mr Reynders: I think that the best thing that can happen for the European taxpayer is more transparency, simpler procedures, and I am convinced that budgetisation will be tremendous cost-effective. Because you budgetise ACP aid—and if today it is 90 per cent poverty-reduction targeted—then it will stay that way. This should not change because you budgetise. I have thought a lot about budgetisation recently, because we have said in the Court's last annual report that budgetisation could be a solution for the problems we have mentioned. It was difficult to get that through the Court. The Court took the position previously that we should not be involved in politics and we should not speak about budgetisation. I understand that position by a lot of colleagues but, the more I think about it, the more I have said, "Please let's budgetise"—for all the reasons mentioned in this document but also for the people in the field. There are presently two accounting systems: one for the General Budget and one for EDFs. In the field, there are two kinds of procedures, regulations and guidelines. It is a great deal of work. If you look at the tables of statistics in

the recently published annual report for 2003—that is, the annual report on the Commission's external aid—they are very complex, because all the time they have to add the General Budget with ACP aid. And that is only one aspect of it. It is not only at delegation level. There is a dual system, which is at the root of the high costs in the delegation. Not only that but the ACP countries themselves have to have the capacity to deal with two systems. Please let us abolish one of these systems if we can.

Q181 Lord Tomlinson: If you budgetise it, with that accumulation of 10 billion in the last five years of commitments, will not a large number of those commitments just be cancelled?
Mr Reynders: That is a political problem.

Q182 Lord Tomlinson: But that will be the budget rules.
Mr Reynders: Not necessarily. You can budgetise those 10 billion of resources not committed yet. From the point of view of administrative efficiency, this would be the best solution.

Q183 Lord Tomlinson: If they are not committed.
Mr Reynders: As I see it, you should not create a tenth EDF. From a legal point of view, the ninth EDF runs until March 2005. However, if you look at the financial protocol, it says at the same time that it covers the period up to 2007. There is a legal discussion there. It runs to 2007 because it has taken up a lot of outstanding money from the seventh and eighth EDFs. So, even from a legal point of view and the need to create a tenth EDF from March 2005 onwards, you could say, "Why should we do that? We know that we will budgetise from 1 January 2008. Why not extend the existing ninth EDF for two years?". This should be discussed with the ACP partners, of course. For me, however, that is a logical approach—but who am I? It is an auditor's point of view—or of someone who really wants to diminish costs. This would be a logical approach to the problem.

Q184 Chairman: You talk about legality and regularity. That is not the same thing as quality of spend. To what extent are you checking on the effectiveness of aid in your operation, or do you leave that to the evaluation service?
Mr Reynders: We have looked to sound financial management of the EDFs. The question of effectiveness then arises. We did that with for infrastructure expenses of EDF and we reached the result that effectiveness could be improved.

Q185 Chairman: So in general terms you are very positive about regularity and legality, but you cannot actually say very much about effectiveness.

Mr Reynders: No.

Q186 *Chairman:* That would have to be for the evaluation people.
Mr Reynders: Not only, also for the court.

Q187 *Chairman:* Perhaps we could now have five minutes on the other half of your presentation?
Mr Reynders: Many things have already been tackled.

Q188 *Chairman:* You are content? You do not have anything else that you wanted to add on ACP or budgetisation?
Mr Reynders: I will just look at my notes. On question (b), when you make a comparison between ACP countries and Bangladesh and India, this is a long story. I think that you are right—there is more help going, but it is not the real problem that we are facing today. I will pass over that. Also, EDF and EU aid is only a small part of the overall aid for these countries.

Q189 *Lord Lea of Crondall:* You mentioned earlier in your presentation that you rely tremendously on the quality of the administrations of the recipient countries. I think you said something like that.
Mr Reynders: No, only for direct budgetary aid, which is a new instrument that is developing fast. All EDF help is going through the EDF framework, based on a national authorising officer. So you need the input of national administration. What I was saying, however, was that, for this new instrument—direct budgetary aid—this does not go, so to speak, through the EDF framework; it is money that is given to the national budget of the country concerned, and then it takes the form of expenditure following the rules and norms of the national budgets.

Q190 *Lord Lea of Crondall:* Yes, but you cannot follow that in the same way.
Mr Reynders: No, we cannot follow that. We do not want to follow that so to speak.

Q191 *Lord Lea of Crondall:* Why do you not want to?
Mr Reynders: Because it is impossible. I think that this is an important question for the future, not directly linked to the ACP group but a topic on which we are making a special report to be published at the beginning of next year. I discussed it at length in the last CoCoBu meeting with Commissioner Nielson. It is a very important topic because the Commission, before giving that direct aid, must have a picture of, let us say, the quality of management of these national budgets. The Commission cannot do this alone. It works on it with all the donors worldwide—also with DfID. It is working with the World Bank and IMF. This is good, because you must have a co-ordinated approach to it by all the donors. To have a view on the quality of management of public funds in these countries involves an enormous amount of work—because it goes from making the budget through to the control, two, three or four years later, by the supreme audit institution in each country. To analyse and to have a good idea of what are the control systems in all of these countries—not merely theoretically on paper but also in reality—involves enormous work. I think that the donor community has to work together to get all the information—and only one piece of information from all the countries, because it is impossible for countries to give different information to DfID from that which they give to the EU and to the World Bank.

Q192 *Lord Lea of Crondall:* Do you think that you could have a staff of auditors for some of these countries or something?
Mr Reynders: They are working on that, to have a co-ordinated approach. I think that it is working relatively well, because all of the donors are aware that, alone, they are not able to have good insight into the quality of management of public funds in these countries. It is impossible; it is too complicated. I think that, for once, there should be a co-ordinated approach.

Q193 *Baroness Northover:* You say that under EDF there is greater flexibility. Could you give me an example of what kinds of projects are now in place which would not be in place under budgetisation?
Mr Reynders: I cannot answer that. I have no concrete examples. There are many, however. Under all the EDFs, you have seven or eight years in which *de facto* to commit, and you can pay endlessly. There are still resources in the sixth EDF that are not yet committed, 15 years later. That is what I call flexibility—and there is no sanction. But the money is not lost; the money is there. Since you know that the money is there, there is no impetus to take the necessary decisions to take up the money.

Q194 *Baroness Northover:* It is not a particularly useful flexibility?
Mr Reynders: As I have said, there are advantages and disadvantages to this flexibility. At the beginning, I was for this flexibility. If you had not had it, these countries would have picked up less money than they have. When the ninth EDF was created in March 2000, it was about 15 billion, with 10 billion coming from the previous EDFs. Ten is the difference between what was available and what has been paid.

This 15 billion and 10 billion, making 25 billion, should have been used from March 2000 to March 2005, legally, or March 2007 *de facto*. Seven years, and 25 billion divided by seven makes 3.5 billion.

Where are we today? We are far from 3.5 billion a year. You have no pressure to commit and to pay.

Chairman: Thank you very much for coming, Mr Reynders, and for giving us your time.

MONDAY 2 FEBRUARY 2004

Present	Bowness, L (Chairman)	Northover, B
	Lea of Crondall, L	Powell of Bayswater, L
	Maclennan of Rogart, L	Tomlinson, L

Examination of Witnesses

Mr Peter Sedgwick, Vice-President, and Mr Dominique de Crayencour, Director of Inter-Institutional Affairs and Brussels Office, European Investment Bank, examined.

Q195 Chairman: May I first of all thank you very much indeed for agreeing to see the sub-committee and give evidence? You will know, I think, the nature of our inquiry into EU development aid and assistance. We are looking at many things, including the reforms that have been made and the position of development aid post the Constitutional Treaty. I think that perhaps none of those things are matters that we would particularly want to press you upon, unless you want to express a particular opinion, having seen our call for evidence. What we would like to do is to hear from you what the European Investment Bank does, what scope there is for it playing a part in development, perhaps replacing general development aid through loans to some of the other countries—some of the countries that are perhaps not amongst the poorest. Before we ask questions, however, maybe you would like to say something to us generally.

Mr Sedgwick: Thank you very much. I am very happy to welcome you here to the EIB. I think that it is possibly the first time—or the first time that I am aware of—that a United Kingdom parliamentary committee has met in these offices, and you are most welcome. I was working out today that it is exactly 20 years since my first appearance before a House of Lords' committee on an extremely controversial occasion, when we were arguing about the nature of industrial policy. My appearance was followed up by an even more rebarbative one by Nigel Lawson. But I am a changed person since then, and I am hoping that we will not repeat those disagreements! I was going to inflict an opening statement upon you. But, given the hour and the fact that it would be better if you asked me questions and I answered the ones to which you actually wanted the answers, perhaps I may make a few points to begin with. Then I and, more to the point, my colleague Dominique de Crayencour who heads our Brussels office and is the main point of contact between the EIB and the Commission, will try to answer them for you. If by any chance we cannot answer specific ones—because this is a detailed area—then we are quite happy to send the material on to you afterwards. Just a few points to start off with. The EIB is a policy-driven bank. The policies that drive it are those that are agreed by the Council and the Commission. So we are rather different to other multilateral lenders like the World Bank, which have a big role in agreeing their own policies and getting them agreed by shareholders and their directors. To a large extent ours are given by others. The second thing I would like to say is that around 90 per cent of our lending is within the European Union. That percentage will go up to around 95 per cent on 1 May, when the acceding countries become members of the Union. Nevertheless, we do have very important lending programmes outside the Union and we have tried to set those out in the table. You may want to ask us about those. I would particularly draw your attention to the Cotonou facility, which is a new way in which the EIB is operating in the ACP countries, and particularly in Africa. The other mandate which has had a tremendous amount of attention recently is the Mediterranean, the FEMIP, where our operations have grown significantly and where the intention is for us to lend about two billion euros a year from now on, mixed with grant aid—some of which comes from the Commission. The next point I would like to make is that, particularly outside the Union, we have a wide range of instruments that are available, ranging from equity to senior debt. We lend on very competitive terms, because we have a very strong AAA rating, and we have relatively small operating costs. We have a staff, for the volume of business that we do, of around 1,100 people. This, by the standards of multilaterals, is very low indeed. So the margin we have to add to on-lend is, by most standards, comparatively low. The next and final point I would make is on co-operation. There are all sorts of strands to this rather general issue. We obviously co-operate with the Commission, not only in terms of devising policies, but quite often in the operations themselves. We co-operate with other multilateral lenders. We never finance 100 per cent of anything. We quite often co-lend or co-finance with the World Bank, the EBRD, or whoever the international financial institution happens to be that is interested in that particular project. We also have a very well-developed policy of co-operation with other financial institutions, whether they be national lenders like, say, CDC in the United Kingdom, or private banks. Those are the things I have said at the beginning, but I am open to your questions now.

Q196 *Lord Maclennan of Rogart:* We were reminded earlier that the EBRD does not have to give direct consideration to issues of good governance, whereas the European aid-giving institutions do—explicitly spelled out again in the Cotonou Agreement. Do you have good governance considerations in mind in looking at loans, or are they raised by the partners with whom you are operating?

Mr Sedgwick: No, they are very important principles for us—good governance ones. We have a variety of policies, the aim of which is to ensure that there is good governance for the projects that we lend on. We have anti-fraud policies; we have very strong procurement policies; we would look at a particular loan project, to see whether that is managed in a proper way. You name it, we have to have some scrutiny of it.

Q197 *Lord Powell of Bayswater:* I see that your current lending is expressed in terms of a ceiling of 1.7 billion for the next four years and in your brochure that you talk about 3.9 billion from 2003 to 2007. Do you actually expect to lend that much or is it just a ceiling?

Mr Sedgwick: You are talking about the Cotonou facility there.

Q198 *Lord Powell of Bayswater:* Yes.

Mr Sedgwick: I think that "both" would be my answer to that question.

Q199 *Lord Powell of Bayswater:* Will there be sufficient viable projects coming forward from the ACP countries to make it possible for you to lend on terms that you would accept, to actually devote that amount of money to them?

Mr Sedgwick: We very much hope so and we are working towards that, but of course the previous question is relevant. There are certain parts of Africa in particular where we have no projects in the pipeline at the moment because of events in those countries. It is perfectly obvious which ones they are. So there is that problem. But we would hope—and maybe I am too optimistic here—that there are certain areas where we have considered projects, which perhaps we would not have done a few years ago. Nigeria is an example. That could go wrong or it could be even more successful than we are expecting at the moment, but certainly it would be our hope that we could have operations there that met all our criteria.

Q200 *Lord Tomlinson:* I want to refer to the same sheet. I have two questions, one a very simple one. Why do you call it "Own resources"? The word has connotations in the context of the European Union

budget. I presume that this is just the expenditure that you are prepared to raise on the capital markets. The more substantive question, however, is about the figure against the Cotonou Partnership Agreement—again, this 1.7 billion. What is it proposed to be used for and why is it necessary to have it, when there is such a huge under-committed resource available to the ACP countries in the ninth EDF and the previous EDFs? Something like 10 billion of uncommitted appropriations in the ninth and previous EDFs.

Mr Sedgwick: The main thing we tried to do with this table was to keep it on one page, so you must forgive us if we took for granted a certain amount of jargon. The "Own resource" has nothing to do with own resources in the EU budget. It is to do with the bank's resources. We have capital from our shareholders, which are the Member States. We are an inter-government institution; there is no Commission shareholding. Like other international financial institutions, a certain proportion is paid in. We borrow on the capital markets and we also have a gearing ratio of 250, which is higher than some of those IFIs which lend mainly to risk areas. So that is what the "Own resources" are. The rest are other funds that are entrusted to us to use. The second question goes a little beyond what I can answer. I cannot give you any sort of authoritative answer on policies to do with the EU aid budget, but it is a longstanding policy that, where there are viable projects, it is sensible for those to be financed from loans and other forms of finance, and we are the chosen instrument for that within the European Union.

Q201 *Lord Tomlinson:* I am interested in why they should come to you when there is this uncommitted appropriation that seems to be available as grant rather than as loan.

Mr de Crayencour: Part of the answer is that there is not the same purpose, the same objective, and the same activity under EIB lending and under the granting of subsidies by the budget. For the EIB part, every envelope in the past has been used. In this particular case of Cotonou, it is now 100 per cent concentrated on private sector operations—which presumably, although I am not a specialist, is not the case for Community budget money. So the lack of utilisation of the budget money—that I do not know and on which I could not comment—is not necessarily linked to a good utilisation of bank money and the respective agreements.

Q202 *Lord Powell of Bayswater:* Could I ask what proportion, very roughly, of applications or proposals from the ACP countries you accept? How many do you agree to?

2 February 2004   Mr Peter Sedgwick and Mr Dominique de Crayencour

Mr de Crayencour: Compared to the requests?

Q203 *Lord Powell of Bayswater:* Yes. Are you taking 10 per cent or 50 per cent?
Mr Sedgwick: It depends what you call a request. Before a formal appraisal process starts, quite a lot of water flows under the bridge. I think that it would be quite difficult to give you a quantitative answer to that.

Q204 *Lord Powell of Bayswater:* There was a time, 20 years ago, when you were certainly only able to accede to a very small number. Do you think that proportion is increasing?
Mr de Crayencour: I think that the answer is on what you consider a request, because we have so many letters, telephone calls, or preliminary dossiers that are very quickly disregarded—if you counted them all as requests, then probably the rejection rate is high. If you only look at the cases where we have thoroughly appraised projects then, because we do not do that and spend the money without preliminary assurances that this is reasonably well constructed, the rejection will obviously be much less. I do not think we have ready-to-wear statistics on this and it would be difficult to build them actually, for that reason.
Mr Sedgwick: There is a perception that operating in the private sector in ACP will be very difficult. So it would not be surprising if the proportion turned out to be lower—if you could measure it.

Q205 *Lord Lea of Crondall:* I think it is fair to say that the European Investment Bank has the best feel of the private sector of the EU institutions, because in some cases you have a minority involvement with some financing facility which has private banks and other equity, long-term loans and so on. Last summer, there was an American study on Africa. You are probably aware of it, but some quite distinguished people concluded that Africa's biggest problem was that they only had 1 per cent of world capital flows. They made some recommendations, pointing out that the big take-offs in the world—like China at the moment, India, and so on—were when there were big surges forward in private investment. That is what Africa does not have, and there is the size of the markets, their being split up, *et cetera*. However, I recall that when we had a debate on Africa in the House of Lords quite a few people advocated that there ought to be an equivalent European high-level study of what would be more conducive for more capital flows into Africa. I would like to put that to you. Would that not be a good idea—OECD perhaps do this as well—to find out what will, if not replace some development aid, make sure that we do not struggle on in this sort of glue that we seem to be in all the time in Africa, and find some

way in which there can be a clear EU strategy to promote private investment in Africa? Have I missed that there is a study or a document like that, which does have a policy that is equivalent to the American one? It does seem to me that this has a great relevance to the complementarity with development aid, which some people do not think is going anywhere at the moment.
Mr Sedgwick: Several thoughts come to mind. Certainly any study which helps one understand how to encourage FDI in somewhere like Africa would be worthwhile. Just to put it in context, the vast bulk of FDI is between developed countries: between the United Kingdom and Europe and the US. Even in those economies that have taken off, it is a relatively small proportion of the FDI in the world. I think that we are conscious of the problems of FDI. The whole problem of trying to increase the amount of private sector activity in Africa is essentially the same one. You come up against problems of governance and problems of whether the private sector is sufficiently robust to cope with this. You come up against the issue, which has been a really important one in the Far East, of making sure that economies are really open to international trade and, if they are not, then it will be quite difficult for FDI. No, I think that we would look—talking from an EIB standpoint—for partners in the private investment projects that we appraise and support. If there was an element of FDI with that, that would be most welcome. That has been something that we have tried to do in other areas. If you look at the EIB involvement, for instance, in the former Communist economies of eastern Europe—whether they are entering the Union immediately or not—we have certainly tried, with our lending activity there, to encourage FDI projects, or an element of FDI in them as much as possible. We will do the same thing in the Mediterranean region, and we will do it, if we can, in Africa as well. Whatever study one has, however, one comes up against these hard issues of governance, the private sector, and opening the economies to international trade.

Q206 *Chairman:* There is criticism that too much of EU aid goes to middle-income countries, not the poorest countries, and the "near abroad". In our call for evidence we asked a question which was: whilst recognising that the Union would want to continue some assistance to such countries for various reasons, could assistance be provided in ways that would free up grant money for low-income countries by placing more emphasis on loans and technical assistance from the EIB? That is a question we posed in our call for evidence. How realistic is it? How would you answer that particular question?

Mr Sedgwick: In a way, I would not. I think that it is a policy decision for Member States and the Commission to make, if they want to transfer grant aid away from middle-income countries and to replace that by loan finance. It is not a decision for us to take. What I do perceive is that in any policy decision taken at a European Union level there is more than one objective. There is obviously the objective of relieving poverty where it is greatest; but there are also policies, which are becoming more developed and more explicit, towards neighbours. The whole drive towards increasing the bank's activity in the Mediterranean region is driven by considerations of that sort as much as by those of poverty. One can see the same thing happening again on the eastern boundary of the European Union. We in the bank expect policymakers always to be concerned with economic development in neighbouring states. May I make one other observation on that? I anticipated this question would come, so I spent this morning having a look at a list of countries that are IDA-eligible. Those are the poorest countries that are eligible for concessionary terms from the World Bank. That list is not the same as it was 10 or 15 years ago. For instance, there are some countries in south-east Europe which are now IDA-eligible after the ravages of war: talking from memory, Albania, Bosnia-Herzegovina, and Serbia-Montenegro. That sometimes is seen by some as not an area where grant aid is a great priority, but there are IDA-eligible countries there. I think that there are no IDA-eligible ones amongst the FEMIP countries, but there are other considerations which have led policymakers to ask us to operate there as well, alongside grant aid.

Mr de Crayencour: There is one other point, which is that in most of these countries where we operate we probably find no investment-grade country. So that there is indeed a potential gap between a poor country, where you would go for poverty alleviation, and an investment-grade country where simple banking loans would suffice. What we have seen so far, and I am not making a policy judgment, but just a pragmatic observation, is that the blend of budget resources with bank loans, in whatever form—and we have plenty of forms to blend a bit of a grant element with loans—is actually a pragmatic answer to these areas where you do not have investment grade.

Q207 *Lord Maclennan of Rogart:* I wonder if you could explain what the mechanisms are under which the mandated budgeted funds are allocated to the bank. Does it vary year on year? Is it related to projects? Is it agreed in advance? How does it work?

Mr de Crayencour: The mandates—

Q208 *Lord Maclennan of Rogart:* The funds that are not raised on the capital market but that are delivered by the governments—is that a variable figure year on year? Is it a programme covering many years? Is it project-related? What determines whether it fluctuates up or down? How significant is it as a proportion of the total expenditure?

Mr de Crayencour: First of all, there are two different situations. Regarding the ACP Cotonou Agreement, you are right to refer to government funds, because this is funded—or guaranteed in this case—for the year's EDF by the Member States. This is not the case for all the other mandates. I draw your attention to the fact that this is funded by the Community budget, not by the Member States' budgets. That said, the mechanism is the same.

Q209 *Chairman:* It is guaranteed by the Community budget.

Mr de Crayencour: And funded by the EIB budget. When there is a grant element attached—and in many cases there is, like in the FEMIP in the Mediterranean where there is budget money also managed by EIB—in all cases, whether coming from the Member States' budgets or the Community budget, they are pluri-annual envelopes. So the mandate itself is based on the number of years. You can see here[1], "Period of validity". The year-by-year allocation of the amount is very much an operational question of EIB programmes: taking into account a smooth distribution over time, so as not to have a peak in one year and no follow-up in the next year. But these are very much operational considerations.

Q210 *Lord Maclennan of Rogart:* And as a proportion of the whole?

Mr de Crayencour: This is difficult to answer. On average, probably it varies from region to region. If I take the ACP Cotonou for instance, we see here that we have from the EDF 2.2 billion—that is, from the Member States' budgets, compared to 1.7 billion of EIB own resources. But this will not at all be the same in other areas. In the Mediterranean, roughly—and I am not sure of the figure—something like 250 million of grants coming from the Community budget are allocated over the period where we will do some 6.5 billion. So you see that the proportions are completely different, and probably in line with the idea that the richer the countries the less the grant element.

Mr Sedgwick: For the Mediterranean we will be seeking—in fact, we have already said we will, as part of the enhancing of this facility that was agreed at the end of last year—extra grant resources from Member

---

[1] On the table handed out during the meeting

State governments, if we can persuade them to let us have them, to enable projects to be prepared.

Q211 Lord Maclennan of Rogart: Can you see any secular changes in the Community funding of that kind?
Mr Sedgwick: Not that I can mention at the moment.

Q212 Lord Tomlinson: I was quickly glancing at the document on financing in the ACP. Bearing in mind you were saying that these are nearly all budgets in the private sector, how would you apply the principle of interest subsidy in that area?
Mr de Crayencour: I draw your attention to the fact that there were interest subsidies in the various Lomé Conventions; they are no longer in the Cotonou Agreement. That is the first point. The second is that—because of fair competition and market rules—they were used systematically as incentives, or technical assistance-type elements for the intermediary institutions, or for the government institutions that were promoting the projects, but never as a direct benefit for a private beneficiary.

Q213 Lord Powell of Bayswater: What proportion of the projects you finance in the ACP go bad? Just in very rough terms.
Mr de Crayencour: In numbers?

Q214 Lord Powell of Bayswater: Preferably a proportion of your total outlay on the ACP.
Mr de Crayencour: I would have to calculate. I just do not know.

Q215 Lord Powell of Bayswater: Is it fairly common or is it unusual? Presumably you do a very thorough appraisal.
Mr de Crayencour: The only answer that I know I can give, without checking figures, is that you have countries getting into trouble and all the projects in the relevant countries following these troubles. That is a fairly standard scheme. Outside that pattern, however, I would need to check. I really do not know.
Mr Sedgwick: The way we try to answer that question, or the way we do answer that question, is by having evaluation reports from an independent evaluation unit, which are prepared for the management of the bank, discussed at the board of directors, and then put up on our website. It is a relatively recent development. It has been going for four or five years. We have just had one on the ALA mandate, which will go up on the website quite soon—I am not sure when. We would try to cover all the operations of the bank over not too long a period.
Mr de Crayencour: There was one on the ACP about a year ago, I think.

Mr Sedgwick: If one were to look at those—they are quite long reports, but then evaluation is a serious business—it is not so many per cent are okay and so many are not. There is a range of things that can be other than expected. Some of those unforeseen developments are not quite so serious; others are quite serious. It is a more complicated business. But, no, one has to face up to the fact that—

Q216 Lord Powell of Bayswater: Presumably there are some bad loans and you have to turn to your guarantors to get restitution.
Mr Sedgwick: Yes, but there I make a distinction between the country going wrong and the projects going wrong. If you have a country which basically suspends all servicing of the debt, it does not necessarily mean that the project has gone wrong. If you hang in there with patience, you can regularise the position once the country has come back onto the rails. But at any one moment there will be some that are not servicing their debt. They are all familiar ones to you—Côte d'Ivoire, countries like that.

Q217 Lord Lea of Crondall: There seemed to be a sense of fatalism in your tone of voice when answering a previous question I asked about Africa. Perhaps I may follow that up. In some parts of the world, such as south-eastern Europe, you are part of the umbrella structure—called the Stability Pact, I think. Do you find that you have some particular comparative advantage as an institution, in terms of banks in these countries, helping within the banking system in some sense, or is that an illusion of my mind? One way into the system in some of these countries may be to improve the quality of the people that could be medium-term bank lenders. This may help with the rather despairing tone, which some of us certainly find in all of these discussions, about how to help change in Africa. Every project that comes up seems to be very hard work indeed. Is there anything that could help? For example, I refer to one of the notes that we have—I think that Tim wrote it, but he will forgive me if I quote from it. Should there be a new AU-EU interface like the Stability and Growth Pact? Should there be some new umbrella attempt to get this together in a different way?
Mr Sedgwick: There are a number of points there. First, I would not regard myself as a fatalist on this at all. As you have mentioned the Stability Pact, perhaps I can start with that. The Stability Pact covered south-east Europe. It is one of the mechanisms for helping the former Communist states and the former Yugoslavia. You mention in particular co-operation with banks. I would say that the co-operation with banks in eastern Europe in general has been very successful. It is difficult to generalise but, after the change in systems from a centrally planned one to what we have now, many of

the banks were in an absolutely terrible state. There have been a variety of policies and actions which have led to those banks being strengthened. You have a lot of shareholdings from western European banks, which have helped to improve the capital structure and the management of those banks. As an institution, we have had a very strong policy, where we can, to co-operate with the local banks, particularly to lend to SMEs—which is a sector which was almost nonexistent 10 or 15 years ago— and we would do the same for small infrastructures. So that has been quite successful, especially in those countries that are just about to join the Union. One hopes that there will be a similar process in south-east Europe for those countries of the former Yugoslavia and the surrounding states there. Of course it is a big jump from there to Africa. There is no point in denying it. You could say that I am a fatalist, but I think that one has to be realistic on this. It is quite difficult to get banking intermediaries in Africa with which to co-operate: either as co-financiers or as institutions to act for us and to distribute loan finance in small amounts, which we cannot do because we do not have the people on the ground. However, that is one of the main objectives. It will be high on our list of priorities for the Cotonou facility. So while not underestimating the difficulty, I would not describe myself as fatalist and I hope that I did not sound as if I was.

Q218 *Lord Lea of Crondall:* Could you add a word on AU-EU in that context?
Mr Sedgwick: I am not quite sure what you mean. Do we need a new institutional structure to achieve these objectives? My first—

Q219 *Lord Lea of Crondall:* The pretensions of the AU are to be, as the years go by, like the EU. And, all right, it is comparing apples with oranges, but that does prima facie come up as a topic.
Mr Sedgwick: The EU will certainly need a dialogue with this structure, if it takes off. I would hesitate before putting new mechanisms in place, however. I emphasise—and maybe I would, being from the EIB—we have the financing arrangements and we have the structures there. The job now is to try to put them in place on the ground where the minimum conditions exist in those countries. I do not disparage higher-level dialogues and arrangements, but our job is one of trying to make what has already been decided effective.

Q220 *Baroness Northover:* I have been looking at what you say here about financing for health and education. In particular, it says that you can support projects in various countries—African, Caribbean, and so on. I wondered what kinds of things you were lending for there. Presumably these would be for, say,

a university medical school or something—which is going to, as it were, pay its way. It will not come in the form of aid. I am wondering what opportunities there would be, great though the need would be in terms of health and education in some of these developing countries.
Mr Sedgwick: It is very difficult to answer that without getting out a list of requests that have come to us and seeing which ones are viable. To change area, to try to give you a flavour of the answer, we have started trying to lend for health and education in the Mediterranean region. There are some quite interesting projects that have come to us and have gone through the decision-making bodies. I am thinking of one, an IT project linked to education in Jordan. In various parts of North Africa one has similar projects, either that are in the pipeline or could be so. With Cotonou, it is a little more difficult to give you a precise feel. However, provided the project was viable, we would certainly be very sympathetic to projects—whether primary healthcare or hospitals, or on the education side at basically all the levels of education. But it is not going to be easy. The reason I gave the example for the one in Jordan was not just because I could remember it, which I could, but because I remember that, when it came to us within the last year, I was very surprised to see that we had got that far that soon—to have a well-articulated project of that sort which we could agree.

Q221 *Chairman:* You and your colleague have made the case for a blend of grant and loan to middle-income countries, and I understand that. But this is clearly not a view that the Department for International Development share, because they have argued and put on record that they would like 70 per cent of the EU external budget to go to the poorest countries. That would effectively mean a shift of two billion euros, or thereabouts, from the middle-income countries to the poorest countries. My question is, would the EIB have the financial capacity to replace that two billion euros of grant to the middle-income countries in terms of borrowing? Would your board of directors feel it was sensible to increase its exposure to the Moroccos, the Brazils, *et cetera?* In other words, although you have pointed out that the amount of grant that is provided to these countries is a matter for the Member States—it is a collective decision—nonetheless, if DfID could increase its exposure to the Moroccos, the Brazils, *et cetera?* In other words, although you have pointed by EIB lending, would this be feasible from your point of view and from the board of directors' point of view?
Mr Sedgwick: I have a number of thoughts on that. First of all, for reasons that I gave earlier, I do not think that you can press too far the idea of replacing

2 February 2004   Mr Peter Sedgwick and Mr Dominique de Crayencour

grant with loan, because a lot of the grant is not financing investment projects. Clearly, whatever the form our intervention takes, whether it be all the way from equity to senior debt, it has to be for a project on which we can get some return. DfID have to win the hearts and minds of other Member States if they want to pursue that agenda. We would have to see, if it was wished to combine that with an increase in EIB loan activity of investment projects, how feasible that was, given all the other demands on our resources—of all sorts, both in the European Union and outside. The only thing I would say is that in the difficult areas, which are not confined to those which are the poorest in the world, you do need some blending of concessional finance with the instruments that we can offer. We have just been talking about health and education. Okay, that was a question about Africa and Cotonou, but I think that there would be limits in the near term on what one could do in the Mediterranean region, which is one that is middle-income, without some grant money for project preparation, and maybe for some interest rate subsidy or upfront grant as well to mix with it. It is going to be quite difficult to pursue that.

Q222 Chairman: For technical assistance you would need it, but that would be quite modest. The World Bank would take the same view, but it would be technical assistance money; they would not be putting grant money into projects in Morocco or Tunisia.

Mr de Crayencour: But essentially—if I understand correctly—the two billion you were talking about are the two billions of grant aid granted today by the Commission under their programmes for, as Peter said, other purposes than investment projects. So it is not only a kind of money substituted by another kind of money but also a kind of action substituted by another kind of action. Can you replace all the necessary education, training, current costs in ministries, to organise themselves—whatever they do, and that I do not know—by hard investment and go away with that? I do not know what the impact would be, but I stress that it is not only the kind of financial resource, but also the kind of action that would be fundamentally changed.

Mr Sedgwick: If we just take the Mediterranean facility, the grant from the EU budget at the moment is used for interest subsidies for the environment; it is for technical assistance, and it is for risk capital. In other words, for those forms of intervention which are of a more risky nature, and you cannot expect to do without that type of blending of grant with it.

Chairman: Thank you, Mr Sedgwick. We are very grateful to you and Mr de Crayencour for coming and giving evidence to us this evening, particularly since it is getting rather late. We do appreciate it very much indeed.

Mandate	Guaranteed by	Own Resources Lending Ceiling (EURm)	Period of validity
ACP African, Caribbean and Pacific countries (Cotonou Partnership Agreement)	Member States	1,700	01.03.2000–01.03.05
Mandates 2000 of which:	Community	19,460	
South Eastern Neighbours		9,185	01.02.2000–31.01.07
Mediterranean Partner Countries MED		6,520	01.02.2000–31.01.07
Asia and Latin America ALA		2,480	01.02.2000–31.01.07
Republic of South Africa RSA		825	01.02.2000–31.01.07
Turkey (Special Action Programme)		450	14.12.2000–14.12.04
Russia*	Community	100	06.11.01–05.11.04
Pre–Accession facility		1,200	up to end 2004
Mediterranean Partnership Facility		1,000	up to 31.01.2007
EFTA Facility		1,700	

*The December 2003 European Council also decided to extend a new mandate of 500 million to Russia and Western New Independent States.

TUESDAY 3 FEBRUARY 2004

Present   Bowness, L (Chairman)   Northover, B
                 Lea of Crondall, L   Powell of Bayswater, L
                 Maclennan of Rogart, L   Tomlinson, L

Examination of Witness

MR MARC FRANCO, Deputy Director-General, EuropeAid Co-operation Office, examined.

Q223 Chairman: Mr Franco, can I first of all thank you very much indeed for seeing us. Very briefly, we are a sub-committee of the European Union Select Committee of the House of Lords that deals with foreign policy, defence and development, and we are doing this inquiry into European Union development aid and assistance. We are looking to try to evaluate how effective the reforms of the European Union development assistance have been and looking ahead to developments with development aid and foreign policy. We have also asked some witnesses how they view the proposals in the draft Constitutional Treaty as regards the position of development aid. We have also looked at enlargement, the future of the ACP grouping, and the question of budgetisation of the EDF. Perhaps, since we are here with you this morning at EuropeAid, we could concentrate on that element. A number of witnesses in Brussels, and in evidence to the Committee before we arrived, have emphasised the improvements that have been made in the delivery of EU aid. I think it is fair to say that we have had some criticisms from some recipients about a lack of meaningful consultation. Perhaps you could start this session by giving us your view of EuropeAid: how it works; whether you feel that it has been successful; answer some of the criticisms that are levelled; and tell us how you deal with the other players in the field—the DG Development, the DG External Relations.

Mr Franco: Let me try to reply to your question in as concise a way as possible, so that you have time for discussion. In order to understand what has happened over the last three or four years, we have to go about 10 years back. By the mid-1990s external assistance, managed by the Commission, was in a mess. Because we had, in a sense, overestimated our capacities and our ambitions, or our ambitions were too high for the capacities we had. I would say that this has been happening gradually over the last decades. However, it became very much so at the beginning of the 1990s with the fall of the Berlin Wall, when a number if important, big programmes were added to our workload—big programmes that were fundamentally different from what we had done before. We are talking there about transformation of the economy, reform of the economy, and other types of topics which we were not dealing with before. At that time I would say that we lacked policy; we had

inadequate structures; we had inadequate procedures; and we were understaffed. What has gradually happened since then, since the Commission realised that something was wrong—and this predates the setting up of EuropeAid, EuropeAid being a last part of a very strong reform process which started earlier—is that we have been trying to put all of these elements right. It is important to put that in perspective. It is not just that we here in EuropeAid have been particularly performing over the last years because we have increased our commitments: this is the end result of a process that happened earlier. What happens at the end of a project or a policy cycle is determined by what happens before. It is not just the guy sitting at the end who gets the blame or who gets the glory for performing better; it is the whole process that changes, and this has a lead time of four years before the improvements come out at the end. That is what has happened over this period. In terms of policy, yes, we have been working quite hard. The November 2000 joint conclusion of Council and Commission on development policy is a clear statement about this. It was the first time that we had an overall statement on development policy. Before that, we were a bit all over the place. We had something in Asia; we had something in Latin America; we had the ACP; we had MEDA, and so on. But in November 2000, for the first time, a development policy came out very clearly. As far as the translation of this policy into activities in programming and projects is concerned, we started getting our act together by what has been called the Relex reform—which is the reinforcement of the programming, the integration of the project cycle, and devolution. This allowed us to improve the structures. We have increased the staffing and we have got our procedures more or less harmonised. It means that the programming services of the Commission, which is Relex and Development, have been reinforced. The programming cycle has been reinforced. For the first time, all the development co-operation of the European Union is programmed in the same manner. There are Country Strategy Papers with a national indicative programme attached. This has been done in a standardised manner. A quality control group has been set up which has read through all the papers. As I said, for the first time there is a harmonised programming process. The quality of these papers has been appreciated also by the Member States, who formulate an opinion on this in the management committees. You can find all of these papers on the website, if you are interested. If your collaborators have not found them for you, I can give you the address. That is one part, therefore. In the process, we have improved the staffing level of Relex and, in particular, here in EuropeAid—which is the second part, namely the integration of the project cycle. We have brought all the elements, all the bits and pieces dealing with external assistance spread over the departments of the Commission, under one roof and that one roof is EuropeAid. You have our organisation chart, so you know that we have geographical directors. They sit together and work together. We make them work together in a horizontal manner by co-ordinating at the level of programming, or transport policies, and so on. We have a number of groups who work at a horizontal level to get people to work together. So that, across the borders of the various programmes, people learn to see what the synergies are, what they can learn from their neighbours, and so on. At the same time— and this was started before EuropeAid was set up— we have standardised our procedures. There used to be close to 50 different procedures in the context of management of the Commission development co-operation. Now we have a total of six or eight different types of tendering for the award of contracts. Standardising it all was an enormous job. It has simplified the life of the officials, but also, in particular, the life of our partners in the countries and of the economic operators in the private sector with whom we work. This exercise of bringing everything together, consolidating the harmonisation of procedures and approaches to sectors, particularly took place since 2001 when EuropeAid was set up. But, at the same time as this integration movement happened, we had immediately to start the devolution process. That was a very tricky business because, first of all, you have to make people feel that they are in a new organisation and have to do things differently; then, the next day, you say, "This is over, guys, because the delegation is now going to do it". I am still surprised that it has been as successful as it has been, in the sense that it has worked. We started the devolution process in 2001 and we had phases of de-concentration in 2001, 2002 and 2003. It will all be over and done with by the middle of this year. This has implied an enormous increase in staffing. I can give you the figures, if you do not have them. It has meant that we had to set up procedures; that we had to train people; that we had to enlarge the buildings, because the personnel has been multiplied by a factor of four or five in some cases. The whole organisation had to be different. It is not just a matter of having more people sitting in more buildings all over the world; it is also a matter of making these people feel

responsible for the programmes they are implementing; training them so that they know what they have to do and, at the same time, putting them in a position of responsibility—because they take the decisions on the contracting and the payments. At the same time in Brussels, where we have let go of the responsibility—and everybody who has gone through this process in Member States or in other organisations will know this—it is a kind of psychological trauma, when people see their "baby" going to a delegation. They handle a project; they do it here; they like their project—and then they are giving it to somebody who will, of course, handle it badly! It is a matter here, in-house, of changing the mindset of people. It has been a tremendous task of management, to ensure that people have their mind focused on a job—but a different job. Not the job of doing the project but of providing the backstop; growing into specialists, who can advise the delegations in the work they are doing. In the process that we are now setting up –apart from all the administrative hassle that it takes to recruit people, train them, and so on—it is a management task to make sure that the head of delegation takes up the responsibility and everybody starts to work differently. It is where the buck stops. They no longer have the option to send the dossier back to Brussels. They can still do it, but normally they are responsible for it. Here in Brussels, it is the task of management to make sure that the kind of "mother-in-law" attitude—looking over the delegation's shoulder, trying to correct, second-guess, criticise and so on— stops; that people take a positive attitude in the whole process and start advising rather than telling people what to do. This is what we have been doing over the last three or four years—slowly getting a situation right which had gone tremendously wrong in the mid-1990s. The results are there, if you look at the bottom line, in terms of the speeding-up of our commitments, contracts and payments. I can give you the figures, or there are some graphs that I can share with you. The quality improvement on the strategy papers is very clear. It is also clear on the project cycle. We have an increased awareness on quality in-house, here in EuropeAid as well as in the delegations. This is supported by what we call by the schematic networks, where people work together, share information. You can also consult it on the website. There is a quality support group website that everybody can check. This is not just theoretical papers. We are practical people. We are the "blue collar workers". The thinking goes on in the other places. We do the job. What we need is not big theory and deep analysis of all kinds of problems in the world. What we need is how to tackle them. That means practical guidelines about terms of reference, how to set up a project. You can find this on the website. This, if you like, is the collective wisdom of people working in-house. They put it on the website and share this information. There is all kinds of electronic mail going on. We have regular meetings with the delegations here in Brussels. They also do it at a regional level. I was in Bangkok two weeks ago and there were all kinds of networks growing up there, because the guys in the delegations say, "We have the same problem. You have found a solution. I am interested in your solution". They start circulating this information. This new culture of learning from others, sharing information, working together, and working on the synergies is really developing. We therefore have these schematic networks. Here we have what we call the office quality support group, because there is an inter-service quality support group to look at the programming papers. Here in-house we have quality support groups in each directorate where, under the responsibility of each director, each programme is looked at twice: first at the identification stage, where the specialists sit round the table and advise colleagues in all the delegations working on the project by saying, "Look at this. Talk to that person. Here is some interesting information. This is how you do it. This is how you don't do it". That is the first step. The second step is, before the project goes to the decision stage, it is also looked at by the same group, which then checks whether it is up to standard and can go to the management committees for approval. In terms of quantity, I think the bottom line proves that we have been delivering. In terms of quality, we are working on it. There are a number of indications that a new culture is growing. As to the question "Are we there yet?"—no, certainly not. There is still a lot of work to do in order to give the European Union, or the Commission as its representative and its manager, the place at the world level that the 10 per cent of ODA we constitute would justify. I would say that, about five years ago, we were rather the pariah of the development world. Nobody spoke to us. Nobody took us seriously. This is changing. Every day you feel that the mentality is changing. We have much better relations now, for instance, with the World Bank—if you take that as the litmus test of how serious you are in this business. There are daily contacts with Washington. Joint business with the World Bank has increased exponentially. I can give you figures if you are interested. In fact, on some topics the World Bank comes to talk to us rather than to a number of bilateral donors, because it knows that we are in that area and have the money and capacity available. I would quote the example of infrastructure, for instance. When, at its last board meeting, the World Bank launched its initiative on revitalising infrastructure, it first had a co-ordination meeting in Washington with all the development banks—plus the Commission. We are the only donor in that area that, particularly in Africa, still has a substantial amount of money, and we can make a

difference. Since then—and this has been consolidated in a conversation between Wolfensohn and Nielson—we have been working very actively with the World Bank on this issue of infrastructure, trying to see how we can blend in; how we can use our money, grant money together with the loan money, perhaps with private sector money, and in that way stimulate sector policies, co-financing—imaginative way of implementing projects, going beyond the pure grant financing that we have been doing historically. This is one example—there are a couple of others that I can quote—where it is clear that, because we have been going through this reform process, people are taking us seriously; we again have a place at the table and we are again being listened to. I repeat that we are not there yet: we still have a lot to do. In terms of the future, the Commission will next week approve the Financial Perspective. The Financial Perspective 2006–2011 covers everything. It covers structural funds, agriculture, et cetera. As you know, there is still a fight going on about whether the budget will be 1 per cent or 1.24 per cent of the GDPs, but the Commission will decide next week which paper it will adopt. In the perspective, however, there is a part on external assistance. The external assistance reform part has been drafted under the chairmanship of Commissioner Lamy. He chaired what was called the Peace Group. President Prodi had groups of Commissioners work together on themes, preparing the substance of this Financial Perspective. Not what are the figures, but what are we going to do when we get the money and do we have other policies. The *Financial Times* called it "the John Lennon group", because they were called Peace, Solidarity, and so on. Commissioner Lamy was chairing the Peace Group, with Patten, Nielson, Verheugen, and all the other Commissioners involved in one way or another with external relations. There are many messages coming out of it but, as far as our business is concerned, there are two very strong messages. First of all, we have to further integrate our instruments and focus them better, in order to implement the policies we want to implement *vis-à-vis* the Third World. It is a matter of getting the policies right, therefore, and getting the instruments more into line with what we want to accomplish with the policies. This will mean a further harmonisation and quality improvement of the work we are doing. Secondly—and this is the big challenge for the future—we have to play a more active role in the co-ordination of European Union assistance, i.e. in working together with the Member States. A lot of things have happened over the last years. Going back four, five or 10 years, Member States did not want to work together with the Commission; the Commission did not want to work together with Member States. A convergence of thinking and action is emerging very clearly at the moment. The second main point of the Lamy paper is that the

Commission has to play this role fully. Not by the Commission taking over from the Member States, however. It is not a matter of the Commission replacing the Member States. There is a complementarity between what one does at the EU level and what the Member States do. One figure indicates very clearly why this is an absolute necessity, and I would say that it is a real missed opportunity if we do not do it. The Commission itself represents about 10 per cent of ODA. I am talking in terms of 2002 figures because I have not seen those for 2003, which may be slightly different. We are the third aid donor in the world, after the US and Japan. The fourth and fifth are in fact Member States. The United Kingdom, France and Germany are fairly close to each other, but less than the Commission itself. It is 10 per cent but, if you take the European Union together, it is 50 per cent of ODA. With 50 per cent of ODA paid for by European taxpayers, emerging from the European Union, it is really a missed opportunity for the Third World and for Europe if we do not capitalise on this because, with 50 per cent, we could have a tremendous impact and influence if we wanted. First of all, however, we have to know what we want. That means we have to work further together with Member States on a common understanding of what development is about and what this policy is about. We have also gradually to intensify the working together at a programming level—i.e. how you translate these policies into programmes. Why do we have 16 strategy papers for Bangladesh—15 from the Member States and the sixteenth from the Commission? Why can we not have one common Country Strategy Paper at the European level? I am not saying that the Commission should draft all of it. This could be two or three Member States together and some could take the lead. There is no problem about this. If we all decide to work together and have a common purpose, it could happen in this way. We could have one strategy paper. If we have one strategy paper, then in this one strategy paper there would be something for everybody to pick up; but it would be done in a coherent form and we would be able to work on the complementarities of what one or the other could bring. To be honest, we are not so good in education. We have education programmes, but DfID is much better in education, and so are the Germans. Why? Because you have an education system that allows you to send the experts and share your own experience in education with other countries. We do not have an education system. Education is not part of the *acquis communautaire*. We do not have specialists. So why does not one of the other Member States take the lead in education? We could take the lead in transport. I think that we do more transport than all the rest together. We have an *acquis* there. We have something to bring to the table. At the level

of the programming, and of the complementarity, this could constitute a growing awareness and realisation of the possibilities of working together; and, at the implementation level, to the extent that countries want to continue to do things separately, okay—but at least let us harmonise our procedures so that we reduce what, in the jargon, is called the "transaction cost" for the beneficiary countries, so that they no longer have to work with 16 different procedures but, at least at the level of the European Union, with one procedure which is the one we all share. I have spoken for a long time about where we have come from, what we have done and where we are going, but that gives you the full picture. Now it is up to you to shoot at me!

Q224 *Lord Powell of Bayswater:* Mr Franco, thank you very much for that very passionate account of EuropeAid and what it has achieved. We have taken quite a lot of expert evidence in London, and it endorses the enormous improvements there have been. On the whole, I think that you would find much of the evidence we have taken very flattering. One or two questions arise from what you have said. First of all, how would you now compare the performance in delivery of development aid between EuropeAid and the best of the national bilateral aid programmes in Europe? Where would you rank it at this stage, recognising that you are in a process which, as you say, is not yet finished? Second, one area we have still heard some criticism of is evaluation: that the evaluation of programmes by the Commission is not yet as strong as it ought to be. The third question is, to what extent would budgetisation of the EDF make a practical difference to EuropeAid's performance? Would it make it more difficult? Would it simplify it? Would it, frankly, make very little practical difference—in the sense that, as far as you are concerned, it does not matter where the money comes from, as long as it comes? Perhaps we could start with those three questions.

Mr Franco: On the delivery side, I would say that, on average, we are probably still slower and, on average, possibly still not up to the top of the performance in the European Union. It is very clear. I would not be telling you even my own deep feelings if I said something different just because I sit here with my Commission hat on. Let me first comment on the quality. There are some areas where we are better. There are some areas, in particular in the area of budgetary systems, where we have more experience and where, in terms of identifying indicators, going for the results-oriented budgetary support, we have gone beyond what some of the Member States or what the World Bank are doing—and the World Bank also recognises that. The World Bank is still stuck with conditionalities which are input or process conditionalities, whereas everybody would agree—and the World Bank is the first to admit it, if you look at some of its own research—that this is not really effective. The only effective approach is that you support a policy of a government and, together with the government, you try to realise that policy. This is not a matter of ticking off a number of measures to be taken, but a matter of making sure that the policy is right and the budgetary resources flow together with the aid resources toward the realisation of results. In this area we are further advanced than any of the Member States, and this is a growing area. In EDF it is more than 30 per cent; in MEDA it must be about 20–25 per cent of our total assistance. In the other areas we are trying to put it on the agenda, because we feel that this is the future of development co-operation, and no one in the business would deny that. This hangs together with what is called "sector-wide approaches", which is also a form of budgetary support but for the development of a sector. As far as the mechanics and procedures are concerned, I would not say that we are further advanced but we are fairly well advanced, and working together very intensively with Member States and with the World Bank, for instance, on sector programmes in education and health. In that case, we are relying on the expertise of the others—because very often we do not have the expertise in-house—but bringing to the table the know-how of how to do it, as we use basically the same kind of technique in sector approaches as we do in macro-economics. This is an area in which we excel and where we feel that this is the right way to do development assistance. It is not by spreading around little projects all over the world, where you plant your flag. It is by supporting governments that have a policy, that know what to do, that have this policy agreed and discussed with donors, and that put their own resources and the donor resources to support the implementation of this policy. That is the only way to success. In many cases, the rest is boy-scoutism. So not as good in quality as the top, but nevertheless a number of areas where I think that we are really listened to and where we are amongst the top of what is available in the world. Regarding speed, we are probably slower, although it is not always easy to compare the speed of implementation. We have particularly heavy financial regulation and rules for budgetary management. That is the first problem. In the European Union we manage commitments as well as payments. DfID in fact concentrates on the management of disbursements. What is the difference? If you manage both, you make a commitment. There is money in the budget; you take the money out of the budget and say, "I'll decide a project". That is what we call the primary commitment. That is when the clock starts ticking. We start building up our backlog, or RAL—*reste à liquider*. The money is set aside for this project. People start working on the project, the terms of reference, and so on. They launch a tender. A year later, a contract is made. That is the secondary commitment. Then the money comes out of this pot

and is put on this contract. Afterwards, the payments take place. If you measure our performance, there is already one year that we can measure which DfID does not measure, because they do not make a commitment. The Germans do measure, and the Germans are slower than we are. If we look elsewhere—I think that it is your system, but it is also the system of the Dutch—they have a primary commitment, a secondary commitment and the first payment on the same day, because they only commit the money the moment they sign the contract. From an administrative point of view, that is the moment you need the money. So are we slower? Probably yes, but it is very difficult to compare on the figures. The figures that we put on the table are not necessarily worse than the figures of the Member States that have the same kind of procedures as we do. So do not compare us with DfID, because you do not have the same points of reference to compare. I take the point that, in general, we probably will be slower in making the concept. Why is that? First of all, we have heavy financial regulation that gives us very strict rules of transparency, equal access to information, and competition. On average, in a Member State, it is much easier to do a direct contract for the implementation of a project, or a kind of an informal consultation. In the United Kingdom, if you want to do something in an energy sector, DfID will know the three or four companies that can do it. They carry out an informal consultation and they take the best. The others do not scream, because they know that their turn will come next time and, indeed, everyone judges that this company is possibly the best one to do it. But this is the judgment of an official; it is not a procedure. When we have to do the same, at the beginning of the year we first have to say that we are possibly going to do a contract in this area—if it is a technical assistance contract. Before we even start working, we have to publish in the official journal and on the internet that, "Yes, it is now decided that we are going to do this contract. Who would like to be on the short list?". Companies then have a month in which to declare themselves and to be put on the short list. After a month we make the short list, which is then used for the tender. Our whole process is much longer. Whereas DfID could possibly do an energy consultation contract in technical assistance in a matter of two weeks, it takes us about three or four months before we are at the same stage. It is because we have requirements of transparency, which means that everybody should know what we are doing; equal access to information, which means that everyone is entitled to the same degree of information on what we are doing—all the possible contenders have to be taken into account potentially; and competition. We have to start comparing bids, and so on. Yes, we are slower, but it is the price of the transparency. If we did not do it, we would spend more time in court than in doing contracts. Whenever we do something with a particular country, there are 14 others that start screaming. Okay, we live with that. Do I mean that this is God-given, carved in stone, and not changeable? We need to think creatively about how the financial regulation functions. In fact, there is a working group which is presently looking at the financial regulation to see how we can make it more flexible, a little more responsive and quicker. That is the story on the procedures. Secondly, speed is also a matter of staffing. As I said, we have been increasing our staffing. Going back five or six years, there were three officials to manage 10 million euro. At the present time, 10 million euro is managed by five officials. This is an increase of two in a period since the existence of EuropeAid—almost a doubling. The World Bank has eight. I do not know the figure for DfID. It is probably of the order of six or seven. The more people you have, the quicker you are. We consider that we now have at least to maintain the level we have, and possibly to increase it—but that is an internal discussion in the Commission. Turning to evaluation, in the Annual Report 2003 there is a chapter on evaluation. The evaluation service works for the whole of the Relex family. There are two types of evaluation—four if we also take monitoring into account. The function has been strengthened over the last years. The evaluation of a project's results is not done by the evaluation service; it is supervised by the evaluation service but undertaken by the delegation. That is where we draw lessons from the experience of project implementation. The evaluation service looks at the more systemic elements. They look at impact on a country—the impact of programmes and of regulation. The impetus that comes from the evaluation service is directed more towards the policy formulation and the programming side, whereas the results of the evaluation carried out by the delegation have a direct impact on the concept of how to do a project. Evaluation is a nice exercise and absolutely essential, but very often its results and conclusions come too late. The project has been completed for a year before the evaluation is started. Over two years have passed by the time the evaluation is completed. In the meantime, the world has changed. It is sometimes very difficult to draw operational conclusions from evaluation. That is why we have worked quite a lot in the past on reinforcing the monitoring of the project implementation, which is an ongoing monitoring using external consultants. We have launched a new initiative—it is also something that the World Bank does—called "results-oriented monitoring". Projects are scored on a number of indicators, such as efficiency and so on, and we look at the score and the evolution of the score over time. There is an explanation of this to be found in the report, and also the scores of the projects in the various areas. In the geographical chapters of our report, we have included the scores of the project and the evolution of the scores, giving some indication of how well we are doing, what are the weak spots, and where, from a management point of view, we should intervene to put the project

back on track. There have been some improvements, therefore. If you want to go into greater detail, we can organise a meeting with someone to explain that to you. In my view, the orientation and the work have been an exercise to make sure that, where there have been shortcomings in the past, now and in the future we catch up with the average of OECD. Budgetisation of EDF would make a dramatic difference. At the moment it is almost impossible to co-finance between EDF and budget lines. If we wanted to finance a pan-African project, if we wanted to give support to the African Union for instance on institution-building across the board, it would be a nightmare. There are three sources of financing. We do not have one line on Africa. We have the MEDA programme for North Africa; we have ACP for Africa south of the Sahara; we have a special budget line for South Africa. If we wanted to finance the African Union from the EDF, we would have to stipulate that none of that money could be used for anything to do with North Africa—or South Africa—because they are budget lines and they cannot be mixed. That is one practical example. The whole system of using the EDF as a fund outside the budget is something that was perhaps justifiable in 1958, when the first European Development Fund was set up. Do not forget that the origin of the European Development Fund is purely colonial. This was to finance the infrastructure in the former French and Belgian colonies. When the European Economic Community was set up, the French and the Belgians thought that it was a good idea of offload some of the costs of the investment in the colonies to Germany, and Germany said, "Yes, we're willing to pay, but we will not do it with the budget. We will set up a special fund and we will pay into the special fund". The special fund still exists. If we go to our partner countries and discuss financial management and budgetary management, the first recommendation we make—and the IMF and the World Bank also make—is "Stop all extra-budgetary funds. All the funding should flow to the budget. There is only one way for funding to get in and one way for it to get out, and that is the budget. Scrap all extra-budgetary funds". But we ourselves have such a fund. We would not be able to give support to ourselves!

Q225 Lord Lea of Crondall: I was very impressed by your point about how can there be 12 Country Strategy Papers for Cameroon, Bolivia, or wherever. I think that argument is pretty unanswerable. How do you find that Member States react to that argument? The reason I find the argument unanswerable is that, in Cameroon or Bolivia, not only do you not have enough people to do it 12 times but, if there are contradictions between what people want, what is their country strategy? How can they get ownership in depth in their country if they are supposed to be doing 12 different things? That is a very strong point for doing more. I was equally taken with the point about countries taking the lead within the family: DfID to take the lead on Bangladesh education and somebody else taking the lead on transport. Incidentally, the question arises here about Africa—mentioning the European Investment Bank meeting yesterday—whether or not transport could play a more strategic role between countries, and so on. This is a division of labour. The central question, however, is do you think that countries are now buying into this philosophy? We still feel some tension with people saying, "The EU is rubbish. Let's spend the money, because we are nearer to the ground", and so on. There are two footnotes to this, and one is statistical. I think that it is very important in our report—and perhaps you can help us—to get the statistics clear. I could not understand, for instance, if the Commission is 10 per cent of the world, how can Europe as a whole be 50 per cent. In a typical country like Britain, if half goes to the EU and half direct, how come it is 50 per cent? Why is it not 20 per cent? I am sure that, without your answering it today, you can provide us with some statistics. You have mentioned World Bank statistics. I would find it very useful to have a clear statistical table showing the totality, and also a clear organisation chart. You mentioned the Relex family. I would love to see it all written down, because I have now become terribly confused as to which is the overall family, and so on. My central point is, even if you do all the strategy papers and get them compatible, presumably the Americans are outside—how does it all come together?

Mr Franco: The starting point of all assistance should be the country's own strategy or plan, or whatever. The guideline we have taken, sometimes very dogmatically, is this PRSP—the Poverty-Reduction Strategy Paper. For us, this has been our frame of reference in which we have defined our own strategy papers. Some Member States have done the same; other Member States have done something different. It is still the case that we are a little bit all over the place. There is no real coherence in what we collectively try to do, although—as I have said, and I think you agree—there is a lot of scope for complementarity between what Member States can do. If we capitalised on this complementarity—with some countries taking the lead in a particular sector in particular countries and others joining in by chipping in with some money, letting the others manage it—it would all be much more efficient and to the benefit of the third country. It would economise on our own administrative resources and collectively we would realise something. There is clearly still some lack of trust to be overcome but, as I said, it is a gradual process. What have contributed a great deal over the last years are the meetings chaired by Mr Richelle, the Director-General for Development, i.e. the meetings of the EU Development DGs. The

meetings take place every three or four months and in fact there is one this week. These are the 15, now 25, Directors-General for Development of the European Union. This is in an informal rather than a Council setting. There are people from the Council involved, but it is informal. What I find amazing is that, at that level, the perception of what needs to be done and the willingness to do it—to harmonise, standardise, work together, work on complementarity, co-ordination, co-financing—are much stronger than at the higher and lower levels. At the higher level, because politicians tend to ask the question, "Will I still be in the picture? Will I still be cutting the ribbon to open the road?". At the lower level you have a task manager saying, "This is my project. I am not going to give it to that guy over there. I want to have my own project". At the level of the Directors-General, however, it is somewhere in between. They are not worried about being in the picture, and they are not worried about giving up a file—because they know that they will get other files in exchange. As there is a lot of impetus now coming from that level, I am fairly optimistic that—not overnight but gradually—a process of gaining trust, working together, setting up joint initiatives, will evolve that will in the end convince the politician as well as the task manager that this is the right way to go. It is a bit unorthodox as a view, but I leave it for your consideration.

Q226 *Lord Maclennan of Rogart:* Can I ask you two questions about possible constraints on effectiveness in recipient countries? Lack of capability to deal with aid programmes, what you can do about it and how you are approaching that. Secondly, corruption.

Mr Franco: For me, the first problem is lack of political will. Capability comes second. It is not just by training people that you make them capable and then, as though by waving a magic wand, everything will happen. There is also the second element of corruption, of course. There are people defending their own interests. For me, that is the biggest problem. By and large, the business we are in is not a successful business. That is being very honest—and do not say it to the press! We all know this. The situation in the world would be worse if we did not do what we do, but if you look at what we have been doing over the last three or four decades, you cannot say that it is the success story of the last century. It is very difficult. In a sense, it depends much less on us than it does on the beneficiary countries. What are the countries that are successful? When did they find the right policies? When did they implement them? A big success—India. What did foreign assistance contribute to India? India had long been the rather slow-moving big country in Asia. Then, 1990–91, economic reform—things start to happen. There was a second wave of reforms recently. They are in China's growth league now. Look at what external assistance has done for India. In terms of GDP, external assistance to India is 0.5 per cent. It is perhaps 1.5 per cent of the total budget. We bring in 40 million a year, which is 0.0-something. We cannot say that we make a difference in India. Nobody can say that they do. The difference in India is made by the Indians. They make the policy, and you see the results. In about 10 years, the number of people below the poverty line has fallen from 45 per cent to 35 per cent. Brilliant! External assistance? No. Indians. I could continue the story and give you other examples of the same kind. What counts is a government that knows what it wants to do, that has a policy, and implements it. We can assist in the process; but if the government does not do it, we cannot do it for the government. It is not a matter of training. Training helps—if the government wants training help.

Q227 *Lord Maclennan of Rogart:* There have been leadership training programmes in eastern—
Mr Franco: Can you train a leader?

Q228 *Lord Maclennan of Rogart:* There have been leadership training programmes in eastern Europe, and it is quite obvious that it has been remarkably successful in a very short time.
Mr Franco: If you are a leader, you can be trained. If you are not a leader or you do not want to lead then, whatever training you go through, you still will not be a leader or a manager. What we can do in those cases is work on civil society, on democracy, the functioning of parliaments, a free press. So that through the ballot box, through the social processes, there is an influence on government and a corrupt government will go. The situation is not hopeless. A year and a half ago I was in Kenya, talking to the ambassadors, and people were saying that it was absolutely impossible.

Q229 *Lord Maclennan of Rogart:* You talked in your opening statement about much greater coherence in the programming, because of your awareness now of what was going on. Has this been pulled together to tackle these problems, which you describe yourself as being among the greatest problems that you face on effectiveness? Where can we look to see what you are doing on governance, on all that list of obstacles you talked about?
Mr Franco: It is an area where we, as well as other donors, are trying to operate through other channels. Over the last three or four years, the emphasis on work with civil society has increased tremendously—sometimes in our normal programmes and also through the democracy/human rights programming, co-financing with NGOs, and things like this. We are also a player in the field, as others are. For me, however, it is the key problem and one which we have

to tackle. If we have not tackled that problem, it is useless to start doing—

Q230 *Lord Maclennan of Rogart:* From our point of view, trying to get information, where is the *locus classicus* that we can look at to see what your policies are and how you are implementing them in these areas?
Mr Franco: I can provide you with some information on the democracy/human rights budget lines; and, secondly, the co-financing with NGOs. Within the programmes—the Mediterranean programmes in particular, also in Asia and, very strongly so, in the ACP—there is money set aside for civil society and the building-up of democracy, human rights, the functioning of parliaments and suchlike. A communication on civil society came out about four months ago. I will make sure that you have it. There is an overview of all the various initiatives we have financed and developed over the last years in that area. It was discussed in the General Affairs Council of November. All the preparatory papers and conclusions of the Council are there, and I can share this information with you.
Chairman: It would be very helpful if your office could let the secretariat have those documents. Thank you.
Lord Tomlinson: I have two questions. I have heard very clearly what you have said, but we hear different things from different people. Clearly, you are not surprised that a number of the recipient countries talk about the Commission as having a concept of dialogue that is one-way; that they do not listen; that there are attitudes of neo-colonialism in the way they tell the recipient countries what is good for them. Inevitably, you must also hear that from certain quarters. How do you respond to that? The second question, in the light of the confusion that there is on development objectives—the focus on poverty on the one hand being seriously diluted by political considerations on the other, and therefore reducing the pot that is available—is can you tell us about the relationship between EuropeAid and the other two directorates general, and how the cut-off in this relationship works?

Q231 *Baroness Northover:* My question follows on from that. The EDF has had a better poverty focus, as we understand it, than money coming through the budget. This question has been raised by a number of people. If there is budgetisation, how do we ensure that the poverty focus will improve, and that the tendency to see aid as a foreign policy tool does not overtake that? I was struck by the fact that you said that in the mid-1990s all of this was thrown into confusion because of the fall of the Berlin Wall and the actions the EU wanted to take in terms of reconstruction there—which is not the same as

dealing with poverty in Africa. I am concerned about how the devolved decision-making is working. Again, this is something we have heard from a recipient country. You yourself have said that you are quite encouraged by how fast this is moving along; but it must be a concern that, if you have to build the expertise in all those local countries, there is a danger of each one having to reinvent the wheel as to how they farm out these projects, how they assess who is going to do this. How too do they resist the pressures locally to take this contractor rather than that contractor? What kind of assessment is made of that to ensure that you do not have corrupt practices creeping in there? I am also concerned, following on from what Bob Maclennan has said, about countries with lack of capacity. You make the point that you want now to support governments who know how to take these projects forward, as opposed to, as you put it, the boy scout approach of putting projects in place. But, after all, the poorest countries are least able to do that. Does that not cause you concern?
Mr Franco: There are a lot of questions there which go to the heart of the matter, and we could go on for quite a while. The question about neo-colonialism is a real one, and we all face it. To what extent do you have to accept what the country tells you? Then do you do it with your eyes closed, or do you have to get involved in a dialogue with them? All the structure-adjustment, budgetary assistance, sector-wide approaches, are based on a policy dialogue. A policy dialogue is a dialogue. You listen, and you talk. All these programmes go with the conditionality. Is this conditionality justified or not? Is it an interference in the policies and the life of this country? Perhaps yes, perhaps no. On the other hand, we are in charge of handling taxpayers' money. We have to make sure that we get the best deal for the European taxpayer— as we have to make sure that we get the best deal for the population in these countries. So we are in the middle, talking to these governments. The question of how far to go or not to go is a difficult one. I do not think that it is easy. Yes, the tone of what one says and the extent to which one listens are important. Sometimes we think we know better, but we do not. Sometimes we are faced with a country which is completely corrupt and incompetent, and we cannot do it. Is there a magic solution? I do not think so. This is the real debate regarding what this business is about. I do not have a reply. I can only share the question, and I think it is a question that is in the mind of all of my colleagues. As we would say in French, how can you make the happiness of someone else? I can accept the question, but I do not have a reply to it. Regarding development objectives, poverty objectives and political considerations, I do not think there is any form of development assistance or international co-operation that does not have a policy component. It is not something that one

should turn away from; it is a reality. External assistance is part of foreign policy. Yes, it has its own objectives and dynamics, but it does not live in a totally different world. It lives in the same world. I think that we all agree that the political will of a country is important. To get the local regime to take a line of sustainable development is important. But when we are talking about interference we are talking about foreign policy. I would not go as far as to utter the words "regime change", but if you are dealing with governments that are not really able to rule their country, then we have to make sure that these governments are being changed. We are not going to bomb anything. That is certainly not what we can do. But, by working through civil society, we can give civil society the opposition, the ways and means by which perhaps to remove this government and to put somebody else in their place. The example I wanted to quote was Kenya, where a change has taken place from a very corrupt regime under Moi to a new regime, which at least tries to move things. That this happened was a small miracle, because it was not so clear that Moi could be removed and that the whole opposition could get together. That it happened, I believe, is also thanks to donors intervening and supporting opposition parties, getting them to work together, and financing a democratic process. Is this poverty alleviation? No, this is almost foreign policy. There is a line to be drawn somewhere, where you say, "No, you can't use your foreign assistance to pursue your short-term, nationalistic, economic interests". That is clear. I think that all the donors are out of this game. There are a few leftovers in old empires, but we are more or less out of this game. What we have to go for is a mature relationship between, let us say, the broader objectives of foreign policy and assistance. Not trying to sit in different corners or in different rooms and not talk to each other, because that leads to disaster. I was in Bangkok two weeks ago, discussing the programmes—but on a bilateral basis with all the delegations that were there. We started with the policy: what it is that we want, what are our policy objectives in our relations with India, China, Bangladesh and Pakistan. Then, from there, how did we programme? Is there a programme reflecting our policy objectives? Then, from the programme to the implementation. Are the projects in line with the programming, and do they have an impact on our policy objectives? This is the normal kind of discussion that we have with our colleagues, and it works out quite well. Okay, there are conflicts, but where in life are there no conflicts and disputes? Life would be very boring if everybody always agreed on everything. It is a natural complementarity, which can function and which functions in most cases. Regarding the EDF, other instruments, and the poverty focus of the EDF—is the EDF more poverty-focused than the rest? EDF is about 30 per cent infrastructure—road building. EDF is about 4 per cent on health and about 4 per cent on education. Is that poverty-focused? Programmes in Asia have about 30 per cent on health and education. Is that less poverty-focused? When is a poverty focus a poverty focus? The thinking about poverty and poverty alleviation is an awareness in-house, but it is something which is difficult to spot. You cannot say that when you are doing something in health, you are doing something in poverty alleviation; or that when you are doing something in terms of roads, it is not about poverty alleviation. A road can be more effective in poverty alleviation than a health project. The important thing is that there is awareness of the issues throughout the house, and that this is being discussed and taken up in all the programmes. Let us be clear, however—not the same way in all the programmes. Where the poverty focus is least present is in the European neighbours, namely the former Soviet Union and the Balkans. There, in our jargon, the focus is on "approximation". That means we want to get our neighbours close to us, and we want to make sure that we set up economic structures and regulations which make it easier for us to trade and to develop economic relationships with them. The focus is slightly different there. There are a number of poverty-related activities, but it is not the overriding objective. The Mediterranean is half-and-half. The Mediterranean is also a neighbour, where we also talk about approximation. The Mediterranean, the western Balkans, and the western part of the former Soviet Union are part of what we call the wider Europe—now called the New Neighbourhood policy. We try to develop good relations with the neighbours and that, in the first instance, is a matter of getting our institutions right. However, we are aware that there are still poor countries in the Mediterranean. In terms of objectives, therefore, the Mediterranean is half-and-half. It is half approximation, and half poverty focus/social cohesion. For the other programmes—Asia, Latin America, ACP—I would say that it is the same kind of overall philosophy that inspires the programme. It is not so easy to check it by sectors. To see whether or not it is focused, you have to go into more depth into

what the programmes and the project mean. I do not think that there is much difference between the EDF and the other programme. Regarding devolved decision-making, yes, it is a problem that, sitting in the delegations, people start to reinvent the wheel; that they are considered to be a small or medium-sized enterprise, independent, and just running their own show—whereas they are part of a multinational, and they have to realise that. We are tying them in, through a management plan, through our networks, through regional meetings. We have a series of regional meetings at the beginning of the year. This is the second year we have done it. That is why I was in Bangkok and Giorgio Bonacci was in Sao Paulo. Next week, I will be in Kingston. We get together the heads of delegation and their operational people at a regional meeting. We discuss for two or three days, in plenary and bilaterally, what they are doing, how they are going about it, what kind of support they need from Brussels. We go through their project pipeline, identifying those issues where they are weak and where they want support. They can get that support either from Brussels or perhaps from another delegation in the region which can send someone. So we are building up these networks, and building up the culture of the new distribution of responsibilities between headquarters and delegation, in order to ensure this synergy and complementarity. Is the work done? No. Are some people still doing the thing all on their own? Yes. Are some people still running to Brussels for cover? Yes. Is this the right attitude? No. Where is the right attitude? In the middle. Okay, let us try to get everybody in the middle, where we have a reasonable degree of independence while nevertheless relying on headquarters for support. This is the process.

Q232 *Chairman:* I think that we will have to break now, Mr Franco. I am sure that we have all enjoyed this morning very much indeed. I am sorry that it cannot continue. Thank you for answering all our questions so frankly and so fully.
Mr Franco: I am not a diplomat and I do not practise the art of the wooden tongue, as they say in France!
Chairman: But it is very much appreciated. Thank you.

TUESDAY 3 FEBRUARY 2004

Present	Bowness, L (Chairman)	Northover, B
	Lea of Crondall, L	Powell of Bayswater, L
	Maclennan of Rogart, L	Tomlinson, L

Examination of Witness

MR GIAMPIERO ALHADEFF, Secretary-General, Ms FRANCESCA VILIANI, Development and Humanitarian Aid Officer, SOLIDAR, and MR OLIVIER CONSOLO, Director, European NGO Confederation for Relief and Development (CONCORD), examined.

Q233 Chairman: As you know, we are conducting an inquiry into European Union aid and assistance. One of the questions we have been looking at is trying to evaluate the reform of European Union development assistance, as well as a number of other questions; but that would perhaps seem to be particularly relevant to you and the evidence which I hope you will be able to give us. No doubt you might also be able to comment upon the future of the ACP grouping and the whole question of budgetisation which is raised. I do not know whether you would like to say something in general terms, or whether you would like to go into questions straightaway?
Mr Alhadeff: I will introduce my two colleagues. Olivier Consolo is the Director of CONCORD, which is the grouping of development NGOs. It brings together 18 national platforms, including the United Kingdom platform, BOND. It also brings in the families of NGOs such as Save The Children, which is joining now, and the other networks such as Eurostat, SOLIDAR, *et cetera*. The EU NGO scene is a little different from the United Kingdom one, in that the brand-name NGOs, such as Oxfam and Save The Children, have all entered into alliances. So CONCORD is our development alliance, and where we all work together. It used to be called the CLONG but, about a year ago, re-formed as CONCORD. The difference was that it brought in, as well as the national platforms, the groupings of NGOs—the Protestant NGOs, the Catholic NGOs, the Non-Confessionals, and other families of NGOs. It also has members in the new countries. It is one of four groupings of NGOs at the Brussels level, the other three being the human rights NGOs, the social NGOs, and the environment NGOs. Those four groupings of NGOs, together with the ETUC—the European Trades Union Congress, now led by John Monks—have formed the Civil Society Contact Group. So it is actually quite a different structure that you find at the national level. On my right is Francesca Viliani. We both work for SOLIDAR, which is an alliance of European NGOs who are involved in social issues, development issues, and human rights issues. We have been on the Brussels scene since 1995. Our United Kingdom members are One World Action and War on Want, and there are NGOs which are linked to workers' movements, trades unions. If you like, that is our specificity across the European Union. As I said, we are both involved in social issues and development issues. One thing on which we have been quite busy is the whole issue of social dialogue, the Convention, the Constitution. So if that is an issue you also want to discuss, we would be quite happy to talk about that as well. We received your questions yesterday. We have talked a bit to our members and we know that you have already received a representation from BOND in the United Kingdom. They did consult with us when they prepared their briefing, but we will send you another briefing this week, if we are still in time. By the end of the week we will send you a note on some ideas that we have on the issues which you raise.

Q234 Chairman: That will be well in time. We would very much appreciate it. Thank you.
Mr Alhadeff: You have asked me for a couple of comments. I am much happier that we get involved in a dialogue between us. Olivier started work about a year ago. Before that, he was working in the field in Guatemala and was very much involved with EU development policy, but from that end. He has quite a lot of background on that side. Francesca has been working in Central America, the Balkans, and the Middle East. So she has quite a wealth of experience. Yesterday we talked to our various members here and got feedback from them. We will therefore give you a bit of a *pot-pourri* of our views, but also their views. By the end of the week, however, we will be a little more considered in our reply to you.

Q235 Chairman: Perhaps we could go straight into questions. You mentioned the Convention. Perhaps we could deal with that at the very beginning, because we have not had very much evidence about it. What is your view about the provisions of the draft Constitution, were it to be implemented? What effect do you think it will have on the development aid situation?

Mr Alhadeff: The main concern that we had throughout was that development aid would be separated from the Common Foreign and Security Policy and from the Common Defence Policy. That was a worry and it continues to be a worry for us. We are looking at—not only from the Constitution but also, at this stage, where the new Commission is coming into place—will there be a Commissioner for development? Will there be that separation between those two? I think that some of the questions you raise seem to suggest that that is also an issue for you. We are sympathetic to the idea, for example, that the policies on the near-abroad and the budgets—for example, on the Financial Perspectives—should be separated from development policy. The aims of the two programmes are quite distinct, and to put them too close together does create a confusion.

Q236 *Lord Lea of Crondall:* How does this relate to the two-tier Commission idea? You have 25 members. Surely all this is in the melting pot, is it not? You have to agree a Constitution at some point, but I am not clear quite where you are coming from. I have heard your comment, but presumably, in practice, you will have to sort out the jobs and the functions in a way where there will be some overlaps and some people doing subsidiary jobs within families of Commissioners, and so on, will you not? Is not that the reality behind all this? Where is the reality and where is what you might call the big labels?
Mr Alhadeff: If you have a Commission in charge of foreign relations and, under that Commissioner, you put a "mini" Development Commissioner, you may end up with a problem. You may find that you have two policies, one serving the other. That is really the concern we have.

Q237 *Lord Lea of Crondall:* It has been put to us this morning—and evidence will be published in due course, but I must not quote it because it is under what we call Chatham House rules—that, to take Africa, governance is the biggest unanswered dilemma. There is conditionality, neo-colonialism, and yet, as somebody said, our taxpayers' money; and whether we talk to EU, AU, and so on. How do you get a grip on that? There is this judgment about interference, and what you do about Zimbabwe, Nigeria, Ethiopia, or wherever it is. I think that there is perhaps a case for saying that it is only when you get a new attitude in government that you get economic growth, which is poverty reduction as a necessary condition, if not a sufficient condition. What is wrong with that? I am being the devil's advocate here.
Mr Alhadeff: That is a kind of Transparency International argument, is it not? That you need to have certain conditions in place for development to take place.

Mr Consolo: My experience over the last three years in the EC delegation, where we spoke a lot about governance—and Guatemala is a very bad governance country—is that if you separate development process and foreign policy from the EC, meaning that the delegates do not have an ambassador role, then it is enough to bring pressure by the trade policy, by the foreign affairs policy, on a government, without affecting the development co-operation between European countries and southern people—not government. I think that there is a lot of opportunity perhaps to cut a little your direct support to the government—without directly affecting the population—through NGO and civil society sectors. There are tools like that, to bring much more pressure at the foreign affairs level—with co-ordination between the EC and the European Member State present at national level.

Q238 *Lord Powell of Bayswater:* My recollection of Brussels is that power follows the budget. Therefore, if you want to be sure that there will be adequate money for real development purposes and that it is used only for that, you will have to have a separate budget line, which separates distinctly foreign affairs purposes from development purposes. That budget line for development will need to be supervised by a Development Commissioner, who is the person who controls that budget. That still appears, as David Lea says, to be completely up in the air: whether or not that will be a structure which will emerge. There is nothing in the draft Constitution that tells you whether it will or not. We shall not know until the Commission jobs are divided up quite how it will fall out. One issue that could be settled would be the budget line for development. Yet I do not see any firm views emerging from the Commission on that. I am told they are about to publish their proposals for the Financial Perspective. Possibly there will be something in that. Maybe we shall learn that later today from Mr Child.
Mr Alhadeff: I think that you are absolutely right. I would go further than that. One of the tragedies for a very long time, in terms of development, has been that, in terms of quality, the Development Commissioners have not been up to the job. I have been here now with three Commissioners. There was one who was good. The following two have not been up to the job and have had a hard time making themselves heard within their own houses, within the Commission, and certainly in the outside world.

Q239 *Baroness Northover:* I was going to ask specifically about budgetisation. We have been hearing a very strong case in many of the presentations we have heard here, from the Commission and various people, in favour of that.

From one of the recipient countries last night, we heard enormous concerns about that.
Mr Alhadeff: Not wanting it to happen?

Q240 *Baroness Northover:* Not wanting to have that, yes. I wondered what your view was.
Mr Alhadeff: The majority of the NGOs believe that it should happen and think the fact is that the Parliament has to be involved in it. They feel that the present arrangement suits Member States, because the Commission does not spend all the money and, at the end of the day, money goes back to the Member States.

Q241 *Chairman:* What do you mean by "money goes back to the Member States"?
Mr Alhadeff: It is reclaimed back. It is unspent money.
Ms Viliani: And also because the disbursement of money is quite late, compared with the commitment, and so of course the Member States gain a few years.

Q242 *Lord Powell of Bayswater:* The rate of call-up is slow.
Ms Viliani: Yes. There are two problems with budgetisation. One is the fact that it is related to the whole discussion about the Financial Perspectives and the maximum ceiling of Commission spending. If this is not raised, it will be a big problem for the Commission to integrate the budget. Also, we do not know what the position of the Commission will be, but we hope that the Commission will go on with the two negotiations—either EDF outside the budget or inside the budget. However, it is too early at the moment for the Commission to decide on one of the two; so we feel that they have to go on with the two negotiations. Regarding the ACP countries, we believe that it is clear that, if the objective of development is eradication of poverty and the commitment of the Millennium Goals, there will be no progress if there is no feeling of ownership by the recipient countries—in this case by the ACP country. For them, this is where there is probably a risk in budgetising the EDF, i.e. in losing part of the involvement they presently have in setting priorities or in the allocation of money. This is why we want to stress the relevance of involving recipient countries, the government, and the civil society in all of the planning activity. This is the only way to be sure that there is a feeling of ownership towards the programme.
Mr Alhadeff: It is still a new process and it does not feel as if it is bedded down. It has these lovely things about involving civil society and governments, but we do not see trades unions being mentioned—that they should be in there as well—and I think that it is all words.

Mr Consolo: Something has been launched by the European Commission called "mezzo dialogue" at country level, involving all the Member States, the European Commission, the government, the southern civil society and the European NGOs, to look for consensus on the main policies that co-operation needs to address in order to achieve these goals—reduction of poverty, *et cetera*. There is a slight fear at EC headquarters level of these kinds of very decentralised mechanisms. We are waiting for the new text, but the new Constitution could create the legal basis for making this kind of experience an obligation in each country—to have a permanent mechanism of co-ordination between Member States, EC, government and civil society.

Q243 *Lord Powell of Bayswater:* To see if I have followed your argument correctly, are you saying, as I think you are, that if the Commission—and later the Council—does not agree to raise the overall budget ceiling, then there is a danger that development spending within the 1 per cent ceiling will be so squeezed that it will be essential to keep the EDF outside, so that the total amount of resource for the poorest countries is still at a reasonable level?
Ms Viliani: Development money is not only EDF, but there are also other budget lines.

Q244 *Lord Powell of Bayswater:* But if the budget is so squeezed by the overall ceiling, you would be in favour of having that and also keeping the EDF outside the budget—if that is the only way to get the additional spending.
Mr Alhadeff: If there is no way to increase the amount.
Ms Viliani: The discussion is timely, because we are discussing the new Financial Perspective for the next six or seven years. This is why we also say that it is too early for the Commission already to decide on which of the two options—not knowing how the discussion on the Financial Perspective will go. I know that they are not too happy about moving the two possibilities, because it is doubling the work. At this stage, however, this is the only possibility for us.

Q245 *Lord Tomlinson:* Perhaps I can follow up what you were saying about budgetisation. Am I being unduly cynical if I suggest to a body like yours that your interest in budgetisation is partly coloured by the fact that you have somewhat more influence with members of the European Parliament, and therefore can lobby your position more effectively with them than you believe you can with the Member States?
Mr Alhadeff: You are obviously talking from your experience! Yes to the second part. It is true that we have a good relationship with the European Parliament. From the NGO side, I have led a campaign to stop the yearly trek of NGOs and all

kinds of lobbying groups, to try to create a new budget line. You will well remember the inter-institutional agreement of 1998 when that was actually stopped. I think that it will happen more. My honest belief on this one is that the NGOs are not approaching it in that way: that the Parliament can be robust; that the Parliament should be involved in the budget; and that there would be more coherence.

Q246 Lord Tomlinson: It has been suggested to us by some of the recipients of aid that they understand the Parliament's position in relation to budgetisation, but they understand it only in the context of it being a power play. They cannot see where the benefit of principle comes, other than a rather fledgling Parliament trying to spread its influence even further.
Ms Viliani: One of the points of budgetisation is to give some control/power to the Parliament. However, it is not only about this; it is also to be sure about the commitment of money and the proper allocation. The ninth EDF has not yet received all the money that the Member States have committed to it. This has a big impact on the capacity and effectiveness of the Development Fund. It is also a way to speed up the procedure. The EDF can be inside or outside the budget but, if the recipient countries are not involved in the planning and the programming phase, there will not be a great result. The two things have to go together. It means a different role, both of the Commission and of the Parliament itself.
Mr Alhadeff: It might be worth seeing that reform also with the division of the money—the clear division made between expenditure on the near-abroad and development. It might clarify things a little bit to do that.

Q247 Chairman: So you would have a separate line for development and a separate line for the near-abroad. Would you include the Mediterranean countries in the near-abroad?
Mr Alhadeff: Yes.
Chairman: Yet a lot of the spending in Tunisia and Morocco is in fact development money, so it is hard to draw the line, is it not?
Lord Tomlinson: And the more so if you do it within the context of a 1 per cent GNI ceiling, which is seriously threatened.

Q248 Lord Lea of Crondall: Do you think that some of your own members are dubious about Brussels? Oxfam is not perhaps one of yours?
Mr Consolo: Not yet.
Mr Alhadeff: It will be one of his very soon.

Q249 Lord Lea of Crondall: I think it is fair to say that there is a certain amount of nationalism, and it is the mirror image of the question that John

Tomlinson asked. Their constituency is not the same as the Spanish constituency. They are Oxfam, the churches, or whatever. They have very distinct cultures in their constituency, and also they feel that they can follow their project, and so on. Yet, on the other hand, we have heard very powerfully yesterday and this morning about the fact that in a recipient country—say, Cameroon, Bolivia—you cannot have 15 strategy papers. Why not? Because: (a) there are not too many people in Bolivia who can keep answering all these questions which people keep coming along and asking, because there may only be four competent water engineers or whatever in the country; and (b) what happens if they all want contradictory things? To me, it is game, set and match because—and this was the secret, I do not say that we stumbled upon, because it is very obviously a model—you can do it more through Brussels as long as the Brits may offer to take the lead on helping the education programme in Bangladesh, and the Germans may offer to take the lead in helping with transport infrastructure across Cameroon's border with Benin, or wherever. My question, therefore, is this. Do you think that, on the whole, there is a pretty strong case for more of a European family doing 100 per cent together rather than 25 per cent here and 25 per cent there? As someone said, with ministers wanting to cut the ribbon, what are you going to do? Have 15 people cutting a ribbon? I do not think that you can cut a ribbon with 15 people holding 15 pairs of scissors!
Mr Alhadeff: I think that there is also a little bit of marketing from NGOs. We have been working quite a lot with our members, trying to get them to see that arriving in this particular place and attaching your own logo is not necessarily the best way to spend money. We came across 16 of our agencies in Nicaragua. There were 300 operational staff in Bosnia. There were six offices and I do not know how many Land-Rovers. We said, "This is nonsense". What Francesca has been doing, therefore, is trying to explain the mathematics of this. You are right. More and more, agencies are coming together. Oxfam are doing it, as is SOLIDAR, as well as all the others. We understand that to operate as a Spanish NGO on your own does not really make sense, but you can be Spanish, British and French together and be more effective. For example, the Germans will do the office/logistics; the Norwegians will do the fundraising, because they have access to certain monies; and maybe the Swiss have the hospital equipment—and the whole thing works. Iraq was a case in point, where one of the members had the expertise and the others fell in behind them—and that was the Spanish, Norwegians and Germans. It is also fair to say that the development NGOs have been in Brussels longer than just about anybody else, except for the consumers. The predecessor of CONCORD had been here 30 years.

Q250 Lord Lea of Crondall: The trades unions were there before them.

Mr Alhadeff: The trades unions are always there before.

Q251 Lord Lea of Crondall: A hundred and fifty years.

Mr Alhadeff: In Brussels?

Mr Consolo: I think that what Giampiero Alhadeff is talking about is the same for the Member State and the government aid. It is a strategic choice: either we reinforce European policies at European level, or we can decide to renationalise some of the policies. It is a political debate that we would like to have with the stakeholders at European level. The role of the EC as a united operation, outside in the smaller and poorer countries, is much more visible than other kinds of co-operation. As the European Union, it is much more visible for the population and for the stakeholders locally.

Q252 Lord Maclennan of Rogart: I would like to ask you about how effectively you think the European development programmes are helping the recipient countries to be capable of putting the aid to good use. If you had a message for the policymakers in the European institutions on that, how would you propose that it be strengthened? The background to the question is that we have heard that, to some extent, aid and development assistance has been reactive, following leads from those who are well prepared to do something about it; but the greatest problems are in the areas where that capability is lacking, and one would like to see how the NGOs perceive that.

Mr Alhadeff: One piece of research done by a couple of our members has shown that a lot of the expenditure is going on issues like transport and infrastructure, and other issues like gender, for example, are being ignored. I have a personal question. I feel that a lot of the emphasis on development has in part been misplaced, even the poverty reduction focus. I believe that the greatest way to fight poverty is through employment. Yet I do not see employment coming through as one of the big turning points, in terms of the poverty reduction strategy. The issue of decent work, which is an important Union campaign, is just not there in the poverty reduction priorities. I am really wondering whether that is an oversight, or just that there has been a bit of a fashion in the last five or six years that trade is going to be the way through. Trade will only affect a small percentage of people.

Mr Consolo: As to the effectiveness of programme aid, I apologise for emphasising this so much, but the co-ordination between the Member State and the EC at national level is a key issue in improving the efficiency of European Union aid. Member States should be given the opportunity—and I know that in many countries this is not the case—to see what the EC is doing at programme levels. Not only to decide on negotiations through the Country Strategy Paper, where the Member States are involved, but also on the implementation—where they are discussing the results, the impact, the re-orientation, the permanent mechanisms. It is something that we could reinforce at national and regional level, and we would have a direct impact on the effectiveness of the aid.

Ms Viliani: For me, the point is really to clarify what are the objectives of development. This is why we also say that it is different from external relations. If the objective of development is poverty eradication or reduction, this can be achieved via the achievement of the Millennium Development Goals. It is clear in this case that some social sectors are the priorities, such as education, health and employment. This is because we say that poverty is not only related to economic capacity; it is also related to access. It has been said that, in a way, the six sectoral priorities of the EU—such as trade and infrastructure—go in the direction of poverty eradication; but if the European Union spends 30 per cent of its money on improving infrastructure and only 10 per cent on education and health, I do not think that this is a way to achieve the goal. It does not mean that it is not effective; it does not mean that the money is not well spent; but it is the fact that the priority of the EU is on infrastructure rather than on the others. I believe that a better co-ordination among the Member States and the European Union is a function of this. It is not only the NGOs that like to have their flag; it is everyone. When I was in Central America after Hurricane Mitch, the Commission had offices and the Member States had their embassies. At one point someone said, "I know that if I need money I have to phone President Clinton. Who do I have to phone in the EU?" There were many different representatives there and I think that it sometimes presents a difficult message to recipients.

Q253 Lord Maclennan of Rogart: I am very interested in all those replies, but there was an ancillary point that I was anxious to get at. What about countries where the government is so bad, is corrupt, is denying human rights, where there is no involvement of civil society, and the prioritisation for aid even by that government is not one that NGOs see is right. How do you deal with that?

Mr Alhadeff: Are you talking about Zimbabwe?

Q254 Lord Maclennan of Rogart: I was not talking about anywhere, because it is a fairly widespread problem.

Mr Alhadeff: I thought that Lord Lea skirted around that when mentioning it. I think that there is a very important role for NGOs there. They should be working in countries that are corrupt and that are dictatorial. There is a long experience of that, whether it is Guatemala or Zimbabwe. There, the onus on the public authority is to decide what is the best channel. You cannot say no to those countries. You cannot say no to those people. You cannot turn your back on the people of Zimbabwe at the moment, going through the hunger that they are. Probably the NGOs are your route in.

Q255 Lord Maclennan of Rogart: How do the European institutions tackle this? What is your message to them about civil society? Should this not be part of their programme?

Mr Consolo: There is perhaps a cultural point in relation to the European institution in this kind of situation. It is a question of strategy. We are all agreed that we need at one point, in 20 years' time, good governance in the southern countries. However, which is the best way to reach that objective? The European institution thinks that the best way is to maintain the relations and the aid through the government, trying to bring about more control, good governance, mechanisms, reform of public policies, *et cetera*. That is the main *discours* we hear at local level. On the civil society side, we think that it is much better to go not only through civil society actors but through, for example, local government, municipalities—other civil society actors, perhaps not NGO but the small firms, the agriculture movement—to consolidate a counter-power to the government. That is our strategy. All our members are working on this strategy. It is not just civil society because we would like to see civil society providing the role of government; but we feel that it is the only way to balance a little the bad governance—by strengthening the civil society side and the capacity to develop social audit throughout the country at local level. It is a question of strategy, and the European institution does not share this approach.

Q256 Lord Powell of Bayswater: Changing the subject, do you think that applying the procedures, the institutional arrangements, and the contractual nature of the Cotonou Agreement to other areas of European aid would be of benefit? Or do you think that actually all those procedures are just so much mumbo-jumbo, a bit of theatre to create a good impression? The limited evidence we have heard from the ACPs suggest a standing disaffection with the arrangements they have, both the parliamentary ones and the consultation ones, and so on. Are they really serving a useful purpose? Or do you think that it would be better to get rid of them altogether and put the ACP countries on the same footing as other developing countries in their relations with the European Union?

Mr Alhadeff: Are they saying that in relation to some of the recent controversies they have had?

Q257 Lord Powell of Bayswater: My experience is that they have been saying it for the last 20 years. It is a standing disaffection, and the fact that they do not really have a proper dialogue with the European Parliament or the European governments—that the European governments just tell them what to do and do not really listen, *et cetera*.

Mr Alhadeff: It is interesting that they then try to replicate the same idea at the level of the WTO. When that was mooted there, I thought that it was a difficult scheme to put into action. The people in the Parliament are very attached to it. Quite a few of the NGOs follow the process. We do not at all. We have tended not to follow the ACP meetings. But Olivier has a problem with the countries that are not in the ACP.

Mr Consolo: Yes. Of course they are the poorest countries; of course we have perhaps to invest more money in these countries; but if we limit the European Union action in this area, we are losing a lot of opportunity to export a development project from the European Union perspective, which is very different from the other donors. If you compare it with Japan or with the United States, we have a specificity. Focusing only on the ACP, we are taking a risk. On the other hand, the kind of agreement we have for co-operation and European aid with Asia, Latin America, MEDA, *et cetera*, is very limited—if you compare it with the Cotonou Agreement.

Q258 Lord Powell of Bayswater: Is it more effective?

Mr Consolo: We would like to see a little more equality, but it is not possible. They have revised the Latin America, MEDA, *et cetera*, is very limited—if questions of good governance and of consultation with civil society. We did lobby, but without a result.

Ms Viliani: The advantage of ACP and the Cotonou is the fact that, for the first time in all of these discussions with ACP, there is a clause regarding the obligation to involve civil society in all the planning and in the review. This is why most of the time NGOs or civil society actors look positively at Cotonou. It is because we realise that it is also a way to improve governance. If the government is obliged to respect civil society in their country, it will involve them in a negotiation. Civil society is quite a broad concept, but this is a means of improvement.

Q259 Lord Powell of Bayswater: If, as it seems to me, there is very little enthusiasm for it amongst the ACP, and no enthusiasm amongst European governments to extend it more widely in these procedures and arrangements, one wonders: why not just put everyone on an equal footing right across the development spectrum?

Ms Viliani: The ACP is also a political agreement. It is different from just a trade agreement.

Q260 *Lord Powell of Bayswater:* But is it really? That is what I am saying. I agree with you that all the panoply of political agreement was there, but it does not really function as a political agreement. They cannot get people to attend the meetings.

Mr Alhadeff: It worked quite well in relation to Doha—on the bananas. You can see that the ACPs were able to work with the EU to get a deal on bananas. But then in Cancun it did not work at all. **Chairman:** I am afraid that we are going to have to close now, before we progress further on bananas! Thank you and your colleagues very much for seeing us.

Supplementary memorandum submitted by Solidar

EU DEVELOPMENT POLICY

1. *Evaluating the Reform of EU Development Assistance*

European development cooperation has undergone significant changes since the late 1990s. The Prodi Commission started a restructuring process of huge dimension (2000 White Paper on reforming the Commission and 2001 White Paper on European governance) and has adopted a statement on development policy. Most of these reforms are responses to criticisms made in a series of evaluations, mainly about the lack of a poverty focus in development policy and about poor organisation of the Commission itself.

The process is not over yet and will definitively be affected by the new events occurring in 2004. In fact a new wave of challenges and changes is on the horizon, both internally and externally.

Internally, 2004 is a year with a tight timetable: the intergovernmental conference on the Future of Europe, the accession of 10 new Member States, the culmination of the de-concentration process, the European Parliament elections, the appointment of a new Commission, the mid-term review of the Country Strategy Papers; and especially the starting negotiations over the next Financial Perspective (next 6–7 year EU budgetary framework).

Externally, the revival of the trade multilateral negotiations after Cancun, the growing preoccupation with security matters worldwide and its consequences on migration and defence policies, the election in the US.

Undoubtedly, the EU has made substantial progress both in terms of organisation and policy. The Community development **policy** is committed to the Millennium Development Goals and its main objective is to reduce poverty. This objective entails support for sustainable economic, social and environmental development; promotion of the gradual integration of the developing countries into the world economy; and a determination to combat inequality.

The new **organisational** structure has created an autonomous implementing agency to manage the cycle aid and to support the delegations (Europe Aid). The deconcentration process is almost completed and the EU Delegations are becoming new key players drafting programming documents, spending money, managing programmes and acting as representatives of the Union. The Cotonou Partnership Agreement has been ratified and now it is being discussed to include the European Development Fund (EDF) into the EU budget under the control of the European Parliament. Finally **new programming instruments**, integrating aid, trade and political dimensions, have been elaborated: Country Strategy Papers (for over 100 countries) and Regional Strategy Papers (around 10 regions).

Nevertheless there are still many problems that need to be addressed and/or solved.

Points relevant for an effective EU development policy:

— coherence and consistency among different policies and instrument should be improved;

   — revision of the Country Strategy Papers should involve a better consultation with recipient governments and civil society;

   — co-ordination with Member States should increase, especially because more power is given to the EU delegation in third countries where also embassies or national agencies of co-operation are active;

— proper allocation of aid to least developed countries;

— the still very low level of aid, far away from the 0.7 per cent commitment;

— slow disbursement of funds (although provisional budgetary execution figures suggest that 2003 saw improved levels of commitments and payments both from the community budget and the EDF).

Country Strategy Papers

The **CSPs** are a relevant instrument of programming and consultation with the recipient countries and civil society. The CSPs are articulated around the six key sectors of the EU: transport, food security and rural development, trade, support for macro-economic policies and access to social services, support for regional integration and cooperation, institutional capacity building and governance. The rationale behind these sectors relies on two assumptions:

— these sectors are the ones in which the EU can provide an added value; and

— the larger the volume of aid targeted to key sectors, the greater will be the impact on poverty reduction.

Consequently, if the CSPs were reflecting the priorities of the EU (eradication of poverty as main one) and the allocation of money was done consequently, they could be used to improve the co-ordination between EU and Member States, but also with other international donors such US or UN agencies. A clear example should be the complementarity with the Poverty Reduction Strategy Papers of the World Bank. Nevertheless the process of elaboration of the CSPs has not been really inclusive, of both recipient countries and civil society; furthermore many crosscutting issues have been marginalised and scarcely mentioned.

In the case of ACP for example, it has been agreed that areas of focus in each ACP Country Strategy Paper should be limited to two sectoral areas (three in exceptional cases), with the idea that these areas would match the EC's priority areas where possible. Though, according to a research realised by EUROSTEP, out of all aid programmed thus far in 71 of the 78 ACP countries that are signatory to the Cotonou Agreement there has been no balance in explicit allocations of aid across the six Community priority areas, with a relatively small amount allocated to the social sectors. Transport receives the largest share—29 per cent. This is followed by structural adjustment—25 per cent. Allocations in the other 16 sectors recognised by the OECD's Development Assistance Committee (DAC) are all below 10 per cent. The percentage of water, health and education combined amounts to 15.5 per cent. The European Commission has stated that aid programmed in macroeconomic sector (which is not recognised by the DAC) may be used for health and education, but additional percentages in these areas derived from the macroeconomic sector are unclear.

Regarding gender equality, it is impossible to determine how much resources have been allocated to this crosscutting issue. However, according to an APRODEV the screening of 40 ACP Country Strategy Papers made at the end of 2001 by the European Commission's own gender helpdesk shows that the concept of gender and mainstreaming of gender equality is hardly found in the CSPs at all. Three per cent of CSPs mention gender in three of four sections of the CSP—31 per cent in two sections and 50 per cent in one section only, mostly in the chapters on EC objectives (terminology), Country Policy agenda and Country analysis.

2. *Looking ahead to 2004 and beyond*

Despite all the discussions taking place on the EU Constitution and the entering of 10 new countries in the EU, the new Commission will be set up later this year and this will mean another step in the reform of the EU with repercussion also on development. We can preview two different options:

1. a stronger Development Directorate with its own Commissioner, and maybe with the reintegration of the tasks of EuropeAid;

2. a stronger External Relation directorate managing the development instrument among other tools.

NGOs strongly advocate for the first option, especially regarding the EU as a global player. Development and humanitarian aid should not become tools of CFSP or any other external policy of the EU; the risk is to undermine the impact of development. A subordination of development and humanitarian aid under the Common Foreign and Security Policy would risk to lose its independence and to put in danger the internationally recognised and accepted humanitarian principles: impartiality, neutrality, independence; humanitarian actions would be transformed in political ones, with all the difficulties related with such a scenario including the danger to transform aid workers in easy targets for rebels or terrorists.

Despite recognising the importance of poverty reduction and human rights, there is an on-going discussion within DAC members [A1] regarding the re-direction of aid away from poverty reduction and towards a counter-terrorism and security agenda. There is grave concern that the counter-terrorism and security agenda risks violating fundamental human rights and further marginalising the poor and disenfranchised. According to the Global Security and Development Network, combating terrorism and combating poverty are not the same thing, while eradicating poverty may reduce the risk of terrorism, counter-terrorism strategies do not necessarily reduce poverty. Articulating this understanding crystallises the need for development co-operation to remain focused on eradicating poverty and protecting human rights—not preventing terrorism—as the goal of development co-operation.

Development policy should be the framework in which donors articulate development co-operation with development countries. Now, EU development policy has its own objectives: eradication of poverty is the main goal of any development co-operation with developing countries. Development countries are the ones listed by the DAC department of OECD and a great focus of the EU should be on the least developed countries (41 of the 48 LDC are ACP). This does not mean that the EU should not co-operate with "near abroad" countries, but it should keep in mind that the objective of the EU development policy is to eradicate poverty, while the rationale behind co-operation with near abroad is more political and related with external relations.

Poverty reduction

The performance of poverty reduction programmes is difficult to assess, because of the fact that poverty is a multidimensional phenomenon. According to the DAC guidelines:

An adequate concept of poverty should include all the most important areas in which people of either gender are deprived and perceived as incapacitated in different societies and local contexts.

Poverty encompasses different dimensions of deprivation that relate to:

— economic capabilities (the ability to earn an income, to consume and to have assets, which are all key to food security, material well-being and social status);

— human capabilities (health, education, nutrition, clean water and shelter);

— political capabilities (human rights, a voice and some influence over public policies and political priorities);

— socio-cultural capabilities (the ability to participate as a valued member of a community);

— protective capabilities (the ability to withstand economic and external shocks, such as hunger, food insecurity, illness, crime, war and destitution).

In the case of the EU an assessment of its results, is even more complex due to the peculiarity of its reality: it is a donor, a global player and the Union of other 15 independent donors and players. Furthermore the internal division among: Parliament, Council, Commission and the division in many Directorate Generals and services do not facilitate the mainstreaming of certain values or objectives.

Many debates are currently going on within the International Community regarding interventions towards poverty reduction, although a few points are essential:

— the reduction of poverty is based on the country ownership, the donors should support the dialogue during the programming phase and promote the participation of the civil society organisations;

— respect for human rights and good governance are critical for an effective partnership in reducing poverty;

— consistency among poverty reduction and the objectives of other policies in different regions (trade and external relations, among others);

— better co-ordination among international donors;

— to keep poverty reduction as the main objective of development policy, attention should be paid to the attempt of introducing new focus as migration or fight against terrorism which link with poverty are implied but not clear; and

— to define and improve approaches for poverty reduction through research, with special attention to the programming documents such as CSP or PRSP (poverty reduction strategy paper).

Adopting a poverty focus as the main objective of the EU development policy should be evident in the level of importance given to different sectoral areas, the allocation of resources programmed in these areas, and the overall design of the programmes.

3 February 2004

The commitment to the Millennium Development Goals require a special attention towards certain social sectors, such as primary education, gender equality and women's empowerment, reducing child mortality, improving maternal health, and combating HIV, malaria and other diseases.

Poverty reduction is not only about growth; therefore any policy that will focus mainly on economic aspects or co-operation will fail. Poverty reduction programmes can be implemented only by the national governments; it is therefore necessary to involve as much as possible the recipient countries. Without ownership there will be no possibility of eradicating or reducing poverty: consultation and common planning with the different stakeholders are key elements. It is necessary to state that governments, as well as civil society, are stakeholders in this process. The mid term review of the CSP is an essential moment for the EU and it is necessary to work out part of the weakness already mentioned (example: inappropriate allocation of money to relevant sectors, low involvement of civil society in the definition of the priorities, lack of specific measures and actions for cross-cutting issues).

CONCLUSION

We can conclude that the process started by the Commission has been positive although can be improved considerably. The key factors for analysing the impact of the EU development policy and its evolution in the near future are:

— the willingness of maintaining development and humanitarian aid as independent policies inside the EU structure;

— the level of commitment to the Millennium Development Goals as framework for the programming of EU aid (correspondence between the policy priorities and the allocation of money);

— the willingness of achieving the Barcelona commitments (0.39 per cent of the PIL to aid);

— the real capacity of improving the existing weakness in the management cycle (more staff, better guidelines, improved dialogue, quick disbursement, simplification of procedures); and

— the evolution of the EU architecture and the weight of the EU in an international setting.

Solidar Member Agencies
Arbeiter-Samariter Bund, Germany
Arbeiterwohlfahrt Bundesverband, Germany
AIF Arbejderbevægelsens Internationale Forum, Denmark
Associaçao de Servicio de Apoio Social, Portugal
COCIS, Italy
FCD Solidarité Socialiste, Belgium
FOS, Belgium
Humanitas, The Netherlands
Instituto de Estudos para o Desenvolvimento, Portugal
IFWEA
ISCOD, Spain
ISI, Instituto Sindacale per la Cooperazione, Italy
ISF Kansainvaiinen Solidaarisuusäätiö, Finland
La Ligue Française de l'Enseignement, France
Lega Provinciale delle Cooperative Bolzano, Italy
Norsk Folkehjelp, Norway
Nord-Süd Institut, Austria
OGB-L Solidarité Syndicale
Olof Palme Centre, Sweden
One World Action, United Kingdom
Schweizerisches ArbeiterInnenhilfswerk , Switzerland
TSL Workers' Educational Association Finland
Solidaridad International, Spain
Volkshilfe Österreich, Austria
War on Want, United Kingdom

3 February 2004

Observers
ICFTU
MPDL

Affiliated Members
UNISON, United Kingdom
Low Pay Unit, United Kingdon
STUC, United Kingdon
Kalayaan, United Kingdon
IFIAS, Belgium
Narodna Dopomoha, Ukraine
INOU, Ireland

EC

Gross Bilateral ODA, 2001-02 average, unless otherwise shown

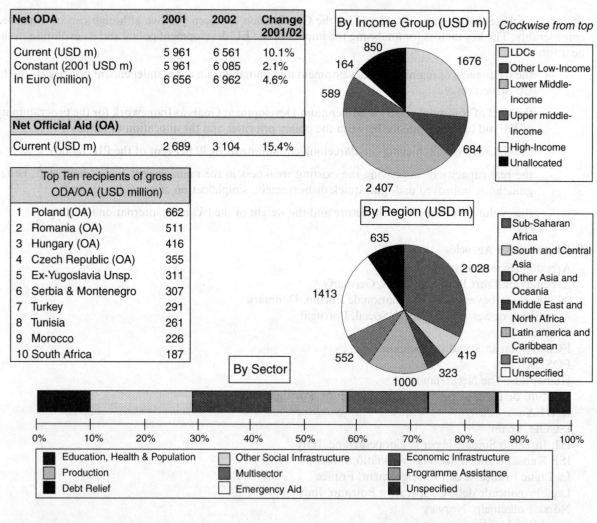

Net ODA	2001	2002	Change 2001/02
Current (USD m)	5 961	6 561	10.1%
Constant (2001 USD m)	5 961	6 085	2.1%
In Euro (million)	6 656	6 962	4.6%

Net Official Aid (OA)			
Current (USD m)	2 689	3 104	15.4%

By Income Group (USD m) *Clockwise from top*

850
164
589
1676
684
2 407

- LDCs
- Other Low-Income
- Lower Middle-Income
- Upper middle-Income
- High-Income
- Unallocated

Top Ten recipients of gross ODA/OA (USD million)	
1 Poland (OA)	662
2 Romania (OA)	511
3 Hungary (OA)	416
4 Czech Republic (OA)	355
5 Ex-Yugoslavia Unsp.	311
6 Serbia & Montenegro	307
7 Turkey	291
8 Tunisia	261
9 Morocco	226
10 South Africa	187

By Region (USD m)

635
2 028
1413
552
1000
323
419

- Sub-Saharan Africa
- South and Central Asia
- Other Asia and Oceania
- Middle East and North Africa
- Latin america and Caribbean
- Europe
- Unspecified

By Sector

0%   10%   20%   30%   40%   50%   60%   70%   80%   90%   100%

- Education, Health & Population
- Other Social Infrastructure
- Economic Infrastructure
- Production
- Multisector
- Programme Assistance
- Debt Relief
- Emergency Aid
- Unspecified

Source: OECD

TUESDAY 3 FEBRUARY 2004

Present	Bowness, L (Chairman)	Northover, B
	Lea of Crondall, L	Powell of Bayswater, L
	Maclennan of Rogart, L	Tomlinson, L

Examination of Witnesses

MR PATRICK CHILD, Head of the Patten Cabinet, MS BARBARA BRANDTNER and MR NICHOLAS BANNER, members of the Cabinet, DG External Relations, examined.

Q261 Chairman: Thank you very much indeed for seeing us. As you know, we are carrying out an inquiry into development policy and external assistance. We have been doing this for some time now. This is the last meeting that we are having after a day in Brussels. We started yesterday afternoon. You will probably have seen the Committee's call for evidence, the concerns that we have, and the areas that we want to look into. I am sure that members will want to put some questions about the reform of development assistance, where development and foreign policy are going, and possibly links between the two. You may care to comment, bearing in mind that there is a new Commission coming and the draft Constitution is wherever the draft Constitution is on the proposals for development aid, the effects of enlargement, the future of the ACP group—whether or not we continue with that—and what seems to be a matter of great concern, espoused with enthusiasm by a lot of our witnesses, the budgetisation of the EDF. Would you like to make some general remarks first of all, or take questions straightaway?

Mr Child: I am happy to do so. First, I should apologise that Mr Patten—who I know would very much have liked to meet the Committee—is unfortunately unavailable. You will perhaps know that this morning he is discussing the case of Ryanair with his colleagues in the Commission so, sadly, he is unable to meet you. Perhaps I could also present my colleagues: Barbara Brandtner who, in the Cabinet, particularly follows development policy issues, and Nick Banner, who is also in the Cabinet and is more engaged in the reform of external assistance, and those issues. I hope that between us, therefore, we will be able to deal with the questions that you may have. I know that you have had a rich programme, including a number of my distinguished colleagues, so I do not intend to second-guess what they have said. Perhaps I could say a few words on how Chris Patten has approached the reform of the management of our external assistance and the substantial progress that we have seen in the last few years. However, it is also a process which is very far from complete and which, as you rightly say, will be affected in the coming months and years by a number of further developments on the EU scene. With regard to the reform, I guess that the late-1990s were

a low point for the management and implementation of EU external assistance. It was a time which had seen very strong growth in the volumes of assistance which were entrusted to the management of the Commission. Successive political developments led to decisions by Member States to channel more and more development and other assistance through EU mechanisms, rather than through national programmes. So we saw, first, the opening up of eastern Europe and the start of the journey towards the present enlargement; and then the opening up of the former Soviet Union and the development of the TACIS programme, which was subsequently mirrored by the very substantial increases in the volumes of assistance to the Mediterranean and the Balkans regions. All that took place in an environment of huge political enthusiasm, but perhaps less hard-headed realism about what was required to implement all those programmes with the necessary quality and timeliness. It was those two challenges, I guess, which were most in our minds at the time when the reform was presented in 2000. You will no doubt have had a comprehensive briefing on the various aspects of the reform. The main elements were the creation of the new department within the Commission, EuropeAid, with responsibility for much more of the cycle of the projects and, in particular, to overcome the problems that perhaps had taken place in the past, where there was a temptation for services with a political focus to announce great ambitions in terms of the sorts of programmes that they would like to implement, without necessarily thinking through adequately the consequences in terms of the nuts and bolts of the delivery. It was that thinking which led to our concentrating responsibilities in EuropeAid for the whole delivery side of assistance programmes. This combines with a process which is of fundamental importance—and which is not yet fully complete— namely, the devolution, or what we call "de-concentration", of responsibility for much more of the management to our delegations in the field, in the partner countries where we are working. That de-concentration process has also allowed us to address one of the other very significant problems that I mentioned earlier, which is the lack of human resources and administrative capacity to deliver programmes. So we have been able to take advantage of the flexibility which exists in the funding arrangements for our delegations, to use more money to ensure that we have the right staff, both in terms of numbers and in terms of professional profile, to deliver assistance more swiftly and of a higher quality than in the past. As I have said, that de-concentration process is still underway. In particular, we have been working, last year and now, with the implementation of the transfer of responsibility for the ACP countries under the European Development Fund, and for a number of the horizontal programmes which are perhaps less straightforward in terms of de-concentration than those which are targeted on a particular country. In time, we will need to draw more conclusions than we have done thus far from the consequences of the de-concentration for the use of resources in headquarters. That brings me to a point that I will come to later, concerning the organisation of the future services of the Commission. I will quickly mention the other main aspect of the reform, which I think has been particularly important for Chris Patten in his work with the services here in the External Relations Directorate-General. This is the need to upgrade significantly the way we approached the programming of our assistance. I think that the new generation of Country Strategy Papers—and the intensified internal arrangements to ensure that the content of those strategy papers is both improved in quality and takes account of all the various themes of the development policy strategy and our other priorities in external assistance—has been widely appreciated by the partner countries. It has also been welcomed by the Member States we discuss it with, and the other actors, in civil society and elsewhere, who are involved in the process of managing external assistance. It has also been a useful focus for improvements in our dialogue with other international donors, like the World Bank and other leading players. It was important to separate that process, we believe, from the nuts and bolts of implementing the projects, and to bring it more closely into the policy agenda that we have for the EU's relations with the partner countries and regions that we are discussing. I think that we still need to go further, incidentally, in improving the overall coherence and the way that we deploy the whole range of policy instruments that the EU has at its disposal, in support of our wider political objectives—both our foreign policy objectives, if you can make that distinction, which are discussed primarily with the foreign ministers and the high representative, and also the development policy objectives which are set out so clearly in the Council's Strategy, adopted in late 2000. To summarise the reform, as I said at the start, it is still very much work-in-progress. We are not yet at the end of the story.

There is much more that we need to do in terms of consolidating the improvements in the country strategies, working more with the representatives of Member States and other international donors in the field, building on the achievement of the de-concentration. We can see very significant improvements, particularly in the speed and effectiveness of delivery in a number of regions. This has been so in the Mediterranean. I would say that we have done well in the Balkans. The Latin America programme last year was a significant improvement on previous years. These improvements are starting to flow through but, as anyone who has been through a similar set of reforms would perhaps acknowledge, this is not something which we can expect to be fully in place, in the sort of timeframe we are looking at. I think that the World Bank, in its own reforms which I guess went in a similar direction, took a period of rather more years—six or so—before the full effects of their reforms were in place. Finally, a word on the future challenges—and, of course, ones which will be more the responsibility of the successors of the present Commission than the present incumbents. You mentioned the three main themes. There is the likely institutional overhaul as a result of the, I would dare to say, ongoing discussions in the Inter-Governmental Conference. Leaving on one side the more controversial issues to do with voting rights, and things which led to the breakdown of the European Council in December, the IGC clearly points to the creation of a new Foreign Minister as a more coherent and central focus of the EU's external relations. This will replace the present, slightly uncomfortable, arrangements with, on the one hand, a high representative in the Council and, on the other, the Commissioner for External Relations in the Commission. We very much hope that the new Foreign Minister will be a genuinely double-hatted figure, to use the jargon. That is, to have a firm relationship with and be properly integrated into the Commission and its decision-making structures, which is important to ensure that the instruments managed by the Commission are genuinely supportive of the political agenda which will be emerging from the Council under the Foreign Minister's other, more political, hat. I guess that, sooner or later—and maybe it will be later rather than sooner—we will have this new figure. That will mean a certain number of changes for the organisation of the services of the Commission, in the way that we relate to the external relations specialists in the Council's Secretariat. There are ideas circulating, which you may have heard of, for the creation of a joint external service of some form. I guess that the final form of that will depend a bit on the preferences of the first Foreign Minister and on the final architecture in the new Constitutional Treaty, when it is adopted and, we hope, ratified. In parallel with that there will be moves, I hope, to transform our 120 or so delegations in the field in third countries into fully-fledged EU representative offices or delegations They would therefore also be taking on—in addition to the significant responsibilities they have at the moment for managing external assistance, and in other areas like trade and policies that are in the First Pillar—the full range of political representation that the new Foreign Minister will have under his or her responsibility. In the future, that will mean changes in the way that the staffing of those delegations is organised and, in particular, much more give and take and exchanges with the diplomatic services of the Member States and also of the Council. That is the first element. Second, there is the work we are doing on the next Financial Perspectives—the financial framework which will be in place between 2007 and, we guess, 2013. The Commission, we hope, will adopt a first set of ideas on that in a week or so. As ever with these big discussions on funding, the primary focus, whether we like it or not, is likely to be on things like agriculture, structural funds, and other internal policies. However, the External Relations Commissioners have been working hard over the last year to ensure that the contribution on the external side is not neglected, and we have designed a strategy based on three main priorities. First, the growing neighbourhood responsibilities of the enlarged Union. Second, the global responsibilities of the EU in development policy through the continued pursuit of the development objectives in the Council's statement on that. Third, the more political contribution that we can make to peace and stability throughout the world. Of course, there are links between these three themes, which are definitely overlapping and complementary, but they are the three axes of our contribution to the Financial Perspectives work. I guess that the profile will show modest but progressive increases in the external budget. You have mentioned one important element, on which the Commission has already taken a position. It is the idea that we should integrate the European Development Fund into the normal budget management systems of the Union. That implies certain changes at the margins in Member States' contributions to the European Development Fund, and a role for the European Parliament in the setting of budget priorities. We also see considerable benefits, however, in terms of improving the management of the European Development Fund and enabling the sorts of improvements that we have made, in terms of timely delivery and quality, to feed fully through into that very important programme. That is an important element to the debate, but it is not the whole story for the Financial Perspectives. Finally, the structure of the next Commission. I think that the only thing which is certain is that there will

be many more Commissioners than there are today. That means there will be rather more Commissioners who are taking an interest and have portfolios in the External Relations family, and I guess that it means that we will have to do even better than we have done thus far in terms of ensuring a strong degree of internal co-ordination and coherence in various different policy areas. Many ideas circulate. I guess that the most often talked about is the idea—prefiguring a bit, in a way, the arrival of the new Foreign Minister—that there should be an External Relations Commissioner who is a Vice-President, with a stronger co-ordinating and overseeing role than Mr Patten has at the moment in the present set-up; and then that there perhaps be Commissioners in different geographical and thematic areas, I guess including an important role for a Development Commissioner. Conclusions would then need to be drawn about the structure of the services working to those Commissioners, with two models. One, which has a lot of commonsense logic behind it, would be to try to group, even more than has been the case so far, the various different services working in External Relations into a smaller number of large departments. That would require more of a challenge perhaps, in terms of establishing how those bigger services related to the individual Commissioners, who, as I say, would be rather more numerous in the system. The alternative would be a more classical and perhaps less imaginative model, but one which might have its attractions for the incoming Commissioners: that each Commissioner would have their own little service dealing with their own particular set of responsibilities, and then there would need to be the necessary co-ordinating mechanisms on top of that. The present Commission has, I think, decided that it would be a good idea to think through some of these issues and offer a blueprint to the incoming Commission. It will be for the incoming President and Commissioners to decide whether or not to take up those ideas. I would say that we are still at a fairly preliminary stage in our own internal thinking on that, but it will be an issue which will preoccupy us over the coming months. I apologise, because I seem to have spoken for rather a long time; but I hope that gives you an overview of the issues.

Q262 *Lord Maclennan of Rogart:* I wonder if I could ask you about the relationship between the European aid and development programme and the national development programmes, in the light of the reforms that there have been. Is there any greater propensity to accept the policy priorities of the European programmes on the part of the member countries? Do Country Strategy Papers or programmes tend to chime with the aid priorities of the principal donors towards these countries? You mentioned specifically, again in the context of the interface between the

Union and the member countries, the proposals for the joint external service. I have not seen it being discussed explicitly in the development field, but it has certainly been put to us that some member countries are better at some things than the Union, and the quality of the service might be better if it drew upon those skills. Is it all much too early to see that kind of convergence developing between the Union and the members and their development programmes, or is it happening? How do you see it?

Mr Child: First, to what extent do Member States feel bound by or are guided by priorities set in the Country Strategy Papers? I would perhaps put the point the other way round. One of the drivers for doing better at doing programming through country strategies and being clearer, operational, and precise in what we say in those Country Strategy Papers, was so that we had an effective vehicle to have a more meaningful discussion, firstly with Member States, and also of course with the partner countries and with others who have a stake in the process. That is both in the interests of learning from the experience and greater expertise that many Member States have than we do in particular areas. It can also help to reassure Member States, in a way, that the country strategies provide an effective way to influence policy at a European level—so that they were perhaps comfortable to give us a slightly freer hand when it came to the implementation. One of the big problems we had in the past was that the various committees of the Member State experts we work with had a tendency to get into the rather detailed, micro-management of the design of individual projects—because, I guess, they felt that it was the only way that they could get a handle on the policy. So, in trying to do better with the country strategies, in setting out a clear basis for discussion on the strategy and on the policy, we could be getting some additional flexibility in downstream implementation. How successful has that been in achieving the results that I have described? If I am honest, it is still work-in-progress. As I said earlier, it is generally appreciated by the Member States, and by the partner countries, that there has a qualitative change in the quality of programmes and, in particular, that the mid-term review process that we are now undertaking is allowing us to get into discussion on some of the important new issues that have emerged and which should figure in those programmes. It is therefore serving our purpose as being the primary instrument that is discussed. Regarding the second question on the joint external service, and what potential input that might bring to the further improvement in the dialogue on country strategies, I think you are right that it is a bit early to say. If, in the time between now and when the joint service is created, we can do more in terms of staff exchanges, we will do quite a lot to overcome the occasional mutual suspicions and lack

of understanding, both on the part of the Commission and its services and also sometimes on the part of our friends and colleagues from the Member States. We are already encouraging the relevant services here to look at that more constructively now. I would mention one other point which is relevant in this connection. Following the informal Council of Foreign Ministers in Evian in the autumn of 2001, the Commission—and Mr Patten in particular—has been urging Foreign Ministers, to take a stronger interest in the relationship between political objectives, the pattern of spending, and the way that we use our financial assistance in support of our political goals. In that connection, we have been pushing very hard for the co-ordination between our delegations—with their new, enlarged, de-concentrated or devolved, responsibilities—and the diplomatic representatives of the Member States in third countries. Often, it is there that we find there is most understanding and experience of the real needs of the country and of the sectors in which we are working. We can have fun—and we do—in discussions in committees in Brussels, and there is a lot of good input that comes from that; but the value added of dialogue on the ground is vastly superior. We are working in that direction. I hope that the joint external service will take us further, but I do not think that we need to wait for that to see benefits starting to emerge.

Q263 *Lord Maclennan of Rogart:* We had it put to us at EuropeAid earlier today that there are areas where the Union has no *acquis*—education, for example—where it would make a great deal of sense to build in, from the start, the expertise of national resources that do have that. Would that be part of your thinking?

Mr Child: I would certainly strongly encourage that, yes. The EU's collective contribution to international development assistance is a very large—50 per cent or so of the overall international development effort. Only a smallish part of that is channelled through the Community budget and the Community instruments. The more that we can all be pulling in the same direction, the better our collective impact. Certainly the Commission should not be in the business of reinventing the wheel in areas where we perhaps do not have the historical expertise or the resources to do that, and should be joining up more effectively with what the Member States are doing. The one caveat that I would mention is that if that discussion comes the conclusion, "Wouldn't it be more sensible for EU money to be channelled through the national programmes of those Member States who have a particular track record in an area or in a country?" Although that makes sense at a certain level, it is also the sort of thing which encounters political sensitivities among those Member States who perhaps have less experience and less of a track record. If there is a decision to channel money through European instruments, it is precisely to overcome that sort of national earmarking.

Q264 *Lord Powell of Bayswater:* Thank you very much for the very full account that you gave. I think that we would all agree that the quality of EU aid has improved very considerably in the last few years. The establishment of EuropeAid was a great step forward. Equally, one of the feelings that we get from this visit, is that the next task is re-structuring at the top level, and you indeed have touched on that. I quite see that it is difficult to give any very clear indications when there is uncertainty over the Constitution, uncertainty over the Financial Perspectives, and uncertainty over the division of Commission responsibilities. But we are now in the last year of the Commission, and you and Chris Patten have both been here for quite a while. Rather tantalisingly, you mentioned "blueprints". Would you like to lift the veil a little on the possible blueprints, and give us you views on how the Commission might be structured in future to deal with developing countries? One senses some concerns, such as, for instance, how do you prevent a new Foreign Minister of the EU being able to raid development funds for foreign policy purposes? All these are arguments we faced in the United Kingdom where we have oscillated between having an ODA which is a handmaiden of the Foreign Office, and having a fully-fledged Cabinet minister in charge of development aid. How do you think these things could best be handled? We are not committing you to a view which the Commission is going to adopt, but just your personal reflections. What is the most effective model likely to look like, in your view?
Mr Child: I think that the debate is very much open and the starting point is whether or not, in a future set-up, it is desirable or possible to have a situation where, as I said, rather more numerous External Relations Commissioners have some sort of more formal hierarchical responsibility to the central figure—the External Relations Commissioner and, in the fullness of time, the Foreign Minister. I understand that that sort of relationship can bring attractions in terms of greater coherence but also the sort of risk that you mention—that policy instruments intended for one purpose may somehow be distorted to another. Although I would add that that argument is perhaps susceptible to exaggeration. There is an intimate link between political objectives, such as securing stability and peace, and development objectives. There is no prospect of having a realistic medium-term development strategy if you have not first stabilised the country. That tension between the two is perhaps sometimes put too starkly. If it is possible to have a situation in the next Commission where you have a cluster, as our jargon

has it, of External Relations Commissioners, led in a fairly strong, formal way by a Vice-President with overall responsibility for external relations. This is one model that the Commission has already been presenting and discussing in the context of the IGC. In that case, I guess that it would be easier to move in the direction of, for example, creating a rather larger department responsible for development policy and the implementation of assistance, and a rather larger department with geographical responsibilities for relationships with the whole world. In essence, that would mean some sort of redistribution of the responsibilities of the present DG Development, in a way which nevertheless had a strong development focus in EuropeAid and, at the same time, ending the rather illogical situation we have at the moment where country desks for the ACP countries are in a different department than the country desks for the rest of the world—which is not necessarily the way you would have naturally have started from. But we have seen the discussion in the Inter-Governmental Conference on the importance that Member States attach to each having their own full Commissioner, and that that Commissioner should have full voting rights. You have to find quite an imaginative way of reconciling those desires—which are politically understandable and legitimate—with the smooth and effective functioning of a cluster arrangement. If you do not manage to make the sort of cohesive cluster that I have described, then it becomes much more difficult to imagine a larger number of Commissioners dealing with a smaller number of services. You will always have two or three Commissioners who perhaps feel that they have a direct line of responsibility to a given Directorate-General; then, if there are differences of view—which, even in the European Commission, do occasionally emerge—then the mechanisms for sorting them out would not be obvious. It then becomes a more difficult discussion. I do not think I have a miracle solution as to what is the best. The lesson I would take away from the present system, however, is that the decision we took to put the programming of assistance with the country desks was the right one, and should not be revisited. If anything, we should be reinforcing the country desks in order to give them more of a handle than they perhaps have at the moment on our other policy instruments—be it external instruments like trade, or indeed the external projection of some of our internal policies, like transport, energy, environment, justice, and home affairs.

Q265 *Lord Powell of Bayswater:* Do you think there is a prospect that the present Commission will leave a last will and testament on this subject? Otherwise, I suspect that the rational organisation will become a victim to the political carve-up of jobs for the boys, as

one has seen in the past. It might help if the outgoing Commission were to leave at least a clear plan, which would have a status alongside the carve-up of jobs.
Mr Child: The clear intention of the present Commission is to do just that. I am of course unable to guarantee that the next President, whoever he or she is, will necessarily choose to implement it.

Q266 *Lord Powell of Bayswater:* But it is harder to ignore, if there is a clear plan which has a certain amount of support in advance from governments, from NGOs, and from public opinion. An incoming President's hands might be tied to a degree in the direction of following the rational course.
Mr Child: Yes, but it would depend on the degree to which such a plan was discussed and agreed with them in advance.

Q267 *Lord Lea of Crondall:* Following the same line of territory, in a sense, we have all been impressed in the last 24 hours by how much thinking outside the box is going on. To me, a strong point is that, in every meeting, we have seen the centrality of the Country Strategy Paper. If you are in Bolivia or Cameroon, or even in Macedonia, nearer home, it is obvious that you cannot have 15 countries dreaming up their own Country Strategy Paper. Game, set and match—self-evidently, you have a delivery mechanism within which there is a common interest in all the 15, or 25, in everybody having the same umbrella. The only thinking outside of the box which can meet that is what we have been hearing—which is very interesting—that Britain might agree to take the lead on health in Bangladesh, and Germany might take the lead in Venezuela on infrastructure, and so on. This leads to other thinking outside the box, does it not? We have all read in the newspapers about how this great new triumvirate of Britain, France and Germany will run the world, but there are all sorts of levels of thinking outside the box, given the sensitivities of different countries. You can imagine Sweden or somewhere else coming into this. If you take a mission in a typical African country, there is a problem that you have 15 country missions and it would be very helpful if some of them were in the same building, for a start. As I understand what you have said about the fledgling links between the foreign ministry type of approach and missions dealing with development, there will be greater synergy if people are somehow part of the same family of diplomacy—even though "diplomacy" is not a word that is very welcome to some NGOs, and so on, dealing with development. But this may have to come. Even on governance, the greatest dilemma that no one has cracked is that you perhaps have to have EU-AU in Africa—so that you can get a negotiation on a thing called Africa, so that governance can come in in a way that does not seem so much like neo-colonialism. I am sorry, that is a very wide range of territory, but it all has to do with this new architecture and I would be very grateful if you could say how much of that you think I have got right or wrong. Would you like to comment?
Mr Child: Your first point was on the proliferation of country strategies, the need to get our act together and to have one set of priorities, and then to ensure that we are all working on the chunks of it where we can most comprehensively add value. It is well established in theory. It is less easy to deliver in practice, of course, given the sensitivities and traditional patterns of working. However, I think that we are moving in that direction already. Incidentally, the de-concentration has given a very significant boost to what was previously sometimes rather symbolic and cursory co-ordination between donors on the spot. Now that many of our Member State representatives recognise that the Commission's head of delegation is often, managing a programme which is larger than their own national programme the advantages of working together through that sort of collective effort are becoming more visible and they are investing more seriously in it. I think that is a good development. It means that the Commission has to be more than usually sensitive to our role in the institutional set-up. We are not in any sense a sixteenth Member State; we are acting in the service of the Member States and of the Union collectively in the country, and it is important that our representatives handle that task in a sensitive and understanding way. An example of how we are, in an individual country, doing just what you say is perhaps in Afghanistan. The two or three top priorities are: drugs, which is basically a strategy that has been drawn up and co-ordinated by the United Kingdom; police, by the Germans; the judiciary reform, by Italy. That is part of the overall country strategy that we have and we have put in place throughout, but it is also mirrored in what is happening to the Member States' actions and their donors. It is a good example and it is one which I would also like to see developing elsewhere. The question of bringing together the diplomatic missions of the Member States—and, related to that, the staff that Member States have based in third countries looking after the management of external assistance through their national programmes—is a complicated one. I do not anticipate an immediate future where all of those national embassies are swept away and there is one central one. That is clearly not politically desirable or likely. There have been some timid moves towards co-location of missions. There is one in Dar-es-Salaam.

Q268 *Lord Lea of Crondall:* Some of the Central Asia republics?

Mr Child: You are very likely right. I think that there is a single building in Dar-es-Salaam which is shared by three Member States and the Commission including the United Kingdom. Obviously, geographical proximity does a lot to help mutual understanding and co-ordination. We are certainly not looking at any sort of complete centralisation of those functions. There will always be foreign policy, and commercial and other responsibilities over which Member States will want to have an independent control. I guess the area where there is most discussion—although it is outside the competence certainly of our DG and of the Union generally—is on the whole area of consular facilities, where Member States, and in particular finance ministries, see potential economies of scale and gains to be had by agreeing that, in a given place, the consular needs of a group of countries are handled by a particular Member State's consular service. It may be that, with growing experience of that sort of arrangement, there is also cross-fertilisation into more sensitive policy areas; but it is certainly not for tomorrow. You made a point on Africa and, if I understand it right, the way in which the collective EU approach could perhaps help us to break through some of the neo-colonial reflexes. Yes, that is true. We perhaps also have to do more in terms of the appointments that we make to our delegations, in some of the African countries in particular.

Lord Lea of Crondall: I mentioned the logic of AU-EU. But I am speaking too much.

Q269 Lord Tomlinson: You have painted this picture of Solana Mark II—double-hatted, being this super-Vice-President, leading a cluster of Commissioners. Where does that leave his relationship with the other part of his hat? It seems that he is too firmly entrenched on one side. I would like you to comment on that. My other question is on the Financial Perspective. As you are lifting the corner on the blueprint, can you lift the corner a little bit on what you see as being the differences in a Financial Perspective predicated on a 1 per cent of GNI, or 1.24 per cent, or the rather more ambitious views that David O'Sullivan put to the working groups on the Convention?

Mr Child: On your first question, the role of the Foreign Minister—forgive me for focusing on the side of the debate which is likely to affect us here most—we expect the Foreign Minister would be Chairman of the External Relations Council and therefore very much engaged in the discussions between ministers on foreign policy. If there is one weakness in the present set-up that I would point to—which I hope this double-hatted figure will be able to overcome—it is the occasional lack of a seamless relationship between, on the one hand, the political orientations coming out of the Council and, on the other, the way in which the various policy instruments managed by the Commission are deployed in support of those objectives—particularly, I would say, in the less sensitive areas. When we have something big—I have mentioned Afghanistan, but like the work in Iraq or elsewhere—there tends to be less of a problem than when we are looking at second-order issues. But, by bringing the two figures together and making sure they are firmly implanted on both sides, that is how we achieve a better coherence. However, I do not think that you should have any worries or doubts about the likely future relationship between the new Foreign Minister and the foreign ministers of the Member States in the Council. If anything, the fear in this building is that you could imagine that the relationship would be too far in the other direction. Your second question was on the Financial Perspectives. The Commission is toying with various scenarios. As I said, internal considerations dominate the discussion: the agricultural policy, based on the decisions that have already been taken for the future of the agricultural reform until 2013; the future shape of structural funds policy, given the very considerable needs that will come from the acceding Member States; and a very strong desire on the part of the Commission to make a significant contribution, recognising that obviously we do not have a full answer, to the whole debate on modernising the economies of Europe, in support of the Lisbon Agenda of a much stronger economic performance by 2010. I think that President Prodi has already made clear publicly his personal feeling that the ceiling of 1 per cent of GNI which is being presented by a number of Member States, is not one with which he has natural sympathy. I guess that, given the pressures on spending the Commission is unlikely to come out with a scenario which is as low as 1 per cent, and therefore we would not have done the calculation on the allocations that might lead to. I think that you raise a very interesting question for those Member States who have signed up to that particular letter. Although I know that the British Government have worked up a number of quite thoughtful, but at the same time ambitious, ideas for the future pattern of structural spending, which would produce an outcome which is compatible with 1 per cent, I am not sure that all the signatories to the letter have gone through the same discipline. Nor indeed am I convinced that, if they were to do that, they would necessarily come out with the same conclusions as Her Majesty's Government. So I think that this is an opening shot in the debate, and of course there will be a number of other Member States—particularly those who perhaps chose not to sign the letter I referred to—who will have rather different views about what the overall level of funding should be. I guess that the Commission will, in its proposals, seek to find a middle way in that debate, which will provide a useful basis for the Council to start discussions, we hope, in the next few months.

Q270 *Baroness Northover:* We have been hearing, as others have said, how encouraging the reforms have been in terms of the delivery of aid and the reorganisation that has happened. What is coming through very clearly from what you are saying, however—certainly to me—is how vulnerable all of this must be, with the reorganisations coming down the track. I was wondering what you think will be the impact of the new countries coming in, without this necessarily being a high priority for them. Clearly, an awful lot depends upon the new arrangements and, in particular, who are the new Commissioners. So much seems to have depended in the past on who the people are and what they have wanted to do. Will that not be even more the case in this kind of situation? How confident are you about the direction of reform—the direction in which you are heading at the moment— and that that can be sustained? How confident are you that it is bedded down sufficiently for it to continue to move in that direction? As a side issue, there is this question about budgetisation, which it seems to me is being looked at somewhat separately from these reorganisations that are coming down the track. Might there not be an argument for keeping funds outside the budget, lest that budget is indeed, as Lord Powell said, raided? Might it not be better to do that?

Mr Child: On the first question—yes, of course. The lifetime of any Commission is what it is—five years— and the time required properly to implement a very significant reform, on the scale that we are seeking to achieve and to see the full results of that in a consolidated way, is inevitably rather longer. So the present Commission, and the Commission as an institution, is always at the mercy of new arrivals with new brooms, having new ideas. Indeed, that has been rather the pattern of the organisation of the External Relations services of the Commission over a long period. There have been more different configurations of Commissioners' responsibilities, defined on geographic, thematic, or other bases over the years, than makes perfect institutional sense. So I think that there is a vulnerability there. Having said

that, the scale of the reform and the conviction throughout the system at the time that it was put in place—at the level of Commissioners, but also throughout the services involved—that the problems we were confronting had become so grave that this was really the final opportunity to get things right, is firmly entrenched in mentalities, and there is a lot of determination to carry the present reforms through. It is nevertheless possible to imagine, in a perfectly rational way, either of the models I have described in relation to the creation of the services of the new Commission—which would not undermine the basic philosophy of the report. That the responsibility for programming should be concentrated with the political geographical services that are looking after the various countries, and that that should be part of a broader effort to co-ordinate with other policy instruments too—trade, and the others which I have mentioned. That the implementation of assistance should basically be the responsibility of the same set of people from the moment that you decide what you are going to do to the moment that you deliver on it, and that should be done not in Brussels but by delegations in third countries—delegations who, incidentally, should also be making a progressively bigger contribution to the setting of priorities in the programming. I think that there is a sufficient consensus over those key elements for us to be reasonably confident that it will not be blown off course on a whim, and that the people who are advising the incoming team—including, we hope, with the benefit of a blueprint from the present incumbents, drawing on their experience—will be sufficient to keep the principles of the reform fully intact, so that the benefits will continue to flow through and the full impact will be established. There may be things that, as we learn from experience, need to be evaluated, and there may be decisions that we have to adjust in another direction; but the core elements of the reform are pretty consensual. That is the way the Commission works. We will have a new Commission President and a new set of Commissioners, and they will take their own decisions and their own political responsibilities.

Chairman: Thank you very much, Mr Child. We are all very grateful to you for giving us so much time, and we also thank your colleagues for joining us.

TUESDAY 24 FEBRUARY 2004

Present	Bowness, L (Chairman)	Northover, B
	Lea of Crondall, L	Park of Monmouth, B
	Maclennan of Rogart, L	Tomlinson, L
	Morris of Aberavon, L	

Memorandum by the Department for International Development (DfID) and the Foreign and Commonwealth Office (FCO)

INTRODUCTION: THE NATURE OF AID AND LINKS WITH FOREIGN POLICY

1. In 2002 the European Commission (EC) was the third largest grant provider in the world. Collectively, EC and its Member States provides half of all official development assistance (oda). In addition, the European Union (EU) is an important political and commercial partner for developing countries. Bringing all this together, the EU could be a tremendous force for good in the fight against global poverty and in achieving the Millennium Development Goals (MDGs).

2. The United Kingdom Government firmly believes that oda is for poverty reduction. Our poverty reduction objective is central to all DfID's efforts. It forms the basis of the 2000 International Development Act and our activities are geared towards achieving the MDGs.

3. Delivery of aid has changed in recent years. Donors including the United Kingdom are increasingly moving away from projects to promoting reforms. Poverty reduction requires sustained broad-based growth and structural change—backing reforming countries where we know aid can be more effective, and finding opportunities to strengthen "poor performers", while maintaining pressure for pro-poor reform.

4. This means we are usually guided by partner governments in designing programmes such as strengthening government systems, enhancing accountability to citizens, and public financial management reform. The private sector also needs support, since investment is key to growth. Aid is also shifting towards multi-year commitments to increase predictability for the recipient government and improve donor collaboration (for example, by pooling budget support and analysis).

5. The way donors have behaved in the past too often undermined these principles. Changing donor behaviour, including our own and the EC's, is an important part of making country led poverty reduction strategies work.

6. Global poverty reduction also serves wider foreign policy aims including those related to peace and stability, migration and terrorism. Post September 11 we live in a changing world with increasing security threats. Development is a prerequisite for a secure and safer world. Development and wider foreign policy aims can be complementary. Our approach to poverty reduction entails working in a broad range of areas including promoting economic growth, democracy, rule of law, human rights, peace and security, and good governance. These can also support foreign policy objectives.

7. Ensuring consistency between different policies which impact on poverty reduction in developing countries is desirable. Evidence suggests that most aid conditionality and aid not developed in line with country priorities and with national stakeholders is less effective. This has led development agencies to use their assistance to respond to, and build on, the interests of the recipient. The use of aid for non-development purposes is not supported by the United Kingdom. Further, we have untied United Kingdom aid.

8. While the International Development Act does not apply to United Kingdom expenditure through the EC budget, the United Kingdom Government believes that our approach to aid domestically should also inform that of the EC. Our objectives for the EC are to improve its aid effectiveness and to increase the amount of its aid going to the poorest countries, with a target of 70 per cent. At the European level HMG will continue to promote:

— using European development assistance to help reach the MDGs;

— applying international best practice on aid in both low and middle income countries;

— policy coherence;

— aid conditionality that promotes both aid effectiveness and aid objectives; and

— minimising the use of oda for non poverty reduction objectives.

9. It will be important to ensure a strong development voice at the European level to promote effectiveness. This has structural, financial and managerial implications including:

— ensuring a clear legal base for development co-operation in any new Treaty;

— creating supportive institutional structures, including a development Commissioner controlling development funds; and

— improving effectiveness, including managerial reforms that promote rational resource allocation, development behaviour according to best practice and clear objective setting and monitoring.

1. POLICY ISSUES

The 2000 Development Policy Declaration

10. The EC's Development Policy Declaration makes poverty eradication the principal aim of its development efforts. This is welcome and has helped us argue for more of the EC's resources to go to low-income countries. It also serves as a statement of intent to which we have been able to hold the Commission to account.

11. However, the Declaration is not the only policy document guiding the use of EC aid funds. There is a complex framework of both thematic and geographical regulations, each with their own objectives and procedures. Added to this are commitments made at international events. As a result, EC development efforts can appear fragmented and inconsistent with different objectives being pursued in different regions and circumstances, with no clear hierarchy. This has led to a lack of focus. We therefore think that now is an appropriate time to review the Declaration, both to assess its continued relevance and to clarify its role in guiding the future direction of EC aid.

Coherence and consistency

12. For Europe, coherence remains a challenge. Many of its non-development policies directly affect developing countries. The most obvious are the common agricultural and trade policies, and the growing interest in foreign, security and migration issues. The new European Security Strategy argues that security is a precondition of development and that new threats require a range of interventions. The Strategy links the foreign policy, development, and security agendas in response to the "new" security threats: terrorism, proliferation of weapons of mass destruction, failed states and organised crime. We recognise that enhanced security is a precondition for development, which is why the United Kingdom strongly supported the recent Commission proposal to establish an EC African Peace Support Facility. Ensuring better policy coherence will remain one of the key challenges for the years ahead.

The draft EU Constitutional Treaty

13. The draft Constitutional Treaty has rightly confirmed that poverty eradication is the central aim of EU's development policy, which should help focus EC aid on the needs of the poorest. The Treaty further argues that the Union's humanitarian assistance should be both impartial and neutral. These are important principles for ensuring that assistance should not distinguish between victims based on gender, race or religion, or the original causes of the crises. It also sets out the importance of making sure that the Union's internal and external policies are coherent with each other.

2. INSTITUTIONAL AND GOVERNANCE ISSUES

14. The reform of EC's external assistance programmes was launched in May 2000, with aims of improving the efficiency and effectiveness of EC aid. The reform was extensive, covering policy, new programming, reporting and financial procedures, institutional reform, and improved quality control. On institutions, the reforms created six entities involved with the management of external actions—DG DEV, DG RELEX, EuropeAid, DG TRADE, DG ECFIN and ECHO. The development of EuropeAid was helpful in uniting the management of aid within a single organisation and facilitating the reform and harmonisation of the Commission's fragmented financial and administrative framework. However, it has also created a rift between policy and programming (DG DEV and DG RELEX) and implementation (EuropeAid). Furthermore, it has marginalised DG DEV, traditionally seen as the "development arm" of the Union, in relation to DG RELEX

which plays an increasing role in emerging areas such as governance, democracy, human rights and conflict prevention.

15. The reform programme also assessed the Commission's staff mix resulting in a recruitment campaign to boost its development policy and management capacity, both at headquarters and in the field. However, it is still under-staffed in comparison with other development agencies and in relation to the size of its portfolio. This lack of capacity is most evident in new and emerging areas, namely governance and conflict prevention. With considerable development expertise around Europe, the Commission should strive to focus its efforts where it can make a difference.

16. Since the abolition of the Development Council, development is discussed within the General Affairs and External Relations Council (GAERC), which hosts two "development-focused" sessions a year, and bi-annual Development Informals convened by the Council Presidency. This has resulted in less time and space for strategic development discussions at EU level. In the case of the United Kingdom, this has promoted closer co-ordination between DfID and the Foreign Office on development issues.

3. ALLOCATION ISSUES

17. Over the last 10 years, the EC has given increasing amounts of aid to middle-income countries as Europe has turned its attention to its neighbouring countries, through programmes such as Tacis, PHARE, CARDS and Meda. This was partly in response to increased EC aid commitments in reaction to events in the Western Balkans and former Soviet Union, together with increased funding of the Mediterranean region. It is true that many of these countries have clear development needs, but these programmes were not originally set up as poverty reduction instruments.

18. It is perfectly justifiable for the EU to be concerned about security, development and prosperity in its neighbourhood. However, this must be balanced against its responsibilities for helping developing countries across the globe. If aid is to support achievement of the MDGs, then it should go to countries where it is needed most and where it can best be used. It is encouraging that EC aid spending is now beginning to move in the right direction, with 52 per cent of aid going to low-income countries in 2002 up from 44 per cent and 38 per cent in the previous two years. This is still below our 70 per cent target (a figure achieved in the 1990s, and more in line with the 65 per cent Development Assistance Committee (DAC) average). The United Kingdom is exploring ideas on how to improve EC aid effectiveness in all developing countries including applying lessons on what we know works best. This could entail an expansion of the role of lending and technical assistance to middle income countries, with more grant funding to low-income countries.

Implications of Enlargement

19. The accession of 10 new Member States in May 2004 could lead to a shift in the Union's development focus as different views and priorities are brought in. The new Member States will want to address the development needs of their neighbours in the East and Southeast. However all Member States have signed up to the existing Treaty and development policy, which provides a strong focus of development efforts on poverty reduction.

4. AFRICA CARIBBEAN AND PACIFIC (ACP) GROUPING AND THE EUROPEAN DEVELOPMENT FUND (EDF)

20. The Cotonou Convention, which covers EU relations with 78 ACP states, is a unique agreement in that it links development, trade and political relationships. The grouping also contains useful joint institutions at ministerial, ambassadorial and parliamentary levels, which provide an increased voice for poor countries. The ACP is funded through the EDF, which has by far the strongest poverty focus of all EC programmes; 89 per cent goes to low income countries compared to 31 per cent for the EC budget. The EDF allocates aid to countries based on the extent of their need and the likelihood of using it well (performance)—principles we would like to expand to the EC budget as well. We fear such principles could get lost with unconditional budgetisation of the EDF.

21. ACP membership is historically based and unique to the EU. Whilst issues are generally worked on at sub-ACP groupings, the ACP as an entity may be under threat from any budgetisation of the EDF, or moves to set up new regional grouping in the future Financial Perspectives. Whatever its future, it will be important to retain the EU's special political and developmental relationship with these countries.

5. RELATIONS WITH MEMBER STATES

22. EC and Member States' aid is complementary and mutually supportive, particularly when it supports the countries' own poverty reduction priorities and is provided in the form of support to the budget. This is the case in a growing number of African countries. EC requirements for field-based co-ordination and new European commitments towards better donor co-ordination and common systems and procedures should also pave the way for more effective aid in the future. Both the Maastricht Treaty and the draft Constitutional Treaty call for more complementarity and co-ordination to improve overall effectiveness.

23. The EC can help bilateral aid efforts, due to its institutional set up and size, such as the scale of its humanitarian assistance, and its global network of delegations. It can play a key role in co-ordination and complementary in the areas of trade and regional integration. It also has long experience in particular fields, for example infrastructure. However, the EC needs to improve the overall effectiveness of its aid that it can fully exploit its comparative advantages.

24. The EC is being asked to support a growing number of new development areas, potentially spreading resources thinly across a range of issues with limited capacity. The United Kingdom would welcome a tighter focus on areas where it can, and already is, adding value. The EC has an important role in bringing all Member States' policies up to the level of the best, in ensuring good Member State co-ordination in constructing a coherent European policy framework towards developing countries, and in aid implementation.

January 2004

Examination of Witnesses

Witnesses: HILARY BENN, a Member of the House of Commons, Secretary of State, MR NICK DYER and MR DANIEL SHIMMIN, Department for International Development, examined.

Q271 *Chairman:* Good morning, Secretary of State. Thank you very much indeed for coming to give evidence to this Committee. As you know, the purpose of our inquiry has been to try and take stock of the reform programme of European Development Aid, bearing in mind that the reforms have been in place now for some two years, and to look at what could be done to make it more effective, and to look at a number of other issues that arise out of the development aid policies. I do not know whether you wish to make an opening statement.
Hilary Benn: I am quite happy to proceed to questions.

Q272 *Chairman:* The Committee will be quite happy to receive any contributions that your colleagues wish to make or that you need to ask them to make.
Hilary Benn: Perhaps I can introduce Daniel Shimmin and Nick Dyer.

Q273 *Chairman:* Can I ask you a question that stands, to some extent, on its own, and that is the vexed question about the articles in the draft constitution treaty relating to development aid? You will know that some of the NGOs have expressed concerns about them as they stand. Are you able to tell the Committee whether the Government would seek to re-open the discussions on those articles, assuming the discussions are re-opened generally on the whole issue during the Irish presidency, or indeed in whoever's presidency they are re-opened?

Hilary Benn: The latter part of your question, Mr Chairman, is a much broader subject, which I probably will not stray into, given the degree of interest there is in the whole IGC process. In answer to the first part, I would say that we were broadly content with the outcome as far as the draft treaty is concerned. We welcome the references to shared competence, the separate chapters for development co-operation and humanitarian aid; the fact that poverty reduction will be at the heart of development co-operative; and the neutrality principle so far as humanitarian assistance is concerned. The thing that has yet to become clear is exactly what the role of the European Foreign Minister would be in the design and management of external activities, and to what extent development and, for example, trade policy are going to be coherent with each other. It partly depends on what the structure of the new Commission is, which I think is the last point I would make in reflecting on the point you have put.
Chairman: We will come back to a number of those issues.

Q274 *Baroness Northover:* I want to ask you about the nature of the relationship between the EU's foreign policy and development policies and how you think they could interrelate and what you think needs to be done in this area.
Hilary Benn: My view is that the two need to complement each other. I know that in the development community, if one might use that term, particularly since the events of September 11 and

what has happened over the last two years, that in some quarters concerns have been expressed that somehow development considerations are going to be forced to take second place to considerations of security and foreign policy. I think that whichever way you look at it, we all have a common interest in tackling poverty, injustice and inequality around the world because if we do not do that, then we are not going to have a safe and secure world in which to live. I think that one of the consequences of the events of the last two years is that in addition to the development constituency, which is rightly fired by moral outrage at the condition of humankind around the world, there is another group of people who are now more open to the argument that promoting development, tackling poverty, injustice and inequality actually does have a contribution to make in the broader sense, increasing the chance that we will live in a safe and secure world. It is not about having a hierarchy of policies; the two have got to work together, and that is the challenge for the EU in taking forward its work in finally reaching decisions on the IGC. We have to make sure that we give appropriate attention to the different needs that there are within those broad objectives. No doubt we will look at this in more detail later, but making sure that the EU spends more of its development money on the poorest countries of the world, which it has not done historically—and in recent years has not done very successfully—is, I would argue, an important contribution to safety and security in the long term as well as being essential for human development.

Q275 Baroness Northover: What do you think the impact of the new accession countries will be?

Hilary Benn: That is the really important question. First, in relation to development policy, they have to make the switch in their minds from having been recipients to being donors. I remember that when I visited Romania, which has aspirations to join, and spoke to the Governor there about the approach to development policy, he said: "It is a very good question and we are going to have to start thinking about it." It is quite a difficult thing to do, to start participating in the meetings of GAERC, faced with all the questions that we discuss on a regular basis, and then to have to take a position on poverty focus and EU development spend—for example, the annual report that the Commission produces on the effectiveness of development policies and what more needs to be done. That will be the first challenge. Member States in general, and the United Kingdom as well, need to talk to them. There are some structures that have been set up to try and help them. The second implication is that the accession states are going to bring with them their own new near-abroad. One of the fundamental issues as far as the EU's external action policies are concerned is the tension

that there is—let us be very frank—between the desire to promote development in the countries just across the border with the EU and, on the other hand, development in parts of the world that are further away. It will mean that we are going to have to re-double our arguments in favour of spending more EU development money on the poorest countries of the world because you are going to have a larger group of Member States that are thinking, understandably, about what is just over the new border of the EU. I think those are the two big challenges that the accession states bring with them to the discussions we are having.

Q276 Baroness Park of Monmouth: Secretary of State, do you feel at all uneasy about the proposal that the African Union has made to the EU for money for a peace support operational facility? Do you feel that perhaps there may be a danger that in following Solana's strategy of robust pre-emption we may find development money being spent in a way that we would not have wished? Secondly, is that not going to complicate the whole position of the Foreign Minister because it is going to extend development money into the area of the CFSP and the ACP?

Hilary Benn: the straight answer to your first question is that I do not feel uneasy. On the contrary, I think that Poul Nielson's proposal to get some money out of the EDF for a peace support facility is a very good idea. Obviously, we need to make sure that the process is right, but I think it is a really practical response to what is a very urgent need. Why? I wholeheartedly welcome what the African Union is doing on the peace and security front. When I was in Maputo in the summer for the AU summit, Thabo Mbeki made a speech and said, "we have got the peace and security protocol; please, Member States, hurry up and sign up to it so we can get it going". Sufficient states have now ratified that protocol. Why does this matter? It is because conflict should concern us, and dealing with conflict and resolving it, and picking up the pieces afterwards, really ought to concern those of us who are passionate about development. Why? If you do not have peace, you do not have stability, and the prospects of any other developments taking place are pretty non-existent. Part of Africa's problem in recent years has been the extent of the conflicts. We happen to be at a moment in history when the number of conflicts is radically reduced. Mozambique in the long term; Angola; there is a transitional government in place in the DRC—fragile, but at least they are talking rather than fighting; and a peace agreement in the process of being negotiated in Naivasha as far as Sudan is concerned—so that is an opportunity. Do we need to build regional capacity around the world to deal with conflict? Yes, we do. Why? If we do not do that, then the expectation and the burden of providing support in certain situations actually falls on a small number of countries, one of which is us. We cannot do it everywhere, so increasing the amount of capacity to do this is absolutely the right thing to do. The AU has had a force in Burundi, which has been doing a very good job. I have recently given some more money to help support that, because funding is a constant issue. ECOWAS took the initiative in Liberia with a bit of support from the Americans, and the situation is better there than it was before. I think it is the right thing to do therefore. We ought to have an interest in it from a development point of view. It is very practical because it is helping Africa to do something that it is beginning to want to do for itself. That is how I see it.

Q277 Lord Morris of Aberavon: I paraphrase what you have said, that there is a tension between the hopes of the accession countries and the needs of the poor countries. Is not the reality that there is a real danger that the interests of the decision-makers who will include the accession countries have a higher priority, and the poorer countries will lose out? Should we not monitor this, and how?
Hilary Benn: The most practical way in which we monitor it of course is looking at the percentage of EU development spending which goes on the poorest countries of the world. If you go back a couple of decades, from a very high proportion of poorer countries in the world, it has gone down and down and down, and it has got down to a low point of 38 per cent. It then went up in 2001–02 by 3 per cent. There have been some interim figures for 2002 but we are not quite sure what the final figure is going to be. That is the nature of the problem. The United Kingdom's policy as far as our bilateral aid is concerned is that we are moving towards a higher proportion of our spending on the poorest countries of the world. By 2005–06 it will be 90 per cent. Why does this matter? If you look at the total amount of aid in the world, it is less now than it was a decade and a half ago, so the amount has fallen; the share of that going on the poorest countries of the world has also declined. So there is less money in the system and a smaller proportion is going to the poorest countries. The United Kingdom's policy of increasing the proportion going to the poorest countries is a contribution that we can make, being only one donor in the system, to try and re-balance that. The EU spends a lot of money and that is why it is important that we should see that proportion increase. However, I do not for one second, Lord Morris, underestimate the extent of the difficulty in persuading others to share that view, because as I said in answer to the earlier question, they bring a different perspective to the table. It is not actually going to make the task easier.

Q278 Lord Lea of Crondall: As a supplementary question on that, Secretary of State, it is often said about the Balkans –we did a report in the House of Lords on the west Balkans, and in a sense it goes back to Lady Park's question—that the spend in the west Balkans in the European family was something like €5 billion a year. Five billion was spent over 5 years on development assistance, one way or another. Two things seem to be necessary to get together, do they not: you have got to get down the military spend as fast as you can safely do so; but in that period, looking at the totality of the European taxpayers' contribution to the west Balkans, you are probably going to be increasing, on that bit of near-abroad, development systems for the reconstruction of the west Balkans, but, as a trade-off, rapidly significantly reducing the military spend. In a sense, you have to look at the total arithmetic. Would that be a reasonable comment?
Hilary Benn: We certainly do need to look at the total arithmetic. Clearly, there are particular issues to do with the Balkans, both in terms of what we as European countries did in relation to the Balkans; and, secondly, by definition, this is very much Europe's back yard as far as that work is concerned. It is not surprising therefore that one sees the figures broadly that you have just described. All I would say is that the international community as a whole has signed up to the Millennium Development Goals. We will be tested, measured and judged in a decade and a year's time on the progress that we have made. We will all gather in New York in the autumn of 2005 at the Millennium Conference, which will ask the question how we are doing. The answer is going to come back that on current trends we are not going to meet many of them. We are particularly not going to meet them because of what is happening in sub-Saharan Africa. Therefore, what contribution is the EU, for its bit, making to this? It is a point I would like to come on later if we touch on the effectiveness of the EU's development expenditure, which I am sure you want to raise. How are we going to make a difference? Looking at the huge imbalance that there is in development assistance per head of population per person in the different parts of the world, it is out of kilter, which is why we in the United Kingdom are arguing very strongly that that should be re-balanced. However, as I said a moment ago, I do not underestimate the difficulty of persuading other people who have other points of view.

Q279 Lord Tomlinson: Secretary of State, can I move you towards budgetisation. As I understand it, DfID, the Foreign Office and the Treasury are currently opposed to budgetisation. Can I ask you two questions about that? is it just the different keys that are being used for EDF funds and the main budget, which would be financially disadvantaged? Is that the main reason or the only reason for opposition to budgetisation? I can understand that from the Treasury point of view, but is it also the DfID point of view that it would involve a switch of part of the development budget to the EDF? But apart from that question are there other issues of principle involved and associated with the general question of budgetisation? Are there any circumstances in which DfID can see budgetisation of the EDF as having a positive influence on development policies?

Hilary Benn: There are two issues. One is cost because, clearly, we are contributing 12.7 per cent of the EDF. After the accession states come in, we are going to be 18 per cent contribution towards the EU's regular budget; so there is a cost difference. The principal issue—money is always an issue, but the principal issue is this question of the percentage of expenditure that goes on the poorest countries of the world. In that respect, the EDF has a much better record because of countries that constitute the ACP states, but it has a much more effective focus on poverty than the EU's development budget generally, and therefore the concern is that if you fold that in and you then have re-created out of the total sum of money available the pattern of spending of low-income countries as opposed to others that we currently see in the EU development budget, we will have moved away from the objective that we have set; and that is the principal concern. Would there be any circumstances?

Q280 *Lord Tomlinson:* If it were ring-fenced, for example for the current pattern of expenditure; would that make it acceptable?

Hilary Benn: That might beg the question in those circumstances what the purpose of the budgetisation in the first place was. There is also the essential division of the political and other mechanisms by which the EU relates to the ACP states; although you could perfectly well keep that arrangement while budgetising the actual expenditure. As things stand at the moment, we are not persuaded for those two principal reasons. Hypothetically, if the EU were to make changes to the way in which the current development budgets are spent that moved in the direction that we are arguing very strongly for, that might be another matter. We are not there at the moment.

Q281 *Baroness Northover:* I wanted to pick up on that. The argument has been made to us that it would be much more streamlined to have it budgetised, to have the same processes applied across what was being done in development aid. Do you feel encouraged by the reforms that things are moving in the right direction—the development of the country strategy papers and the devolving processes that they

are developing? Do you feel that under those circumstances there is some weight in their argument that things should now be budgetised and all put together so that that can be carried forward?

Hilary Benn: There are two parts to your question. One is the reform process itself and how it has been coming along. The second one remains: what would be the percentage of spend out of, for the sake of argument, a development pot that included budgetised EDF financing, and where would that then leave the percentage going on low-income countries? That is not necessarily linked to the effectiveness with which the money is then spent. As far as the reform process is concerned, it was much needed, as I think everybody recognises. I think it is making reasonable progress, although there is some way yet to go. There has been reasonable progress in the sense that I think the EU has done pretty well in doing the things that it said it would do as part of the reform process. For example—the terrible jargon, the de-concentration—the devolution of responsibility to country office is wholly sensible. It reflects very much the approach that we increasingly take as a government organisation. You do not have to think about it terribly long to realise why it makes sense: you have people on the ground who know the country better, and they have built up relationships. We in DfID have a very high level of devolved responsibility, and I see the benefits of that every time I get the chance to visit a country and talk to my colleagues there. Forty-eight out of the 78 have been de-concentrated so far, and they have got another 30 to go. That is the first thing. They are paying out the money quicker; there is no question about that. I am told that on average 75 per cent of all invoices are now paid within 60 days. This, I am reliably informed, constitutes real progress. An example of that is Kenya, where they have now got a fully decentralised office. The average time to process payments has gone down from 50 days to 8 days. There are therefore real signs of progress being made. The other part of that is the annual report, which is beginning to reflect greater attention being paid to the effectiveness of expenditure, because there are process issues and then there is the effectiveness of the progress. The thing that is missing, which would be the next stage, is how the EU would relate all of its development effort to achievement of the Millennium Development Goals. If you were to look at what would be our forthcoming departmental report, what would figure very prominently in there is assessing progress towards the Millennium Development Goals in the particular focus countries that we have agreed with the Treasury as part of our PSA target we are going to be measured on to see what progress we make. I would say that that is the next stage. So they are looking quite effectively at the projects and trying to judge whether they are successful or not; but better co-ordination between that and achievement of the Millennium Development Goals is one priority, and the second is more effective co-ordination with other donors within countries. That is not just an issue for the EU; it is an issue for us as well.

Q282 *Lord Morris of Aberavon:* Secretary of State, what would be your preferred outcome on the current negotiations at the next set of financial perspectives? Is there any possibility or prospect of a separate development budget that could be provided for providing aid to the poorest countries? I ask that against the background that there was a great deal of newspaper reporting six months ago or thereabouts that money was going to Iraq, whether it be for us or Europe or both, and was going to Iraq at the expense of aid to the poorer countries. Was that true or not?
Hilary Benn: No. In relation to the United Kingdom, if are you asking—

Q283 *Lord Morris of Aberavon:* I am asking on both.
Hilary Benn: To deal with the United Kingdom first, we have the commitment, as I explained a moment ago, to move towards 90 per cent of our budgetary spending going on low-income countries. One result of that has been that we are balancing our expenditure, and that means that some of the programmes that we have had in middle-income countries, ie, less poor countries, we have been reducing in size and in some cases coming out of those countries altogether. That was a process that was already taking place. Most of the money that we have put into this commitment of £544 million to Iraq's reconstruction between April 2003 and March 2006 has come either from central contingencies across the Government or DfID's contingency reserve; and a small part of it has come from re-allocation within our middle-income country budgets. I would argue that what we are doing in Iraq at the moment is very important and right. That is not to say that there still will not be a very considerable middle-income country programme, in particular through the work that the European Union does, and to which we contribute. Your first question was about the financial perspectives. The Commission has made its proposals. There is not as much detail as we would like to see, but they are on the table. Broadly speaking, they are reasonably good suggestions about trying to simplify our budget. We welcome the proposal to create a single Economic Cooperation and development budget with a focus on poverty reduction. We are concerned about the proposal to increase the volume of expenditure. We want to see the EC stick to 1 per cent of gross national income. However, I think it provides the beginning of the opportunity for a debate, and one has these three things working together: the IGC wording, what is going to happen

to the Commission structure, and the debate about the financial perspectives. I suppose the big issue is this: how can we, within those three opportunities that we have now got, try and ensure that the EU does spend more of its money on poor countries, which we want; and that it does so in as effective a way as possible, in other words to build on progress. There has been real progress as far as reform is concerned, but on both of those issues there is still a very long way to go.

Q284 *Lord Morris of Aberavon:* Given that there is poverty everywhere and it is a question of giving priority to one against the other—and I make that comment regarding our aid—what is the bottom line if you look at all the sources of money for Iraq, whether from here or from Europe? Have the poorer countries suffered or not?
Hilary Benn: I can only speak with most authority about what the United Kingdom has done, and I have described to you the process that we went through in order to protect a higher proportion of a growing United Kingdom aid budget, which is very important, going to the poorest countries of the world. Clearly, when we met in Madrid in October, and $32 billion was committed in grants and loans and a mix of the two, there was a very strong expression of international commitment to supporting Iraq, which currently—according to the best classification we have—is a low-income country as we speak today, although it is expected that it will very rapidly get above the threshold. That is the World Bank's working assessment. Why? It is because it has been impoverished and brutalised and traumatised by the last 30 years' experience. I make no apology for the fact that we have committed the resources that we have. We have a moral responsibility, and if we give the support now—which is the crucial point—for the reconstruction of Iraq, so that people feel their lives are getting better and the political process can work—then Iraq has natural resources in abundance and a highly educated population, and all the capacity in the world, if those two were sorted, to come out of the last thirty years and actually chart a much better future for itself without requiring continuing assistance from the international community in the form it is currently being given.

Q285 *Lord Lea of Crondall:* In response to the last point and the first reply to Lord Morris from the Secretary of State, you mentioned in passing the 1 per cent ceiling aspiration of the whole of the European budget, 1 per cent of the whole European national income. Do you see it logical—a problem in fact—if we were to want to see more of our development spend go via multilateral resources, via the EU in this case, the arithmetic would show that if 1 per cent was somehow correct in year 1, and by year 5 you wanted to have more going through the EU, for the same amount of taxpayers' money you would have logically increased the level of the EU budgeting. This raises the general question of how much should go through the EU. We have just been shown the draft of the transcript of the report of the House of Commons Scrutiny Committee that you attended on 4 February, and there is quite a theme along that line of questioning there. "Why should so much go and why can we not spend it better ourselves?" You gave the interesting answer: "We cannot all go to these countries and say we have got a plan for them, and then the Dutch say they have got another plan." I would like you to enlarge on that because it is a very central point for our report, and a second important element, which is the limited number of competent people in a typical African country, for example. If you take the number of 15, and they all turn up not only have they got contradictory views, but they have got a lot of people rushing around, with a limited number in that regard. As long as the pattern is developing, is this not a logical case for saying, "we want to explain to the British public why more money has to go via the EU and certainly not go retrospectively"?

Hilary Benn: The first two answers I give are that given the current circumstances, where in the past, by the EU's own admission, development spending has not been as effective as it might have been, and that is why there is a reform process; and secondly, given that the proportion going to the poorest countries of the world has declined over the last decade and a bit, has begun to turn up questions in which direction it is now going to move; and compare that with, as far as our development of bilateral programmes is concerned—I think we do a pretty good job. We could always do better. Certainly, we have a very clear focus on the poorest countries of the world. You can see why one would argue, in the hypothetical situation that you put, that one would need to see very significant further progress on both of those fronts before saying "we want to put more money through the EU rather than bilaterally". The second answer to your question is that there are certain areas in which the EU has got what you might describe as a comparative advantage, as one sees reflected in a lot of the programmes that they are working: trade and regional economic integration is a very big issue for sub-Saharan Africa in particular, where we can see some moves now taking place to integrate regionally—and that is a process that we want to encourage; there is macroeconomic assistance, transport, some infrastructure, and some work on good governance. I think that those are areas where the EU should focus its efforts. Obviously, it does some work on health and education in support of the good governance and macroeconomic assistance,

including budget support. The third thing I would say is that the really big challenge for all of us is to make sure that whoever we are, whether we arrive as the EU, the United Kingdom, the Netherlands or whoever, is that what we do pays really close attention to what the government of that country itself has determined are its objectives. The poverty reduction strategy paper is the mechanism for making that happen. There has been a lot of argument and persuasion to get the international system to rally around that. The second challenge is to make sure that the way in which we provide our support reduces transaction costs and minimises the burden on hard-pressed ministries. There is no area in which that is more strongly illustrated than tackling HIV/AIDS, which is, in sub-Saharan Africa in particular, a really big development challenge which cuts right across everything. As a world, if we are not capable of dealing with that, then the prospects for development in some countries is very bleak. Malawi loses more teachers every year to AIDS than it trains, so there is a fundamental problem in that country. Whether it is our increasing bilateral spending on HIV/AIDS work—and we are the second largest donor in the world at the moment, and we have increased that seven-fold since 1997—whether it is the global fund or the Americans with the new money they are putting in the system, the discipline has got to be on all of us to work in a way which supports developing country governments. That is why—repeat after me what we call the three ones: one policy for tackling HIV, one strategy; one body in the country responsible for doing it; and one mechanism for reporting. If we really sign up to that, as donors, whoever we happen to be, then we maximise the chance of increasing the amount of money in the international system to fight HIV, which is a good thing—the global fund has levered in more cash. The growing public attention and global commitment can then be turned into change on the ground.

Q286 *Lord Tomlinson:* Secretary of State, can I take you back to an answer you gave to Lord Morris? You used the words "stick to 1 per cent of gross national income". The present financial perspective, which takes us through to 2006, is not 1 per cent; it is 1.24 per cent of GNI, or 1.27 per cent of GDP. It is only the expenditure currently being held at 1 per cent because of the frugality of the European Parliament in its votes in the budgetary process. I can understand the letter that has been signed by the Chancellor, Mr Gordon Brown, and maybe privately I welcome it, but there is nothing to stop the European Parliament this year using the old financial perspectives in actually voting non-obligatory expenditure up to a limit of 1.24 per cent of GNI, is there?

Hilary Benn: The actual payment, as you say, is currently 1.01 per cent.

Mr Dyer: To some extent the Council has to agree the budget as well.

Q287 Lord Tomlinson: Not on non-obligatory expenditure. On non-obligatory expenditure, which is essentially everything except the Common Agricultural Policy, the European Parliament have the final word, and even if there is a dispute the President of the Parliament signs the budget when it comes into effect as it is. Therefore, they could in fact, if they are provoked excessively, blow 0.24 per cent additionally on non-obligatory expenditure.

Mr Dyer: If they got through the Council process and the conciliation process.

Q288 Lord Tomlinson: They do not have to go through a Council process, though, do they?

Mr Dyer: A conciliation process.

Q289 Lord Tomlinson: At the end of the conciliation process, if they fail to agree they have the last word, do they not? I think it is important to make sure that we understand the same figures, because 1 per cent is an aspiration of the Chancellor and it is not a reality in the current financial perspective.

Hilary Benn: It reflects the actual current level of expenditure.

Lord Tomlinson: That is right.

Q290 Baroness Park of Monmouth: I simply want to put on record how utterly I agree with what the Secretary of State said in his evidence to the Scrutiny Committee on the DRC, when he points out that there has never been a state design—not rebuilding something that has never been there and trying to persuade people that the Government actually does something for you. I was deeply impressed by that; it has got the DRC in a nutshell.

Hilary Benn: It is very kind of you to say so. Indeed, I was merely replaying back to the Committee on that occasion what President Kabila said to me when I met him in Kinshasa in December. The scale of the challenge in that country is enormous. Historically, we did not have a very good presence because it did not form part of our Anglophone African inheritance, so to speak. But we are increasing our aid programme there. We are looking to establish a fully devolved DfID country office by 2005 because my very firm view is that given what I said earlier about the opportunity we now have with peace breaking out across significant parts of Africa, the international community has a real responsibility in those circumstances to say, "we will come and support you in return for continued establishment of that peace". It is not "whatever you do, we will help you"; this is support in return for success in

establishing that peace and taking it forward. We could not forgive ourselves if we did not take the opportunity there is, given that this is a continent where 3 million to 3.5 million people were killed, frankly before the television cameras went into Bunja last year. If you asked most people in this country to please name the African country where 3 million to 3.5 million people had been killed in the last decade, in what some people have described as "Africa's hidden first world war", frankly very few people would have been able to identify the DRC as the place where it was done. I can only repeat that it is an enormous challenge, but it is right that the international community should be coming in. I think I am right in saying that we are now the third largest bilateral donor in the DRC, and I think it is right that we should be giving that help to a very complex and difficult process that President Kabila and his colleagues are having to take forward.

Q291 Lord Maclennan of Rogart: Secretary of State, in the written evidence, which was very helpful, and in what you have said this morning, you have either directly or indirectly drawn attention to the questions that are uncertain at the moment about the future shape of institutional arrangements.

Hilary Benn: Yes.

Q292 Lord Maclennan of Rogart: I would like to seek to come to terms with what your thinking is in these areas. The strands which have come out of what has been submitted in writing include such things as the fact that the Commission is under-staffed in comparison with other development agencies and in relation to the size of its portfolio. It has also been shown that it is to some extent as a result of deliberate reform processes and regulatory policy programming implementation; there is some suggestion that DG Dev is marginalised; and finally, as evidentiary of the problems that have come up, there has been the issue of the abolition of the Development Council. Does this have a significance? We have had it put to us that it has resulted in less time being spent on key development strategies at EU level. Some of your policy stances, and those of government, appear to flow—and I am thinking particularly of your earlier answers on budgetisation—to the failure to arrive at strategic policies with which you are in agreement. I am sorry that that is a rolled-up question, but what are the institutional changes which you would like, focusing on particularly the question of the Foreign Minister's role, which you said was uncertain? What would you like? You said it was uncertain about the structure of the Commission. What would you like? Perhaps that is enough!

Hilary Benn: Firstly on staff, it may have been Baroness Northover who talked about skills that the Commission has got as far as development is concerned. Part of the challenge that the EU is facing in its reform programme is that you need very different skills if you are processing invoices and running programmes in Brussels to working in a devolved country office, rolling up your sleeves and getting to work on development. One of the problems, frankly, which the Commission has faced in making the transition from one approach to the other is finding sufficient people with the right skills to do that work. That is partly a training need and partly a problem arising out of transition. We need to acknowledge that. That is the first thing, having the right number of people with the right skills. Secondly, as far as the structure of the Commission is concerned, this is all very much up in the air, but since you asked me the question I will do my best to answer it. My view is that there is a very strong case for having policy and implementation together, as far as development is concerned. I say that partly because DfID is a department where we make a policy, we do the implementation and we do the humanitarian aid; and it seems to work reasonably well. It is a bit dysfunctional to have them separately. Whether that would be the outcome or not, to be honest I do not know. However, what is essential is a strong development commissioner who is responsible not only for policy but he or she should also be able to oversee effective implementation; but I do not see how you can divorce one from the other. That would be my aspiration as far as that is concerned. On the Development Council, clearly there was an agreement reached in the greater scheme of things, which reduced the number of councils in the interests of streamlining. That is what happened and that is where we are. We now have the two specific meetings as part of GAERC, where the focus is on development. In practice, at other meetings, development issues are also on the agenda for discussion. The onus is on us, as development ministers, to make sure that we use the structures within the new streamlined arrangements for making sure that development is up there alongside the other foreign policy and security considerations. I believe very strongly that this should not be about a competition within a hierarchy. Each has its place and we need to make sure we are working to make them complement each other as effectively as possible, and not subordinate one to the other.

Q293 *Lord Maclennan of Rogart:* Where does the Foreign Minister come into the picture as far as you are concerned?
Hilary Benn: Partly that will depend on precisely on the structure of the Commission and we are going to have to wait and see what the outcome is on that front. Clearly, you want to have a Foreign Minister who understands the development argument and the need for broader development around the world; and

you need a Development Commissioner who understands that there are perfectly legitimate interests as far as the near abroad are concerned in regard to foreign policy and security. I suppose I come back to the point I made right at the beginning in answer to one of the first questions. This is the world as we find it. I do not think the development interests and the development community should be anxious about having to engage with broader issues of foreign security policy because I think the development community has a really strong argument to make about the long-term security and foreign policy benefits of tackling poverty, injustice and inequality around the world. If we look at states where that has not happened, which begin to fail, and where there is a breakdown of law and order, you get conflict. We then deal in Europe with one of the consequences, which is refugee flows. We live in a world now where, increasingly, events that occur in one country affect other countries; so anyone who ever argued in the past, "it is all very unfortunate; let's pull up the drawbridge and hope it will all go away"—that is not going to work. Therefore, providing you get it right I think that the two can sit alongside each other very effectively. That is my view.

Q294 *Lord Maclennan of Rogart:* For the avoidance of doubt, can you say what you would like to see as far as the Foreign Minister is concerned? You have said it is in the air and we know you cannot predict the outcome, but what would be preferable in terms of the relationship between the Foreign Minister and the Development Commissioner?
Hilary Benn: I think the most preferable thing is that there should be a strong development commissioner with responsibility for policy and implementation, because I think that is the most coherent thing to do so far as development is concerned. In the context of the IGC, as I said, I think that is a reasonably good outcome. In practice it is going to be about how the two work together and how the principles that are set out in the IGC, assuming it is agreed in the form as far as development is concerned in which it is currently drafted, work with that to take it forward. What would be problematic is if you broke up Commissioner responsibilities that cover different bits and pieces, because I think that is a less functional system and one where you have very strong development interests.

Q295 *Lord Lea of Crondall:* Secretary of State, concentration on poverty may be a false argument if it is felt that some people are not concentrating on poverty and instead concentrating on governance or economic growth or foreign direct investment. India over the last ten years—they have now 7 per cent per annum average economic growth—reduced the number of people on the world development goals in poverty from 45 per cent to 35 per cent, and I guess that something similar is happening. Therefore, is it not a false way of putting the argument to say you are or you are not concentrating on poverty? Is not the real problem—and I take the continent of Africa—that of course we want to meet the Millennium Development targets, but all these questions of governance, transparency, corruption and so on are terribly important? Therefore, what we are circling around is the objection of neo-colonialism and so on. Can you comment on how far it would help to have more umbrella policies under perhaps the African Union, AU/EU, so that you would really get through to what would create foreign direct investment, as well as domestic capital formations, simply because you find it more acceptable to get these policies in and moving without being accused of being imperialist and neo-colonialist?

Hilary Benn: I am tempted to say that your last comment is always a risk that we run in certain quarters (I am sorry—that was a joke!). I do not think there is a conflict between saying we are interested in poverty reduction and questions of good governance, dealing with corruption and promoting foreign direct investment, because we know that all three of those, and lots of other things, are absolutely fundamental to making progress. That is the truth. The argument is about whether we should be focusing more of our effort in the poorest countries of the world where, if we make progress, we have the best chance of achieving the Millennium Development goals. I happen to think that that is entirely the right policy, but the truth is that if we are going to make progress towards the Millennium Development goals it is not just a question of the total amount of aid within the system. In one sense, if it was just a question of the total amount of aid, if you could get the money it would be easy to fix. However, it is not just that, although it is important. Why has Kenya just seen an increase in the number of kids going to primary school? It is because it has been able to abolish its user fees, and we made a contribution of money, alongside others, which has helped to make it happen. That is progress. That is moving us towards the MDG on getting 130 million kids around the world who are not currently in primary school into a classroom with a desk, a textbook and a teacher. Debt relief is part of the answer. What we are going to do on world trade is of fundamental importance because if we can sort out agriculture and get the World Trade talks back on track and reach agreement, depending on which estimate you take the benefit that would flow to poor people in poor countries would be worth three times the value of all of the aid which the rich world currently gives. If you do not deal with conflict, what are the prospects? Do you want to come and invest in a country where there is a war going on? No, you do not. If you have not got the war, can you get a long

lease on the land; can you enforce a contract; will you face problems of corruption? These are all of the things that need to be done which maximise the chance that development in a country is going to take place, so I do not see a contradiction between us being interested in poverty and governance and everything else over here; they are all part of understanding better the things that need to happen and what countries need to do for themselves and what we can do to help them to maximise the chances that people are going to be lifted out of poverty. China is a very good example because it is in the process of economic development, which has meant that China is the one country in the world that has lifted more of its citizens out of abject poverty in the last generation than any other on the planet.

Chairman: If members agree, I think we do want to cover the rather different point which is reflected in Lord Tomlinson's point about the EIB, but I am conscious of time as far as you are concerned.

Q296 *Lord Tomlinson:* We have had a lot of discussion today about poverty focus. What do you think therefore about the possibility of getting greater poverty focus from the EU development budget if there is a possibility of using other EU instruments such as EIB loans but dealing with the needs of the middle-income countries and thereby leaving the European Union development budget for greater poverty focus? Is that a feasible objective in relation to poverty?

Hilary Benn: I think it is a really pertinent question, and it is one of the things that we think is good in principle because clearly the middle-income and some of the relatively better-off countries are in a different situation to those that are the very poorest. Therefore, looking at a graduated system of support would be a good direction in which to move. I think that is good in principle. How you would do it in practice is another question. It would assist us in dealing with the problem we have identified in answering your questions today.

Q297 *Lord Lea of Crondall:* The EU Annual Report on Development Assistance and its continued lack of focus and fragmented development profile: how do you square that with your diversity of aid programmes? Can you comment on the relationship of those two?

Hilary Benn: The fact is that we have now got this, and I think I am right in saying this is the second year in which they have produced this. In my previous incarnation in DfID, when I was Parliamentary Under-Secretary of State, I attended the Development Council, where the first report came. I remember Poul Nielson saying: "This is not perfect but at least we are making a start." I think we should congratulate the Commission on what it is now seeking to do. It is still quite long, but that is perhaps an unfair criticism and I had better make sure now that our departmental annual report is not quite so long, or I will be taken to task on this! I come back to what I said in answer to a previous question: there needs to be greater focus on performance and the difference that it makes. Frankly, this is the challenge for all of us in development because we focus a great deal on process. That is for the very good reason that if you get the process right, then you can get the outcomes that you want. However, in the end what matters is the difference it makes and how you quantify and measure this, because we are spending public money, and it is the best way of going back to the world out there and saying, "this is what we have been able to do for what we have spent so far; if you think this is good and it is making a difference, can we have some more?" That is part of winning the wider political argument for development assistance, which is important in the United Kingdom and in the wider world, given that the world is giving less development assistance now than it was a decade and a half ago. I made an earlier point about linking it better to achievement of the MDGs because that would be extremely helpful. With the work they are doing on activity-based budgeting (ABB), that will help. I do not know whether Nick wants to say something about how he feels that process is coming along. That, too, is a step in the right direction.

Mr Dyer: It is, and they are committed to introducing ABB. This is the first year it has been introduced. We are working with the European Commission to try and make sense of what we can get out of the process. I think the ABB is a step in the right direction more akin to something like our Public Service Agreements/Service Delivery Agreements (PSA/SDA)—where you can start seeing objectives and making links between objectives and activities. It is very much a step in the right direction. I do not think they have got it right yet but certainly it is an innovation.

Q298 *Baroness Northover:* Picking up the point about poverty focus, you have been somewhat critical of what the EU has done. I would like to ask you about your view on their country strategy papers. You have obliquely said that it is extremely important that there is a poverty focus when you are working with the governments. Is that an oblique criticism of the kind of country strategy papers that they are coming forward with, or would you fully support what they have done? After all, we are not going to move to a position where there is going to be this co-ordinated approach within each country if you do not agree on what the countries in question need to do.

Hilary Benn: It was not intended as an oblique criticism because I think they are a step in the right direction. As you have just stated in asking the question, part of what we all need to do is to look at the country with which we are working and ask ourselves what we identify as the needs, and what is the particular contribution that our development programme, whether the United Kingdom bilaterally or the EU through its own country strategy paper, can contribute. We should also look at what other people doing because it would not be sensible for us all to do everything in a particular country; and where we can pool our effort, for example through a sector support programme in health and education for instance, or where we reach agreement across donors that we are going to move towards budget support, clearly there have to be the right circumstances. If you come to the view that the government has got a good credible plan, a poverty reduction strategy paper is in place, it knows what it wants to do and has mechanisms for spending the money and using it effectively, but they lack the cash to make things happen, to get more kids into primary schools and improve the availability of healthcare whatever, then there is a strong case in those circumstances for saying, "okay, let us give them budget support in those circumstances". I think it is a step in the right direction. When I talk about the need to be coherent in the way we behave and to harmonise, that is a comment I direct at everybody, not at the EC, because in some countries you get a strong sense of a greater or lesser degree of harmonisation co-ordination. It is a principle that everybody signs up to. If you say, "we need to harmonise, everyone will go out and nod their heads" but the question is: do we do it? It includes us and it includes other countries as well.

Q299 *Baroness Northover:* Do you see the EU as playing a leading role in deciding that that in a particular country maybe they are going to co-ordinate things, so that the United Kingdom has a commitment in terms of developing schools and Norway something else; or do you think we are a long way off that?

Hilary Benn: There are clearly examples where donors have pooled their money through sector support arrangements, and there are examples where donors have pooled their money through budget support. What tends to happen is that there is a different set-up in different countries. It depends partly on the personalities of the individuals who are the country representatives or heads of departments. It is important that they should meet together on a regular basis and should share and exchange information. They should work as hard as possible to make sure what each of them is doing supports where the country itself wishes to go. It is entirely sensible to divide up the work. There may be circumstances in which the EU will lead in particular areas. I think it matters less who leads in which particular area in a country. I would not be in favour of imposing around the world the fact that the EU is going to lead on that and the United Kingdom on that, because I think we need to have regard to country circumstances and the fact that donors would have been there for a period of time and built up strengths and relationships with government departments. I think you need to build on that but always ask the question: "Are we co-ordinating and harmonising the work we do in a way that will maximise the difference that our money, effort, passion and commitment makes on the ground". That, in the end, is the real test.

Q300 *Lord Tomlinson:* There is just a small point arising from that, because you have laid great emphasis on coherence and co-ordination. Going back to the question that Lord Maclennan asked, are you satisfied that in post enlargement Europe, with the now inevitability of a much larger coalition than some of us would have liked to have seen, that you are necessarily at the level of the Commission going to get greater coherence? I would have thought that bearing in mind the empirical evidence of having more commissioners to whom they have to give something to do, there might be less coherence at the level of the Commission. Are you taking steps to try to influence advance decisions in that?

Hilary Benn: I think my modest contribution to that bigger political question would simply be to reinforce the point I made in answer to Lord Maclennan: as far as development is concerned, what matters to me is that we get an outcome which ensures that there is coherence between the different bits of development. That does not necessarily solve the problem as you have put it, Lord Tomlinson, as far as how the rest of the responsibilities will be divvied out. That is the thing that I am focusing on because that will make the difference.

Q301 *Baroness Northover:* Are you focusing on a particular person coming down the track? Obviously, Chris Patten has had a major influence, and a lot may very well depend on who replaces him.

Hilary Benn: I am not focusing on a particular person; I am focusing on trying to get the right structure, and it will be for others to determine who the particular person is.

Chairman: We have covered the area fairly well, but you mentioned the ACP in answer to one of the questions about its structure, and we have also touched on the Balkans. In the last few minutes, I will first ask Lady Northover to pursue the ACP issue briefly and Lord Lea afterwards so that we would at least have covered those topics specifically.

Q302 *Baroness Northover:* You have been emphasising your poverty focus, so what is the future for the ACP? Is there not a case for treating all low-income countries on a similar basis as far as development aid is concerned?

Hilary Benn: Currently, about 90 per cent of the EDF goes to low-income countries. The most fundamental principle is that the assistance should be allocated on first of all the basis of need and, secondly, performance. You clearly want to support countries that are taking steps—going back to the question that Lord Lea asked me a moment ago—in relation to governance, corruption and so on. In the end, this has to be a partnership between the EU and developing countries themselves, and we should give support to those countries and also to the countries that are taking the steps that they want to take, which all of us know are going to maximise the chances that the lives of their people will be improved. There is clearly a lot of work underway at the moment on the negotiation of the partnership agreements, which is going to take some time. We need to see that process through. Also, progress has been made in trying to make sure that the EDF money is spent more effectively and more quickly. I simply come back to the point I made earlier that compared with the development budget generally, it does have a much higher focus on the poorest countries of the world, and that is something that we need to preserve. That is really important.

Q303 *Lord Lea of Crondall:* I am sure there are good reasons for increasing the share of the EU Aid to developing countries from 50 per cent to 70 per cent, but on that argument why do we not just put poverty as such as the criteria? Why do we not put more money into North Korea? Clearly, there must be some conditionality. Can you comment in conclusion about how far there is a necessity of a negotiation where you say effectively "there is the money" and put the money on the table"? There must be some sort of relationship between the flow-back, before you say, "there is another one".

Hilary Benn: On this central issue of conditionality, which of course figures very prominently in a lot of debates that we have about development, then there are very few people who say that there should not be any conditionality at all. The best example, to make the case for some conditionality, is when General Abacha was in charge of Nigeria and the international community gave Nigeria in aid about $1 billion during the period of his rule, and he and his family it is estimated nicked from the people of Nigeria $3–4 million. This is a problem. The question is: what is the right type of conditionality? That is the way that I would put the argument. The Bank and the fund increasingly accept through this mechanism called the Poverty and Social Impact Analysis, the argument that taking decisions about support and aid and programmes that they are going to do, that they should take account of the effect of what they are proposing and the effect it would have on poverty within the country concerned. I think one of the things we need to do is to make sure that the Bank and the fund are consistently undertaking those PSIAs and, secondly, to ask the very legitimate question: "What have you decided to do differently now, having done it, having looked at the impact of what it was that you were proposing to do in the first place?" That is the real test. Thirdly, what we do should support the poverty reduction strategy plans which countries themselves have drawn up. In the end, we have to be able to demonstrate the progress. If corruption is not tackled or your customers do not collect the revenues that are owed, it makes sense—and we do work in some countries—to encourage customs organisations to be more effective in collecting money. If you collect money, you have got more in the pot to then spend on health and education. There are more controversial questions that are to do with spending money on state-owned enterprises that are losing cash hand over fist. Any government in the end is going to have to make a choice in carrying on spending that money; or you could say: "If we did not spend it there, then we would have more available to do other things." None of this takes away from the choices, which, in the end, developing country governments have themselves got to make about what they want to do. In the end, they have the greatest incentive and interest in trying to solve these problems because it is about their people, their country and their future. We have got to make sure that the support we give is applied in a way that maximises the chances of that happening and also demonstrates to our communities that the aid we give makes a difference—and it really does, but we have to work harder to demonstrate that.

Q304 *Chairman:* As far as the freeing-up point, how realistic do you think it would be to persuade the whole of the EU that they should reduce their aid to the Balkans and the Mediterranean, bearing in mind the interests they have in what you referred to as "Europe's back yard"?

Hilary Benn: That is the fundamental question, which runs right through everything that we have discussed this morning. It is not a euphemism, but I think it will be quite a challenge not least in relation to your question and that of Baroness Northover about the impact of the accession states, because it does inevitably change the balance. We might as well be honest and open about it; it changes the balance. All we can do is continue to make the arguments that I have tried to make today about the Committee about why this matters, and why, if you take a broader and longer term perspective so far as security and foreign policy is concerned, it really does make sense that we should be doing something about poverty, injustice and inequality around the world. We all have an interest, and even though some countries may see their immediate interest in relation to their immediate near abroad, for reasons that we can quite understand, as far as the future of the world is concerned, this is something that together we really do need to do.

Q305 *Chairman:* Secretary of State, thank you very much for giving us so much time. It has been a very interesting morning. I can assure you that we could have kept you very much longer but we are aware that you need to go away.

Hilary Benn: I do hope it has been helpful to the Committee.

Chairman: I am sure all the members have found it helpful.

WRITTEN EVIDENCE

Memorandum by Dr Anna K Dickson, University of Durham and Dr Peter Clegg, University of the West of England, with research assistance from Chris Savory, University of Durham

1. The European Community's Development Policy, and the associated Declaration agreed by the Development Council in November 2000, provides a rationale for the EC's continued engagement with the question of development and the importance of poverty eradication, and highlights the key criteria that will define the EC's development policy in the future. The focus of this evidence is to highlight the position of the Caribbean within the EC's development agenda, which has been increasingly marginalised and downgraded in recent years. An indication of this can be seen within the EC's Development Policy statement, which makes reference to sub-Saharan Africa and southern Asia, but no explicit reference to the Caribbean region.

2. The EC's Development Policy statement correctly identifies sub-Saharan Africa and southern Asia as particular hard hit areas with regard to poverty and its related outcomes, such as chronic malnutrition and high levels of communicable diseases. It is right to focus on those areas of the globe which have the greatest development needs, and that a significant amount of development aid should be channelled towards them. However the omission of the Caribbean in the EC's Development Policy Statement is an unfortunate oversight as the Caribbean, now more than ever, is facing a series of important developmental and poverty related challenges which require EC support.

3. The evidence concentrates on a number of policy areas of particular importance to the Caribbean within the context of EU International Development Assistance, namely the issues of poverty reduction, development policy coherence, the relationship between middle income countries, aid disbursement and poverty, and the place of the Caribbean within the ACP grouping.

4. *Question 1b. To what extent have poverty reduction and the agreed cross-cutting issues, including the environment, gender, human rights and good governance, been incorporated into country programmes?*

Country programmes in the Caribbean reflect a variety of aims and objectives for resource allocation in the 9th EDF. Policies to promote poverty reduction are paramount. For example, in Belize under the National Poverty Elimination Strategy and Action Plan (1998–2003) 88 per cent of the total expenditure is for rural development where 42.5 per cent of the rural population lives below the poverty line. In Antigua 90 per cent of EC aid is intended for education, in St. Kitts, the comparable figure is 85 per cent while in Trinidad and Tobago 80 per cent of funds are allocated for tertiary education. In Dominica 100 per cent of funds are intended to improve road infrastructure complementing previous EDF initiatives in eco-tourism, and agricultural and economic diversification. In Grenada 90 per cent of EDF funds have been allocated to tourism. In St Lucia 90 per cent of EC aid is intended to help build a new hospital. These *foci* all contribute to poverty alleviation.

5. There is also evidence that some of the agreed cross cutting issues have been incorporated although they only account for a small portion of allocated aid in the 9th EDF. For example, in 2002 the EU Initiative for Democracy and Human Rights (EIDHR) gave €1.1 million to the Commonwealth Caribbean Death Penalty project run by Penal Reform International. Such regional initiatives are good examples of EU initiatives designed to promote Human Rights in the Caribbean. However the Caribbean region receives less money for human rights projects than either Africa or the Pacific because of the long history of democracy in the region. For example while the EIDHR approved 56 projects (worth €38.6 million) to promote democracy in 2003, 24 were in the ACP states but only two (worth €1.57 million) were in the Caribbean. Further, there are environmental conservation programmes in Belize, Guyana and Jamaica. While Jamaica's country strategy paper also includes a good analysis of the status of women in society and an evaluation of the country's gender policy, St Kitts has an EC funded Information Technology programme which is targeted at young women.

6. *Question 1f. How much progress has been made in bringing about greater coherence between development and other policies affecting third countries?*

Despite a commitment to greater coherence there are still inconsistencies between the policies of DG Development and those of other Directorates, most notably DG Agriculture and DT Trade. The issue of market access is key for progress in development. Developing country agricultural exporters, including the Caribbean, need access to European agricultural markets if trade is to provide a means to lift poor countries out of poverty. The barriers imposed by the Common Agricultural Policy (CAP) (tariff escalation, quotas, limited or no entry for sensitive products, high tariffs in, for example, sugar, dairy and livestock) mean that aid offered by the EC is offset by blockages to additional agricultural exports. In addition subsidies (decoupled payments) paid by the EC to European farmers generate exports surpluses which impact negatively on world market prices, as well as on local markets, effectively contributing to increases in rural poverty. Additionally the Caribbean region is being particularly hard hit by the loss of the Commodity Protocols of the Lomé Convention, which have historically provided valuable market access for key agricultural exports.

Agriculture is not the only area where joined-up thinking is missing. In textiles the EC maintains tariffs in excess of 15 per cent for developing country exports as well as the right to restrict any surge in imports under the WTO safeguard system. Insufficient progress has been made in improving coherence between development and other policies, such as agriculture, affecting third countries.

7. *Question 2i(b). Has the relatively large amount of aid that continues to go to middle income countries been at the expense of aid to the low income and the very poorest countries?* There are two issues to consider here. Firstly the relationship between the ACP as a whole, and other regions which receive EC aid, and secondly the nature of aid disbursement within the sub-regions of the ACP. In terms of the amount of aid given to the ACP *vis-à-vis* other regions, we would argue that the ACP has slowly lost out with regard to the disbursement of EC aid. For example, the percentage of the total aid budget that the ACP states received has decreased from 44.7 per cent in 1986 to 33.1 per cent in 1997. During this period aid to central and Eastern Europe went from zero to 18.4 per cent. Such statistics indicate that the ACP has fallen down the pecking order with respect to aid disbursements, with potentially damaging consequences for development in general and poverty reduction in particular. The second issue relates to the balance of aid provision within the sub-regions of the ACP. Here there has been a slow re-focusing of aid away from the Caribbean and towards sub-Saharan Africa. Aid to the Caribbean region has decreased by nearly 25 per cent since 1990 and the majority of Caribbean states now receive less aid than they did in 1990. In some cases the drop is significant. The trend here is a move away from providing aid to middle income ACP countries to benefit the poorest countries within the ACP group.

TOTAL EDF ALLOCATION TO THE CARIBBEAN 1985–2000 (MILLION EURO)

Country	1985	1990	1995	2000
Antigua	6.1	7.3	4.5	3
Bahamas	22.6	38.7	4.5	4.5
Barbados	14.2	33.5	37	6.8
Belize	15.4	24.2	35.7	8.8
Dominica	11.6	28.2	56.3	35.4
Dom.Rep		170	210	236
Grenada	12.3	24.7	13.3	9.4
Guyana	31.9	73.9	60.4	38.9
Haiti		276	236	239
Jamaica	77.6	156.8	221.9	100
St Kitts/N	7.6	4.5	7	4
St Lucia	17.2	45.1	52.5	46.1
St Vincent	32.9	46.5	42.3	39.7
Trin&Tob	32.3	122.8	24.2	17.9
Total	**281.7**	**1,052.2**	**1,005.6**	**789.5**

Source: http://europa.eu.int/comm/development/body/country/country en.cfm#

8. We would, however, warn against marginalising the middle-income countries of the Caribbean in terms of aid provision. The rationale for the change in aid focus is clearly articulated within the EC's Development Policy statement. Here the emphasis is on least developed and other low-income countries, and the attempt to reduce poverty, close the inequality gap, and address the exclusion it creates. However, many of the aims and objectives of the EC's statement can also be applied most convincingly to the Caribbean region. Indeed, the increasing economic, political, and social problems facing the Caribbean at the present time, as well as ongoing economic and environmental vulnerabilities associated with small size, do correspond to a great extent to the priorities and provisions of the EC's development policy. There are two issues of particular concern for the Caribbean, when issues of development and poverty reduction are considered.

9. The prevalence and effect of HIV/AIDS in the Caribbean must be acknowledged by the EC within the context of its development assistance. The prevalence of the disease in the Caribbean at 2.4 per cent of the adult population is second only to sub-Saharan Africa. It is estimated that around 500,000 people are living with HIV/AIDS with the highest prevalence of, and the number of deaths from, HIV/AIDS amongst the economically active age group of 15–49. New infections in 2001 amounted to 60,000, while AIDS deaths reached 42,000. AIDS is now the largest cause of death among young men, while young women are increasingly being infected with the HIV virus. In Haiti, Guyana, Turks and Caicos, Belize, Bahamas, and the Dominican Republic, the epidemic has spread to the general population. Jamaica and Trinidad and Tobago have concentrated HIV/AIDS epidemics in high-risk groups, but they are set to spread more widely to the rest of the population. The EC has a central role to play alongside other donor organisations in making sure the HIV/AIDS situation in the Caribbean does not worsen, and that prevalence rates do not begin to compare with those in sub-Saharan Africa. This is a case where limited action now can stave off a serious public health crisis in the future, which would have serious implications for poverty and economic development in the region. Indeed, the EC in its Development Policy statement highlights HIV/AIDS as a key issue to address. World Bank research suggests that HIV/AIDS has a substantial negative impact on

economic growth. While a separate Caribbean Epidemiology Centre/University of the West Indies report from 1997 estimates that Jamaica and Trinidad and Tobago will suffer declines in their GDP of 6.4 per cent and 4.2 per cent respectively by 2005 as a consequence of HIV/AIDS.

10. The second issue of particular concern for Caribbean development, which is acknowledged in general terms by the EC, but must be given specific policy focus relates to the fact that any attempt to tackle poverty must encompass the notion of vulnerability, including natural disaster risk. The issue of vulnerability for the Caribbean is a real and ever present one, and must be recognised by EC policies. Small states, and particularly small island states face a number of additional constraints *vis-à-vis* larger states as they seek to address the problem of poverty. These constraints include: small population size, openness of their economies, income volatility, limited diversification possibilities and a high level of export dependence, susceptibility to natural disasters and economic change, and a limited institutional capacity. Research has been undertaken by a number of organisations such as the Commonwealth Secretariat, the Caribbean Development Bank, the UN, and the World Bank to quantify and highlight the problems facing small states. There are 12 "small states" in the Caribbean and these countries, despite their relatively high *per capita* incomes do suffer a number of those particular and specialised problems. The EC should acknowledge these constraints on Caribbean states when considering future aid policy. Relatively high *per capita* incomes should not necessarily mean a sharp retrenchment of aid funds for the region.

11. *Question 2i(g). To what extent has aid to the middle income countries tackled poverty issues in those countries?* As can be seen from point 4 above, specific projects in Belize, the Eastern Caribbean and indeed elsewhere in the Caribbean have incorporated a concern, for poverty reduction. The results of such programmes have been generally positive. Assessing the EC's regional strategy paper for CARIFORUM and the strategy papers for individual Caribbean states, it can be argued that in general the results of aid programmes have been positive and mechanisms for accountability have been functioned reasonably well. We would argue that good past performance of the Caribbean with regard to EC aid should be acknowledged, and that current record is important when considering future disbursements.

12. A further illustration of the success of EC paid policy with regard to poverty reduction in middle income Caribbean countries is that a number are now classified as having high Human Development Index ratings by the UN. However, we would argue that such improvement cannot and should not lead to complacency on the part of EC development policy. The situation is still very difficult for certain Caribbean countries, and in some cases the position has worsened in recent years. Since 1998, for example, Dominica, Grenada, St Kitts-Nevis, St Lucia, St Vincent and the Grenadines, and Trinidad and Tobago have fallen out of the high UN HDI classification. Indeed, there is other evidence to support suggestions that poverty in the region remains high and that access to some basic services remain absent. A World Bank report in 1997, for example, found that Belize, Dominica, Guyana, Haiti, Jamaica and Suriname had high levels of poverty, with between 33 per cent and 65 per cent of their populations living in penury. Other research highlighting the continued problems of poverty includes Caribbean Development Bank Poverty Assessment Reports; a 2000 Jamaica Survey of Living Conditions; and studies by the United Nations Economic Commission for Latin America and the Caribbean. Since these reports have been compiled the situation has worsened further, particularly in the Eastern Caribbean. In Dominica, for example, a deteriorating fiscal deficit, growing unemployment, and a decline in traditional export earnings, have all led to an increase in poverty. There is a risk therefore that middle-income countries will slip back to low-income status if the present problems are not arrested. Elsewhere in the Caribbean, such as in the Dominican Republic, serious economic crises are precipitating social dislocation, unemployment and growing poverty. Once again if prevention is a key element of EC policy, action to stop Caribbean states falling back into poverty must be given proper consideration. Therefore, although progress has been made in terms of reducing poverty in many Caribbean countries, and sometimes to great effect, the difficult international economic situation at present, including the loss of traditional export markets, means that continued EC support is important. Without it there is a real danger that these countries will slip back to low-income status and greater poverty.

13. *Question 2iii(a) Does the ACP grouping have a future? What is the particular benefit for the EC or for the ACP countries themselves of continuing as a group?* We have already warned against the marginalisation of the Caribbean within the context of EC development assistance, and one important process of potential marginalisation that needs to be counteracted concerns the threat to the coherence of the ACP group and the Caribbean's place within it. A strong and united ACP group, with the Caribbean playing a full part, will help the region retain its position at the heart of the EC's development thinking. This view can be supported by a number of specific arguments relating to the nature and development of the ACP group.

14. The strength of the ACP group is numerous negotiations with the EC illustrates the need to resist attempts to split the ACP—the *sui generis* nature of the first Lomé Agreement was in large measure attributable to the emergence and solidarity of the ACP. Similarly the negotiations surrounding the creation of the Single European Market in Bananas bears testimony to the strength that can be derived from ACP unity. The solidarity gained with the creation of the ACP group was hard won, and has lasted 30 years. The institutional memory and way of operating for the ACP is a great asset, and the cost of losing it would be significant. For the Caribbean in particular, and the ACP more generally, the unity of the group is key in order that the ACP can defend its development gains acquired under the four Lomé Conventions.

15. The ACP does not exist solely on the basis of the Cotonou Agreement. The ACP is an internationally recognised alliance of states underpinned by the Georgetown Agreement. Only the ACP itself can split the

group. Recent signatories to EU-ACP co-operation, such as South Africa and Timor Leste have separately signed the Georgetown Agreement. These countries became members of the ACP group not by signing the Lomé or Cotonou agreements, but by signing the Georgetown Agreement. The membership of Timor Leste is an illustration that a newly independent state recognises the merit and benefits that can be accrued from having common purpose with a group of developing countries. Further, Cuba is a signatory to the ACP group but is not party to the Cotonou Agreement. Therefore, we would argue that the ACP as a group derives its strength from its own independent institutional and legal structures, and not from its relationship to the EC. It is therefore not the right of the EC to dictate to the ACP its future structure and coherence; that decision lies solely with the ACP itself.

16. It is important to recognise the growing independent influence of the ACP away from the ACP-EU framework. A good example being the activities of the ACP before, during and after the WTO Cancun ministerial meeting. Here the ACP was active in working closely with the Group of 22 developing countries during the negotiations. For the Caribbean, such a close working relationship with countries from Africa and Asia, allow their concerns to be better represented on the international stage. A related issue concerns the more general representation of ACP interests internationally. The recent banana case, the ongoing sugar dispute, and the agreement between the US and EU on rum market access all highlight the increasing importance of the WTO in particular when it comes to trade policy. Under such circumstances it is vital for the Caribbean and the ACP more generally to make sure their interests are recognised when issues of importance are raised within international economic and financial institutions. Indeed, the EC has itself recognised recently the importance of such an ACP presence, with the Community funding a Geneva-based ACP office to help the group deal with matters arising at the world body. In reality, therefore, the influence of the EC with regard to the integrity of the ACP is only of marginal significance. The ultimate decision on the group's future can only come from the ACP itself. Indeed the recent activity of the ACP within the context of the Cancun negotiations, for example, illustrates the continued viability of the group. We would argue that in a more uncertain international economic climate, a strong and united 79 member ACP group has a crucial role to play in relation to the EC and beyond.

17. *Conclusions*: The evidence submitted has focused on the role and place of the Caribbean in EC development policy. We have argued that the region is at risk of being marginalised in this policy because with the exception of Haiti, Caribbean states are classified as middle income. However despite their middle income status there is a danger that some states will fall into the LDC category, as markets they previously relied on (sugar, bananas, rum) disappear with the dissolution of the Commodity Protocols, if prevalence rates for HIV/AIDS increase, and if aid volumes are further reduced. It is incumbent upon the EC to take steps to prevent this, in keeping with its commitment to poverty reduction.

18. Aid to the region has largely focused on poverty reduction indicators such as education, health, and basic infrastructure. In this respect the EC has a good record, which should be built upon with due recognition given to the specific economic and environmental vulnerabilities facing small island states. However the continued lack of coherence between development and other EC policies does undermine the effectiveness of EC aid.

19. The ACP group retains its own *raison d'être* independent of the EC. It is a valuable collective forum for otherwise weak states. The ACP states have declared their commitment to the group and there is no compelling reason for the EC to disregard this.

19 January 2004

Memorandum by the Embassy of the Federal Democratic Republic of Ethiopia

EU INTERNATIONAL DEVELOPMENT ASSISTANCE

1. EVALUATING THE REFORM OF EU DEVELOPMENT ASSISTANCE

European Development Policy

(a) To what extent the joint Declaration agreed by the Development Council in November 2000, which set out the main objectives of EC development assistance, had an impact on the allocation of aid?

— The Joint Declaration had a considerable impact on aid allocation of the EU. The Declaration sees poverty reduction as the central focus for EU assistance. Accordingly the bulk of the 9th EDF allocations to the ACP countries goes to poverty and poverty related sectors.

(b) To what extent have poverty reduction and the agreed cross-cutting issues, including the environment, gender, human rights and good governance, been incorporated into country programmes?

— They are incorporated to a large extent. The development programmes of the ACP Countries under the Cotonou agreement, the 9th European Development Fund Country Strategy Papers (9th EDF CSPs) have poverty or poverty related sectors as focal areas of cooperation. Taking the case of Ethiopia, the 9th EDF CSP has as focal areas of cooperation, the Transport Sector,

Macro Economic Support, and Food Security. The Macro Economic Support, a direct budget assistance, is in support mainly of the health and education sectors.

(c) Has the intention to make EC aid, to a greater extent than before, conditional on performance as well as need, been brought into effect?

— Yes. EU aid is no more based only on needs, but also on performance. According to the new cooperation agreement of EU with the ACP. The Cotonou agreement, aid allocation is based on an assessment of each country's needs and performance, with the possibility of regularly adjusting the allocations upwards or downwards. The performance-based management of EU aid has already been introduced in the programming of the 9th EDF.

Coherence and consistency

(d) Has there been progress in bringing about more coherence and consistency within the EC aid programme.

— To some extent there is coherence. In the Country Strategy Papers it is stipulated that resources outside the EDF, ie budget line resources which are provided outside the Cotonou framework, will be used to finance the focal areas of cooperation, supplementing the EDF allocations.

Commission

(g) How successful in terms of improved efficiency and effectiveness has been the new organisational structure for EC aid introduced in 2000? Is there a case for improved rationalisation?

— With respect to the cooperation under the Cotonou framework, the agreement was signed in 2000, it became effective only in 2003. Except that CSPs for most of the ACP countries have already been concluded, implementation has not yet fully started. It is not, therefore, possible at this early stage to make judgement on the efficiency and effectiveness of the aid. However, we have noticed that some of the programmes such as FLEX (support to compensate losses in export earnings) are facing difficulties in their implementation. Due to the complicated new procedure of FLEX, it has become difficult to access the funds for this programme.

(h) Are the quality, skills and number of staff now commensurate with the size of the overall programme?

— Due to the deconcentration policy, the European Commission is expanding the size of its Delegation Offices in some of the ACP Countries through the recruitment of new staff. As most of the staff members deployed are young recruits with insufficient experience, and as they are not adequate in number, it is true that the size and quality of staff is not commensurate with the size of the cooperation programme.

(i) How much progress has there been in simplifying financial procedures so as to speed up disbursements without taking undue risks?

— Although it is early to give full judgement of the situation, off hand we can say that no progress has been made. For example, Ethiopia's 9th EDF CSP was signed before 2 years (February 2001), but nothing has been disbursed so far from the 9th EDF funds. This is partly due to the delays on the EC side in the preparation and approval process of projects and programmes.

2. LOOKING AHEAD TO 2004 AND BEYOND

i. *Development and Foreign Policy*

(iii) *Does the ACP grouping have a future?*

(a) Although the Cotonou Agreement was only signed in 2000 and is supposed to run to 2020, questions are being increasingly asked whether the ACP grouping of countries continues to make sense as a Partnership for the EC. What is the particular benefit for the EC or for the ACP countries themselves of continuing on this basis?

— The principle under Cotonou is that development is political. The ACP–EU Partnership Agreements main focus is reducing, and ultimately eradicating poverty. Therefore the development (poverty) issue is a political issue which cannot be addressed by globalisation. That is why both the EU and ACP have determined to maintain this unique arrangement.

30 January 2004

Memorandum by Global Witness

INTRODUCING GLOBAL WITNESS

1. Global Witness investigates the role of natural resources such as oil, diamonds and forests in funding conflict and corruption (see www.globalwitness.org). We aim to promote improved governance and transparency in the natural resource management sector to ensure that revenues are used to promote peaceful and sustainable development.

2. Using first-hand information and evidence to document the issue, Global Witness has achieved real change on issues previously deemed totally untouchable, for instance revealing the role of the logging industry in funding the genocidal Khmer Rouge and introducing transparency and good governance in the sector as a criteria for non-humanitarian aid disbursement in Cambodia, and spurring the creation of the Kimberley process to stem the trade in conflict diamonds from Africa. In 2003, Global Witness was nominated for the Nobel Peace Prize for its work on the conflict diamond issue.

3. In 2002, we launched the Publish What You Pay (PWYP) campaign with George Soros and his Open Society Institute. The PWYP coalition now numbers over 180 developed and developing country NGOs and calls for the disclosure of net payments made to national governments by oil, mining and gas companies in every country of operation ("revenue transparency") and the disclosure of such revenues by governments ("Publish What You Earn") in order to promote the financial accountability of governments for the natural resources that they hold on trust for their citizens. Such transparency will help to end the extended conflicts fuelled by diamonds and oil in countries such as Angola.

4. In March 2004, Global Witness published a report *Time for Transparency* looking at corruption and mismanagement of natural resource revenues in five countries: Angola, Congo Brazzaville, Equatorial Guinea, Kazakhstan, and Nauru.

Context to Publish What You Pay *campaign*

5. Oil, gas and mining industries are important in over 50 developing countries, home to some 3.5 billion people and where 1.5 billion of those people live on less than $2 per day. Twelve of the world's 25 most mineral-dependent states and six of the world's most oil-dependent states are classified by the World Bank as Highly Indebted Poor Countries with amongst the world's worst Human Development Indicators.

6. The reason for this "paradox of plenty" is that dependency on extractive resources tends to lead to unaccountable state institutions. The political structures that accrete around resource-rich economies generally fail to bring about social and cultural changes that lead to long-term investment in social development. Those governments tend to use low tax rates and patronage to dampen democratic pressures and spend an unusually high fraction of their income on internal security. World Bank research suggests that states that are dependent on oil and mineral wealth face a much higher chance of civil war and conflict.[1]

7. The UNDP Human Development Report 2002 confirms that resource rich but non-transparent countries have the highest levels of economic mismanagement and failed development as measured by the discrepancy between their rank HDI and GDP.[2] The Human Development Report calls for "a second wave of democratisation" to assure transparent government and equitable development across the globe to tackle such development failures: revenue transparency is a central component for this democratisation process. Similarly, the recent IMF Review of National Poverty Reduction Strategies concluded that openness and transparency within countries and international development partnerships are critical for successful poverty reduction efforts.

8. Sources within World Bank, the IMF and elsewhere will confirm the magnitude of the resource revenue misappropriation and diversion in some of these countries. Information on Angola suggests that almost US$1.7 billion per year from 1997–2001 is unaccounted for.[3] In Equatorial Guinea, the entire government income from oil—about US$135 million or 90 per cent of the country's foreign export earnings—may be disbursed offshore and remains unaccounted for in the state budget. In Congo Brazzaville, according to the IMF, none of the national oil company's after-tax income (US$43 million in 2001) has been transferred to the budget. Information from the Sudan suggests that the oil revenues and the incremental cost of the Government's war in the south are both between US$700,000–1 million a day. At least US$4 billion of Nigerian government funds—some 90 per cent of which came from oil—were stolen by General Abacha during his dictatorship and deposited into offshore accounts.

9. It is clear that despite the resource wealth extracted Africa, over 300 million Africans live on less than a dollar a day; life expectancy is 48 years and falling; one-third of children are malnourished; and 40 per cent

[1] World Bank Development Research Group Policy Research Working Paper No 2355. May 2000. Greed and Grievance in Civil War.

[2] Rank HDI for Equatorial Guinea is some 73 places below rank GDP, Gabon shows a discrepancy of 44 places, Angola has a discrepancy 36 places, Algeria is 22 places, Vanuatu is 18 places and Cape Verde is 17 places lower in rank HDI and so on.

[3] Global Witness. Forthcoming report on Angola. Global Witness' March 2002 report "All the Presidents' Men. The Devastating Role of Oil and Banking in Angola's Privatised War" contains extensive details on the offshore structures and mechanisms for revenue misappropriation.

of children have no access to education. In the Great Lakes region, 5 million people were killed in violent conflict in the last decade, most of which is directly or indirectly funded by resource extraction. One-fifth of the world's small arms are circulating in Africa and South Asia—the world's two poorest regions—and both have seen increases in military expenditure driven by unaccountable revenue streams.

10. Although mining and oil companies are not responsible for the way in which their royalties and fees are spent, Global Witness and other PWYP coalition members believe that they do have a clear responsibility to disclose the payments made for those resources so that the citizens of the countries concerned can, themselves, hold their government and institutions accountable. The publication of net payments made by oil, gas and mining companies to national governments disaggregated on a country by country basis would offer the citizens of these countries the opportunity to hold their government accountable for how that money—amounting worldwide to billions of dollars annually—is spent.

11. In some countries, especially where ruling regimes are unaccountable to their population, state institutions that govern resource management exercise their powers as a form of private property rather than as a public service. A central reason why such "grand corruption" and the misappropriation of state funds is possible is non-transparency over state budgets and revenues. If companies working within such countries do not publish what they pay to national governments, it is impossible for civil society to call their government to account over the management of rents earned from their resources.

Publish What You Earn: the role of bilateral and multilateral donors in requiring host government transparency

12. Lack of transparency imposes a further cost on the international community. The illicit diversion of oil and gas revenue causes serious shortfalls in state budgets that can only be made up, if at all, by grants and loans from abroad. This imposes a heavy and unnecessary burden on international humanitarian agencies, economic assistance agencies and official lenders, nearly all of whom receive funding from the North. This money should be used for positive development outcomes, rather than to fill in the gaps caused by the misappropriation of oil and gas revenues by corrupt officials.

13. The donor community already accepts the principle that it should promote good governance in recipient countries, and the use of conditionality to promote transparency is a consistent and logical extension of this principle. For example, the US Government's International Anti-Corruption and Good Governance Act, passed in the year 2000, amended the existing Foreign Assistance Act to add "the promotion of good governance through combating corruption and improving transparency and accountability" to the list of major US foreign policy goals. The Bush Administration's Millennium Challenge Account initiative also placed good governance at the core of its fund disbursement criteria.

14. The World Bank Group (WBG) and the International Monetary Fund have a particularly important role to play in promoting revenue transparency because of their technical expertise and central role in macroeconomic restructuring. So far, their engagement has been sporadic and piecemeal.

15. The WBG not only disburses development assistance directly but is also involved in direct investment in the extractives sector through its International Finance Corporation (IFC). An internal evaluation of WBG's performance in January 2003, subsequently passed to Global Witness, highlights the failure of its current approach. It states that due to the "links between poverty and poor governance . . . increased EI [Extractive Industry] investment is likely to lead to bad development outcomes for many if not most of the Bank's clients [original emphasis]."[4] The report calls for "a fundamental reorientation of the Bank's work . . . away from prioritizing the attraction of new investment and toward capacity building and technical assistance focused on strengthening the government's capacity to maximize the benefits and minimize the risks of existing EI investment".[5]

16. The World Bank Group, like other multilateral donors, could achieve this policy reorientation by mainstreaming a requirement for revenue transparency across all its engagements with countries where extractive industries are significant. In return for Bank technical assistance and structural adjustment loans for the oil, gas and mining sectors, or for macroeconomic purposes, governments should be obliged to mandate the disclosure of receipts from oil and mining by state agencies and the disclosure of all such payments to the state by extractive companies. The IFC and the Multilateral Investment Guarantee Agency, a Bank unit that guarantees investment against political risks, should also require that all companies receiving their support should publish their payments to states.

17. Indeed, the July 2003 report of the Bank's own Operations Evaluation Department, titled "Extractive Industries and Sustainable Development" suggests that the "Bank should vigorously pursue country- and industry-wide disclosure of government revenues from EI and related contractual arrangements (such as production sharing agreements, concession and privatization terms). It should work toward and support disclosure of EI revenues and their use in resource-rich countries".[6] This recommendation is echoed by the

[4] Operations Evaluation Department. 21 January 2003. *Evaluation of the World Bank Group's Activities in the Extractive Industries. Factoring in Governance.* World Bank, Washington DC. para 5.1.

[5] *Ibid.* para 4.11.

[6] World Bank Group. 29 July 2003. *Extractive Industries and Sustainable Development: An Evaluation of World Bank Group Experience. (Four Volumes). Volume I: Overview.* Report No 26373. World Bank Group, Washington, DC. p 14.

Extractive Industries Review (EIR), a two-year multistakeholder consultation which was initiated by the Bank and completed its report at the end of 2003. The EIR not only endorses the OED's call for urgent action but also recommends that the World Bank work with partners such as the Publish What You Pay coalition to promote revenue transparency worldwide.[7]

18. Similarly, a 2002 WBG and IMF Review of its National Poverty Reduction Strategies concluded that transparency within countries and international development partnerships is critical if efforts to reduce poverty are to succeed.[8] Despite this, both the Fund's Oil Diagnostic revenue tracking exercise with the Angolan Government and the IMF/World Bank audit of oil revenues in Congo Brazzaville have lacked any commitment to publish publicly any results, nor is it clear how those results will be factored into a future assistance programme.[9]

19. The case of Congo Brazzaville also underlines the lack of "joined-up-thinking" in the aid policies of multilateral and bilateral donors. While the IMF has recently suspended negotiations with the government because it has not fulfilled its commitments to improve fiscal management, and in particular to implement transparency in the oil sector, the World Bank and other donors have given positive signals to the government that it will be able to access further debt relief. Congolese civil society groups have recently lobbied the Fund and the Bank stipulating that no further non-humanitarian aid should be forthcoming without the implementation of the government's existing commitments to improve revenue transparency and the attachment of strict conditionality to any new money. They have also called for independent civil society to be genuinely consulted in any poverty reduction strategy process.

20. The generally piecemeal and unsystematic approach of the World Bank and IMF and other international and national aid-giving bodies to date would seem to undermine the IMF's efforts to promote a code of good practice on fiscal transparency more widely amongst its members. Given that oil income is critical to the macroeconomic performance of countries like Angola, it is deeply concerning that the Fund would consider a restructuring programme without a clear requirement for disclosure of basic monies due to the state.

21. Unless donor governments and the international financial institutions commit themselves to mainstreaming a requirement for revenue transparency across all their lending, development and technical assistance programmes, they will inevitably fail to address the underlying reasons for poverty and macroeconomic mismanagement in resource-rich-but-poor countries. Instead, they will simply perpetuate a vicious circle of using the money of Northern taxpayers to cover up some of the symptoms.

Conditional Development Assistance from the European Union

22. It is important that the implicit risks and costs of non-transparency to the EU's development agenda are recognised. If unaccountable revenues are misappropriated, moved offshore or used to prolong conflict, so European objectives of development assistance are undermined and taxpayers will further be required to fund reconstruction and humanitarian assistance that corrupt governments should be providing themselves.

23. The Cotonou Agreement has set an important precedent by recognising that the fight against corruption is a fundamental element of future development assistance and makes explicit reference to corruption as a major development problem. As Cotonou Article 9(3) notes, good governance is the "transparent and accountable management of human, natural, economic and financial resources for the purposes of equitable and sustainable development. It entails clear decision-making procedures at the level of public authorities, transparent and accountable institutions, the primacy of law in the management and distribution of resources and capacity building for elaborating and implementing measures aiming in particular at preventing and combating corruption. Good governance ... constitute[s] a fundamental element of this Agreement".

24. The recent communication from the Commission on Governance and Development (October 2003) reaffirmed that fighting corruption is a key element of good governance. Corruption is "very often a tax on the poor" according to the Commission, which recognised that "combating corruption ought to be done within the framework of broader support to strengthen good governance and democratisation processes".[10] This means fighting corruption "not only in cases of corruption involving Community funds but also more widely, in any country where the Community is financially involved and where corruption constitutes a serious obstacle to result-oriented development strategies".[11] In relation to Angola, the communication specifically cites Publish What You Pay as "a useful instrument in this context".[12]

---

[7] Final Report of the Extractive Industries Review, December 2003. *Striking a Better Balance*, Volume 1, p 47.

[8] Joint IMF and WBG Development Committee. 11 September 2002. *Poverty Reduction Strategy Papers (PRSP)—Progress in Implementation*. Report DC2002-0016, International Monetary Fund and World Bank Group, Washington, DC.

[9] Although a summary of the Angolan Oil Diagnostic has now been produced.

[10] Commission of the European Communities. 20 October 2003. Com (2003) 615 final. Governance and Development. Communication from the Commission to the Council, the European Parliament and the European Economic and Social Committee. Brussels, 2:6, 31.

[11] *Ibid, 2:6, 34.*

[12] *Ibid, 4:2, 79.*

25. Global Witness would like to support, firstly, the Commissions' emphasis on the need for a more coherent and systematic approach by European donors: "Progress should be made on coordination and complementarity between the EC and EU Member States by adopting common policy principles in this specific area".[13] Secondly, we would emphasize the need for EU aid to "foster civil society's capacity to participate in policy-making processes and debates".[14] Overall, Global Witness believes that revenue transparency is perhaps the most basic measurable criterion of good governance in developing countries whose income is almost entirely reliant on resource extraction.

Transparency is a Corporate Governance and Energy Security Priority

26. Policies to require revenue transparency are also in the interests of developing countries, investors and the international community more broadly. The Commission's communication on Governance and Development of October 2003 states that "weak governance (in terms of inefficient administrations, lack of accountability and financial transparency, corruption and inefficient financial systems and other state failures) represents a major disincentive for investment".[15] As Enron and similar scandals have demonstrated, a company that manages its finances in a non-transparent way also poses a clear risk to the interests of its investors. As Global Witness' forthcoming report on PWYP will show, in Kazakhstan and in Congo Brazzaville, American and French companies using non-transparent means to win future gains that are turning out to be highly insecure: indeed, some of the contracts are so opaque that they are subject to continual renegotiation. Investors need to be reassured that companies are not winning business with methods that could be counter-productive in the long term.

27. This point is very clearly highlighted in a recent statement by 38 major North American, European and South African investment houses which manage some US$3 trillion in funds and hold significant stakes in all the main international oil companies. They state: "legitimate, but disclosed, payments to governments may be accused of contributing to the conditions under which corruption can thrive. This is a significant business risk, making companies vulnerable to accusations of complicity in corrupt behaviour, impairing their local and global "licence to operate", rendering them vulnerable to local conflict and insecurity, and possibly compromising their long-term commercial prospects in these markets".[16]

28. There are other business benefits to greater transparency. Investment analysts may need information on company payments to a state so as to calculate the in-country costs of doing business, to work out the profitability of investments and to identify company subsidiaries in particular countries that are under-performing. The higher the level of disclosure, the better investors will be able to safeguard their own interests.

29. More broadly, the instability triggered by mismanagement of oil revenues can pose a major threat to energy security. It also threatens the prospects for transparent and accountable government, whose promotion should be a foreign policy priority for the energy-dependent US and for EU countries. West Africa is one of the world's fastest growing sources of oil and gas and West African countries that are not transparent about their revenues currently supply about 15 per cent of American oil imports, a figure that the US National Intelligence Council expects to rise to 25 per cent by 2015.[17] Production from the potentially unstable Caspian region is expected to double in the next decade: this production may be more important to European energy security and any future disruption of supply would have a knock-on effect on world oil prices.

30. As a recent report by the US African Oil Policy Initiative Group argues ,"the US should not be partnering with unpopular, undemocratic regimes. On the contrary, proper foreign policy would bolster American values with our allies and encourage democratic development [. . . .] African oil is not an end, but a means: a means to both greater American energy security and more rapid African economic development."[18] Revenue transparency is essential to achieve these objectives and should also be a priority for other industrialised countries and regional bodies such as the European Union.

[13] *Ibid,* 5: 95.

[14] *Ibid,* 4:4, 87.

[15] *Ibid,* 2:11, 53.

[16] *Joint statement by* ISIS Asset Management, Banco Fonder, Boston Common Asset Management, Calpers, Calverts Group Ltd, CCLA, Central Finance Board of the Methodist Church, Christian Brothers Investment Services, Co-operative Insurance Society, Deutsche Asset Management, Dresdner RCM Global Investors, Domini Social Investments, Ethical Funds, Ethos Investment Foundation, F&C Management Limited, Fidelity Investments, Frather Asset Management, Henderson Global Investors, Hermes Investment Management Limited, Insight Investment Management, Jupiter Asset Management, Legal & General Investment Management, Local Authority Pension Fund Forum, Merrill Lynch Investment Managers, Morley Fund Management, New York State Common Retirement Fund, Nottinghamshire County Council, Progressive Asset Management, Railpen, Sarasin, Schroders Investment Management, SNS, State Street Global Advisors Limited, Storebrand, Trillium Asset Management, University Superannuation Scheme, Walden Asset Management, 17 June 2003. *Investors' Statement on Transparency in the Extractives Sector.*

[17] African Oil Policy Group. 2002. *African Oil: A Priority for US National Security and African Development.* Institute for Advanced Strategic and Political Studies, Washington DC. p9.

[18] *Ibid,* p7.

CONCLUSION

31. The goal of revenue transparency is fully consistent with international and EU objectives of accountable government, corruption prevention and democratic debate about issues of resource management. Businesses will benefit too. Requiring transparency would have the effect of protecting companies from allegations of complicity with corrupt governmental practices, providing a level playing field exists that requires disclosure from all the main competing parties. Finally, revenue transparency is a vital first step towards alleviating the crushing poverty of the ordinary citizens in many resource-rich developing countries. Transparency is a necessary condition of good governance, and should be recognised as such by international financial institutions when they allocate taxpayers' money. Aid disbursement and investment in extractive industry projects should take place only within a coherent policy framework that makes such investments consistent with poverty reduction and development goals.

24 January 2004

Letter from the Embassy of the Republic of Hungary

Thank you for your letter of 9 December 2003 in which the European Union Committee asked for written evidence where appropriate in response to the inquiry into EU International Development Assistance.

As you might be aware, international development was not a focal point of the association between the EU and Hungary. During the process of economic and social transformation Hungary was mainly a recipient and not a donor of international assistance. Due to the successful transition and the current status of our relationship with the EU, Hungary is in the process of transforming itself from a recipient to a donor country and has just started its donor activities. But as an acceding country we still have fairly limited experience with the international development activities of the EU. The month we have spent observing and participating inside the EU structures since April 2003 do not yet provide us with sufficient knowledge to comment on efficiency and coherence. I suppose we need a little more history as a fully-fledged member to do that.

Nevertheless, we would like to contribute to the work of Sub-Committee C, so please find attached the Hungarian position on certain relevant questions and a short summary of the Hungarian international development co-operation policy.

HUNGARIAN POLICY FOR INTERNATIONAL DEVELOPMENT COOPERATION (IDC)

On becoming a member of the OECD and as part of our preparations for EU membership, the principles established for the nature and delivery of Official Development Assistance (ODA) of the Development Assistance Committee (DAC) of that Organisation have become an important component of our foreign relations.

While considering the principles and political practice of the OECD and EU development strategy, the Hungarian IDC will be based on national interests and characteristics will form part of foreign relations and will be aimed at the social and economic development of countries eligible for ODA and those countries in transition. Hungary intends to form a development partnership with countries that are important to its foreign and security policy and foreign trade relations (regional stability, geographical proximity, traditional and active foreign relations, extensive social and political contacts, well-founded economic and commercial structures, etc), that are well known to Hungarian social and economic actors (knowledge of local characteristics and needs, command of languages) and where its IDC efforts are duly received.

On the basis of Government Decision 2319/1999 (07.12.), the Ministers of Foreign Affairs, Economy and Finance drafted a Concept Paper proposing a new approach to international development co-operation (IDC) for the Republic of Hungary. The Paper proposed that Hungary replace its practice of delivering its contribution to ODA as a series of *ad hoc* and decentralised initiatives with a practice adapted to UN, DAC and EU standards. The Paper proposed that the Ministry of Foreign Affairs (MFA) would draw up the annual plan for the delivery of IDC and would act as the interdepartmental co-ordinator. On 24 July 2001, the Government approved the Concept Paper. In the context of institutional development, the International Development Co-operation Department was established within the MFA in November 2002 to execute all IDC activities. 2003 marked the Department's initial year and it will manage Hungary's IDC programme in a manner intended to reflect the practices of donors as established by the OECD and EU.

PARTNER COUNTRIES AND TARGET AREAS—SELECTION CRITERIA

In view of our relatively limited financial means, in comparison with the total flow of ODA from OECD Member States, and the requirement for the exposure of Hungarian assistance, Hungary's IDC resources shall, at first, be concentrated in only a few partner countries.

These partner countries have been and will be selected according to strict and consistent criteria. The assisted country shall meet the general co-operation conditions of the donor community and of international organisations (UN, OECD DAC, IMF, World Bank, etc). At the same time, the selection of these countries shall ensure coherence between our political, security and economic objectives on the one hand, and the practice of development co-operation on the other. The programmes are intended to contribute to the sustainable social and economic development of the partner countries and to the reinforcement of bilateral relations equally.

SCOPE OF IDC ACTIVITIES

Together with other member countries, Hungary shall employ the definitions of Official Development Assistance established by the DAC of the OECD. The most important areas thereof are as follows:

— Technical co-operation (essentially education, technical training and the transfer of experience)

This is where Hungary has the greatest experience. The exchange of experts and the provision of opportunities for university and post-graduate education have improved our relations with the developing world for decades.

— Project type development programs

It is expected that partner countries will possess poverty reduction or strategic development plans which they share with donor countries as they seek partial or total funding and implementation of specific projects. At the same time it is noted that the success of development projects depends on their more general effect on economic and social conditions and sustainability.

— Humanitarian assistance

Humanitarian assistance can take two forms: responses to natural catastrophes, and assistance to the victims of man-made crises. In both cases however, it is usually necessary to be able to respond urgently to unforeseen circumstances. Political considerations are often of secondary importance when offering humanitarian assistance as it is provided to everybody and anyone in need, under the *aegis* of discrimination-free assistance. At the national level therefore, facilities for offering and delivering quick assistance will have to be formed. It is foreseen that the resources dedicated to Humanitarian Assistance by Hungary will be channelled through NGOs capable of delivering aid quickly and proficiently and distributing it where needed.

— Credit with aid included

Within the frame of bilateral assistance forms, OECD allows the extension of credits with aid to ODA countries, subject to the observation of strict regulations. Hungary has not yet taken the opportunity of subsidised credits and the government decree to regulate this topic is currently in the preparatory stage.

DEVELOPMENT AND FOREIGN POLICY

i. The countries of the Western Balkans have arrived at a difficult and complicated period of their development. To advocate the successful preparation of the countries in the region for EU membership as early as possible remains a priority for Hungary. The exchange of our experiences and technical know-how gained during the period of political and economic transition would greatly contribute to the political stability in the region and would promote good governance.

iv. *EDF and Budget*

Hungary in principle, accepts the arguments of the Communication from the Commission to the Council and the European Parliament towards the full integration of co-operation with ACP countries into the EU budget.

Hungary deems it important to bring the assistance to ACP into the mainstream of EC aid and also to make resource allocation mechanisms more flexible.

Upon formulating our final position however, other factors will also be taken into consideration, such as the exact figures of the alternatives (10th European development Fund or EDF budgetisation) and a clear picture on how this issue will affect our net financial positions.

Hungary would welcome if it could participate as a full-fledged EU member in the discussion and decision making procedure on the full integration of co-operation with the ACP countries into the EU budget.

12 January 2004

Memorandum by the International HIV/AIDS Alliance

The International HIV/AIDS Alliance is a United Kingdom based international non-governmental Organisation that supports community action on HIV/AIDS in over 40 countries. The witness, Wanjiku Kamau is the European Policy Advisor for the Stop AIDS Alliance, a project of the International HIV/AIDS Alliance and the Dutch based Aids Funds.

1. We are writing in response to the recent invitation to submit written evidence to the Upper Chamber of Her Majesty's Government on the important issue of the EU Development Policy and External Assistance.

2. The volume of European development aid has been growing over the last few years and in our view that these increases must be supported with corresponding improvements in the efficiency and effectiveness of these resources. It is important that all efforts are made to ensure stronger accountability of European Community aid to the EU's stated objective of poverty reduction.

3. We offer, for your consideration, evidence on three main aspects of EU Development Policy; the changing priorities and focus of European Community Aid, our analysis of the low priority accorded to spending on social sectors and particularly to health-sector, and finally we offer our opinion on how the European Commission might "regularise" the allocation of EDF resources to multilateral initiatives like the Global Fund to Fight AIDS, TB and Malaria.

4. The International HIV/AIDS Alliance believes that this is an important time for EU Member States and their parliaments to focus their attention on the EU's development policy as a number of important changes are due to take place over the next year that could profoundly change the priorities and direction of Community Aid. As a development organisation focused on supporting the response of communities to the AIDS pandemic we are particularly concerned that the leadership role that the EC plays in combating AIDS, TB and Malaria is not lost during this time. Most notable of these changes are the adoption of a new constitution, accession of 10 new Member States, the negotiations of the new Financial Perspective, and the budgetisation of the European Development Fund. *The International HIV/AIDS Alliance recommends that the Committee extend the scope of its inquiry to consider the implications of all of these changes, and not just budgetisation, and take a detailed look at how all these processes are likely to impact on the fulfilment of the EU Development Policy objectives.*

5. There is evidence of increased influence of foreign policy objectives in the allocations of EC funding. In spite of the EU's stated commitments to channel aid to the poorest countries and then to the sectors that benefit the poorest in those countries, recent decisions taken suggest that the priority is to direct EC aid to Europe's "near abroad" and middle income countries on the Mediterranean and Eastern borders while diverting scarce development resources away from low-income and least developed countries. This trend is mirrored by the move of EU Member States' own national, bilateral official development assistance towards increased "selectivity" and "conditionality". This trend to divert resources from the poorest countries is likely to have a negative and serious effect on countries that are highly affected by AIDS.

6. The European Parliament has set a goal to spend 35 per cent of EC aid on health and education. Currently it is estimated that only 3 per cent of the EDF is spent on health and only 4 per cent on education. Our analysis suggests that the preference to direct significant proportions of EDF resources to ACP governments in the form of macro-economic budget support is largely responsible for this situation. *While not wanting to constrain the ability of governments to set their own priorities the International HIV/AIDS Alliance urges the members of the House of Lords Committee to consider how the EC could include, as a key element in Country Support Strategies, clearly articulated sector-specific indicators and outcomes.* The proposed indicators would serve to reinforce the policy priorities set out in the EU's Development Policy Statement (2000) and while allowing national governments to determine their priorities, would also provide an appropriate "policy steer" in the directions to which EU members are already committed. This would bring the spending of EC aid more closely in line with its commitments to the European Parliament and Council.

7. The International HIV/AIDS Alliance would also like to draw attention to the high level of dormant funds within the EDF and the strategies we believe should be employed to remedy the situation while getting much-needed resources to ACP countries. While there is no agreement about the volume of unspent funds that have been rolled-over into the 9 EDF from the 6, 7 and 8 EDF's it remains an undeniable fact that disbursement of funds continues to fall well below projections even in the current year. While we welcome the European Commissions initiatives to accelerate the rate of disbursement of EDF funds we would also draw the attention of the House of Lords Committee to the fact that the EC has recently successfully allocated funds to the Global Fund for AIDS, TB and Malaria and to support the Highly Indebted Poor Countries Initiative (HIPC). These two allocations demonstrated clearly that reserve funds can be effectively allocated and efficiently spent through multi-lateral initiatives. We believe that the AIDS pandemic poses a severe threat to development in many ACP countries and would *urge that the Committee support recommendations to allocate further resources from EDF reserves to the Global Fund for AIDS, TB and Malaria.*

8. The Global Fund has already made considerable progress and is starting to prove its potential. As a mechanism to attract and disburse resources it has succeeded in significantly increasing the resources directed at the three diseases that affect the world's poorest people. Furthermore its success in attracting high-quality proposals, mobilising resources and dispersing them effectively has transformed expectations. It has delivered positive change on the ground in areas of the world worst affected by these three diseases.

9. It is important the European Union Member States and the Commission act together to support the Fund continue its good work. At the EU Summit in Thessaloniki President Prodi, Prime Minister Blair and President Chirac promised the world that the EU would meet its moral obligations and ensure that at least one billion Euros a year are provided from Europe.

10. The International HIV/AIDS Alliance has called on the Irish Presidency to take forward with urgency an initiative that would lead to the *recognition of certain countries as "highly affected by AIDS". This category would include all least-developed countries that also have an HIV prevalence rate of over 5 per cent.*

11. In order to ensure that EDF resources reach the poorest countries, *the International HIV/AIDS Alliance has proposed that countries in this special category should be able to apply for higher levels of EDF funds (to be directed to their health sector)*, but most importantly has asked that the European Union Member States should provide fast debt relief to these countries.

12. The International HIV/AIDS Alliance would like to thank the House of Lord's Committee for considering our submission, We would be happy to present the evidence orally if the committee deems this necessary. We are also able to provide case studies examples should the committee require such evidence.

12 January 2004

Memorandum by the Jamaican Mission to the European Communities, Brussels

1. HAS JAMAICA SEEN AN IMPROVEMENT IN THE DELIVERY OF EU AID IN THE PAST 5 YEARS AND IF SO, HOW?

Jamaica has not seen a marked improvement in the delivery of EU aid in the past 5 years. From as early as 1999, a restructuring process was embarked on in Brussels as a mechanism to assist in the delivery of EU Aid. However, this process resulted in lengthy delays in accessing timely information and was further compounded by the lack of clarity on issues regarding the interpretation of various guidelines. Even with the introduction of deconcentration lengthy delays have still existed.

There is still some inflexibility on the part of the EU in facilitating the implementation process. More stringent guidelines have been implemented by the EU to ensure greater accountability on the part of ACP States in utilising EU resources. However, communication of the new guidelines has been very slow and has been only partially available at times to the NAO. This has proved very taxing and has pulled extensively on the limited human resources in the National Authorizing Office (NAO).

2. HOW MIGHT AID DONATION FROM THE EU BE IMPROVED (WITHOUT BEING INCREASED)?

The recent introduction of deconcentration by the EU is expected to assist in a reduction in the approval time for documentation submitted to the EU. The process should contribute to greater efficiency and facilitate quick discussions on technical issues. It is also an expectation that there will be greater dissemination of information through the local Delegation in regards to new developments in Brussels. While it may be too early to assess the deconcentration process, there is still much concern regarding availability and interpretation of new guidelines introduced.

We continue to recommend that discussions be held with the ACP States prior to the implementation of new guidelines to ensure greater clarity and a similar interpretation by all the parties involved. For example, the EC's proposals on the revised role of the NAOs were not presented to the Development and Finance Committee, though they had been sent directly to the NAOs. Yet at the November meeting of the Joint Responsible Officials of the DFC in Brussels, the EC had sought to pass a decision in support of the new modalities. Fortunately, a few ACP Ambassadors had been briefed by their NAOs and were able to block that attempt. To date, as far as we are aware, the document has not been submitted in Brussels. Still, the matter is on the agenda for the ongoing regional consultations. These are essential in the partnership and also because too often the evolutionary process of experience dictates interpretation and modification of the guidelines.

3. WHERE COULD THE EU DO BETTER?

There is room for improvement in the area of communication between the EU and Jamaica. Making guidelines available to the NAO on a timely basis and having the necessary training in place to facilitate accurate and similar interpretation by both parties would enhance the partnership process and facilitate implementation. The EU could be more flexible in regards to resolving difficulties in project implementation which would ensure that the spirit of the partnership process is maintained.

4. HAVE THE RECENT IMPROVEMENTS IN THE EU AID BEEN SUFFICIENT?

There has been some improvement in the EU aid although there is scope for continued improvement. The following two areas have been identified as positive improvement in EU aid.

(a) The introduction of the concept of a Country Support Strategy (CSS) (to accompany the National Indicative Programme under the 9th EDF. The CSS which provides the basis for the formulation and review of the co-operation programme which targets resources towards the needs identified by Government and the EU.

(b) The EU should be commended for its thrust in providing budgetary support to ACP States. Under the Support to the Economic Reform Programme I, II and III Jamaica has benefited from budgetary resources which has been critical in the face of its macroeconomic situation. This has allowed Government greater flexibility to increase discretionary spending in the social sectors and ease the debt burden.

However, the introduction of the 9th EDF represents significant changes to the operation of EDF resources. The preparation process for the EU was insufficient to cope with the new regulations. For example a response to Jamaica's request for emergency assistance under Envelope B was long delayed due to the absence of associated guidelines for releasing Envelope B assistance.

5. DO MEMBER STATES GET GOOD VALUE FOR THEIR AID MONEY DONATED BY THE EU?

It is our opinion that the EU Member States have received good value for their money. Firstly, the Government has ensured integrity and proper accountability of resources employed to projects. These resources have assisted Government in achieving its economic developmental objectives in the area of infrastructure and poverty reduction. With the introduction of the CSS, resources are targeted at the needs identified and agreed by the EU. Funds are therefore channelled towards programmes such as:

— the Poverty Reduction Programme which targets poverty through a community based approach in the lowest quintiles;

— the Support to the Economic Reform Programme which provides budgetary support that facilitates discretionary spending in the social sector given Government's macroeconomic situation;

— Eastern Jamaica Banana Support Programme which provides assistance to farmers in areas of food production, marketing and other support services;

— Assistance to Transport Sector, EJASP and STABEX provide funds for road improvement. EJASP and STABEX have assisted in the rehabilitation of roads especially farms/feeder roads which will enable the transportation of agricultural crops to the markets; and

— Private Sector Development Project aimed at increasing firms' competitiveness to export to international markets.

6. SHOULD THE EDF BE BUDGETED?

While budgetisation may have some merits we are concerned that given the EU's track record of annualised development cooperation with other countries and regions, the new system provides no guarantee of improved management of the external assistance. Instead, it carries the risks of restrictions and limitations in partnership, co-management and ownership with the increased role of the European Union Council and Parliament. In addition, the advantage of the "flexibility" of the budgetised EDF to the EU could be a disadvantage to the ACP, as it would allow the EU to re-allocate funds between different geographical regions at will. It would also permit the EU to more easily reallocate ACP designated resources to meet EU's international commitments.

The compatibility between the multi-annual projects which dominate ACP/EU cooperation programmes, and the strict time lines within which the annualised budgets operate will also present a considerable challenge under the proposed measure.

The management of funds by the European Commission through the General Budget is opposite to that which exists under the EDF's as part of the ACP-EU Partnership Agreements. Under the new financial regulations governing the EU General Budget, the EC is singularly responsible for implementation of projects/programmes and ACP governments can only participate in the implementation process after receiving verification from the EC. Verification will involve the country providing full disclosure of its management of the fiscal budget and the legal status of those departments involved in the management of the Budget. In contrast, project implementation under the EDF as part of the ACP-EU Partnership Agreements assumes partnership between the Commission's Chief Authorising Officer and the ACP's National Authorising Officer. In this regard also, budgetization poses a threat to the spirit of partnership that has characterized the ACP-EU relationship over the past quarter century. This is the spirit which has defined as exemplary, the ACP/EU development cooperation.

12 March 2004

Memorandum by the Embassy of Portugal

1. EVALUATING THE REFORM OF EU DEVELOPMENT ASSISTANCE

'European Development Policy'

(a) The Declaration agreed by the Development Council in November 2000 had some impact on the allocation of aid, pushing for more focus on poorer Countries, thus pursuing the main objective of EC development assistance—poverty reduction.

(b) They have been gradually incorporated into country programs, what is also identifiable in the commitments made internationally (Doha, Monterrey, Barcelona and Johannesburg) and the will to implement the Millennium Development Goals.

(c) Yes, to some extent, but especially in the framework of the EDF.

Coherence and consistency

(d) Yes, there has been progress in bringing about more coherence and consistency within the EC's aid programs, not only through the agreement on broad development objectives, but also through the introduction of new instruments like Country Strategy Papers and Country Fact Files.

(e) Yes, particularly the Country Strategy Papers have been an important instrument for local co-ordination.

(f) There has been some progress. Even though recognising that it is a difficult topic, awareness of coherence has been gradually increasing. However, development policy is not preponderant over other policies and, often, it is difficult to conciliate opposed positions or interests.

Commission

(g) Taking into account the dimension of the reform, it has been successful. Improvements can be identified in programming, local co-ordination, evaluation, financial management and implementation of projects. EuropeAid and the Quality Support Group have been playing a decisive role.

(h) In what concerns EDF, there is a lack of human resources in Headquarters, in Brussels, and also in some ACP countries.

(i) There has been progress in simplifying and speeding up disbursements. However, the speed in implementation still has to be improved. The harmonisation efforts have been a great impulse for this.

(j) There has been some progress in achieving better reporting: the Commission has been coming forward with an annual report about the global aid effort. However, in what concerns the budgets, we think that there are still too many different budgets making it more difficult to achieve transparency and to bring them into line with clear objectives.

Governance

(k) If the system that has started to be applied—two GAERC per year dedicated to development and informal meetings of development Ministers—is maintained, then there is no down-grading of input or oversight. It might even allow for a great coherence with other external policies. Up until now, all the Presidencies have been guaranteeing this system, however, it is still too soon to evaluate if the arrangement will keep.

2. Looking Ahead to 2004 and Beyond

1. *Development and Foreign Policy*

EU assistance and CFSP

(a) To some extent, yes. If around EU there are stable and prosperous countries, the Union gains security, trade partners—to sum up, economic and social stability around it and inside its frontiers. However, this priority should not be at the expense of the poorer Countries, which are more vulnerable to crisis due to their fragility.

(b) It is true that a large amount of aid continues to go to middle income countries but that does not necessarily mean that it is at the expense of Low income and very poorest countries.

(c) It should be both. Firstly it needs to be part of foreign policy, thus guaranteeing coherence with other policies affecting third countries. At the same time, development aid has its own specificity, requiring some autonomy to guarantee that aid is truly directed to countries in need, in accordance with the commitments assumed related to poverty reduction and the Millennium Development Goals.

(d) Not necessarily, even because, in many places, they are a pre-condition for poverty reduction.

Aid to the 'near abroad' and other middle income countries

(e) Yes, especially because the enlargement will bring new 'near abroad' which will be a new priority for EC assistance and maybe that is the only way to guarantee that this assistance really tackles poverty in those countries.

(f) Yes, if effective and efficient, that would be desirable.

(g) Only recently has the poverty focus started to be applied in these countries.

(h) It might be too ambitious.

Development in the Constitutional Treaty

(i) The new draft Treaty that is being negotiated is quite close to what Portuguese initial ideas were, in what regards development cooperation. It ensures poverty reduction as the main goal of EU development policy and reinforces the Commission's co-ordination role, emphasising the complementary relation between Member States and the Commission.

II. *Enlargement*

(a) It is quite obvious that enlargement will create more difficulties, especially in achieving agreements. Besides, EU aid policy might also be affected, as the new Members do not have the same concerns and experience in development co-operation. Despite this, we hope that in the long run it will bring positive results, not only increasing their awareness and attention to the poorest countries, but also making poverty reduction their priority too.

III. *Does the ACP grouping have a future?*

(a) Appearing as a group give ACP countries advantages.

(b) ACP do benefit from larger amounts of aid but India has been growing rapidly, and even refused certain aid supports. ACP countries are mostly African countries, and Africa is the continent where achieving the MDGs seems to be most difficult.

(c) The best way to treat countries is, in our view, on a regional basis but taking into account their development status (in between regions and inside the regions).

(d) It has been very effective, especially the quite unique Parliamentarians joint consultative arrangements. These bring mutual understanding and promote parliaments role, and consequently democracy, in ACP countries.

IV. *EDF and Budget*

(a) EC have been making progress. Firstly, there is greater co-ordination in the field and secondly, the introduction of Country Strategy Papers.

(b) Yes, EC programmes have added-value *vis-à-vis* Member States bilateral programmes: greater coverage as it is a worldwide player; greater impartiality as it is almost a multilateral donor and also playing the role of aid co-ordinator.

(c) d) It is not that clear that budgeting EDF would bring about more legitimacy and transparency, as the Commission states on its recent communication. Two solutions are possible: budgetise but include a series of safeguards regarding these resources so as to preserve the good aspects of EDF; or maintain EDF as an autonomous instrument and work on improving the quality of co-operation with ACP.

February 2004

Memorandum by Saferworld and International Alert

INQUIRY INTO EU DEVELOPMENT POLICY AND EXTERNAL ASSISTANCE

Saferworld[19] and International Alert[20] work together on a joint programme to support and enhance the EU's ability to prevent violent conflict. Saferworld and International Alert have been engaged with the EU as policy advisors and advocates since the mid 1990s and provide analysis and practical expertise to the EU and Member States drawn from experience in conflict affected regions. The joint work culminates in the production of annual reports detailing how the rotating Presidencies can ensure that the EU strengthens its commitment to, and impact on conflict prevention.[21]

---

[19] Saferworld is a foreign affairs think tank which aims to prevent and reduce armed violence, increase human security and create conditions for sustainable development.

[20] International Alert is an independent, non governmental organization which analyses the causes of conflict within countries, enables mediation and dialogue to take place, sets standards of conduct that avoid violence and helps to develop the skills necessary to resolve conflict non violently. IA conducts policy-orientated research and advocacy aimed at promoting sustainable peace.

[21] Past Presidency papers include *Ensuring Progress in the prevention of violent conflict: Priorities for the Greek and Italian EU Presidencies 2003* Forthcoming publication January 2004: *Strengthening global security through addressing the root causes of conflict: Priorities for the Irish and Dutch Presidencies.*

SUMMARY

In 2003 most violent conflicts took place in Africa, the world's poorest continent.[22] Conflict causes poverty and in turn poverty, social and economic exclusion increase the risk of violent conflict. The EU through its development, trade and foreign policies has the potential to play an important role in the eradication of poverty and the prevention of violent conflict in a coherent manner. The link between conflict and underdevelopment is now well recognised and the EU is committed to mainstreaming a conflict prevention approach across its wide range of instruments. The challenge facing the EU remains turning the rhetoric into reality and retaining the EU's commitment to a conflict prevention or human security approach in an increasingly "hard security" driven geopolitical climate. This submission suggests that in order to achieve this the EU should:

— Redirect development assistance towards the poorest countries.

— Increase the emphasis on conflict prevention and good governance in the EC aid budget.

— Further mainstream conflict prevention across all areas of policy.

INTRODUCTION

In approaching conflict prevention it is important to distinguish between two broad categories of actions. These have been defined by the Carnegie Commission as (1) operational prevention (measures applicable in the face of immediate crisis) and (2) structural prevention (measures to ensure that crisis do not arise in the first place, or if they do, that they do not recur). Our emphasis in the submission is on structural prevention.

Over the past 10 years the EU has developed a strong policy commitment towards structural prevention as reflected in "The EU Programme for the Prevention of Violent Conflict", developed at the Gotenburg European Council in June 2001.[23]

In addition to policy commitments, a number of institutional developments have also taken place. These include the establishment of a Conflict Prevention Unit within the External Relations Directorate, of the Commission, which is tasked with mainstreaming conflict prevention priorities across community policy (eg trade, development, environment).[24]

However, much more remains to be done to put commitments into practice. In addition, implementation of the structural approach has not taken place as fast as developments within operational or short-term crisis management prevention.

THIS SUBMISSION CONCENTRATES ON DEVELOPMENT AND FOREIGN POLICY QUESTION (21 A-D)

a) *There has always been a strong political/foreign policy element in EC aid. This has increased over the past decade with increased aid to Central and Eastern Europe, the Balkans and the Mediterranean countries, and with greater emphasis on governance and conflict prevention. Is this desirable?*

b) *Has the relatively large amount of aid that continues to go to middle income countries been at the expense of aid to the Low Income and the very poorest countries?*

The increase over the last decade of amounts of EC aid to middle-income countries in Central Eastern Europe, and South Eastern Europe and the Mediterranean at the expense of the poorest countries is not desirable. It is inconsistent with the principles of EU Development policy and fails to reflect that, in a globalised world, it is not only instability in the "near abroad" which has an impact on the EU. In 2002 this trend continued—with the total of pre-accession community budget aid representing six times the amount spent in Asia.[25] The process of enlargement has no doubt contributed to this trend, in order to facilitate the accession of new members this May. Whilst increased stability in the region is welcome, this should not be at the expense of efforts to support development and peace within the EU's wider external relations.

— The EU should provide a greater concentration of resources to low-income countries to ensure that the aim of poverty reduction is met within the EC's future development budget.

---

[22] See P5 *Conflict Barometer 2003* Heidelberg Institute for International conflict resolution http://www.hiik.de/en/main.htm.

[23] The EU has produced a total of nine documents detailing the EU's commitment to conflict prevention, these include: the *Council Common Position Concerning Conflict Prevention Management and Resolution in Africa*, May 2001 and the *Implementation of the EU programme for the Prevention of violent conflicts*, at the Seville Council in June 2002.

[24] Other institutional changes include the Council Policy Planning and Early Warning Unit, PPEWU has provided an important capacity for analysis and initiatives in support of conflict prevention. Council CFSP working groups such as the Political and Security Committee and the Africa group have begun reflecting on conflict prevention, as witnessed by the increasing number of CFSP instruments used in conflicts such as the deployment of EU envoys and troikas in South Eastern Europe.

[25] The total amount spent on pre accession aid for Sapard, ISPA and Phare programmes plus Malta, Cyprus and Turkey totalled 3,494.21 million euros while total aid to Asia was 574.87 million euros (2003 Annual Report from Commission on the EC development policy and implementation of external assistance in 2002).

(c) *Should development aid be used as an instrument of foreign policy as is suggested in the High Commissioner's "Security Strategy" presented to the European Council at Thessaloniki in 2003, or should it be an autonomous policy with its own objectives and rationale?*

Development aid should not be used to further narrow political interests but it is vital that the EC and Member States are more coherent in the design and implementation of development and foreign policy. Poverty reduction and conflict prevention should be guiding principles of all EU policy instruments.

Today's geopolitical climate does present a threat to the progress made by the EU in developing a coherent conflict prevention and poverty reduction approach. Concerns over the politicisation of development aid for use in the war against terror are legitimate and real. For example, NGOs have gathered evidence to show that development funds are being diverted from the poorest countries to those deemed sufficiently aligned with the "war on terror"[26] and countries are loosening controls on their arms exports despite human rights concerns. To address these challenges, coherence across EU policies must be better addressed and safeguards put in place to protect development and structural conflict prevention.

ENSURING COHERENCE

The European Council agreed that "all relevant institutions of the Union will mainstream conflict prevention within their areas of competence"[27] but a lack of political will and the pillar structure of the EU have prevented effective implementation.

As decisions related to external relations and conflict prevention are generated and implemented in all three pillars, the pillar structure poses particular challenges. Similarly the division of responsibilities for programming and implementation between the Directorate Generals (DGs) of the Commission (eg EuropeAid, DG Relex, DG Dev, DG Trade, DG Enlargement and ECHO) can hinder the process of mainstreaming conflict prevention within sectoral and geographical units and a delegation level, where programme development and implementation takes place.

The EU should work towards reform of the pillar system. The first two pillars should be brought closer together. We support the merging of the position of High Representative and Commissioner for External Relations into a single job of EU Foreign Minister, but are aware that safeguards need to be implemented to ensure coherent policy decisions are taken (see next section).

—   The EU Foreign Minister should be supported by a Deputy, who is responsible for the further co-ordination of all EU external actions.

—   The EU should establish joint planning and progress meetings between regional working groups, the Political and Security Committee and the DGs from the Commission to facilitate mainstreaming and effective co-ordination.

—   The EU should ensure that country and regional task forces are used more in the formulation and implementation of inter pillar strategy papers for key priority countries, particularly in bringing together relevant staff from DG Relex, DG Development, the Council, DG Trade, ECHO and relevant Member States.

SAFEGUARDING DEVELOPMENT

The eventual agreement on the Constitutional Treaty of the EU is likely to have further financial and structural implications for the EU's external relations and development policies. The proposals to create a Foreign Minister, to possibly reduce the powers of the EU Development Commissioner[28] and the budgetisation of EU-ACP co-operation (the European Development Fund or EDF), offer opportunities for greater harmonisation of development and foreign policies but also pose challenges.

As outlined above, the creation of an EU Foreign Minister could improve coherence and effectiveness across foreign and development policy. This Minister will have budgetary control of all external relations, humanitarian affairs and development funds. It is therefore important to safeguard against the possible subsuming of development and conflict prevention funds for narrow political agendas. A Deputy Minister responsible for coherence would go someway towards achieving this. In addition, the position of Development Commissioner must be retained and guaranteed voting rights.

---

[26] Oxfam have noted that levels of humanitarian aid are being provided to "priority" cases such as Iraq and Afghanistan but not to others. eg Nearly half of all the funds given by donor governments in 2002 to the UNs 25 humanitarian appeals went to just one country Afghanistan—admittedly very poor, but top of list of priorities are war on terror. The remaining 24 countries had to struggle on what was left. ("Beyond the headlines" Oxfam 2003). They also note there have been increases of military assistance to countries on side in the war on terror despite human rights concerns eg post September 11 US Government provided £3.8 billion military aid to 67 countries to support counter terrorism but half were criticised by US State Department for their poor human rights record.

[27] EU Programme for the Prevention of Violent Conflicts 2001.

[28] It has been reported that to take account of enlargement, of the 25 new Commissioners only 15 will have voting rights. The rest will become sub commissioners with no voting rights.

Budgetisation of EDF funds into the Community fund would ensure improved transparency (parliamentary scrutiny would be required) and efficiency (through improved speed of allocation). However, safeguards should be implemented to guarantee that budgetised EDF funds will continue to reach their ACP recipients and that the innovative qualities of the Cotonou Agreement, such as the principles and obligations for ownership, consultation and partnership, are retained.

The establishment of a separate development budget heading for development within the EC community budget, as proposed by the United Kingdom International Development Select Committee in 2002[29] and the suggestion by CONCORD[30] that a separate sub-heading for Development Cooperation should be created within Heading 4 in the Financial Perspectives, may go some way towards preventing the use of development funds for purposes other than the reduction of poverty.

Conflict prevention should however be acknowledged as a legitimate use of development funds, particularly if requested by the poorest countries. The request by the AU for the EU to support the development of a Peace Support Operations Facility (PSOF) in Africa with European Development Funds (for which they have shared ownership) is a good example of this.

The facility aims to be more than simply a military standby force, but also encompass a wide range of actions from conflict prevention actions such as mediation to post conflict reconstruction. Many have expressed concern that the EU should not use EDF Funds to support the facility, but the Council have agreed that the use of EDF funds will only be an interim measure and will not be used to fund troops or military equipment. Furthermore the EDF Committee will be consulted on individual operations and further work is to be undertaken while working out the objectives and implementation modalities as to which activities will be eligible for ODA funding and which will not.

— The position of Development Commissioner must be retained with guaranteed voting rights.

— If EDF funds are budgetised, the EU should develop effective safeguards to protect the geographical poverty focus and partnership qualities of EDF funds.

— Development funds should be available for wider conflict prevention and peace-building activities including support for good governance initiatives, security sector reform, early warning, disarmament, demobilization and re-integration of ex-soldiers, small arms awareness-raising and education.

d) *Whilst good governance, political stability and conflict prevention are necessary for development, will the new emphasis on these objectives mean a down-grading of other development objectives, particularly poverty reduction?*

Greater emphasis on conflict prevention and good governance within the EC Aid budget is desirable. Violent conflict and a lack of good governance are two of the main obstacles to poverty reduction. Beyond the direct consequences of military and civilian deaths and displacement, conflicts have long-term political, economic, environmental and social costs including the erosion of political institutions, reduced state capacity to provide basic social services, destruction of livelihoods, loss of food production, forced migration and destruction of natural resources.

Corruption, unaccountable state institutions, a lack of rule of law and repressive security forces have also fuelled poverty in many countries across the world. An emphasis on conflict prevention and good governance in EC aid should not, therefore, be seen as "downgrading other development objectives, particularly poverty reduction". Rather peace-building and strengthening good governance are important pre-requisites for poverty reduction in many of the poorest countries. It is desirable therefore, for all EU development assistance to be "conflict sensitive" that is, to maximise its potential to contribute positively to conflict prevention while delivering on its core mission of poverty alleviation.

Progress is being made with mainstreaming conflict prevention across development policy. Since 2001, the EU conflict prevention unit has developed for desk officers and EC delegations staff the *EC Checklist for Root Causes of Conflict,* which aims at increasing awareness and early warning action in regions prone to conflicts; the checklist is also designed to ensure that EU policies contribute to conflict prevention and resolution. The checklist refers to about eight political, economic and social conflict indicators to inform the users. The checklist is reviewed when country and regional strategy papers are drafted and, on the basis of the conflict analysis, attention is drawn to conflict prevention focused activities that external aid should target.

In addition, the linkages between poverty and conflict prevention have been recognised within regional co-operation agreements such as the ACP-EU Cotonou Partnership Agreement, which defines trade and aid co-operation between the two regions. Conflict prevention and resolution are explicitly mentioned in a separate article—article 11. However there is no implementing mechanism for article 11 and conflict prevention is not listed as a key issue, nor a thematic or cross cutting issue within the Agreement. It is welcome that the

---

[29] In the Second Report *"The Effectiveness of the Reforms of EC Development Assistance"* April 2002, it states *"We would welcome progress towards a separate budget heading for development, in order to make it clear which funds are earmarked for the elimination of poverty".*

[30] CONCORD is The European Confederation of NGOs for relief and development.

guidelines for the 2004 mid-term review of the country strategy papers acknowledge this point and list conflict prevention as an "area not adequately addressed in the initial programming".[31]

To effectively mainstream conflict prevention it is essential that all areas of EU policy such as trade and actions by the private sector, also address the root causes of violent conflict. Further mainstreaming of conflict prevention across other areas of EU policy is therefore required.

— The emphasis on conflict prevention and good governance in EC aid budget should be increased to help further the goal of poverty reduction.

— More capacity-building is needed to ensure that staff in the delegations and in the Commissions have the relevant training to conduct conflict analysis and, that this analysis takes place at all stages of the programming cycle from early planning through to evaluation.

— The EU should further develop conflict prevention mainstreaming across other instruments (eg trade, CFSP, ESDP, environment) by developing effective peace and conflict impact assessments that extend beyond development programmes.

14 January 2004

---

[31] Guidelines for 2004 mid-term reviews under the ACP-EC Partnership Agreement, p. 6.

Printed in the United Kingdom by The Stationery Office Limited
4/2004   940043   19585

ISBN 0-10-400441-X

9 780104 004418